# About the author

Damian spends his time teaching English in a large further education college. He lives in mild tranquillity in the remote mountains of Staffordshire. He has a beautiful wife, four darling children (Sarah, Thomas, Katie and Harris), a son-in-law who knows a thing or two (Richard) and three grandchildren he would rather not name. Pies still play a prominent role in his life, and he has a large collection of antique pies that will one day be turned over to a museum. When not writing he lets his mouth do the talking, and this has worked well for several years.

JULY 20<sup>TH</sup> — A GOON LANDING

Damian Carter

JULY 20TH— A GOON LANDING

Vanguard Press

A CIP catalogue record for this title is

available from the British Library.

ISBN 978-1-80016-418-5

*Vanguard Press is an imprint of*
*Pegasus Elliot MacKenzie Publishers Ltd.*
www.pegasuspublishers.com

First Published in 2021

**Vanguard Press**
**Sheraton House Castle Park**
**Cambridge England**

Printed & Bound in Great Britain

# Dedication

For Thomas and Anne,
now enjoying eternal pies and pipes.

# Acknowledgements

Thank you to Sadia, for constantly checking.

# Part One — The Landing
## 1965

Anne paced up and down the landing, visibly wheezing, possibly due to her pipe habit or as a result of the imminent birth of her third child. Thomas, her husband, was outside trying to change a flat tyre on his Austin Value. Anne had already successfully hatched two children, but she knew this one was going to be trouble. When Anne had first suggested trying for another child, Thomas had been reluctant, preferring instead to spend the money saved on a Ford Grappler. Anne had always wanted a child with a large nose, someone to share her love of truffle hunting — a child who would appreciate woollen clothes, not through duty, but because they loved hand-knitted garments. As the contractions grew, if that were possible, Thomas was tightening the final nail in his ambition to purchase a new car; that would have to wait. The cries emanating from the vicinity of the front bedroom were now so severe that it was feared that the infant would be born oblivious to pain. The three older children, Stephen, Janine and Paul, were in the back room huddled around a small wireless, waiting for news on the arrival of the new rival for their parents' pity.

It was the year when The Rolling Bones, Britain's greatest geological export, brought a spirit of rebellion to a nation still desperately clinging to crepe soles and quiffs, grasping the final crumbs of rationed fun, indeed, struggling with a '50s hangover. The mildly white-hot heat of 1965 was sure to set the world alight. At the start of the year, the nation mourned the passing of Britain's war leader, Winston Haystack, and many citizens felt that it was a time for a changing of the guard. A new horizon beckoned, with the hope of dazzling light and technicolour noise; a surge of confidence in a nation, if not reborn, then at least brought back from the dead; a wave of optimism so strong that it would change perspectives and alter perceptions, and riding that wave of hope and optimism was a child named Damian.

Born to a poor family in the lower reaches of the Pennine hills in Yorkshire, young Damian enjoyed his birth like only a newborn baby could, crying. His father, Thomas, was already the proud owner of three part-worn children, and this instalment of fatherhood was surely his last chance of getting it right. Damian's siblings were a mix of both varieties, and his eldest sibling, Stephen, was the fourth living thing to hold young Damian. It was a bond that would last until one of them died. His other siblings, Janine and Paul, would in time paw at the newborn infant, but that is always the case with middle children.

Damian's mother, a proud woman with an iron ankle, was known in the area as Audrey, but her real name was Anne. She had light blonde, mousy brown hair and a strong whiff of motherhood. Anne was an emergency hairdresser who was always on call. No matter what the time, she would wait by the fire, puffing at her pipe, on standby for an emergency trim or beehive. The people of Yorkshire were known for their elegant hair and love of expensive hairspray, even if this meant going without meals. Anne always had a sandwich bag in the house, for emergencies, long before collecting dog shit became fashionable. This marked her out as a radical and free thinker, a dangerous thing to be in 1960s Yorkshire, where even some partially educated people still believed in witchcraft and horoscopes. She was the Jammie Dodger in a jar full of digestives.

Thomas worked as a rule and was employed as a wool tester in a mill town full of mills. Long hours and even longer minutes meant that Thomas sometimes worked over a day in less than twenty-four hours. His love for his children was without question and was a lasting gift that just kept on giving. However, a life close to wool took its toll on his health and fashion sense, and for years to come he was plagued with a distrust of sheep and a love of man-made fabrics. This would eventually lead to semi-madness and a life waiting by the door for unexpected deliveries, but more of that later in a decade or two.

It must be remembered that in 1965, few working-class people could afford birthdays, and so were often either very young or very old. Damian was no exception, and his birthday, July the twentieth, was only a rough estimate as to when he was delivered. With the absence of clocks, it was very difficult to give an accurate date of arrival. On the day he was allegedly born, Neil 'Moon Walk' Armstrong was busy practising for his cavort on the moon in four years' time, and moon boots were top of everyone's must have list. Moon boots have gone on to play an insignificant role in both fashion and Damian's career choices. In later life he would toy with the notion of becoming Yorkshire's premier moon boot retailer, but that potential business lay way off in the future. Before he even took his first swig of Yorkshire air, Damian's extended family found that they were unable to stretch to a suitable birth gift, so on day one, Damian's journey had a foreboding feeling of poverty. His gran, who was female, knitted him a cot using only twine from a disused sack, and this sufficed for the first few weeks of this infant's life.

Damian was blessed with a plentiful supply of aunties, whose knowledge of wool and tabards had led to a life of spinsterhood and contentment. They gave him love and wool as an infant, and a lifelong passion for chutney as an adult. This menagerie of relatives wished the baby Damian well and drank into the early hours of the evening, celebrating the passing of the past.

By late August of the year, the family decided to give the child a name, and many suggestions were made by both interested parties and strangers. Before his final birth name was settled on, suggested names for this ludicrously attractive young child included Macaroni, after his great uncle Waldo, Nick, after a shaving accident and Sally, if he turned out to be a girl. His parents whittled down a very long list of possible names and arrived at two: Gerard and Lucifer. These were good, strong, traditional Yorkshire names, but breaking with tradition, his father vetoed both and instead adopted the 'scar the kid for life' method, which produced Damian, pronounced in a variety of ways, depending on the prevailing mood of the room. His mother, a huge fan of Lee Marvin, Lee J Cobb, and Lee and Perrins, plumped for Lee. So, when the infant arrived at the font for the ritual dip, his full moniker was Damian Lee Carter the first of Undercliffe.

The ceremony was an affair to remember, with the good and the grateful from far and wide squeezing into the Methodist chapel to witness what would be one of the most memorable naming ceremonies since unsliced bread was rebranded.

Sadly, both his grandfathers had survived the First World War, but were not present at the naming ceremony. His paternal grandfather loved horses, serving with distinction in a top-secret stable on the Western Front. At the end of the conflict, he continued with his love of all things equine and set up a street corner horse advisory service, only stopping when he died in 1946. Damian's maternal grandfather supplied chutney to the troops via a revolutionary pipeline that ran under the Channel. He too went on to do great service in regional chutney development and lived a fruit-filled life. Both had little impact on the outcome of the war.

It was a gloriously cold day, and as the wind whipped its way across the low-slung hills of West Yorkshire, the naming ritual dragged on as the stammering vicar struggled to annunciate consonants. As the assembled conglomerate of misfits awaited the holy splash, the babe in arms lay still, placid yet restless, dull yet possessing an inner sparkle. Few of those present are still alive, and those who have managed to cheat death are fast approaching the borders of death, but it was said at the time that the vicar almost cried when he washed that forlorn babe in the biblical bath of baptism. In the eyes of the world, and those who were still awake, Damian was now officially a name. The vicar was subsequently defrocked and spent a long and successful career as an undertaker and part-time DJ.

As summer turned to winter, and birds flew with greater urgency, infant Damian started to explore his pre-colour world. A world of greys and smudge, where each sky looked in desperation for the night, where colour was something of a pre-war luxury for the upper echelons of society. Home life for Damian centred on the washing cycle of his mother's pre-loaded twin engine mangle, which churned out noise day and night as it attempted to keep up with Damian's demands for pristine nappies. Quickly finding his feet (at the end of his legs), Damian was growing very quickly into an annoying little boy, with his unreasonable demands for food, warmth and light. Anne and Thomas, already worn down to bitter husks by their three other parasites, felt that Damian was a burden that could well drive at least one of the two to madness or drink, or both, or none. Thomas, a stoic character whose crowning achievement to date was shooting floating mines in World War Two, considered moving into the family garage to get a reasonable night's sleep. This was only dismissed as impractical when he realised that the family garage had been stolen the previous winter. A truly heinous waste of criminal time. With the constant jibber-jabber of young children, in a time when online gaming and other such technological advances were a thing for sci-fi fanatics, the only way to entertain his boisterous brood was to stick them in the privet hedge that bordered the family hovel. The privet hedge was a truly northern gift to the world and represented the pinnacle of nature in this part of Yorkshire. Damian would later recall the happy hours he spent inside that hedge, searching for who knows what with his equally confused siblings.

As the ageing months of 1965 gradually slipped away, Damian had the prospect of his first Christmas, with all its attendant joy and tom-tittery. Finding presents suitable for a five-month-old child can be a burden too far, or a step too heavy, and Thomas and Anne vowed one late November evening never to spoil their children with the superficial fripperies of consumer indulgence, so the kids were assured of a very frugal Christmas. Lightly boiled oranges would pass as presents, along with a sturdy length of twine, which could be used to wrap itself. Kids love twine and oranges, and these two staples of pre-TV served the family well throughout the decades that followed. Sometimes the oranges would be large, if the wool harvest had been a bumper one, and sometimes a satsuma would have to be shared by all four siblings. They never contracted scurvy at Christmas, so perhaps that is a lesson for today's parents. That winter of late 1965 was the seventy-fifth coldest on record, with temperatures hitting freezing on two occasions. As the family gathered together that December, events in the wider world appeared briefly in the window of their lives, yet the fleeting nature of such events had little impact on their orange and twine celebrations. The escalation of fighting in Vermont, the continuing rise in hemlines and the discovery of gravity in South America might well have been headline news on the front pages of the tabloids, but there was an abundance of peace, love and vitamin C in the Carter household. Outside their rotting front door, a wider world faced many pressing challenges which would affect young Damian as he grew bigger, but for now, the family suckled on the metaphorical juices of the orange. Another year older, but would they be wiser?

That first Christmas morning was a magical moment for Anne and Thomas, as the children's noses lit up with the smell of oranges and twine was ripped to reveal more twine. It was almost Dickensian in its unbridled simplicity. For Christmas dinner they ate the traditional Yorkshire dish of dripping and bread served with a garnish of potatoes and roughly chopped meatballs. Damian, who still had no teeth to speak of, nuzzled a mashed-up meatball and swore to himself that meatballs would be an integral part of his life. As with many family Christmases across the land, problems occurred, and Damian's first Christmas was no exception. His father, Thomas, had been diagnosed with a rare medical condition as a child — Stupicus Elbowus, or ill-fitting elbow, which had affected his life in many ways. He was unable to clap or wave with enthusiasm, find short-sleeve shirts that could cover his hideous elbows or lean on a fence (he could of course sit on the fence). Whilst in the navy he had been court-martialled seventeen times for not saluting — a promising naval career cut short due to this misunderstood and debilitating condition. In the future, ill-fitting elbows would no longer draw cries of derision and loathing, but in the 60s, when few people had access to Google for self-diagnosis, he was treated like a pariah, his awkward gait a constant reminder of life's cruelty. This condition flared up at times of great anxiety or during cold snaps, and the winter of 1965 was a very anxious time. He would take himself off to the family garage, or what remained of it, and gently lean against a broom, wishing for some miracle cure or unguent. This would bring some relief but did not remove the social stigma.

Boxing Day, with its abundant twine and relatives, was a special day as it meant a trip in a motor car to see in-laws and relatives. The day started early with the ritual cleansing to mask the smell of orange. The children would be wrapped up tight and packed away in the boot of Thomas's Ford Gripe, a sturdy model of the era with twin doors and a patchwork roof. The excitement was almost unexplainable, as disappointment was always lurking around the corner, but the children's iridescence and flamboyance meant that the day would be tiresome and difficult. The drive to the relatives' house was relatively short, but in the boot of the car the children would squabble over who would sit on Granny's lap, or who would sniff the mince pie first. Anne, a keen passenger, would often smoke her pipe on these short journeys to ease the travel sickness, whilst Thomas would hum along to Mario Lanza on the car wireless, the patchwork roof gently flapping in the wind.

On arriving at the relatives' house, the children were quickly unpacked from the boot and escorted to a quiet part of the garage until such time as it was felt appropriate. Thomas, who was both sociable yet uncomfortable in social situations, would often disappear at this point to check the air levels in the car, or dispense soap on its outer casing. He harboured resentment on account of their garage still being visible and not being stolen. His disappearances would quite often take the whole day, so he would miss the awkward silences and tepid food that was the standard for these visits. The relatives were a collection of well-meaning people related to Anne, whose enthusiasm for tabards and preservatives meant that chutney was always on the menu,

17

often accompanied by a cold meat of some sort. As a baby, Damian would avoid meat, but when it came to chutney, he could eat a jar without taking a breath.

Boxing Day was a time for extended family, and Damian's family certainly were extended. His uncle had worked as a travelling soothsayer in the '50s and could stretch reality beyond what was considered acceptable. His gran would always extend a warm welcome to Christians and atheists, and Auntie Ronda could extend a holiday if it meant another trip to see a well-preserved preservative museum. Auntie Marge had a love of balloons that would often leave her lightheaded and deflated, but she was always the instigator of after-dinner entertainment. Party games, the pastime of the bored and idle, were often played during these visits. A family favourite was the mitten game, so called because a mitten was integral to the game, the objective being to perform as many mitten-related tasks as possible in a prescribed time limit whilst wearing an ill-fitting mitten. The game provided hours of fun as relatives dropped food, soiled carpets and generally sullied what would otherwise have been a perfectly agreeable afternoon. Damian, who watched these games as only a five-month baby could, slept the sleep of the careworn. His siblings, flitting between house and garage, were fed and garnished with low cost presents and when all the presents had been suitably discarded, it was time for the ritual rolling out of the hostess trolley, atop which sat a gratifyingly grotesque mince pie. Lovingly made by Gran, its ingredients were a family secret, which was probably a godsend. Auntie would slice the pie into seventy-seven pieces. Any leftover pie was taken to the local churches to be shared amongst the tasteless and hungry.

The family would usually leave the relatives around quarter past late, ready for the short drive back to their hovel on the dark side of town. Thomas would miraculously return to the relatives' house just before it was time to leave. Damian had spent the whole afternoon suckling on a softened crust of mince pie, oblivious to the tension and rivalry that the mitten game had caused. The remaining siblings would be removed from the garage and repacked into the boot of the car whilst Anne would sit in silence as she puffed away on her pipe; Thomas would warble along to Mario Lanza; the patchwork would flap. Routine is such a reassuring drug.

As the new year approached, many people liked to reflect on the passing year's events and look forward to new hope and experiences. Thomas and Anne were no exception, and 1965 had been a momentous year from the very start. In January Anne had discovered she was pregnant yet again, and the prospect of yet more washing had sent her into a downward spiral of despondency. At twenty-six, she wasn't old. You can understand her dilemma, but Thomas was always there to support her, elbows permitting. At the start of the year Thomas had started to consider a career change, moving away from the demanding wool business which had crippled his wardrobe. On New Year's Eve 1965, Thomas received distressing news from a colleague; job losses were on the menu and Thomas was the main dish. The wool business had shrunk drastically following an outbreak of heat and taste, which saw many people opting for cotton and polyester, and rayon as the number one clothing fabric. Nudism was also on the rise. Wool belonged in the bottom draw of textiles, and Thomas was one of the first victims of this new-found fashion for comfortable clothes. Thomas, who was not forward in going backward, faced a terrible dilemma — fight for his job in the world of wool, knowing that wool had been and gone, or step into 1966 and search for new challenges that would allow him to treat his family to a weekly tinned pie. Driving was his passion, indeed, he loved cars so much that he changed cars more often than underwear, but could he ever dream to find work as a driver in a highly uncompetitive jobs market? He had hands and eyes, and was no stranger to seats, so he certainly had all the necessary skills to become a driver. However, he hated heights and was worried this could hold him back. On that dark night, as the new year crept in, Thomas made a momentous decision; for his kids he would suffer in silence and become a driver, despite his fear of heights. His children, his wife, his elbows, they all deserved a brighter future, and Thomas was not going to let them down too badly. Damian knew nothing; he slept throughout these incredible changes, waking in the new year a day older but none the wiser.

# Was it all over?

As we cast our collective minds back to 1966, possibly the crowning achievement of the year was the England football team winning the World Cup alongside Thomas finding non-wool based employment. However, it is a little-known fact that the roots of that footballing triumph were laid in a sleepy suburb of Bradford. Anne, who was a lifelong woman, loved football. As a girl she had played in the West Riding 'Ladies and Gentlefolks under 14' Methodist League, where her agility both on and off the pitch soon caught the eye of budding football coach Albert Charm. Charm, a graceless man with eyebrows that screamed backcombing, was a smooth tyrant of a man. He moulded his Methodist ladies into a hardnosed group of evangelical tacklers, willing to sacrifice dignity in search of a win. Anne was catapulted into a world of long shorts and knee-length boots, and her ability to play in all weathers meant she never needed an umbrella. Who knows how far she could have gone were it not for her twenty pipes-a-day habit, which meant she could only walk in very short bursts and smelt like the inside of a tobacconist's? Years later when England took to the field to play in that memorable final, it was Anne who first noticed the similarities between the England manager's name, Alf Ramsey, and the coach who had spotted her talents all those years ago, Albert Charm. As Hurst scored the winning goal, Anne knew it was all over as far as her footballing ambitions were concerned, but she also knew that if she had been brilliant at football and a man, she could have been scoring that historic winning goal. Carter, Charlton and Hurst might have been names that resonated through the annals of pipe-smoking footballers. Bitter is the taste of what could have been. Of course, young Damian was unaware of this, and the nearest he got to a football was when his eldest brother, Stephen, rolled him into a ball and kicked him across the front parlour.

Damian was a curious child, and it was in February that year that he first discovered a love of curtains. As anyone who has a remote interest in home furnishings will tell you, the 60s were a frightening time for home interiors and haberdashery in general, yet despite this apparent slump in good taste, Damian was drawn to the vivid swirls and colours that adorned the windows in that cramped hovel he called home. An added attraction, which sadly we see very little of in modern Britain, were the fly splattered nets, which offered some relief from prying eyes but were perfect breeding grounds for envy and petty rivalries. Thomas and Anne loved their home, as only two people with low expectations could, but it could never have been described as a palace. With its squinting windows, a hole in the wall that served as a door, and an unduly flimsy roof that was a friend to the elements, it was little wonder that the whole family took comfort in home furnishings and interior décor. Damian's sister, Janine, had an eye, and using her innate sense of the visually ridiculous, could transform a room into a flamboyant tale of ill-judged soft furnishings. Sequins, velvet and wool were all combined to produce a look that was described at the time as ominous. It is little wonder that Damian's nearest sibling, Paul, spent the first five years of his life completely oblivious to soft furnishings. Paul would only respond to black and white and wore grey most days. For Thomas and Anne, home furnishings provided a welcome break from the drudgery of everyday life, but the impact on their children was harder to quantify. It is safe to say that none of the children ever truly had potential, as most of it had been misplaced alongside an ill-advised scatter cushion or over-elaborate throw. A piss-poor diet also played a significant part in their lack of discernible hope.

The hovel had two lower decks and a mast that served as a lookout for when the local meter reader came knocking. On the lower deck there was a galley kitchen and two portholes, along with a cabin that could double up as a sitting room. The kitchen had all the essential fittings needed to make pancakes and strong tea, and on a Wednesday, there was also running heat and water. The bathroom had a portable toilet and a sink that doubled up as a bucket, which was used to cleanse the children as and when their smell became overwhelming.

The kitchen was the hub of the house, where the family would gather for hot meals and cakes. Cakes, the joined-up crumbs that painted a picture of happiness, much loved by many, were the only source of fruit and vegetables for the Carter children, and came in the form of Anne's experimental cakes and fancies. Anne's fifth love, after Thomas and three of the children, was baking, and young Damian was introduced to the world of sponges and buns from a very early age. Anne's drop scones were often dropped; her Victoria sponge was often left in the bathroom; her flapjack had industrial qualities, yet she persisted with her baking. Damian, spoon in one hand and measuring tape in the other, would help Anne measure ingredients, whisk eggs and beat flour. For a baby his age, it was incredible, but there was something hypnotic about the smells that emanated from that cramped kitchen, churning out barely edible treats for a family sorely in need of treatment. Thomas, who was handy with a ladle, would often sit in the corner of the kitchen, ladle in one hand and spoon in the other, ready to digest Anne's experimental creations if needed. His ability with a spoon was innate, and those who witnessed his thoughtless stirring could only marvel that he did this despite being inflicted with ill-fitting elbows. The pain was immense, and the cries of agony, often occurring following a robust slice of cake, would leave him bedridden for minutes. He would stagger upstairs, spoon in one hand, cake in his pocket, and quite literally climb into bed and sleep awhile. Damian, ever the curious child, would gurgle curiously, not knowing how or why his father always carried a spoon. Thomas was born shortly after the First World War, and like many children of that era, lived a hand to mouth existence, and a spoon was an essential piece of kit for a child growing up in the 1920s. The spoon was Thomas's comfort blanket, and as a grown man, he was unable to desert that spoon.

Thomas loved music and employed his ears in an efficient manner to fully appreciate the nuances of Mario Lanza. In 1966, Vinnie Despania released his seminal album, 'Strangers in the Porch', which was a success for both Despania and his record label. Loosely based on visitors, or people who might be found in a porch, the album featured unforgettable classics, such as 'There's a Mousetrap in my Hall', 'Lady in a Hat', and the bestselling 'Pick up the Towel, Mac'.

As he grew, Damian began to explore, and would often be found in the dog's basket, snuggled up with the family pooch, Remus, a long-haired, short-tailed basset whose temperament was rather like a set of taps; warm and tepid. Imbued with legs, the dog would often frolic and at times, bark along to Vinnie Despania. Paul, Damian's nearest sibling, would sleep in the dog's basket as a way of drawing attention to the fleas in his long blond hair. A small child at birth, Paul was a rumbustious toddler whose calculated sulks meant that he was forever being sat on a naughty step. In most households, a naughty step would have to be installed by a highly skilled operative, but Thomas met a man in the local park who was selling naughty steps at very low prices, or it could well have been very low steps at naughty prices. Suffice to say, Thomas purchased a job lot and stored them in what used to be the garage. Occasionally Paul would take a seat on the naughty step uninvited, and gently hum along to Mario Lanza. It was clear that he had his father's musical ears. Paul was very fond of Damian and would often spend hours throwing small peanuts at the infant's head. Janine, Damian's sister, would join Paul on the step and quietly hum a Despania classic to soothe both her younger brothers. Thomas and Anne encouraged this primitive bonding, believing that it would foster a strange pack mentality in their brood. Damian, the runt of the pack, would in later life sometimes only respond to dog whistles and 60s easy listening. This type of advanced child rearing was seldom seen in the mid-

60s, and it is little wonder that emergency counselling was needed for all three of the younger children.

Thomas was quickly settling into his new role as a short distance lorry driver. This job meant that he never had to travel more than five metric miles from his home and was always home before dark. He was employed by the Yorkshire Lighting and Illumination Society as an electricity delivery driver. If there were power outages, blackouts or general mishaps with the power supply, Thomas would be sent to deliver urgent power and light to needy householders. Each working day began with a roll call, for no apparent reason, followed by hours of waiting for a call from control, before being dispatched to some lightless house with residents in need of illumination. It was a nerve-racking job transporting live electricity, and the stress could be seen across Thomas's furrowed arms. His truck was fitted with a seat, for comfort, and a large plastic sheet to cover the electricity. On many occasions, Thomas would arrive at an incident only to discover that he had somehow lost all the light and arrived with only an ill-lit truck. Those were the risks he had to take in order to keep the people of Yorkshire illuminated. Consequently, Thomas aged rather undramatically, if not at all, and his elbows, his Achilles heel, meant that any turns in the road would leave him in agony for minutes. Like many men of that generation, he left school with few formal qualities. He could read and count to seventy-two, but his geography and general understanding of physics was limited. School for him had been a series of beatings at the hands of cruel and large-handed teachers. School meals consisted of a warm towel dipped in lard, followed by a cold towel dipped in dried custard. Rickets was rife, and the only hope for many of these boys was a life with a travelling circus or the workhouse. Thomas chose neither, but instead spent his teens guiding horses with his father, who incidentally was also called Thomas. He lived by his wits, and it was these wits that stopped him getting too lost on the mean streets of 60s Bradford. Many men tried to deliver power, but few could do it as adequately as Thomas. He was marked out for mediocrity and a long career in all things electrical. All this power meant that he could put food on the table, and this meant Anne could take food off the table and store it in a more suitable place. The children were treated to fancy food, the likes of which they had never even heard of, let alone seen. Tinned fish, tinned bread and tinned eggs were all on the menu, and very soon the whole family would suffer from bowel disorders and scurvy.

# Warped expectations

The Stains released their thirty-fifth album in this year, with many fans running out of ears and unable to listen any more. Jimmy Pendrix joined the Dave Clam Quartet, and Peculiar Clark didn't walk in any subways on her way downtown.

In rural Bradford, Damian and the Carters were busy planning a family holiday, the first for many years due to genetic travel sickness and parochialism. Thomas, ever the wondering heart, fancied somewhere far afield, like Scarborough or Paraguay, whereas Anne wanted somewhere that would enable her to indulge her love of slumming it. Unfolding his road map of Britain and the isles, circa 1912, Thomas quickly eliminated several possible destinations through a process of prejudice and ignorance and came up with a very short longlist which was in time reduced to a very short shortlist of two possible destinations: Scotland or Wakefield. Anne loved the idea of Wakefield, with its fields and wakes, but Thomas decided that Scotland offered so much more, and without Anne's knowledge, booked a week's self-catering holiday in a run-down cottage outside Dumfries. It cost Thomas several pounds, not including transport, but the cottage seemed to have a range of amenities that would make this holiday a holiday to vaguely remember. Anne, it turned out, never wanted to go to Wakefield, so the die was cast, and the Carters were heading north.

Thomas had replaced his Austin Pilgrim for a newer Austin Suffragette, which came with bench seats front and back, and a real leather windscreen. Quite often Thomas would chain the Suffragette to the railings at the back of his garage, in fear of having it emancipated. The touch of luxury afforded inside the Suffragette meant the journey up to Scotland was still a bloody nightmare, but the windscreen never once misted up, meaning

Thomas at least felt he could see where he was going. The three older siblings spent the journey counting, in the hope that they would run out of numbers, whilst young Damian perched his little arse between Thomas and Anne, giving him a bird's eye view of the rolling slums of West Yorkshire. As the journey stretched out, Damian was witness to the glorious slums as they spewed out before the Suffragette: disused mill towns with drab chimneys, tower blocks in rows and overtly hairy dogs hunting children in the grimy back streets. Damian's main concern was to not vomit on Anne's expensive cardigan, but he failed. The next three hours of the journey were spent with windows down and hoods up, as Thomas attempted to alleviate the joyous aroma of vomit from the velour seats of the Suffragette. The car's value had depreciated substantially, and Anne's cardigan was left somewhere on the A56 in a layby strewn with cardigans. Obviously vomiting on journeys was a popular thing in the 60s.

The holiday cottage was truly a monument in under-renovation, dilapidated being the watchword. Its only selling point was that it had a roof and was near a farm that sold free-range milk. Every morning the children were treated to breakfast, which meant a full day of fun with no further meals until the obligatory fish supper from a local chippie, where a slap-up fish supper was less than a month's wage. The kids lapped up the wonderfully greasy chips, whilst Anne mused on her pipe. Thomas, binoculars in hand, would wistfully scan the coast in search of German mines, perhaps reliving a wartime memory or reading the very small, small ads. His love of binoculars was fuelled by his myopia, and he always had a pair to hand when reading road signs. Obviously, this made him socially awkward, and he would often leave the house without the binoculars and then find himself unable to read even the largest of large print. How he remained employed was a mystery.

The week in Scotland was the pinnacle of holidaying on a very small budget. Trips to the beach with a shared bucket and spade, long walks around a roundabout and seagull baiting were all legitimate ways of avoiding spending any money. At no point were the children ever in danger of enjoying themselves, which gave Thomas and Anne little satisfaction. The journey back was uneventful to say the least, with stops at all the highlights on offer along the M6 corridor. Penrith to Lancaster, Preston to Colne — all these places were passed and not explored, and the children lapped it up, believing that this truly was a road trip to end trips. On arriving home, Anne immediately popped the kettle on whilst Thomas went to his secure debriefing room in the garage to dismantle his dreams. The children tucked up in bed, it would be another five years before the Carters once again hit the road and vomited.

By the end of the year, young Damian had started to listen to a wider variety of music, partly due to the development of his ears, but also in part due to Stephen's love of guitar-based rock. Pendrix, Slapton and Palmerston were all musicians who passed him by, but he loved the music of Peculiar Clark, The Doolicans, and of course, that boy band to end all boy bands, The Slunkeys. Stephen had a steam powered, wind up gramophone, purchased via the small ads, which allowed Damian to aurally witness classic music at a very young age. As night drew in, he would sit on the kitchen table and whistle such classics as Don't Sweep in the Subway, Get Off My Yellow Submarine, a classic folk song which would bring any submariner to tears, and of course those 60s classics, Rat on a Hot Tanned Pouffe and Putrid in the Sty with Diamante.

Whistling has long been a way of attracting attention, and from an early age Thomas instilled into all his children the importance of a good, strong, hearty whistle. Paul was whistling before he could talk, and Janine went on to be a world class whistler, like her mother. Damian too showed an aptitude for whistling which he would practise in the garden, at one with the birds and local sheepdogs. In later life it enabled him to easily fit in, as a man is often judged by the quality of his mother's whistle. Indeed, Damian did consider a career as a window cleaner, which would have allowed him to indulge his love of whistling all day long, but a fear of ladders put paid to that little dream. Suffice to say, music in the Carter household was an eclectic mix of rock, pop, old time folk, medieval chanting and Dean Martin. Anne would often visit the ruined abbeys of Yorkshire to experience chanting in its purist form. Pipe gently tucked behind her ear, she would chant in the morning, in the evening and even chant on public transport. She was often excluded from social gatherings and found making new friends difficult, but she never turned away from her love of a medieval chant. Paul loved jazz and would listen to Piles Mavis for hours on end. It must be remembered that Paul's ears were extremely small, so he would often have the gramophone turned up to max in order to get the full rush of that syncopating jazz. In later life he did toy with the idea of buying a tuba, but due to awkward toes, he could not use the instrument with any confidence as he was liable to overbalance at any moment. A tragedy for him and the planet.

As Stephen became more and more of a rocker, Anne and Thomas noticed a change in him. His hair became unused, simply sitting atop his head. His ears, usually so clean, were now filled only with noise and guitar. He started wearing clothes that suggested personal hygiene was optional, and he no longer ate his full quota of pies on a Sunday. He was growing into a rebellious teenager, which for Anne and Thomas proved to be a difficult time. For Damian, who by this time was able to control a trike and no longer soil his trousers, this change in Stephen went unnoticed. Children can be so unobservant unless they are very religious.

Like many parents in the 60s, Thomas and Anne were shocked by the changes that had taken place within teenage culture. Ginger beer and wholesome bike rides had been replaced by long hair and satin trousers. Thomas loved man-made fabrics, but a satin vest was one step too far for him. Anne, who had enjoyed ginger beer during the war, with its pungent dried egg overtones, usually kept at least ten bottles in case of an emergency. Her pipe-smoking was her first addiction, but ginger beer ran a close second. Teenagers in the 60s, and Stephen was a prime example, wanted to try new soft drinks, experiment with skin-altering fabrics and listen to mind warping music. Stephen had started to hang around with a long-haired crowd of ruffians, whose names struck fear into Anne's pipe-stained fingers. Carlos, Jed and Marco were names that belonged in a 60s leather museum, not to friends of your son. Stephen had adopted a high-pitched walk and would often spend hours in the bathroom singing French pop songs into a toilet brush. Thomas, whose wits were artificially enhanced after a torpedo accident during the war, adopted a silent but stoic approach, preferring to watch and learn before banning his eldest from France. Thomas had travelled, and was not averse to spaghetti, but when it came to his son, he was determined to make sure Stephen didn't go off the rails and become a full-blown victim of French fashion and fads.

Stephen had started to write verse in the hope that it would be put to music, and some of the lyrics stayed with Damian for years. Stephen would often strum on his two-string guitar and attempt to compose the next big thing. This made a lasting impression on Damian, who always assumed that guitars had four strings.

### Blown along by the wooden breeze

*Blown along, couldn't breathe,*
*Blown along by the wooden breeze.*
*Blown along, blown along,*
*Wooden breeze couldn't breathe.*

*Tree tops leaning, stone faced sun,*
*The wind and rain have begun.*
*Whips me up, takes me on,*
*Wrapped in cold, summer's gone.*

*Blown along, couldn't breathe,*
*Blown along by the wooden breeze.*
*Blown along, blown along,*
*Wooden breeze couldn't breathe.*

Hair like wire, brittle skin,
Frostbite forming on my chin.
Chilled and sodden, eyes of ice,
The weatherman said it would be nice.

Blown along, couldn't breathe,
Blown along by the wooden breeze.
Blown along, blown along,
Wooden breeze, couldn't breathe

Lying bastard, fooled us all,
The mystic with his weather ball.
Cloud and rain, snow and hail,
The wind grew strong, it blew a gale.

Blown along, couldn't breathe,
Blown along by the wooden breeze.
Blown along, blown along,
Wooden breeze, couldn't breathe

Step outside, feeling raw,
Walking now, such a chore.
Weather like my spirits rage,
Vivid colours, never beige.

Blown along, couldn't breathe,
Blown along by the wooden breeze.
Blown along, blown along,
Wooden breeze, couldn't breathe

Wooden breeze, takes us all,
To higher plains, where grass is tall.
Wooden breeze, hard and trunkey,
I think my granddad was a junky.

These lyrics reflect a bigger problem that existed beyond the Carter family hovel. For many years, people had relied on gossip and hearsay for their weather, but with the explosion in television ownership and windows, people were now able to get their weather gossip from almost anywhere. Thomas blamed the counterculture and the lack of trustworthy gossips. His own father, Thomas the Elder, was a very taciturn man, but he understood the need for weather. Stephen explained to Thomas that he at no point thought his granddad was a junky, but Thomas was none too happy with the direction in which Stephen's experimental lyrics were heading.

Thomas grew up in an era when margarine also served as a gentlemen's fragrance, so the notion of his eldest son becoming familiar with the weather and understanding the principles of cold fronts sent a shiver down Thomas's heavily burdened spine. Stephen was obviously under the influence of external forces that could see him develop into a mature and well-rounded adult, so it was important for Thomas to at least inflict some mild psychological issue onto his eldest before his influence waned. Food was the key to most people's stomach, so Thomas set out to reward his children with top quality pies whenever they pleased him. His cunning plan would see his children become mildly addicted to pies and mushy peas. They loved their father beyond words, but his cruel introduction of the pie into their innocent guts meant that in adult life they would be forever foraging for a pie at inopportune moments. For the children, pie was their father's love; Anne gave them pipe smoke and tweed. Stephen grew into a pie-loving fiend, and would often eat two, sometimes three, without blinking. He would then feel guilt coupled with fond memories of Thomas. In the evening, the children would be arranged around the family chair, where Thomas would dish out pie and love in equal measure. It was a very northern household, and as the children greedily munched on a crust, Anne would be busy ironing the family towel to ensure that the children dried without creases. Huge plumes of pipe smoke would obscure her vision, but she would know that her husband and children were somewhere in the room due to the frenzied grunts and scrapes. Anne's grandmother had been a stickler for a good crease and would iron her own legs before long journeys to ensure she travelled by the straightest route. She died at a young age thanks to blisters on her shins which became infected with death. At the time it was attributed to her rusty iron, but recent studies point to a severe case of burnt shins.

# Say 'cheese', you little bastard

During those first years of Damian's life, there was a revolutionary evolution in music, social attitudes and scientific endeavour, and it is fair to say, he played a small but very insignificant part in the events that unfolded in that unforgettable period. Sir Terrence Spade produced the experimental play 'The Excavator', a ground-breaking piece centred on the corrupt nature of trench digging. Received with a mixture of apathy and a lack of interest by the critics, its central themes of warfare and waste chimed with several people who bothered to visit its opening night, but its central message was lost on many who just thought it was about digging a trench. Damian, who by this time had become a fully-fledged pedestrian, followed the unfolding turmoil as and when naps would permit. He had little understanding of the conflict in Vermont, nor the geo-political power struggle between the two great superpowers. He did have a very nice trike that occupied his time during those long, hot winter evenings, and he would often sit around the TV and watch the piano with his family. He loved music, as did sixty per cent of his family. His brother Paul was numb to the melodies that wafted through the kitchen on a Sunday afternoon, but his sister, Janine, could often be seen jiving to the latest tunes as they blared out of the family wireless. It is a little-known fact that Thomas Carter invented the whisper in response to this cacophony of noise and movement, a counter-revolution to the counter revolution. Thomas, who was afflicted with many things, found the increase in music and noise in general upset his delicate elbows, and would often sit in the confines of his prefab garage in search of tranquillity. As with most inventions, there are many conflicting versions of how the whisper came about, but it is fair to say that Damian played a very tiny bit part in something that went on to transform private conversations, secrets and gossip. His father had only one vocal cord, which was both fragile and unusually flexible, which meant Thomas could reach the highest and lowest notes when singing a range of songs — the downside being that his vocal cord was liable to snap at any time, leaving him hoarse and emotionally broken. In response to this, he developed a complex system of nods, winks and barely audible utterances. It was this final innovation that caught on in the bars and cafés of Bradford, and soon Thomas was renamed Whispering Tom, the Wizard of Words. Of course, with hindsight, it seems amazing that no one had discovered whispering prior to this date, but as with most inventions, it takes someone with vision, one vocal cord stretched to its limits, and four children, to push an idea from the turgid slopes of theory to the exhilarating hills of practice.

It was around this time when Damian first asked his father how high the sky was. The pithy response from Thomas, that clarified a confusing and complex area of astrophysics, illustrates why Thomas was such an enigma. He told his newly qualified pedestrian son that it went all the way to the top. This satisfied the limited curiosity of Damian and meant both could continue with other distractions in an otherwise very mundane month. However, that cordial settlement of fact and truth was nearly ripped asunder when Armstrong and Aldrin shattered the surly bonds and landed on the bloody moon. An event few had believed to be in the realms of fantasy, it coincided with Damian's fourth birthday. As he woke on that sunny morn in late-mid July, few people on this ball we call earth would have more of a connection with that event than young Damian, junior space cadet. Thomas had built a small observatory in the cellar of the family hovel, and on the historic day, father and son positioned themselves near a very powerful pair of reading glasses and scanned the little patch of sky they could glimpse from the cellar. Hoping to see Armstrong or the other one, they charted every moving thing that flew, walked or skipped past that cellar window. At one point, when Thomas was applying a powerful unguent to his elbows, Damian was sure that he had seen something or someone stepping on the moon, but he couldn't be sure and didn't want to look stupid. Even as a four-year-old he was fully aware of the insignificance of his little patch of hovel on earth, and imagined up there on the moon strange alien creatures puffing on magical pipes and speaking in grunts and clicks. This also sounded a little bit like Anne, who had been suffering from a rather oppressive bout of phlegm, afflicting her knitting and limiting her to fifteen pipes a day.

Like most parents, Thomas and Anne wanted to record and capture the stunted development of their children, so that in years to come the children could reflect on how awful their childhood had been. Most people living in the area could not afford to have their image captured professionally by a professional, but many at the time used primitive drawings and thumb marks to replicate what they might look like if there was a camera strong enough to trap their hideous features. Wealthier folk might employ a portrait artist or a sculpture, but these avenues were unavailable to Thomas and Anne. However, fate's fickle finger pointed its tarnished nail, and Thomas was the lucky winner of a competition offering free portrait sittings with a semi-professional snapper. Thomas had entered the competition at the local working men's club believing the top prize was a week's holiday in Hornsea on the east coast of Yorkshire. On winning the prize, his immediate reaction was a mixture of shame and disappointment. Shame that he had misread the prize categories and disappointment because he had a real love of pottery, and he knew that Hornsea was the epicentre of cutting-edge pottery and pottery-based memorabilia. Despite this obvious reluctance to engage with the idea of a family picture, Thomas arranged a sitting, and on the allotted day the children were suitably prepared to have their grubby faces captured in wonderful black and white. Stephen and Janine were resplendent in flared clothes, with garish designs taken from a wallpaper catalogue, whilst Paul and Damian wore matching tee shirts with a tree motif, along with best short trousers with a splendid tartan design which complimented the wallpaper, which was also of the tartan variety. There was a group photo, with all four children sitting together, arranged in a higgledy-piggledy fashion by the boss-eyed photographer whose left eye was constantly scanning the room for flies, whilst the right eye blinked incessantly. Stephen sat at the front, with the remaining children scattered around a crushed velvet cushion at his feet, rather like badly dressed spaniels at the court of King Charles II. There then followed two more photo opportunities. Janine and Stephen perched on a rather attractive card table, looking into the middle distance, rather like a lighthouse keeper squinting at a vivid sunrise. Paul and Damian then had their turn, which was an underwhelming disaster. Damian was required to sit to the left of Paul, with a gormless gaze which said so much about the content of his mind, whilst Paul endeavoured to smile for the two of them. The resulting picture has been studied by anthropologists ever since, and is a telling reminder, in this time of selfies, that perhaps some people just don't take a good picture. Suffice to say Thomas and Anne were shocked with the results, and the pictures had pride of place in the family cellar. Damian still has a copy of that picture, and even today when he looks at the two brothers sitting side by side, he feels amazed at Paul's ability to smile so well. Many people are born with a smiling gene, some take smiling lessons, but what Paul has in that photo is a smile that speaks volumes. It says help, it says why, and it says aren't my tartan trousers lovely. A smile can convey so much. Obviously, no relatives clamoured for copies, and Thomas used the remaining copies to make paper thin gaskets for his 1963 Austin Pilgrim, which had an intermittent oil leak.

There was, as is the case in many of these tales, a silver lining. Thomas, ever the collector of tat, discovered a new focus for his tat hoarding — broken cameras. He was able to amass a huge collection over the ensuing years of cameras that looked to be in working order but were in fact pointless. This impacted on Damian's future, as in later life he refuses to have his picture taken but is often found behind the lens taking terrible out-of-focus photographs that would shame even the ineptest snapper. Also, following Thomas's obsessive search for tat, Damian now cannot spend any time scouring newspapers for bargains, meaning he spends too much money on overpriced tat and not enough money on under-priced tat.

Visceral cries in the night were not an uncommon occurrence in Damian's little part of desolation, and quite often he would sit awake listening to the wails of despair that emanated from the rows of terraced houses that dotted the street. Thin curtains and even thinner skins meant that life easily hurt the residents of the neighbourhood. Thomas was witness to the pain and would often stalk the deserted streets in the hope of capturing the pain on celluloid for posterity. Puntix Gloom Capturer in hand, he would click away under a sordid street light, unaware that the flash couldn't capture sound. Holed up in his very dark room, he would spend hours developing reasons for the wailing, all the while trying to work out how to get the film out of his Gloom Capturer, a Russian-made camera that was designed to be used by left-handed photographers. Those nights when the wailing became a chorus of despair running through the dirt-encrusted streets, when hope had long left the area in search of light, Thomas produced some of his least memorable snaps, capturing the utter hopelessness of taking pictures without the proper equipment. Anne, pipe in hand, would offer Thomas a pie and a tea on his return from these nocturnal photo shoots, knowing that Thomas would soon tire and resort to buying different tat.

Damian, holed up in the attic with Stephen and Paul, having been allowed his own bed since his discovery of the toilet, witnessed very little of the pain, but imagined a world of monsters and evil, intent on avoiding unflattering photos. The attic hole was a cold place, with three part-furnished beds, a carpet waiting to be threadbare, and a window that also functioned as a hole. Like most four-year-old boys, he wanted to be like his dad, so took to wandering the landing at night making clicking sounds. He was also the proud owner of a dysfunctional trike, which lacked its full complement of wheels. This made riding the trike a challenge, and Damian confined his time on the trike to riding in the back yard, avoiding dog turds and crashes with a deftness that was appreciated by very few. At the rear of the house was a dirt drive, used by all the residents to access the less desirable entrances to their hovels. At the front of the house was the ex-shoe museum, now being used to store vast vats of lard in case the Russians attempted to impose a fat embargo on the UK.

As the decade neared its end, two little boys frolicked with two equally small ponies, and Damian looked forward to new teeth, bike riding with confidence and school. Attending nursery had equipped him with the minimum of social skills needed to avoid any serious mishaps, and he understood the importance of not pissing his pants in the classroom. He couldn't read and numbers were simply a way of expressing bathroom habits. School would be a whole new set of challenges, and as he whizzed around the back yard on his two wheeled trike, he could only imagine the adventures he would have, the friends he would make, and the under-achievement that awaited him.

# Tiny steps

Anne was born in the late '30s, and she grew up in a time of great uncertainty and hardship. As a baby she had spent most of her time wrapped in a gas mask to be protected from the smell of the dried eggs and pickled bread that was standard fare in the early '40s. A shy and retiring girl, she had sparkled brightly at school, only to miss out on an opportunity to attend Hair College for Serious Young Ladies, in Huddersfield due to her attachment to the gas mask, and was forced to take a job in the local pipe factory. Her school friend Celia was the daughter of a wealthy magnet and pipe manufacturer, and was able to pull strings, punches and pranks. Anne was soon working in the finishing department at 'Smokestack & Sons', Yorkshire's premier pipe producers, responsible for ensuring that every pipe that left the factory had two ends, a middle and a free book of matches. The work was undemanding, and Anne would spend hours dreaming about the day she could finish with the pipes and pursue her hare-brained scheme to work with the hair of the rich and famous — coiffure to the cultured. Reality soon bit when the whole factory went up in smoke in mysterious circumstances. She was laid off and had to find a job quickly to fund her twenty-pipes-a-day habit. She had always been rather good with children, so decided to retrain and become a nursery nurse, which is how she met Thomas, a single father looking for childcare.

Damian didn't really feel the impact of Anne's unusual work-life balance and never fully understood why his mother would sit by the clockwork phone waiting for work, either as a hairdresser or nursery nurse, or as a nursery nurse caring for infant hairdressers. It was in this year that Anne added a third rung to her already overstrung bow after she set herself up as a children's entertainer. Her nom de guerre for this new enterprise was Lester the Jester, the juggling queen. She couldn't juggle, didn't own a unicycle, nor did she know any jokes suitable for the under tens. What she could do was use her pipe to make interesting smoke shapes, such as De Gaulle's silhouette, the Vatican, and Naples by moonlight. The bookings trickled in and she was soon filling smoked filled rooms with smoked filled silhouettes. Her rates were very low, due to money shortages, but her clients would sometimes pay in kind — perhaps half a kipper for an hour of smoke shapes, or a pair of lady's shoes, size nine, for two hours of De Gaulle and Churchill. Damian loved to go to her impromptu smoke displays, where he would sit, mouth agape, laughter on the tip of his tongue as he coughed uncontrollably due to the heavy smog. Anne, weather permitting, could often be seen outside the busier shops and pubs in the city centre, her three younger children in tow, bag of pipes at the ready, freestyling smoke displays in the hope of earning some extra coppers to put towards a new sewing machine or meal. If it was raining, she would mime the silhouettes as the smoke tended to dissipate, which was also the case when there were high winds. Still, on a good night she could make at least three shillings in old money, which equates to around seventeen farthings in pre-decimal what-the-fuck-are-you-talking-about money.

Damian liked nothing better than seeing his one breathing grandparent and looked forward to the weekly visits when he would be treated to heat, light and running water. His grandmother was a small woman with a big heart and possessed a beautiful hostess trolley, capable of carrying three hostesses. She would treat her herd of grandchildren to boiled sweets, bacon rashers and bananas. His favourite time with her was when she would read him stories from pre-industrial magazines, charting tales of derring-do and drudgery. She read 'The Spindle', a mill-themed magazine for ex-mill employees; 'Hope and Drudgery', a chutney digest featuring all things chutney; and 'Candlewick & Twine', a hodgepodge of shite and home baking. At the back of each magazine were short stories aimed at children who lacked visual stimulus. Damian would beg his gran to read and reread these stories, and he had two favourites that stayed with him, despite psychotherapy. Below is a brief flavour of the shite that soaked his infant brain:

# Iona and Henrietta make chutney — a cautionary tale!

*Iona was in the garden with her twin sister, Henrietta, picking gooseberries off their grandfather, who tended to collect pointless fruit. The girls adored their grandfather and loved gooseberries. Iona was confident that this batch of gooseberry chutney would be the best ever and wanted to enter it into the Frichton and District Gooseberry Chutney Championship, the third most prestigious championship in the area. Each year the twins would harvest the green gold in the hope of triumphing in some random and pointless chutney festival, but they were always pipped at the post by the horrible girl who lived three doors down from their grandfather, Ida Jar. Jar was the only child of Sir Derek Jar, chairman and majority shareholder of Frichton's Chutneys and Preserves. He was to judge the competition and would surely give the much sought-after rosette to his daughter. How could the twins hope to compete?*

Suffice to say, Damian was enthralled by such tales of chutney and cheating, and when at the end of the story, Iona utters those immortal words, "Henrietta, and now she has stomach-ache," Damian would fall about laughing.

The second story, 'Harry the Haberdasher', was a humdinger of a tale about a regional needle and twine spy ring that was in the pay of an unnamed foreign power, stealing haberdashery secrets and selling them to the highest bidder. Harry was a humble needle and twine salesman who somehow had become entwined in a web and had to thread his way through the complicated maze of haberdashery espionage. Thimbles and needles seemed so glamorous to Damian, and he would sit for hours with his gran, soaking up the mysterious world of international needle theft, illicit ribbon exports and general twine tom-tittery.

His gran would often take him to Bradford's world-famous twine museum, where the interactive exhibits let children touch twine, needles and ribbons, and the gift shop offered an array of haberdashery-based pencils and pencil erasers. The bus journey would take two minutes, and there never seemed to be many visitors, so Damian and his gran had the museum to themselves on most occasions. The building was originally an eighteenth-century barn but had been renovated to resemble a twentieth century barn, with opening doors and running light. Sadly, the museum was burnt to the ground in 1970, leaving no trace of the exhibits and memories that had been made there. Damian only discovered that it was gone in 1997 when he was planning to take his own parasites on a wondrous tour. He was bitter for weeks.

Damian had been inadvertently dipped in a vat of gormless as a child, meaning that quite often he would look as if his jaw was overly slack, with little activity going on upstairs. Anne had worried that when he started nursery, the teachers would spot his intermittent gormless disposition and only let him play with softer toys. Damian was due to start nursery school in the September as Anne believed it might encourage Damian to develop his anti-social skills and be more aware of the outside world. Thomas, who had recently purchased a Ford Slump, a box of a car with flaps for doors, believed that Damian would be better served joining the navy and getting to grips with basic car maintenance. Anne, pipe in hand, would remind Thomas that his youngest was only four and way too young to be messing around under the bonnet of a Ford Slump, despite its easy-to-use user guide. Suffice to say, Damian went to nursery, where he was introduced to children whose names differed from his own, as did their hair, teeth and general appearance. Shaking off the gormless was a trick Damian used when he wanted attention or food, and discovering that nursery had toys opened his eyes to a world of fun and colour. The nursery, St Fragrance the Blessed, was a Victorian establishment and still had many original fittings. These included a water-powered slide, a brick-built head teacher, and hessian blankets for nap time, which took place most afternoons for the nursery teachers. This is when the kids could run wild and destroy the cheap toys. Like most children of the era, television offered a world of rampant imagination, often mingled with recycled stories given a modern twist. Damian would spend long periods perched on the edge of the family dog, watching his favourite programmes and for a few minutes at least, escaping the damp and grey of pre-colour Bradford. Several programmes of the period are still remotely irrelevant today, and Damian's top five were:

## The Vegetable Rack

This animated offering was set in a vegetable rack in a small hotel kitchen. Pete Potato and his chums, Mr Carrot, Doris Cauliflower and Susy Pea, would get up to mischief and hi-jinks whilst all the time retaining their naïve charm and avoiding certain death at the hands of the wicked chef, Monsieur Gruff. Pete was a short-sighted spud with poor eyes, and he relied on Mr Carrot's impossibly brilliant vision to cheat death on an hourly basis. Doris, a rotund and quite frankly grub-ridden cauliflower, brought very little to the table, but her bubbly florets added a light-hearted touch to an otherwise dour serving. Susy was a soft-centred girl, obsessed with love and romance. She had a secret crush on Pete, and seeing him made her feel mushy. Pete was a homosexual potato, and had very little time for Susy's nonsense.

The interplay between the four badly-drawn characters and the cruel-hearted chef, always on the lookout for a veg to boil, made this riveting TV for any child who had a passing acquaintance with cooking.

## Shrill and Annoying

Puppets were the pathway to happiness for kids growing up in the 60s, and Shrill and Annoying were two glove puppets guaranteed to send anyone over the age of four into a rage, but for those whose judgement was suspect, they represented the pinnacle in puppet technology without the need for strings or wire. Shrill was meant to be a kind of thoughtful aunt who resented children, whilst Annoying was plagued with minor ailments that meant she was forever moaning about twinges and sneezes. A touch of consumption afflicted her in one episode, and on another occasion, she suffered from an outbreak of an overly irritable bowel. These ailments would send Shrill into a spiral of abusive rants, directed at the cowering Annoying, her flea-infested agent, and the deplorable ruling class who had let a once great country sink into a mire of mediocrity. Damian loved the subtle undertones and non-deadly puppet violence.

## Captain Half-Heart

Set in the highly toxic world of international spying, Captain Half-Heart cleverly tapped into the worries of a generation living in fear of nuclear destruction by a rampant unseen red enemy.

Half-Heart was a spy working for the Ministry of Safety, with a special mission to be completed on areas such as food waste, unsafe electrical appliances and of course that perennial of parental worry, road safety. The captain would swoop on some unsuspecting rogue appliance and make it fairly safe or ensure that most of the children in a small area knew the difference between red and green when presented with a set of traffic lights. His work was monotonous and offered very little opportunity, but for a child with little or no imagination, it kept them safely slumped by a small black and white TV set.

## Gaston the Ghastly

Cut to medieval Wiltshire, and the castle of Gaston de Ghastly, evil overlord to a cowed and downtrodden peasantry. Originally made by a small Norwegian TV production company, it was dubbed into French and redubbed into broken English for broadcast to those infants keen on modern foreign languages and history. Set in Wiltshire, thanks to its proximity to Oslo, Gaston the Ghastly would have his evil plots thwarted by ill-educated, poorly equipped outlaws who somehow never died, got sick, or ate. The dubbing was truly atrocious, and quite often the voices sounded vaguely stoned or at least a little drunk, and despite thousands of complaints from Norwegians and the French, it was still promoted as an excellent way to learn about Norwegian history and French culture, despite being set in Wiltshire. Damian loved the opening sequence, when Gaston would appear on the castle walls, chicken leg in hand, berating a peasant for some trifling misdemeanour, overlaid with the catchy theme tune, 'Gaston, Oh Gaston'. Damian remembers the words to this day, and has produced them below for all you nostalgic buffs:

> *Gaston, oh Gaston, please set us free,*
> *Gaston, oh Gaston, I'll hide up a tree.*
> *Gaston, oh Gaston, where can he be,*
> *Gaston, oh Gaston, he's hid up the tree.*

## Causeway to Curiosity

This semi-educational offering mixed fun facts with old people who had little or no understanding of the demographic they were supposed to be speaking to. Presenters Ralph Certainty, Avril Tweed and Dan Groan had been selected as the face of fun facts on the basis that they were extremely cheap and appeared to know a little about some things.

Ralph had served for fifty-five years in the army and had very little time for those who couldn't stand by their beds, load a musket or march into the face of the Hun with steely determination. This on-screen persona frightened many children away, and his explanation of battlefield amputation was considered a little too graphic for the pre-school audience. Damian loved it! His wispy hair (he had one) was a trademark, along with his tree stump of a nose which had been disfigured by a bullish tin of bully beef at the battle of El Alamein.

Tweed had been a researcher for a food hygiene company when she was spotted by a television producer polishing a cabbage to remove unwanted bacteria. Her obvious attention to detail meant she was great at explaining science and shit to kids who didn't really give a fuck. Her ramblings on disease, food poisoning and the possibility of choking on grapes meant that quite often people would send in food to her to try on screen. She was hospitalised on two occasions: once when she demonstrated the dangers of raw chicken, and also when she nearly choked on uncooked chestnuts soaked in paraffin.

Dan was the youngest of the trio and had enthusiasm seeping from every orifice. This made him appear slightly oily, and he had been arrested previously for looking like a seedy pervert. He was never charged. His brief was to perform the really dangerous stunts and activities that Ralph and Tweed refused point blank to do. He too spent weeks in isolation due to a very severe touch of near death, and on one occasion broke several bones in his inner ear. He had metal plates fitted in most parts of his body, and he weighed far too much for a man with a drug habit. Damian was transfixed by this melange of shit and would eagerly stay awake just to stare at Ralph's hair, or listen to Dan's cries of pain.

## Part Two — Brown and beige
## Lice to the left, lice to the right

School, the home to words, numbers and that perennial torment, head lice. In Yorkshire's schools, head lice were the unwanted for the unwashed. A plague that every head accommodated, not through choice, but as a welcome source of companionship. The routine method for handling this scourge was to round up the head lice using a series of clicks and bird calls, and then corral them in specially built nit enclosures, where they would be held awaiting collection. Each Friday, weather permitting, the by now sleeping lice would be loaded onto waiting trucks, and then be transported to the coast where they would be used to power wind turbines. This inexpensive yet highly inefficient source of energy was never fully funded, so it is yet another reason why the 70s were racked with fuel shortages and industrial disputes.

Damian entered school knowing very little. He could tie shoelaces, but knot his own, if you will excuse the pun. He could count very little and the final third of the alphabet was a theory that had yet to be tested. His first school was in fact a nursery — Didley Hull Infant School and Nursery. This squalid building perched on the outskirts of nowhere and consisted of three buildings, a collection of teachers and some pre-war camp beds. Snoozing and napping were encouraged, and it was in this bleak world that Damian made his first tentative steps into education. It would be a long journey. The head lice would remain a constant reminder of his loneliness, but his awareness of letters soon provided comfort and inspiration.

As Damian's curiosity for the world increased, he was able to explore his environment and discover new and magical things. It was on a trip to Manningham Park in early April that Damian's curiosity took a severe knock; thankfully, he did recover as an adult, but it left mental scars on the young child. Manningham Park, birthplace of the swing, was a low-cost entertainment centre located in the north of Bradford and Anne, hairdressing appointments permitting, would often take the three younger children there on tepid afternoons for hours of dreary fun and games. She would rise at the crack of dawn and prepare a picnic, fill a thermos with tea-infused tomato soup, and check the bus timetables. The three children, suitably attired in early 70s woollen garments, would don their nylon anoraks and head off to the bus stop, marvelling at the wondrous sights they spotted on the way to the park. Occasionally they would glimpse other children looking equally despondent, with harsh woollen shirts and scuffed knees. These strange sights were exotic and new to the three children, and Anne's ability to make her offspring look vaguely clean was a source of pride. On arriving at the park, the priority was to find a suitable patch for the picnic rug. This could take some time due to the copious amounts of dog turds that inhabited the park. Anne was a stickler for not having dog shit on her woollen blanket, and never compromised in her search for a clear bit of grass. On this occasion, it only took fifty minutes to find a suitably unblemished spot of park, and she then laid the blanket on the ground and unpacked the goodies from her Morrison's carrier bag. The picnic always included a range of three-day-old buns, some jam tarts with fluff on and the obligatory jam sandwiches. Damian loved jam sandwiches, and for him, the jam sandwiches were the highlight of the trip. On this fateful day, Damian and his brother were perched on the clean corner of the picnic blanket when they spotted a rather angry group of geese making their way to the playground. Damian loved birds, and one day he would eat one, but on that day the geese turned nasty. Of course, the geese 'were just being playful', but Damian has been consistent in his story, maintaining that at no point did he stare at the geese or whisper any derogatory remarks about goose shit or overblown ducks, and that the geese's response that day was a complete overreaction to jam sandwiches. Suffice to say, it turned very ugly, and when one of the geese made off with the last jam sandwich, it brought the sky down on Damian's love of picnics, parks and geese. He cried for three weeks and refused to sleep with the lights on. The following five years were harrowing times for Damian, as he struggled to come to terms with the loss of the sandwich, and with geese. He would wake in the night, sandwich in hand, geese attacking his deformed feet. It was a nightmare, or at least a slightly troubling dream, which would disturb the sleeping family in their slumber. Cries rang out throughout the house as Damian battled with imaginary geese in his sleep. It was only the intervention of a renowned quack, who lived three doors down from the family, that eventually brought about an end to these night terrors. 'Face your fears' is an overused platitude, and Damian was not ready to do that, so the quack moved Damian's bed to the far side of the attic, bought several pairs of ear plugs for the family, and normality and peace were restored. Now as a grown man with grandchildren, it is easy for Damian to reflect on this episode with a crooked smile but living through those dark days has left him with a lifelong fear of soft pillows and eiderdowns. Life is a strange mistress.

House moving, or moving house, is never a simple process. Thomas and Anne had lived in the same hovel for the last five years, and never ones to shy away, they felt it time to up sticks for a different kind of hovel, more suited to their obnoxious brood. Space was at a premium, following the recent moon landing, so the couple confined their search to areas near local parks and poorly performing schools. Education was something that other people did, so the children were guaranteed a poor start in life. After viewing several houses, Thomas and Anne realised that there was an abundance, so narrowed their eyes and searched harder. Eventually they found a rundown area with many disappointing aspects — perfect for their ever increasing need to be further away from prying eyes and the police. Thomas, criminal to the bone, was not specifically wanted by the police, but he lived in hope and would commit small mundane crimes on a weekly basis, often drawing his children into his illicit schemes to have a selection of fall guys.

The house they finally chose, a terraced detached (it was part of a terrace, but the builders had given up once they realised what a shit location it was built in), needed a thorough rebuild, but Thomas and Anne's budget couldn't walk, let alone run to any decent renovations. It had two doors, front and back, a selection of windows and several rooms. At the top of the house there was an attic, perfect for storing children and far enough away from neighbours to diminish the grievous aromas. There was room at the side of the house, on what could only be described as a driveway, for two poorly maintained Triumph Bedmites. At the rear was a yard, with integral path and room for a metal bin. Thomas and Anne secured the house with nails and quickly packed all their old tat in readiness for the move. The children were only told of the move three weeks after it had taken place, which meant Thomas and Anne saved several pounds on food shopping, but the kids were a little emaciated.

Settling into their new home, the Carters quickly developed poor relations with all their neighbours. Adjacent to their new hovel was a row of four terraced slums, back yards resplendent with weeds and crap, and to the rear of the house was a single-storey bungalow with a rather fetching garden shed, made entirely of wicker. On the right-hand side were two sturdy garages, each containing copious amounts of three-week-old vegetables — ripe pickings, so to speak. Thomas and Anne were no social butterflies, more social moths. Nobody liked them, but they were always fluttering around after dark near dim lights. Over the coming months, Thomas, the children and the smell would all cause disputes with their new neighbours. The bungalow was occupied by a divorcee, Mrs Spittle, a ball of a woman with large hair and evil hands. Most days she would walk the perimeter of her potted garden, ensuring that her boundary walls were not penetrated by boisterous girls. She had a son, Martin, who was gregarious during the week but extremely introverted at weekends when he was required to share his toys.

Martin was around twenty-one, and the proud owner of several things which he refused to share with anyone, lest they be soiled by grubby hands and minds. Thomas hated them. The first house of the terrace was owned by a Mr and Mrs Suttball, who had a son, Amos, a rather disturbing child whose insipid voice was reminiscent of a beaver's fart. They were deeply distrustful and spent most of their time queuing at the local church in the hope of salvation. Thomas hated them. The second house in the row was occupied by a spinster, Miss Hurtle, who was forever tearing around the local area buying teabags. She believed that the Marxists would take over the world and ban tea, so dedicated her life to stockpiling tea, loose and bagged. Her home was very cosy, if a little damp, and she would spend hours at the kitchen window, staring into the glass, fearful of the Marxists. Thomas liked tea. The third house was owned by a young couple, Doris and Arthur, who had no children but did own several small pets. Arthur was assistant manager at a pet supply business, whilst Doris spent her time nurturing injustices. The house smelt like a dog's graveyard, with faeces liberally dotted around the back yard. Their seven dogs were called Shitty, Ploppy, Farty, Gunther, Rayon, Denim, Acrylic and Sediment, and they devoted themselves to the shit of these pets with love and disgust. Thomas hated dogs. The final house was home to Mrs Cakehole, a surprisingly ugly woman with a sordid past. She had spent much of her youth as a member of the Marxist party, in a collective on the outskirts of Santiago, near Rotherham. Her extreme views had resulted in her expulsion from Rotherham in 1957. She had joined a travelling group of Marxist entertainers and travelled the north, doling out sadness and despair. She had recorded several songs about her life on the road, and she is still remembered in Wakefield as that fuck-ugly Marxist. Thomas liked the Marx brothers.

As the family settled into their new home, Anne busied herself with pointless activities, all the while puffing on her pipe. Her baking attracted derision, yet she persisted and produced some truly disgusting cakes: chocolate and cheese, pea and jam, and a favourite of Thomas's, bacon and egg turnover. The last recipe, something that Anne had thrown together in the early hours of Easter Sunday, was both savoury and sickly. Whipped bacon would be mixed with pan-dried egg, and then incorporated in a very runny batter mix. It would then be left to fester for several hours to allow the flavours to intensify, before being cooked at a ridiculously high heat until it was extremely burnt. Anne would then shave off as much of the crust as possible, leaving behind a wonderfully abhorrent cake that really could put hairs on your chest.

The children had settled into their respective berths with little obvious complaint, although Janine did have her own door, and was able to wake up to light in the mornings, whereas the three boys shared a freezing afterthought of a room, with the tiniest of windows and no obvious means of access. Damian was given what could only be described as a bed in the corner, along with an eiderdown, a pillow, and several old, World War Two blankets, that had seen better days. The attic had sloping ceilings, which meant it was perfect for anyone with a sloping head, but the boys all had more angular heads, resulting in several head injuries along with fallen plaster from the decaying ceiling. In the winter, the attic hole was freezing, and in the summer, it was also freezing, due to Stephen's insistence on leaving the attic crevice open to allow him to smoke. Stephen was a born athlete, but he had started to poison his body a few months earlier and was now smoking at least some cigarettes each day. Thomas strongly approved of nothing and was quick to point out the dangers of anything. He believed most children's toys were death-traps, so his attitude to smoking was equally as irrational. He advised Stephen on the health benefits of cigarettes, took several bites from a lard sandwich, and then continued to read his Readers' Digest. Of course, in the early 70s, many people smoked, and it was viewed as a rite of passage for many gullible fools. Cigarettes were plentiful and matches even more so. Damian heard that at school you were given cigarettes by the teachers and encouraged to smoke one between every lesson to build up your immunity to life. Thomas had started smoking when he was very young, and took to it with ease, displaying a natural flair for mild inhaling and exhaling. During the war he had stopped smoking for health reasons, but on resumption of civilian life he had quickly fallen back in with cigarettes, and they were his lifelong companions. On some mornings, when food was short, he would rustle up cigarette surprise, a simple dish of tobacco and eggs. The kids lapped it up and were soon chronic.

# Milk it and they will come

The long, outstretched arm of the law was never too far from Thomas's nefarious activities, and for the Carters it meant many days in hiding, be that in the shed, emotionally, or if necessary, in the boot of a Ford Fugitive. The newly formed Uniformed Slightly Serious Crime Squad had no radar, but if they had possessed such fancy equipment, then Thomas would have been a very small blip on a very large screen. His ability to infringe by-laws was well known, and his criminality was a burden that Anne was fully aware of when he stole her wedding ring to pay for the Ford Fugitive. His schemes, plans and mind-blowing escapades were hatched in the cubbyhole under the stairs. On most evenings he would retire to the lair, pencil in hand, and work by candlelight to stave off starvation. Not wanting to lead his eminently leadable children into a life of criminal ineptitude, he would plan his villainous endeavours after the watershed, in the knowledge that three of his children were extremely heavy sleepers. Many of his schemes were doomed from the outset due to incompetence and over-ambition. Occasionally he would hit on an idea that would mean he would be able to pay at least one utility bill and feed the kids more than one meal a day. The Carters were regular shoppers at Morrison's, and Thomas devised a plan that would allow him to borrow food from the shop without fear of prosecution. In a time when yoghurt was considered a luxury beyond the grasp of pie-eating folk, and muesli was something that was eaten in exotic locations, Thomas devised a plan so simple and so elegant that it was doomed to fail or succeed. He planned to have his three youngest children shoplift the elegant food, his rationale being that nobody would think that three bedraggled urchins from a hovel in Bradford would possibly steal such fancy items as Dundee cake, glacé cherries, yoghurt or any fish-based products.

Tinned fish was the preserve of the well-to-do who played golf and drove reliable cars. Suitably prepared for the heist of the century, Janine, Paul and Damian were driven to a Morrison's on the far side of town where their grubby coats wouldn't be recognised and sent into the shop and told to plunder. Janine was sent in the direction of the tinned fish due to her larger biceps and natural affinity with the sea. Paul was told to focus solely on Dundee cake and walnuts, whilst Damian went off in the direction of the chilled aisle in search of yoghurt.

Suffice to say, the plan went like clockwork. Rammed to the brim with decanted yoghurt, Damian had exotic flavours such as strawberry, cherry and banana secreted into the lining of his anorak. In his hood he had a family pack of muesli, and snaffled just for the thrill was a bumper box of After Eight mints — Anne's favourite. Janine hit the mother lode, managing to grab an incredible array of tinned fish products, ranging from red salmon to yellow haddock, blue whale to black squid — a rainbow of fish products. Let the good times roll. Paul was almost caught when several walnuts slipped from his grasp as he left the supermarket, but thanks to some quick thinking, he ran like fuck. He had got away with three extra-large Dundee cakes and a tube of tomato puree, along with a half-eaten loaf of premium white bread and two tubs of margarine. On seeing the bounty, Thomas was ecstatic; they would eat like kings for the coming months. Of course, for every success there was an equal and opposite failure. What Thomas saved in grocery spending, he spent on trying to maintain the hovel to a level fit for habitation. Very soon the roosters came home to roost following a very over-indulgent feast of tinned mackerel and glacé cherries, accompanied by a very heavy tomato-based gravy. As the old adage goes, 'cherries on a Monday, blocked toilet all week long'.

Somethings couldn't be done easily. So when Thomas stood in the bathroom with his junior-sized plunger, he knew this blockage would not shift itself. With a degree of trepidation, he attempted to persuade the blockage to move of its own accord, knowing full well it was futile, so when Damian, and then Paul asked to use the toilet, Thomas had to act quickly. Placing the plunger on the edge of the bath, he ran downstairs, grabbed the key for the Fugitive, and went to see if he could purchase an industrial-sized plunger from a very resourceful man down at the local working men's club. A regular at the club, Jeff Shift, knew a man who knew a man who might have a family-sized plunger, but it would cost. Shift was himself a licenced plumber, with wrenches, tool belt and an enthusiastic approach to all things toilet-related. It was his night off and Thomas could ill-afford the ridiculous call-out charge. Whilst Thomas waited for the plunger, Damian and Paul had retired to bed and assumed that it would be okay to piss in the neighbour's back yard, egged on by Stephen. Needs must when the devil drives.

*The Tweezers*, so called because they were mean pluckers, were a 60s tribute band formed at the end of the '50s. Realising that they were ahead of their time, they disbanded in 1961 only to reform in 1971 in the hope they could now capitalise on the musical wave that had washed over the previous decade. They performed on the northern club circuit, covering such bands as *The Chocolate Haze, Velvet Undergarment and the Robe*, and of course *The Weevils*. The lead singer of *The Tweezers*, Tommy Goat, was a raucous chap with a beard to match. He had grown up in the same street as Thomas, and when he opened a photographic studio at the start of the year to supplement his earnings (The Tweezers had hit a barren patch), he was on the lookout for children who could smile in order to promote the studio. Paul was known throughout Yorkshire for his dazzling yet enigmatic smile, and he had often been compared to the Mona Lisa. His ability to crack a smile regardless of the circumstances was a gift that kept on giving. In the previous year he had attended a series of workshops at the Shipley Smile Academy, where his natural exuberance and affability were immediately spotted by the principal, Miss Gloom, and he was used as the face of the academy throughout the 70s. Initially Paul had to exhibit his full range of smiles, so Tommy could catalogue them into the correct category. Smiling was a very misunderstood area of human behaviour in the 70s, and many people assumed that if you smiled too much you had mental issues. Paul was able to produce the full range of smiles, all of which came completely naturally to him. His 'dumbfounded yet happy' smile was very popular with his teachers, as was his 'hidden turd' smile, often used when he was younger. The more sophisticated smiles, such as the 'condescending bastard' and the 'supercilious' were the favourites of the righteous and religious. Tommy was very pleased with most of Paul's smiles, but two of them were not included in the catalogue, the 'angry bishop' and 'cheesy but charming', as they were deemed inappropriate for families and those with sensitive eyes. Tommy's studio thrived, in part due to Paul's smiles, and he was able to invest in several Airfix models on the back of the money earned.

Toys in the 70s were a different world, with action figures, toy soldiers and cowboys and Indians, a firm favourite with Damian and Paul. Both boys would dress up as model aeroplanes and throw toy soldiers at Thomas to get his attention. Those carefree days were a time of imagination and rationed fun, where every last giggle, chortle or mirthful glare had to be accounted for otherwise there would not be enough fun for the whole year. Thomas never played with his children, preferring to spend his time tinkering with crappy cars or buying tat from all over the West Yorkshire area. There was no tat too expensive, no distance too far if it meant he could justify a drive to Keighley or Halifax, or on rare occasions, over the border into Lancashire. This would only happen if the tat was of the highest quality and its provenance questionable. On those rare occasions when he sat with his two younger sons it would be to play a hand of gin rummy or pontoon. Damian loved the pretty colours and images that decorated the forty-seven-card pack that Thomas had picked up from Dewsbury market at a very reasonable price.

Milk: the water of life, giver of calcium, mother of cheese. Milk not money makes the world go round. The humble cow with its udders of love, providing young girls and boys all the calcium needed to ward off brittle bones and rickets. Damian loved milk, especially the little bottle of milk he would have every morning at school, along with a malted milk biscuit and a smile full of despair. This was the year when many cows faced deportation, and even though Damian was not directly affected by the expulsion of so many pretty cows, as he was only six years old, his bones felt it, contracting a little bit to preserve what little calcium they held.

Didley Hull School was a hive of low achievement and underwhelming damp, and the withdrawal of free school milk saw a drastic reduction in pupil activity. Their fragile, calcium depleted limbs became mere receptacles of flesh and the teachers were powerless to prevent this floppy-limbed mass of calcium junkies from falling and tripping due to their inability to stand for any length of time. Damian had been drinking milk for many years and felt the reduction in calcium hard, unable to leave his bed for the first three weeks of March. Anne, deciding that mother knows best, took to raiding milk from a local dairy farmer to ensure her children were not confined to office jobs. No one wants a child who is desk-bound. Having suffered with calcium shortfalls for months, Anne decided to take drastic action to prevent her children's bones from completely crumbling into dust, only held in place by a thin layer of skin and fat. Setting Thomas the task of finding a cheap and affordable cow, Anne believed they could kill several birds with one rather large stone. It wasn't usual to see second-hand cows advertised in the local paper, certainly not for under five pounds. Thomas scanned the small ads, desperately searching for that mythical Friesian, Guernsey, or Jersey at a push. Each evening involved a dash to the newsagents to get the small ads hot off the press in the forlorn hope that a farmer somewhere had an unwanted cow for a knock down price. Thomas, magnifying glass in hand, would scour the ads, often finding animals, but not one that he wanted to extract milk from or even touch. There were several ads for part-worn snakes needing a comfortable home; two ads extolling the virtues of rearing free-range tortoises; and an exotic gentleman from Lincolnshire who was trying to sell his herd of llamas to a Peruvian loving family. It seemed hopeless until Thomas spotted a small ad offering a litter of cows at a ridiculously low price. The farmer in question stated that the cows were from their mother, possessed a full set of legs and udders, and would make an ideal birthday gift or pair of shoes. Thomas was on the phone like a shot, explaining that he couldn't understand why the cows were going for such a low price. Despite this, Thomas jumped in his Austin Lactose and headed up the A657 to try and land the deal of the year; a complete set of cows for under ten quid.

Arriving at Low Top Farm and Animal Rescue Centre, Thomas swept down the driveway in his Lactose and screeched to a halt near a rusty-looking man by a shed. Once the hasty introductions were concluded, Farmer Shaft (that was his name) took Thomas to a smaller shed located at the bottom of the farmyard. As the shed door swung open, Thomas was greeted by five yapping little cows with big eyes and furry tails. They looked a little like sheepdog puppies, but Farmer Shaft assured Thomas that these were a rare breed of dwarf cow whose milk was highly prized by athletes and dogs alike. Thomas immediately offered £7.37 in cash, stating he would take them today and ask no awkward questions. The deal was done, and Thomas was the proud owner of a bundle of dog—like cows. Of course his next problem was to give the five dog-like cows names that matched their personalities. On the drive home he ruminated on several possible names, but thought that his children might want to join in and choose a name too, giving them a sense of responsibility in their otherwise depleted existence. They could also take the cows for walks and train them to perform tricks for visiting relatives and vets. Parking up outside the Carter hovel, Thomas left the dog-like cows in the boot of his Lactose and went to drag his sleeping children out of bed; it was better to sleep than think about the long summer evenings without milk. Damian loved dwarf dog-cows, having seen a picture of one in a book at his underfunded school. Paul was a little nervous around larger animals, and Janine would eat most meats without questioning their provenance. Stephen was ambivalent, believing that they didn't have room for five more mouths but also loving the idea of frolicking with the young dog-like cows. Thomas explained to the kids that he had bought the dog-like cows to provide a suitable source of lactose for their calcium deficient bones, and he needed suggestions for names for the calves currently barking in the boot of the Lactose.

Damian sat and thought whilst Paul practised his smiles. Janine was gnawing on her bowl of crusty porridge, and Stephen immediately decided on a name for his dog-like cow: Butterpat, after his great-grandmother, Patricia. Janine, who loved all things mechanical, decided on Corkscrew-Sewage Pump, as she felt it reflected the flamboyant nature of her chosen puppy-like calf. Paul, after some deliberation, decided that he would like to call his Cheese Puff Ball, after his favourite snack. Damian pondered and was undecided. On the one hand, he wanted to give his, a short powerful name, such as Gut, Snack or Hat. On the other hand, he felt that his puppy-like calf deserved a name that reflected its personality and obvious characteristics. He had toyed with Smells Like a Dog — Shits Like a Cow but felt it would be a little too long for its name tag, and Slightly More Dog than Cow, which was accurate but lacked mystery. Finally, after two minutes of deliberation and reflection, he plumped for If Milk Were Free We Wouldn't Need this Beast; short and pithy. The last pup was given to Anne as a belated anniversary present, and she named it Bastard Shithole Beast because of its loving nature and propensity to crap everywhere.

As the animals settled in, it became obvious to most disinterested observers that Thomas had bought five puppies from a farmer in Colne, yet Thomas persisted with his morning routine. First, he would rise before dawn and make his way down to the 'milking shed', with cut down stool and rinsed out mop bucket in hand. Then he would patiently tease and cajole the beasts into their milking stance. Avoiding the piles of shite which had accumulated over the week, he would then spend hours looking for anything that looked remotely like an udder. His fruitless search for calcium was to last for seventeen weeks until he realised that he really had been sold a pup, so to speak, and he needed to re-house them and find alternative milk supplies. Damian had mixed emotions on the matter. He had grown fond of Bastard Shithole Beast, as had all the family, but mucking out half a ton of dog shite on a weekly basis was too much, even for the hardiest of seven-year-olds. Furthermore, the cost of feeding, fettling and buying saddles was prohibitive, so it was not even possible to ride the beasts to school and save some money on bus fares. Thomas, with a heavy heart, admitted defeat, and sold all five beasts to a butcher in Colne who promised to give them a loving home. Thomas even made a small profit of £1.29 on the transaction, so bought two pints of full fat milk to celebrate.

Damian's school was a grubby little hole adjacent to a dual carriageway and opposite an abattoir. This made it the ideal hunting ground for childhood illnesses and scabies. The school nurse, Miss Pulse, was a stickler for germs and infections, often insisting that she would not see a child until they had at least two communicable infections. With the ongoing shortages of calcium that had so bedevilled the nation, school nurses had been given the responsibility of pumping, injecting or secreting calcium into their young and feckless charges. The government had invested a considerable amount of money in ensuring that emergency supplies of calcium were available if ever the nation faced shortages. Utilising some old vats of calcium that had been retained following the end of hostilities in 1945, the boffins at the Ministry of Calcium and Vitamins had also built several underground vitamin storage tanks that could be used if scurvy reared its ugly head. The Minister responsible, Sir Eustace Bugger-Hall, announced that with the nation's bones at such a brittle juncture, it would be necessary to roll out the emergency calcium programme. School nurses were sent to the front line in this battle against floppy legs and emaciated expressions.

Miss Pulse took her responsibilities very seriously, insisting on every child performing a series of lunges, thrusts and stretches in order to ascertain their emotional well-being. Damian, fragile both in mind and body, had been practising lunges in readiness for this very eventuality, so when Miss Pulse called his name outside the school shed, he was fully prepared to lunge. Stepping inside the infirmary shed, a place full of history and garden tools, Damian was asked to take off his shoes and give Miss Pulse twenty lunges. He froze, unable to perform even a half-hearted lunge. Panic crept across his brow, and realising he was in danger of leaving the infirmary shed as a category D lungeless loser, he threw himself into some violent arm swinging, whilst at the same time whistling the 'Dad's Army' theme tune. He then attempted a very energetic thrust, ripping his undersized trousers and letting off a violent fart. Miss Pulse's faced throbbed, her heart raced and her thyroid went into overdrive. No child, regardless of their lack of basic calcium supplies, should ever fart in the presence of Miss Pulse. Removing a large needle from under her captain's hat, she organised the needle, overloaded with nutrients and pure, grade A, undiluted calcium, and threw it in the general direction of Damian's arse. Brittle bones or no brittle bones, Damian was an agile child, and ducking like he was born to quack, the needle shot past his arse, ricocheted off a garden shovel and entered some very soft, flabby flesh. An eye-watering scream rang out through the corridors of the school as the needle sunk ever deeper into Miss Pulse's already obvious nose. She had accidently secreted raw calcium into a calcium-overloaded nose, and the effects were immediate. Her already large legs began to swell, her hips, already suggesting child-rearing, now shouted out brood delivering, and her nose, a powerful advert for cosmetic surgery, now took on a calcium life of its own. Often the excuse for carrying excess weight, 'big-boned' really did describe Miss Pulse. That much calcium, ingested through the nose, would normally kill a wild herbivore, or at least make it feel a little queasy. That much calcium would stop a small group of under-privileged children from having weak bones for one whole month. Miss Pulse just soaked it up and grew stronger. Her nails, normally stunted and unsuited to digging for truffles, now resembled talons. Her teeth, previously a small collection of decaying tombstones, now stood proud and erect, exploding from her mouth like shards of marble. Her weak frame, with bandy legs and a bow-like back, transformed into a labyrinth of fortified, high-density limbs, struggling to break free from the grey skin that held her together. Miss Pulse had got herself racing. Damian fled from the infirmary shed and hid in his safe place near the school's garbage disposal facility (bin).

Still shaken by the milk-based trauma, Damian asked Thomas if he really needed the book learning, or could he just make up an alternative alphabet and counting system and do away with school altogether. Thomas, a free thinker and wide-brained man, was all for allowing his youngest to stay at home. They could share hours of fun, messing with rusty car parts and oil; sifting things that needed a good sift; and generally arsing around in between Thomas's bouts of inflamed elbows and heart attacks. Anne, whose liberal approach to child rearing meant that until Damian was five, he wasn't sure if the sky existed, wanted to see all of her children have an education of sorts, with or without pens and paper. She insisted on the children going to school for a period of time, but as she worked in a primary school, was emotionally and professionally torn — educate her children and keep her job or let them run wild and be happy and keep her job.

Janine and Paul were now attending middle school, where the knowledge was centred on the middle, whilst Damian was still at primary school. Each morning, cheap school bag slung over a fence, the children would head off to school, with a packed lunch and worn PVC shoes (they could be cleaned in a twin tub), ready for a dreary day of indoctrination. Janine and Paul would drop Damian off at his school and then continue on to middle school. Damian would furtively scurry, like the rat he was, to his safe place by the school's hygiene department (the outdoor cleaning store), until the playground guards had marched the inmates into class. Then, avoiding the guard animals and security fence, he would slip out of the school gates and head off home. Once an inmate was logged as missing from school, the alarm was raised, and the school would go into lock down. This was a time before CCTV, so schools employed sketch artists to draw the best bits of the action in and around school. Damian had to cover his tracks and leave a false trail for the dogs which would be released to hunt down the fugitive child. Skirting round the glue factory and along the side of the disused toilet paper recycling centre, Damian hurried along the dried-up railway line. The route meant that he would avoid the sweet shop, which was monitored for illicit children, and he would come out at the back of a fishmongers, throwing the dogs off his scent once again. He would then climb into the back of a milk float and hide beneath the crates of full fat until finally jumping off four yards from his home.

He would then clamber over a small wall opposite his house and wait for the signal from Thomas giving him the all clear. Once the school had contacted Anne about Damian's escape, she would call Thomas and tell him to retune to channel seventeen and wait for the allotted call. Providing the truancy officer was still off sick with varicose veins, Damian was then free to spend the day with Thomas, arsing around. If the truancy officer had bothered to come into work, the 'sudden ailment plan' would kick in and Damian would be tucked up in bed with a used biro acting as a thermometer. This cunning ruse enabled Damian to spend many a happy day with his father, bonding over pork pies and brown sauce, sharing a love of hub caps and chrome, and visiting numerous scrap yards in search of a starter motor for a Ford Fugitive. Obviously, this impacted on Damian's progress at school, but if the school had tested him on his knowledge of hubcaps, pork pies or the history of chrome and its uses, he would have come top of the class. Thomas told Damian that rules were there to make people feel better about themselves, a lesson lost on Damian as he picked at the crust of a rather succulent pork pie. School was a place of restrictions and rot, and Thomas wanted his children to experience a different kind of education. An education that would equip his children with enough elbow grease to turn their hand to any chrome tarnishing problem. An education which would let them fully appreciate the hand-raised pie. An education that wouldn't require a child to fester in a classroom when there was a scrap yard to be explored. These were life skills beyond any book or university educated la-di-da types, whose understanding of the intricacies of chrome was minimal; whose ability to find, never mind change, the starter motor on a Ford Fugitive was a non-starter; whose appreciation of lard-based pastry was limited due to defective palates and prejudice.

Thomas had been employed part-time at a local ice-cube factory, but when the business went into liquidation, he found himself once again looking for a job that would match his very particular set of skills. Whilst searching for the perfect job, he was able to spend many hours at home, undertaking pointless domestic activities, but in the main, arsing around. Thomas and Damian would jump in the Fugitive (if it started), and as these were pre-safety days, no seat belts were necessary, only the trust of a son and the good eye of his father. Speeding along the highways and dirt tracks of West Yorkshire, whilst the busy workers were locked away in their worlds of futility, the pair were free to roam and explore the wondrous world that was Bradford in the morning. Taking a right at the end of the street would take the pair through the local council estate, with its pre-fab despondency and bitter smell of decay. Beyond the estate, charmingly called Holme Park Wood, lay the happy hunting grounds of the scrap yards, luring Thomas for a bargain he would not be prepared to pay full price for, preferring instead to attempt to bamboozle the trader with technical lingo and sleight of hand. Taking a left took you to the bright lights of Bradford city centre, with its dual attractions of a functioning railway station and a very good fresh fish market. On some days it would be fish and trains, on others the thrill of haggling with an oily, one-toothed scrap-dealer with hate in his heart and cash in his pocket. Whilst in the car, Thomas would listen to Mario Lanza, the voice of a generation. If Lanza was not available, Thomas would retune the wireless to Radio Northern, where men with flat vowels and even flatter feet would prattle on about the wool harvest, the price of a barrel of lard and the latest pop tunes to offend their hair-filled ears. Damian never fully appreciated the wit and wisdom that these northern fellows offered, but Thomas was a regular caller to the programme, often coming home just so he could make an indignant call on a point of fact. When the presenter of the mid-morning show, Gus T. Wether insisted that deep sea fishing was no different to breeding sheep, Thomas felt compelled to turn around and drive the seventeen miles home in order to make his point. Below is Damian's recollection of his father's contribution to the debate that was raging in the bars and tea rooms of Bradford that wet Wednesday afternoon.

Damian's recollection is kindly reproduced thanks to his vivid imagination.

*Good morning, Gus, or can I call you Windy? My name is Thomas, but you may call me Mr Carter. As I recall, you and your ilk, with your thrifty beards and heavy-duty vowels, are funded by the Wool Marketing and Wearers Association, an organisation hell bent on undermining the fishing industry in this country. As a wearer of wool myself, it is with a heavy heart that I have called today, on account of all the cholesterol, but I must give the fisherman's side of the argument. I was a loyal servant of the sea for nearly six years, chopping up and down the rough seas in search of pike, perch, carp and alike, and not once did I ever find one in the North Sea. Elusive buggers, yet I have fond memories of my time aboard the good ship Brine. Not once did I see a sheep farmer catch a fish in all my time at sea, yet here you are, badmouthing the humble fisherman for his lack of understanding of the wool trade. I served a wool harvester for several years, and I can assure you that I stole my fair share of quality wool in that time, but I never worked as hard as I did whilst aboard the good ship Brine. Long waves and intermittent rain meant I shrunk by over half a foot, and with the onset of winter I was sodden pretty much all the time. Three years I spent trying to dry out. Doctors said I contained more water than a fully inflated cucumber. On account of all the water, I didn't need to drink for seven months. I paid a high price to hunt for fish to put on the tables of the average sheep farmer in the street. Nowadays I stay away from the sea following doctor's orders. My physician says that if I so much as dip a toe in any sort of briny water, I could balloon up to thirty stone.*

*I think I have said my piece, so I would bid you good day and ask you to consider your words carefully.*

Thomas delivered this in a West Cornwall accent and won the hearts of all the fisherman who might well have been tuned in that day. Those days of Damian's spent wasting time with his dad were happy and carefree. Every child should be so lucky.

# The pensioner and his angry banana

Opposite the Carter hovel was a collection of low rise, single-storey kennels for the elderly. They had been built to prevent Damian and Paul from playing football opposite their house, and as such, the two boys resented the crusty pensioners who occupied these dreary dwellings. There was still a small patch of grass where football could be played, but it became a battlefield, a war between a pack of feral boys and an old man with a banana for a telephone.

On warmer evenings or when the rain wasn't too heavy, Damian and Paul would slip on their PVC trainers and a hand-knitted jumper and call for all the local boys in the surrounding area for a game of footie. Using the woollen jumpers as goal posts, and double checking for dog shit, the boys would kick off, and that is when battle would commence. The old man who lived opposite this scrubby patch of grass objected to the noise the boys made. His name, Arthur Crumple, still haunts Damian today, and has ensured that Damian never uses and never will use a banana to make phone calls. Crumple would watch the boys from his front room, net curtains twitching, and then pick up his banana phone and ring the banana police to report a disturbance. When the boys didn't move on, he would come to the front of his oh-so-low bungalow and threaten the boys with his by now half-eaten banana phone. The boys would protest, protest some more and then move on, only to return in half an hour. The dance, this ballet between young and old, happened every day, and Thomas and Anne supported the boys, stating that it was a free country and that old git could shove his banana phone where the sun didn't shine. Bradford? Of course, with all conflicts, there is a period of intense manoeuvring and feints to try and put the enemy off balance. Sometimes Crumple would use a plantain or a cucumber;

on other occasions the boys would mime the football match, sans football. This only intensified the heat that only needed a spark to start a full-scale war.

Crumple had served as an aircraft warden during World War Two, seeing action and aircraft in Norwich and Bury St Edmonds. He had retired to Bradford for its Spar and the clean air. He was a very disappointed man, who took his frustrations out on his neighbours, his banana phone and the local boys. The local Spar wasn't as well stocked as he would have liked, and the air was polluted with particles of wool and sheep breath. His wife had left him in 1947, and he had struggled for the last twenty-five years to find his place in the world until now. He was the villain who would end up in court following a serious assault of Damian and his sensibilities. Who could have known that football could lead to such violent behaviour? Certainly not in the 70s when football was a gentleman's game.

The day of the assault was like no other and is etched into a tree near the hovel. Damian, Paul and several other like-minded boys had made their way to the scrap of grass to play football, avec football. Crumple was nowhere to be seen; his nets remained still, and the banana phone was not spotted. The boys tore around, hoofing the ball with abandon, caring not if they scored, as it was just so nice not having to keep a careful eye out for Crumple. They dropped their collective guard, and were soon playing other games like tig and hide and seek, in between the occasional shot at goal of course. From behind a disused shed, Crumple appeared, banana phone in one hand and a fist full of anger in the other. Making his way toward the ball, Crumple intended to snatch the ball and deny the boys their fun. Damian spotted the danger immediately, and using his more efficient foot, flicked the ball to Paul, who then gave it back to Damian to hold. Crumple strode up to Damian and demanded that he give him the ball immediately. This was never going to work with Damian, who could be a little shit at times. Point blank refusal was his only option, which infuriated Crumple, his face turning a beautiful crimson colour and his banana phone looking decidedly overripe. Lunging at Damian, Crumple attempted to snatch the ball, but Damian, nimble as a foal, skipped to one side and let out a little fart. Crumple swung round and smacked Damian on the side of the head. As the ball dropped, Crumple grabbed at it and threatened the other boys with more of the same. Damian turned and faced Crumple, swearing that one day he would write an embellished version of events that would see him drummed out of the local bowls club and ruin him if he was still alive. Brandishing his banana phone, Crumple gave an evil laugh which sent shock waves through his leather trousers. Marching off with his prize, Crumple seemed invincible.

The boys were deflated, not unlike the ball. Damian and Paul quickly made their way home, a journey that took thirty seconds, and raced into the back parlour to disgorge the horrendous events that had just occurred. Anne, resplendent in a fetching blue and green pinny, velvet pipe in hand, told the pair to calm down and breath awhile. After what seemed like ten minutes, Anne was fully informed of the facts and asked the boys to peel some turnips for tea while she pondered on the next course of action. Thomas would be home soon, if the Austin Triangle didn't have a flat tyre again, and his reaction would dictate whether Crumple was beaten to death with a large turnip or a civilised approach was to be adopted.

Thomas was extremely protective of his children, and in the past had been provoked over the treatment of Stephen at the hands of a hot water fanatic, so Anne was worried that he might do something that they both would live to regret. As the Austin Triangle scraped up the drive, Anne went to the door and was soon in deep conversation with her husband. Thomas's face gave nothing away, but as he strode across the street, rolled up Reader's Digest in hand, it looked as if Crumple would be facing a thrashing by bi-monthly journal. What happened next surprised no one. Thomas rapped at the door of Crumple's bitterly lit bungalow, and when he came to the door, banana phone in hand, Thomas simply stated that he would see him in court and that no one struck his children. What a hero. He marched back to the hovel, gave his sons a hug, and asked if the turnips were ready.

As the court date approached, jumpers were frayed and nerves were knitted. Since the incident, Damian had changed, and had taken to wearing more pastel colours and fewer woollen items; it was summer after all. The Carters' solicitors, Twist and Turn, had assured them that like the door to the office, it was open and shut. Damian was required to give testimony, but Thomas and Paul would be there, as would the boys who had witnessed the sordid farrago of an incident.

On the appointed day, Thomas started the Ford Redemption (the Triangle was a three-seater and unsuitable for a family of six) and they headed off to have their day in court.

Arriving at Bradford Magistrates' court, Thomas parked the Redemption and made his way to the reception area, his two youngest sons in tow. They were seated in a very busy reception area, full of miscreants and ne'er-do-wells (solicitors) and told they would be called shortly. Damian felt calm, knowing that Thomas would be with him in the witness box. Paul was practising his serious but friendly smile just in case he was cross-examined by a hostile defence solicitor. Anne had prepared some turnips and peas to stave off the worst of the hunger pains, and a thermos full of strong tea for Thomas, who functioned better with a strong, sweet tea. Crumple was nowhere to be seen, so when they were called by a clerk, Damian was a little confused. Was Crumple to be hanged in his absence? Taking their seats next to Mr Twist, the three sat in silence as Crumple was led in. With striped pyjamas, shackles and shaved head, he really was going for the prisoner look. His hound dog eyes remained focused on the clerk's feet, and throughout the proceedings he never made eye contact with Thomas or Paul, and certainly not Damian. He reeked of shame and guilt in equal measure; a hasty action had cost him his banana phone, his jaunty hat (he misplaced it a few weeks before) and his reputation; the trial hadn't even started.

As the magistrates entered, the whole court rose in unison, Crumple maintaining his defeated demeanour. After a few formalities and birthday wishes to Mr Twist, who was forty-nine, Damian was called to the witness box. The clerk explained that Thomas would sit behind him, but he must explain what happened in his own words. He was given a bible, and he passed it to Thomas for later, and he then swore an oath, promising to embellish the truth. Questions were asked and Damian's clear and angelic delivery had the court in raptures. He still had a scar from where Crumple had struck him (thanks to Anne's work with an eye liner) and when a tear welled up in his beautiful green eye, the whole court seemed to lift him up and hug the little cherub. Thomas reassured his son throughout, and when his evidence was complete, Paul was called. Smiling one of his most popular smiles, the 'butter would never melt in this orifice' smile, he told a tale of fear and anger, cut and thrust. He embellished and exaggerated so well that the actual incident, if Paul was to be believed, lasted for two days. The court loved him, and he was followed by several other witnesses to back up the facts. Mr Twist then called two expert witnesses, to hammer home the two final nails in Crumple's criminal coffin. The first was a psychologist from Viana University, Doctor Chump, who had been brought in to examine Damian and assess the long-term psychological impact on Damian's development. The good doctor stated that incidents like this could leave a child afraid to eat fruit, scared of answering machines and distrusting of octogenarians. The next expert witness was an optician who had also done a part-time course in ball technology. Doctor Squint was asked if it were possible that the ball had hit Damian, and not Crumple. He said it was highly unlikely, as he looked askance at the door. When asked if he could see, he confirmed that his eyesight was okay and was not relevant to the case. Doctor Squint also maintained that no fruit, regardless of size, could have done that kind of damage to Damian's face (he was born that way). When it was suggested that Doctor Squint was giving evidence in the wrong case, an adjournment was called to let the participants catch their breath. After the break, Crumple was to give his testimony.

Head bowed and pyjamas looking soiled, Crumple struck a tragic figure in the dock. His voice was weak, and as he tried to dodge and evade the fruit that was occasionally lobbed at him from the public gallery, it was clear that he was looking for any way to avoid the death sentence. He stated that the incident was a figment of a disturbed child's imagination; he stated that Paul's smile was no replacement for truth, to which Paul gave his best 'you're fucked now, old man' smile. As his testimony continued, it was clear for all those who were present that day that Crumple was guilty. Despite his twisting and turning (the name of the solicitors he had used), the magistrates arrived at their decision before he had finished giving his feeble defence. Sentencing was swift and harsh, with Crumple given a two-hundred-and-fifty-hour community service order, a fine of thirty-five pounds, and instructions to say sorry to Damian in a sincere manner. Justice had been served, and as the boys left court with Thomas, they reflected on the invaluable lesson they had learnt; Crumple was actually ninety-one and could be taunted with impunity now; fuck him.

The following months passed in a blur, due to a mix-up over some ointment for Damian's weepy eyes. The other big pastime for Damian was knock down ginger, which was banned in many countries, but was positively encouraged in these parts of Yorkshire. Despite its name, it could be played by anyone, regardless of hair colour. Legal shenanigans aside, 1972 was a seminal year for TV court room dramas, and Damian would spend hours glued to his seat. This involuntary gluing (Stephen was the number one suspect) enabled Damian to enjoy such legal classics as 'Let Him Swing', a tough, no-nonsense court-based epic fixated on the illegal importation of playground equipment. These slides and swings were death traps in the wrong hands, and tough, no-nonsense legal beagle Hank Kneescrape was determined to make playgrounds a safe haven for kids and paedos alike. Pitted against unscrupulous swing and slide importers, Kneescrape adopted a crouching position and kicked the living shit out of anyone he suspected of being a wrong 'un, whilst still having time to perform essential legal paperwork and stay just inside the law, or at least close by. Another favourite that Damian enjoyed during this gluey phase was 'Helmet & Bob', two tough, no-nonsense bounty hunters. The pair would squirrel away in a seedy office, hunting down fine dodgers and debtors. The underbelly of law enforcement fascinated Damian's idiotic mind, and he saw himself pursuing a legal career, with ermine and silk, along with a fetching wig and briefcase. Of course, Helmet and Bob only wore wigs on their nights off, and the only cases to be seen were headcases who were determined to fight justice and park with impunity. Only Helmet and Bob stood between parking serenity and gridlock, and to Damian they were the unsung civil superheroes. One final TV drama that would leave Damian feeling slightly uncomfortable yet excited at the same time was 'Write to me from Cell Block P', a harrowing three-part series following the struggles of a newly qualified solicitor who had been sent down for fiddling his gas meter. The main character, Hoarse Buttalive, was faced with near certain violence for being a solicitor, and during each episode he was beaten off camera and slumped in his cell. The only solace he had was writing dreary letters to his fiancée Ima, recounting his travails and meals in dreary detail. Ima, tears soiling the letters, would long for the day when Hoarse would be released, and they could move to Kettering and open a small legal practice away from prying eyes. For Damian, this sophisticated take on the criminal justice system opened his eyes to the dangers of crying near paper. He also understood what slopping out meant.

# A slap-up meal in Yorkshire!

Rabid ineptitude had stalked Thomas for several years, and his unwillingness to pay full price for anything often meant corners weren't just cut; they never existed in the first place. Any scheme, project or household task could be reduced to a miserly rehearsal of a half-arsed job. At the start of the year, Thomas had bought yet another new second-hand car, this time the evergreen Austin Deciduous. With sleek seating arrangements, space-age boot and acceleration that would put wrinkles into any face, Thomas should have bought the new Ford Lightspeed, but drawn to the Deciduous by its two doors and insipid bench seating, along with a price that screamed shitheap, Thomas couldn't resist. Driving the car home from Shipley, it was apparent that three wheels were out of kilter with a fourth wheel, and steering was performed using a series of levers and pulleys. The one working windscreen wiper was currently not working, and despite reassuring Anne that it was the perfect car to ferry his ever-annoying children from place to place, Anne had her reservations to consider. First and foremost was the colour. Anne was no Picasso, but even she realised that a lime green car was just a little too outrageous for 70s Bradford. Thomas took on board the observation and decided to repaint the car, himself, using a small brush he found in the boot of the car. The colour he chose was the bluest of sky blues, based solely on the fact that he had three tins of sky-blue gloss paint left over from his Jackson Pollock phase. Taking the car to a secret location somewhere near his brother's house, Thomas spent three weeks scuttling between the two houses, carefully adding coat after coat of paint until finally he was ready for the big reveal. He prepared the children, informing them that they would soon be the envy of all passengers, whisked from location to location inside The Blue Goddess. Damian, whose love of all things blue since before he fully understood colour, was excited at the prospect of The Blue Goddess. His three siblings were not so; Stephen, on seeing the car, observed that its pallid appearance had taken the residual value of the car to next to nothing. Thomas, who was currently standing next to nothing, took this as a personal slight against his handiwork. Paul, who still suffered from acute unawareness, merely shrugged his shoulders and continued to smile at his father. Janine, normally such a placid and retiring girl, merely stated that maybe it would have been better to scrap the car and buy another more jocular mode of transport. Anne, who was ever the diplomat, puffed hard on her pipe and gripped the door handle tightly. The car was an abortion of a dog's dinner, but to say so would have broken Thomas's heart, so instead she merely observed that blue was indeed a colour. Thomas was crestfallen, knowing that this far from ringing endorsement meant he had to start looking for a replacement car, but in the meantime, he would have to drive the streets of Bradford only at night with the headlights switched off.

The year was also significant for many other reasons. Kung-Fu, a very popular form of dressing, was everywhere, and Bruce Lee led the field in karate-based movies. Damian loved films and would spend hours with Thomas watching black and white classics, such as The Maltese Sparrow, The Magnificent Six and the unforgivable Herbie Rides a Horse. Thomas had no truck with colour films usually, but even he could appreciate the artistry of Bruce Lee, and quite often the whole family would settle down on a Saturday evening, dressed in white pyjamas, adopting the Kiba Dachi in readiness to chop and kick any intruder who was foolish enough to knock on the back door before The Duchess of Duke Street had finished. Sadly, Bruce Lee died later that year, on Damian's birthday, and this had a lasting impression on Damian, who from that day forward refused to wear white pyjamas and never adopted the Kiba Dachi again. He continued to watch films, sometimes with Thomas, but sometimes with other people who also watched films. Over the coming years his library of knowledge on cinema expanded very little, but his eyesight deteriorated significantly, meaning he could no longer read the subtitles.

Pork pies also became more important to Damian's life that year and have always been a source of happiness and cholesterol. The humble pork pie was originally created to store trinkets and small change, but when an enterprising butcher happened upon some spare pork at the back of his garrulous walk-in fridge, he decided to experiment with the meat and placed it inside a wonderfully fatty crust, and hey presto, the pork pie was born. The Carters always referred to the pork pie as a Kevin Stickie, so called because of the local butcher whose real name, following a spell in police protection, was Kevin Stickie. Stickie had a way with pork and cold-water pastry and could craft a pie in under ten minutes. His attention to detail was haphazard, but what he lacked in finesse he made up in spades with sheer enthusiasm and sweat. Stickie would spend hours experimenting with pork, and most Fridays, long queues could be seen outside the local off-licence, which was across the road from Stickie's the butchers. The Carters would share a family pie, which could, if sliced thinly, feed a family of seventeen. They always had mushy peas as a side, along with mint sauce and just a hint of wind.

It was also the year that his grandmother Ida turned seventy, and a whopping family knees-up was not on the cards. Anne's family were not ones for slap-up nosh in fancy restaurants, preferring the more intermittent and simpler environment of an obscure restaurant. Believing that it would ease his anxiety, Thomas had purchased a Ford Rhino, a beast of a car with a powerful horn. As they drove to Ida's seventieth birthday meal, it became obvious that the car was severely flawed. Not only would it not turn right, but the giant horn obscured the driver's view of pretty much everything, including the steering wheel. Using only his ears, eyes and Anne, he was able to steer the Rhino to within a mile of the restaurant; from there the family walked. The restaurant, The Frisky Farrier, specialised in traditional horse-themed dishes, something that appealed to Thomas's equine sensibilities. The restaurant was owned by a retired blacksmith,

Titus Knut, who had made a small fortune in the '50s after creating horseshoes for Shetland ponies, which he patented and sold to a giant American blacksmith conglomerate. He was a man who loved food almost as much as he loved forelocks, the heat of the forge and the smell of the anvil. The restaurant itself was horse themed, with forelocks and anvils casually littered around the main dining area, and in the very small bar there were saddles instead of stools. It was very much a niche restaurant, and many customers would leave before the dessert as the heavy smell of horse sweat could be off-putting.

Thomas shared this love of all things equine, and would spend hours on his CB radio (call sign Marengo) chatting to weird and wonderful characters who vaguely understood the concept of social skills. When not on his CB rig, he would write long, horse-themed poems, inspired by his youthful experiences around stables, horses and carts.

*Kindly repossessed by the council estate of Thomas Carter*

*The Fair Farrier*

*Smell of hay, stable door,*
*Count the legs, one to four.*
*Champion gee-gee, off to trot,*
*All its shoes, it has got.*

*Crisp the air, cold the morn,*
*Out to ride, early dawn.*
*Saddle on, rider ready,*
*Not too fast, nice and steady.*

*Over fields, lanes and track,*
*The early sun on their back.*
*Gallop, gallop, steady there,*
*The gentle breeze in their hair.*

*Going faster, going quick,*
*To the saddle you must stick,*
*Over hedges, high and wide,*
*Let us go, let's ride and ride.*

*Unsteady foot, a shoe is lost,*
*To replace, it will cost.*
*A pretty penny, do not doubt,*
*The horse, its shoe is without.*

*To the farrier, he will fix,*
*On his anvil, he will mix,*
*Iron, metal, hit down hard,*
*Just behind the stable yard.*

*It's done, its ready, shod the horse,*
*Fit it on, not too much force.*
*Smithy's done, the horse has shoe,*
*But it's done a fucking pooh.*

This was a poem that Damian knew by heart as Thomas would often recite it at bedtime, complete with sound and visual effects.

Attending the meal that day were Damian's uncles, aunts and cousins, so it promised to be a day to remember. Anne had dressed the children in their finest woollen underwear, complete with woollen hat, shirt and trousers hand-knitted by the woman with the withered hand at number thirty-eight (if only she could knit herself a new hand). The children had cooled down a little thanks to the walk, but woollen clothes are generally considered to be a ridiculous choice for children. Thomas had insisted they wear wool, so when they sat down for starters, Damian, Paul and Stephen were like sweaty sheep on a day out. Janine had managed to smuggle in a hand-operated fan, so she looked serene and cool as she wolfed down her horse-shaped prawns. Damian and Paul had chosen the horse-shaped nuggets to start, whilst Stephen went for melon with horse-shaped lettuce leaves. Thomas and

Anne, sans pipe, went for deep-fried meat with a balsamic drizzle and horseradish. Ida, who neither drank nor cursed, nibbled away on a dock leaf, happy to see her extended legs under the table. After the lone waiter had cleared away what was left of the soiled napkins and cutlery, it was time to pick their main course. Damian fancied the rather elaborately named 'Spirit of the retired farrier with new potatoes and hand-brushed peas', whilst Paul opted for a seahorse fish cake with ketchup. Thomas, Anne and Stephen went for the pickled saddle of lamb on a bed, and Janine for a fetlock of fried fish with a piquant salsa. As they greedily guzzled the equine edibles, Ida nibbled on a shoot of arrowroot, content in the knowledge that she wasn't paying for all this grub. The desserts were a mixture of horse-based ice cream or pony-based pies. Damian loved ice cream, which for him represented the pinnacle of ice-based desserts, along with ice pops, ice picks and ice packs. The pies came in three flavours: Pit Pony Surprise, a charcoal infused melange of over ripe fruit; Shetland Mess, utilising very short pastry and even shorter fruit; and Shire Syllabub, soaked with lashings of Guinness to give it a bitter and unpalatable aftertaste. The whole family desperately ate their desserts and headed for the toilets, whilst Ida continued to chew serenely on yet another shoot of arrowroot. The bill for the whole meal was a whopping £32.53, and it was decided by the more responsible members of the family to pay in full. Bill settled and vomit removed from most of the woollen garments, Thomas, Anne and the children jumped in the Rhino and headed home to enjoy the delights of a pie supper with homemade mushy peas. That truly was a meal fit for a seventy-year-old.

# The best falls of your life

Like most households in those dark days, light was at a premium, and when the Carters had their first windows installed it was akin to opening the sky to eyeless visitors from a troglodyte convention. Whole new colours were visible inside the family home, and Anne, ever the proud housewife, felt that some home improvements were needed to mask the unsightly stains and growths which had until now been hidden in the shadows. Thomas, a very unreceptive home improver, immediately travelled to the local newsagent to buy a copy of the Telegraph and Argus, Bradford's premier evening newspaper. At the back, nestling between wanted adverts and a burgeoning lonely-hearts section, were the 'under a fiver' adverts. Here, ill-advised purchases could be recycled for ridiculous prices to unsuspecting fools looking for a bargain piece of tat. Thomas had always appreciated fine art, and the works of Botticelli lingered in his imagination, as did the Venus DeMello. Scanning the pages with a fevered brow, Thomas quickly honed in on an item that would, if he could get it for less than a fiver, transform the Carter family home. It was a three-foot bust of Benny Piecrust (pioneer of the pie), in marble, with only a few chips and some residual moss on the neckline. Thomas immediately rang the number given, and within hours that very same bust took pride of place on the now very crowded mantelpiece. This purchase re-ignited in Thomas a love of tat that would endure. He quickly set about finding more exquisite examples of 70s icons. Within a month Thomas had managed to purchase, for less than the price of a second-hand Ford Farce, a bust of Danny Pea (pea enthusiast), matching busts of Reg Gutslap and Brian Horsewhip (from the highly disappointing TV show, 'Pie, Pie from Him'), and a six-foot-tall statue of Barbara Gargle (singer and reputed to eat sixteen pies a day). His eye for a bargain truly was astigmatic, and soon the house resembled a stonemason's rubbish bin. Anne could see very few merits in this obsession, yet she did little to prevent Thomas's manic collecting. Each day he would eagerly search the paper, looking for some long-misunderstood politician or failed TV star to add to his already outrageous collection of statues and busts. Thankfully, Edward Heath put a stop to it, following the miners' strike of that year.

With a shortage of power, and Thomas's lorry sitting in a garage somewhere, due to fuel shortages, Thomas turned to alternative sources of heat and power. One cold January evening, after a fruitless search for a bust, he chanced upon a three-bar electric fire that was advertised as being in reasonable condition, with only two bars working. This was Thomas's eureka moment, and he was out of the door like a man possessed. On his return, he installed the said fire in the back parlour, and immediately, the effects were barely noticeable, although the fire did hum a little. All four of the children huddled around that fire, marvelling at the monstrosity, yet drawn to its lacklustre heat. They would survive the strike, Mr Heath! Toasting stale bread became the new family pastime on those long winter evenings after a hard day's learning. Thomas fashioned four toasting forks from an old coat hanger, and the children would eagerly crisp the already crisp bread in front of those two vivid bars of energy, and then smear them with dripping, knowing that low cholesterol was a thing of the future.

Gymnastics reared its flexible head in this year when Damian was introduced to the concept of stretching, flexing and generally twatting around in shorts by his orthopedically challenged P.E. teacher, Mr Flummocks, a lithe man if you consider being able to stand up unassisted to be lithe. Damian had been transfixed by aquatic gymnast Mark Spitz at the 1972 Winter Olympics, but when Mr Flummocks confirmed that Spitz was actually a swimmer, Damian decided that he wanted to do the other type of gymnastics not involving water. As luck would have it, the school had several old mattresses, some heavy-duty rope and a vaulting horse that had been used for storing grit and sand. The gym equipment meant that Damian, and his good friend Mark, were ready to learn how to flex, stretch and jump in a graceful manner. Mr Flummocks, who had no formal education but possessed a keen eye for mediocrity, chose Damian and Mark for their imposing stupidity and willingness to break bones. Lesson one involved floor exercises and both boys knew where the floor was, so it was a good start. They had to learn the cartwheel, the Arab spring and various other complex manoeuvres which would then be performed until perfected. Cane in hand, Flummocks perched on a disconnected toilet and made the pair repeat their pitiful attempts at gymnastics, slamming the cane hard against his wooden leg when they appeared to be flagging. Praise was a morsel kept for the pupils who didn't fill him with loathing, so Mark and Damian had to be content with grunts and the occasional globule of spit heading in their general direction. Damian's Arab spring was seasonal, needing more spring and less winter; his cartwheels were flat, and his floor exercises belonged in the basement. Pushing the boys didn't help as they kept falling over, so Flummocks adopted a softly-softly approach, threatening the boys with toilet cleaning or litter picking if they didn't fucking apply themselves. Satisfied that they had peaked, attention was turned to the vaulting horse, a seven-foot wooden shire of a beast with only a solid cranium between it and a wheelchair. Damian took to vaulting like a duck to running, and was soon flipping, flopping and generally flying at the vault with abandon. He possessed a natural ability to fall well, meaning his visits to the school nurse were frequent but not too time-consuming. Mark was unable to master the vault and suffered some ruinous injuries as he repeatedly hit the wood rather than clearing it. Thankfully, he had soft hair, which prevented serious injury, but he never rode again and forswore never to work in the timber industry. They then moved on to the rope, which was designed to strengthen their puny upper bodies. Flummocks had greased the rope to alleviate some of the more severe rope burns but suffice to say that the pair of budding gymnasts needed plentiful amounts of chafing cream when the rope tasks were completed. They shimmied and slipped for hours, writhing on the snake like twine until they lay slumped on a mattress. Flummocks pushed them hard, meaning they had to get up again. The training was a relentless rollercoaster of routine, honing the boys until they were ready; for what they weren't sure.

Damian opted to take two proficiency badges but was spotted on his way out and had to give them back. Despite this, he was chosen to represent his house in the inter-house gymnastic event, the premier gymnastic event of the year — in fact the only one. Donning a pair of plimsolls, a fairly clean white vest and some white shorts borrowed from Paul, he was ready to compete for the glittering prize: Best Gymnast in Year One. On the morning of the event, Damian woke as per usual, dressed, ate his regulation bowl of tepid porridge (diet is key to an athlete's success), dressed and made his way to school. To say he was nervous would be an over-statement. He was too stupid to be nervous, so when he arrived in the school hall and saw that the whole school had turned out to witness this clash of titans, he was unable to control his feet. Damian suffered from a debilitating condition known as Morton's toe, or Greek feet, meaning his feet were very inefficient. This affected his balance, his diet and his ability to understand and follow simple instructions. Flummocks was nothing if not sadistic and had spotted Damian's inefficient feet from the outset and decided they would make suitable entertainment as a sporting failure. Morton's toe is a little-known condition; sufferers spend long hours in shoe shops trying to find ill-fitting shoes that do not draw attention to their hideous gait and faces. As Damian sat on the narrow bench, shivering as the hall was cold, he witnessed some amazing feats of stretching, flexing and jumping. The grace and poise of the headmaster was a thing to behold. Then the hall went quiet; you could have heard a fart drop, and Damian's name was called. As he stepped on the mattresses that served as mats, his mouth seemed moist — not too moist or too arid. His palms were as expected, next to his fingers, and his mind was in tune with the moment. What followed was a dazzling display, interspersed with a transient mix, an over-arching cavalcade of a dog's dinner. Damian writhed around on the mattresses, attempted an Arab spring and lost a plimsoll, tore his shorts doing a cartwheel, and could only manage a backward roll thanks to an ingrowing armpit (something that Thomas also suffered with). He had chosen the music to accompany his routine himself. Eschewing convention, he had plumped for 'Marcellus O'Reilly and his Penny Whistle', a haunting marching song that his father would often hum. Believing it would encapsulate the grace and elegance that he brought to the mattresses, Damian had practised long and hard with the volume turned down in his back yard. However, when it came to the real performance, the music was played way too loud, and he couldn't hear himself fail, flail and fall repeatedly. Experience is an unforgiving bastard. He then had to complete two different vaults without breaking a major bone. Damian had chosen two very difficult vaults, thinking that this would impress the two partially sighted judges who ran the music department on a Thursday and Friday. His first vault, The Lunge with Triple Cry and Fall, had never before been attempted in daylight, so it was no surprise when Damian completely mistimed his run up and smacked head first into the face of the vaulting horse. The judges kindly let Damian stop the bleeding before he attempted his second vault, The Headless Horseman. This was inspired by a 1930s Boris Karloff film that Damian had seen the week before, and although it was not a recognised vault, Damian felt it offered the judges a glimpse of the future now.

The audience were wild, and some say it was only because of The Headless Horseman and Damian's sacrifice on the altar of aesthetic athletics that children no longer have to witness such shit at school. Thunderous applause would have been nice, but all Damian got was last place and fifty lines for making an arse of Mr Flummocks.

Satisfied that he would never represent his country in vaulting, Damian turned his attention to other destructive distractions, and was soon chosen to play a part in the school summer production. Mark had landed the lead role thanks to his plentiful hair and ability to walk and talk. The production was part-musical, part-whimsical exploration on the themes of litter and littering. Mark was to play a park-keeper with very low self-esteem, and Damian was the leader of a gang of villainous litterers, whose malevolent littering had brought the park-keeper to his knees, both metaphorically and literally, as he was picking up a lot of litter on his knees. The lead character, Mr Fragment, was a middle-aged man with a sack and a paunch. His nemesis, Jonny Junk, was a punk whose trail of debris, dross and detritus made him public enemy number one. The action took place in the park over a half hour time span. There were several songs, written by the partially sighted music department, and possibly the most memorable was the rousing foot stomper, 'Mr Fragment's in Bits'.

Kindly reproduced thanks to the partially sighted music department being unaware of it being reproduced:

*Mr Fragment's in Bits*

*Pieces of paper flutter on the breeze,*
*Litter does flitter it brings him to his knees.*
*His picks at it, no help he has,*
*He bags it up, no help he wants.*
*'Cos he's the Lord of Litter, the King of Clean,*
*No ifs no buts no in between.*
*'Cos he's the baron of the bins, oh he is oh so smart,*
*With his dandy brush and his handy cart.*
*The dog turds, the cans, banana skins,*
*Wherever there's litter no one wins.*
*So pick it, bag it, and throw it away.*
*Don't leave that litter for another day.*
*'Cos he's the Lord of Litter, the King of Clean,*
*No ifs no buts no in between.*
*'Cos he's the baron of the bins, oh he is oh so smart,*
*With his dandy brush and his handy cart.*
*His brush is broken, wants a new one now,*
*This litter is causing an unholy row.*

*If it ain't cleaned, you dirty gits,*
*Mr Fragment will be in bits.*
*'Cos he's the Lord of Litter, the King of Clean,*
*No ifs no buts no in between.*
*'Cos he's the baron of the bins, oh he is oh so smart,*
*With his dandy brush and his handy cart.*

The song brought a house down, but the closing ballad, a reflective look at why litter is so messy, was a tear-jerking power ballad to staunch any reckless littering. Again. it was written by the partially sighted music department, and is called 'Drop if you Dare':

*Drop if you Dare*

*I had a piece of chewing gum, it lasted all my life,*
*I loved it so, I chewed it much, I loved it like a wife.*
*We went for walks, we laughed we cried, we wanted so much more,*
*But never, now, or in the future, would I throw it on the floor.*

*Drop it, don't drop it, don't drop it, don't you — don't you dare,*
*Make chewy, make chewy, on the floor so rare so rare.*
*Peppermint, or spearmint, I'll even try the menthol,*
*But throw it on the floor oh no, you must be fucking mental.*
*We are as one, we masticate; we chew the fat together,*
*But throw it on the floor not now, not never.*
*Drop it, don't drop it, don't drop it, don't you — don't you dare,*
*Make chewy, make chewy, on the floor so rare so rare.*

A short and elegantly crafted song, it was hummed throughout the school well into the autumn term. Mark got most of the plaudits for his thoughtful portrayal of a man tormented by his tortured relationship with litter, and his inability to come to terms with the death of his three hamsters. This part of the play was lost on a significant section of the audience, but watching from the wings, Damian appreciated Mark's nuanced and subtle representation of a hamster loving park-keeper in an emotional zoo. Damian was briefly laughed at for his performance, but his low-key presence (at one point he stood for a full three minutes without wittering any of his lines) suggested that his acting prowess was rather like an undeveloped cheese, tasteless and in need of maturity. The partially sighted music department went on to write some top forty hits, including 'I Only Have Pies For You', 'Old Red Pie is Back', and that perennial classic, 'Take that book off your face'. Mr Flummocks continued to be flummoxed, and gymnastics was dropped from the school curriculum.

As the new school year progressed, charity was always on someone's mind, and that year Blue Peter decided it would be a good idea to collect wood to build a home for wayward puppies. Damian, who never really liked puppies or wood, or Blue Peter for that matter, decided that this year he would collect something for Blue Peter as he wanted to make a difference to someone somewhere. He couldn't send puppies through the post as that was considered cruel, so he decided to collect twigs, planks and small wooden chairs and send those off to the do-gooders down in London. Mark was a willing helper, and the two idiots would walk for hours in search of twigs that could fit in a reasonably large envelope. The chairs and planks were saved for Bonfire Night, that annual celebration of failure. They did send five twigs off, sans stamp, but never got a thank you from the presenters or the puppies they helped. Turning their whole attention to having a huge bonfire, the pair would go chumping, a ritual whereby anything remotely combustible which was not nailed down was collected for the bonfire. This presented huge opportunities to re-furnish your front room, earn some extra money and have a half decent fire in the process. The two boys managed to get a rich velour three-piece suite, only slightly soiled, two Formica encrusted tables, a cheese grater, and what looked like a Victorian toilet brush, all in one night. Rivalries were intense, and gangs of feckless boys would roam the streets in search of tat to burn; indeed, quite often, Thomas would join them in the hope of finding an occasional table and chair set. In many parts of the country, Bonfire Night was viewed as a pagan festival; an antiquated ritual that had no place in modern Britain, but as the miners' strike had proven, you could never have enough tat for burning. Traditional food was served on the night, and Anne was always keen to experiment with obscure recipes that she had found in the inside cover of the Encyclopaedia Britannica. Her favourite was pickled pie with cinnamon, a mouth-watering mixture of pork and pickling spices. Damian preferred the sweeter toffee turnips. Anne would make tray after tray of toffee every autumn, storing it at the back of the airing cupboard in Janine's bedroom. This meant it would stay ripe well into the new year and provide an alternative source of vitamin T for the children (vitamin T only existed in Anne's mind). The turnips were washed and de-seeded before being roasted over charcoal for several hours to soften the fibres. They were then passed through the eye of a large knitting needle to ensure they were the correct size, then flash-fried in margarine to ensure they contained plentiful amounts of cholesterol. The final part, the dipping in the toffee, was done on demand, which meant that well before November, Anne was preparing vats of strong, dark toffee for her toothless brood.

Fireworks were handed out to the children so that they could experiment with danger, and Thomas would light up Anne's pipe, signalling that the fire could commence. Burning well into the night, the neighbour's house was finally put out by three very efficient firemen. Thomas apologised to his ex-neighbour and retired to his room to contemplate the tat he hadn't torched. Anne would decant the toffee into Tupperware tubs and send them to relatives dotted around the city, regardless of whether she liked them, or whether they liked toffee.

# Graveyards of the mind

Anne was a ferocious reader, and she would often sit in her tweed armchair, pipe at the ready, with a well-thumbed book perilously close to her failing eyes, devouring the words as if her life depended on finishing the book before bedtime, and at more rabid moments, chewing the spine of a classic to satisfy her appetite for words. She couldn't appreciate the works of Dickens, Bronte or Austen, but despite this, had taken to wearing a bonnet in the style of Miss Bennet from Pride and Prejudice. Thomas believed Austin to be a make of car but had never heard of the Pride or Prejudice model. Anne was told that a bonnet offered protection from hair-borne parasites, which were rampant in the 70s. Bonnets also gave the illusion of spirituality and godliness, even if your soul was a dead certainty for the burning halls of hell.

The Carters as a family were godless buffoons, dribbling empty hope on the periphery of worship. Thomas had a deep distrust of anything that was vaguely organised, or organised vaguely, and this resulted in an aversion to all the holy books and scriptures. Thomas's explanation of why Moses crossed the Red Sea had left his witless children confused and paranoid, and when he went into detail on the merits of the canapés served at the Last Supper, it only succeeded in making the children hungry. He also argued that it was less of a supper and more of an evening meal, but this was lost on the children as they sat at his feet, chomping on dry Weetabix.

Anne, who at no point in her life had been possessed by demons, was raised as a Methodist, attending chapels with her equally devout family. To the children, Methodism was a way of life which they weren't prepared to follow, preferring instead the freedom of believing in the more approachable deities. Celestial matters were for the birds; the children worshipped Santa and the

Easter Bunny, which incidentally was the name of a folk band from Shipley. At Easter, they would pray to Cadburys or some other chocolate-based deity, begging for just a nugget of milk chocolate, and at Christmas time they would sacrifice what little dignity they had and camp out at the foot of their parents' bed. Paul and Janine would whittle small wooden figurines in the hope that these pitiful oak icons would appease the god of gifts, whilst Stephen, no lover of tradition, would write a carefully crafted tune to charm the Santa spirits. Damian looked on in awe, amazed at the lengths his siblings would go to in order to get some tat. Damian had seen Jesus in a film and realised that Jesus was a dead ringer for his great uncle Harold. Thomas had told Damian to never trust a man with a beard unless he was a sailor, as all the world loves a sailor, so as he flicked through Anne's 'A to Z Guide to Bearded Men', he was astounded how many had been or were associated with religion. He had been taken to Sunday school on one occasion, and found it very wholesome and humiliating, due to his ignorance. Whilst the other children had sung Victorian chants with almost demonic enthusiasm, Paul, Damian and Janine had sat quivering in silence, hoping for it all to stop. When Anne came to collect them, they swore on all that was unholy to never mention church, God or religion for the foreseeable future, or until such time as they had to take an oath.

As children, they all spent many hours in and around graveyards. This could be for a variety of reasons, but the main one was the proximity of the library to the local graveyard. Anne, pipe in hand, would browse the large print section in search of larger words to impress her fictitious friends from the book square (circles didn't exist in the 70s). With her failing comprehension, the only words she fully understood were several profanities her colleagues sometimes used when talking to the children at the nursery, and some technical words used at pipe gatherings. The children would at first wait by the door, until the noise police would inform Anne that her children were in danger of waking the dead, so she would tell them to go and play in the graveyard and be of some use. Children can be so creative when left in a graveyard on a dark Friday evening in Bradford. One of their favourite activities was hunt the corpse, whilst Damian's personal favourite was tattiest tombstone, which was both simple to play and allowed the children to read the moving epitaphs. Damian was fascinated by the messages written on some of the tombstones, and he would often bring a small notebook to record some of the more tasteless memorials. Several stayed with him, and to this day he can recall two such epitaphs that inspired him throughout his life:

*Albert Clippings,*
*Loving hairdresser, customer and father.*
*Husband to his wife, and forever*
*in search of...*
*Born 1932*
*Died 1974*
*Missed in a sad sort of way.*

*Gerald Stork*
*Giant of a man, midget in the mind.*
*Much despised and thank God the*
*Fucker is dead.*
*Sadly he lived too long...*
*Born 1932*
*Died 1974*

He discerned from these two tombstones that they both lived for forty-two years. Damian planned to live longer, write his own epitaph and invest in marble.

When the children were allowed to browse the books in the library, they were amazed by the musky smell given off by the librarian, Miss Chunk. Anne would be scanning the shelves for large print Westerns, enabling the children to peruse the huge variety of Thomas the Tank Engine books — row after row of engine porn, disguised as innocent tales of talking locomotives. The vibrant colours and lurid titles meant that Damian was instantly blinded, resulting in a love of braille books, which was a short-lived love, as his sight returned after less than a minute. Each week the children were allowed to select one book to paw at, and Anne would then tell the excited children that she couldn't afford to borrow the books this week as the repayments were too high. She usually went home with a sack of large words, and the children would look forward to the following Friday when they could once again frolic in the foetid grounds of the graveyards whilst Anne stole one page at a time from War and Peace.

Thomas was never really one for book learning, having been forced to leave school at the end of the day. He didn't realise he was free to return the following day so started working at the very early age of ten. Thomas and his father, also called Thomas, would roam the streets of Bradford, horse in tow, delivering alcohol to the thirst-ridden residents for a penny a pint. This illicit yet fundamentally flawed enterprise led to the two Thomas' being put on a most wanted list in and around the Undercliffe area of Bradford. They were forced to lie low for an afternoon until the local constabulary realised that there were far more important crimes to investigate. Bradford in the early '30s was a hard place to live, with villains such as Monty Mush, the Manningham Maniac, who was wanted for a series of tree-related crimes; Sidney and Edward Butterflap, whose unspeakable crimes made a mockery of the many mimes who operated in and around Bradford's markets; and possibly the worst of a very hotly contested field of felons, Hatty McFluff, who was wanted after an outbreak of spots at a local ointment mill. Thomas and Thomas were small fry in comparison, and they soon reverted to legal crimes, of which there were many.

Aside from the library visits, the main entertainment for Damian and his siblings in those pre-fun years came from the TV. Although they only had a black and white view of most issues, TV represented a world of opportunity and escape for children who sometimes never saw the clouds due to all the pollution and lack of hope that dogged their every waking minute. The children all had their favourites, and this was reflected in what they watched.

Stephen loved music, and would often watch the Old Grey Thistle Test, where his clandestine love of west coast rock saw him listening to bands such as *The Cornish Patties*, *Clary Cork and her Wind Duet*, and the outrageously unglamorous *Nina Falmouth the Foulmouthed Florist*. Janine loved period dramas, like 'The Sweeney' and 'Coronation Pete', whilst Paul was content to watch 'Vision What!', a brilliant children's programme that offered northern kids the opportunity to appear on TV and talk shit. Damian was content to watch Laurel and Hurley, Charlie Chuplin or Harold Floyd with his father. Those hours snuggled up on a one-seater sofa, cold chip in one hand and a thinly disguised sandwich in the other were some of the most remarkable days of his childhood. Board games played a very small part in entertaining the children, and Thomas and Anne preferred to create their own games to encourage self-motivation and inner turmoil. Thomas was a genius when it came to devising simple yet divisive games that would leave his children if not in tears, then certainly emotionally scared. He would sit alone in his redundant shed and craft games that stretched and challenged the repressed minds of his three youngest children. Stephen would never take part in the games; only observe.

Anne's bonnet did many things, but the one thing it couldn't prevent was illness. Anne had been experiencing sharp pains in her pipe, and the family doctor, Doctor Flap, diagnosed an ingrowing pipe. Anne knew she would have to undergo a pointless and time-consuming procedure. She checked into Bradford Oil Hymnfirmary, so called because the hospital was built on the site of a Methodist oil refinery, and the quacks soon got to work on her hideous pipe infections. The procedure was actually quite simple; Anne was put under a blanket and the pipe was removed using only mirrors, a little smoke and some kind words. The recovery period was critical, and in Anne's case she was confined to a small room for just under two weeks to face constant criticism. This was a very difficult time for Thomas, who had to be both mother and father to his feckless children. Whilst Anne was in recovery, Thomas had the children strictly rostered to perform household chores. Damian was keen to take on some responsibility, and when Thomas gave him the twin roles, de-greasing the cooker and de-greasing the toilet, he was like a pig in grease. The elder children were given equally onerous tasks; Stephen was in charge of toilet roll requisition and outside catering requirements; Janine was given the vacuum and was permanently on call for emergency crumb elimination, whilst Paul was allowed to fill the kettle for the constant supply of tea needed for Thomas. Thomas's biggest headache was catering for his four hungry kids, whose dietary requirements could be ignored. He decided to focus on fish and potato-based meals, which meant Stephen was on constant standby to nip to one of the two local chippies: The Sullen Sailor or Colin's Cod Pieces. The Sullen Sailor was poor on quality but good on price, whereas Colin's Cod Pieces was a mouth-watering aquatic adventure; indeed, sometimes the fish was so fresh it wasn't cooked. It was very expensive for the basic cod and chips, but The Times and Daily Telegraph were used to wrap up the orders, giving them an air of sophistication. The Sullen Sailor relied on donations of old wrapping paper and copies of the conservative party manifesto in the hope of keeping its prices lower than a bottom feeder in the Mariana Trench. The Sullen Sailor was owned and operated by Gilbert Guppy, a sprightly man in his late fifties who was married to an equally odious woman, Gloria Guppy. They had been preparing soggy battered fish for years; it was in their blood. Their approach was one of resentful acceptance coupled with pig ignorance. Stephen had a very acrimonious relationship with the Guppys following an incident with an undercooked chip. The matter was finally resolved out of court, yet Stephen still persisted in visiting the shop at least seven times per week.

Thomas struggled to occupy his children during those summer months as Anne was gradually nursed back to pipe-smoking health. He would often push the kids into his Austin Python and hit the open road. He had always loved follies and monuments, and his copy of the definitive guide to the monuments of West Yorkshire, 'Ponting's Points of Interest', was a well-thumbed volume of inane facts about little known places in and around Shipley. He loved to pack a thermos and several pork pies and set out very early to visit his favourite monument, 'The Hapless Sailor', on the outskirts of Baildon. Built by an incredibly ambitious architect whose talent exceeded very little, it was designed to recognise the contribution made to the fishing industry by the people of Baildon. Thomas had worked as a deep-sea fisherman after he was demobbed from the navy at the end of World War Two. His love of all things aquatic and nautical meant that his obsession was foisted onto to his passive children. He knew his way around a net and could sniff out a pickled herring at forty yards. The monument itself was severely underwhelming, and the three children sat in the back of the Python, scattering crumbs in the hope that Thomas would let them get out of the car. If the weather was good, they would be allowed to roam near the monument but not paw at its rusty plaque. The monument had been at the centre of a protracted legal dispute between the townsfolk of Baildon, and the equally townsfolk-like townsfolk of Basildon. Both towns had a rich aromatic odour, akin to a fish's boudoir, and both had a long tradition of sea shanties, either sung in estuary English or sung with the flat vowels of West Yorkshire. Enchanting sea shanties are a miserable British tradition, and the recipes for successful shanties were closely guarded secrets. Thomas had penned several himself and was known for his Melville-esque delivery, a haunting mix of wailing and groaning. One of Damian's least favourite shanties was the enigmatically titled 'The Carp on the Bow is a Freshwater Fish'.

(Kindly repossessed thanks to the council estate of Thomas Carter)

*Oh carpy, oh carpy, your scales are so fine,*
*You wash over me like a fine British wine.*
*Oh carpy, oh carpy, your fins are so strong,*
*Oh how can our love be considered so wrong?*
*Oh carpy, oh carpy, what a beautiful tale,*

*I love and adore every scale.*
*But high blows the wind; fuck me it's a gale,*
*I can't see old carpy, not even a whale.*
*The crashes and splashes bring death near to you,*
*Oh carpy, oh carpy, what the fuck should we do?*
*Saltwater fish, they frolic all day,*
*But freshwater carps have no time for play.*
*Oh carpy, oh carpy, you're all out to sea,*
*The rivers the rivers, where you want to be.*
*Oh carpy swim harder, head for the coast,*
*You're the freshwater fish that I love the most, the most, the most.*

Of course, the shanties of Baildon and Basildon had their merits, but the legal dispute over 'The Hapless Sailor' led to a landmark ruling by Judge Francis Fickle, stating that the monument belonged to no one group of townsfolk, and therefore should be shared between the two towns on a bi-weekly basis. Thomas had planned the trip perfectly, as he never liked driving south as a rule, preferring instead east, west and north, in no order.

As Anne readied herself for discharge, Thomas quickly swept the house with a fairly new broom, dusted the younger children and polished his car's hubcaps. Stephen had gone to The Sullen Sailor the previous evening to buy a slap-up fish supper for the homecoming mum. Stephen had bought a fish special, twice the size of a normal haddock, along with three fishcakes, three extra-large tubs of mushy peas and a bucket of chips. He had left them in the fridge and planned to re-heat them on the bonnet of his Ford Refuse; Anne loved chips. Anne had been advised to go home and avoid pipes for at least three hours, or until such time as seemed appropriate, and she was given a prescription for several low smoke NHS pipes, which emitted a low hum. She was also given three weeks' supply of strong glue and a rolled-up newspaper, which on reflection was very thoughtful of the nurses on Ward 76; Anne had made some new friends. As Thomas drove to the hospital, his mind raced his car, and the car won. How would the children feel after not seeing their mother for such a short time?

How would he fit a sofa into a very inadequate boot, and had Stephen got enough chips? These questions, along with the responsibilities of being full time, had severely affected Thomas's ability to recognise up from down, left from right, and right from wrong. His children didn't really notice any change in their dad, although he would sometimes drift too close to the kerb at speeds over ninety miles per hour. Arriving at the hospital discharge department, Thomas spotted Anne, pipe in hand, chatting to a snaffle of pipe smokers. She looked relieved to be released and skipped over with a new sense of hope in a small envelope, kindly given to her by a passing optimist.

# Play it long and run like fuck

Damian had reduced his wearing of short trousers over the previous two years, and now preferred to leave his knees where they belonged; under a fetching pair of flared jeans. However, he quickly had to re-evaluate this decision later in the year, during the long, hot, languid summer, which saw water being imported from abroad and the outright banning of lederhosen. Of course, at the start of the year, Damian had other things on his mind.

He was in his second year at Highfield Muddle School, a small tatty facility located at the back of a Ford dealership. Adjacent to a disused railway line, and surrounded by industrial smells, the school offered a terrible environment for young minds to be fed facts and fumes. His teacher, Mr Williwontee, was a brick of a man, with an indecisive haircut but a very forgiving waistline. He was seldom without his hair and had played rounders professionally as a teenager. This meant that Damian and his good friend Mark would spend hours in the segregated playground, ball in hand, despair in heart, tossing balls at lifeless pupils who despised rounders. Mr Williwontee inspired hope in the pupils, and this, Damian would reflect on, only made life's disappointments harder to take. Most mornings started with a school assembly, where the head teacher, Mr Guillemot, all beak and no hair, would give a reading on the dangers of some aspect of life. Never overtly useful, the children had to stand in line, eyes to the front, ears on standby, until Guillemot had finished his tongue exercises. This was followed by the deputy head, Mr Starling, a devout man with little time, who would lead the hymns, his deep baritone voice tunelessly echoing around the hall. Finally, he would give prizes to pupils for a range of achievements. Quite often these prizes were piss-poor, such as a pencil with 'hands off' scratched on, a bucket of milk that he had found on the bus, and on one occasion, a cold bag of chips that he found in the back seat of his car. His selection method of winners was done using a hairdryer and a balloon. He would inflate his ego and then dry his permanently wet hair, using the balloon only if the power gave out. Once his limited hair was dry, the balloon would be tossed with abandon into the faces of the eager fools on the front row, and the lucky catcher would be awarded a prize.

Damian yearned to win anything. Being one of life's losers was not a destiny that fitted in with his very ill-judged career path. He played football for the school team, displaying his wonderfully inept legs to a whole new audience. With his silky shorts and fluid bowels, he would skirt, patrol and avoid the channels on both the left-hand and right-hand side of the pitch. Mark was captain of the team, and he inspired fear in opponents with his unruly gait, insipid running style and over-attractive curls. Their P.E. teacher, Mr Quail, was a bearded man who loved the rugged outdoors. Wearing only skimpy shorts and Wintergreen, Mr Quail could be seen most mornings berating the local infant schoolteachers for wearing coats. He was a hard fucker. His coaching methods were very unorthodox, and he faced criticism from all sides. He insisted that the boys in the team must train in slippers and pyjamas, in the belief that it would fend off inconsistency, whilst he also was not averse to throwing fruit at those players who underperformed or were crap. Damian was often hit on the head by a kumquat or kiwi. The team had been playing some extremely unattractive football, so dull and tiresome that quite often the pyjamas were needed for the few idiots who turned up to cheer on the hapless collection of feet. Despite this, they had reached the semi-final of the 'under-12 Tong & District Interdenominational Bi-annual Cup', a tournament so prestigious that only those truly in the know knew. The school was awash with rumours, speculation and raw sewage, and the day before the big match, Mr Starling held a special assembly. As the hall filled up with heaving sweat and puberty, the team took their place on the improvised stage, which was in fact a plank of wood with a curtain draped across. A hush descended over the assembled audience as Mr Starling took to the stage. Boys and girls would have been a reasonable opening, but instead he began to whistle the tune from The Magnificent Seven. As one, no one joined in, so he continued with his witless warbling until Mr Quail discreetly pointed out that it was not a seven-a-side tournament for under sevens. Quickly changing his tune, he dived straight into a sermon from the book of Job, offering Old Testament advice in the hope that it would strike fear into the opponents. The line that struck a chord with Damian: "and lo, there was a bush that caughteth on the foot of the centre back, stirring God's rage" was particularly relevant to the team, as the centre back was called Rose and he was prone to tripping. Rose, along with Dave Dumpling, Simon Abscess, Gary Barry and goalkeeper John Jump, all suffered from nerves, and would spend the hours before the game feeling very nervous. Mr Quail had tried various remedies to alleviate some of the nerves, from a good shouting at to a vigorous session of hypnotic babble. Nothing seemed to make a difference, and the team had become a veritable bag of psychological wobblies. During that lacklustre speech by Starling, it was obvious to Damian that he must be the cool calm one and demonstrate a steely-eyed determination not to shit himself. As the team listened to Mr Starling, the whole school were enthralled, but the assembly was cut short when a first-year pupil, Darren Earlobe, a fragile and feeble-minded dunderhead, had an attack of the vapours and passed out. The crash as he smashed into Miss Righteous-Ninny, the R.E. teacher, could be heard three streets away, and so the assembly ended abruptly whilst the teachers scrambled around looking for Earlobe's teeth, which had been dislodged as he hit the holy head.

On the day of the big game, Damian woke late and thought it was Wednesday; days were still a problem in the Carter household since Thomas had insisted on using the Julian calendar in conjunction with a series of candles and sundials. As he dashed around the back room looking for his wooden football boots, Anne sat in the one usable armchair, puffing her pipe. She turned to Damian, pipe in hand, and gave him a knowing wink. This

104

lifted his spirits and he quickly snaffled down a loose collection of crumbs and some warm spittle, and made his way to Mark's house, where the remaining members of the team were due to rendezvous. Mark never gave team talks, but instead preferred to let his luxurious hair do the talking. With a wistful flick the team knew that they were ready to win or lose. The game started with a bang following an inadvertent firework launch, and soon the two teams, Highfield Muddle and Muddlefield High, battled for control of the channels located somewhere in the pitch. Playing deep, but not too deep, the long balls looked peculiar, and it wasn't obvious if anyone knew the rules of the game. Mark, at the forefront of the action, dived hither and thither in search of the ball, but due to its elongated appearance, mistook it for an egg and ran past it. Damian was playing a holding role, which meant he was unsure whether to move or not move. His teammates looked shell-shocked, and it was obvious that their opponents were better equipped to run, with sleeker legs and an altogether more aerodynamic appearance. Indeed, the striker had such a smooth head that he was mistaken for the ball on three occasions. As half-time approached, Mark was still haring around the pitch with a bit between his teeth — God knows why — and it looked as if it would be all square at the break. Their opponents managed to force a corner in added time, and as the ball arced its way into the goalmouth, the substitute goalkeeper went AWOL. Bruntington had been given the goalkeeping role due to his hands and owning some gloves. Suffering from a severe lack of height, Bruntington came for the ball, but standing at a mere three feet, seven inches, he had little chance of reaching it. However, as he turned to see where the ball was, a shot was fired in, hitting him on the arse and ricocheting into the net. Disaster. Mr Quail screamed from the touchline, demanding more hither and thither and less shit, but before the boys could react, the half-time whistle blew. During the break, Mr Quail had a stall set out, and explained the finer points of stall setting out, which did nothing to improve the mood within the team. Who the fuck needs a stall at a football match? Drawing on no experience at all, Mr Quail encouraged the boys to follow the lead of Mark and show less aggression and more skill. Try as they might, as the ball remained a reclusive fugitive from their feeble feet; the game slipped away, the final result reflecting their innate inability: 23 − 1. Maybe next year?

Like most ten-year olds, Damian had a very sketchy understanding of airborne viruses, so when he was informed that he was due a TB jab, his mind began to race. What could TB mean and was it only him who was due this onerous injection? Speaking to Mark, who was a meticulous bullshitter, it turned out that TB could stand for several things: Tony Bennett, Ten Bulls, Tiny Buttons, Terrifying Bees, and Totally Bald. Mark's hair was legendary, and Damian had beautiful locks too, so why they needed an injection to prevent baldness wasn't clear to begin with, but when they had time to reflect, perhaps their elders were trying to prevent the tragic loss of hair in later life. In the 70s, hair was at a premium thanks to the miners' strike and a poor harvest. A government report, commissioned by the hirsute Roy Penkins, had found that those with a full head of hair would live a life of uninhibited joy and bring future economic benefits. Damian and Mark fancied some uninhibited joy, so approached the forthcoming jab with a mixture of excitement and immaculate grooming. On the day of the jab, Damian wore a very fetching turtleneck sweater, something that Thomas loved, and Mark went for a rather lacklustre tweed tracksuit. Both had combed their hair in the style of the day, The Barry Ribb. Ribb and his siblings were an inspiration to most ten-year-old boys, with their falsetto warbling and high-waisted gait: you could possibly discern by the way they moved that they were women or men, to paraphrase a chart-topping hit of the era.

The injections were to be administered in the art room, as it was felt that the creative environment would have a calming effect on the more hysterical pupils. At the door stood the history teacher, Mr Goose, a fierce man with a moustache allegedly made of iron, and Miss Partridge, the art teacher, whose one claim to fame was having one of her drawings featured on Blue Peter. The school nurse, Miss Antipathy, had a gruelling disposition, lacking the basic human qualities of kindness, compassion and functioning brain. As a nurse she fitted the uniform and had all the requisite equipment: a sharp knife, a tube of multi-purpose ointment and some twine for broken limbs. What she lacked was patience, so to speak, and the ability to perform routine injections. As she stood by the slowly drying papier-mâché figures, made by the hysterical children earlier in the day, her cigarette jauntily hanging from her lips, Damian started to feel a little worried about the whole process. Perhaps baldness wasn't such a bad thing; it never stopped Churchill having a successful singing career. Mark, glued to the spot thanks to a split tube of PVA glue, allowed Damian to go before him, whilst Mr Goose yanked hard at Mark's plimsolls. Miss Antipathy stubbed her half-smoked cigarette out in a petri dish, and produced from her pocket a handkerchief, which was moistened using some Dettol and axle grease. As Damian rolled his sleeve up, beads of sweat appeared on the nurse's face; she was overdressed for the occasion and should have removed her fur lined boots. Explaining that most things in life would hurt, she rammed the needle into his quivering arm, and in the process inadvertently stood on his foot. The scream could be heard thirteen streets away, and at first it was believed that his foot would be unusable in the future. Fortunately for all parties, Damian always wore sturdy footwear, regardless of what society dictated, and the nurse had lost some weight, now weighing a very trim seventeen stone. As he limped away, tourniquet wrapped round his left toe, he glanced back and witnessed Mark, plimsoll in hand, screaming for mercy and demanding to see the manager of this shoddy establishment. Even in times of stress, Mark was extremely well mannered and articulate. Suffice to say, Mr Goose stepped forward and explained that if Mark didn't leave now, he would have injections in both legs, his back, feet and forehead. Discreetly leaving his dignity behind, Mark joined Damian in the playground where they compared congealed blood and reflected on the merits of plimsolls in medical situations.

As the long summer walked slowly into autumn, Damian's thoughts turned to the rich turnip harvest that would not pick itself. Thomas and Anne were not vegetarians but believed that vegetables were an inadequate replacement for a top-quality pie, or a tin of refried meatballs in a rich tomato sauce. Despite their conflicted thinking, the previous March had seen them furtively planting vegetables in the hope that they could reduce the household food bill. Times were always harder, but with a plentiful supply of root vegetables, Thomas and Anne hoped to ward off the worst of the hunger pains. The vegetable patch consisted of three rows of turnips, two rows of strawberries and a single row of parsnips. Thomas had discovered that the neighbouring garage was rammed full of decaying vegetables, and after some lengthy negations with the owner of the garage, was given directions to a local garden centre. He honed in on the bargain bucket seedlings and made his way home; it was only when he was in the car that he realised that he had stolen the seedlings, and immediately accelerated away, changing his route home and growing a very dapper beard.

Harvest time was a Carter family affair, with all the children rising early for a hearty breakfast of tea and hope before they made the arduous journey through the kitchen to the back yard. The organisation was done using a time-honoured method which meant the children had to scratch around in the dirt searching for nuggets of food while Thomas and Anne, like tyrannical gang masters, sipped tea and puffed on their various nicotine sources. A good harvest would mean they could eat well for the next two days. Anne would fashion meals using only ingredients and food, and the children would make suggestions on dishes that should be avoided. Damian's least favourite dish was parsnip flan with strawberry gravy. Although it was riddled with nutrients, most of them were lost once Damian had vomited. Thomas and Stephen preferred the turnip roll, whilst Janine and Paul favoured rumbling stomachs and severe cramps. The neighbours, all lifelong luddites, would watch enviously as the large carrier bag of produce was taken into the kitchen in readiness for the feast.

The old ways were preserved in this way, and even now, Damian is often seen in his neighbourhood with a small bag of turnips which he shares with the local workhouse as a way of giving something back to the community.

Stephen was now fully in charge of his own facial hair, along with most of the hair on his head. He was a massive Marc Dolan fan and would spend hours perched atop a pair of platform shoes, longing to be a twentieth century boy. His love of music was nurtured by neither Thomas nor Anne, who thought it was a fucking racket, but undeterred, Stephen would experiment with all types of music. He had managed to purchase a very large and cumbersome gramophone from a nearly useful shop on the better side of town. It had cost an astronomical £7.37 and getting it home on his 50cc scooter had proven to be a real challenge. After several near misses and a fractured foot, the gramophone took pride of place in the boys' attic hole. Here Stephen would listen to all the unpopular artists of the era, who might never have achieved popular recognition, but who lived in hope of uncritical acclaim. Artists such as Bathroom Rim, a neo-classical rock ensemble, Herb Virus and the Lone Trumpets, a truly awful brass collective, and possibly his most played artist, Cosmetic Underwear Salesmen, a rather obscure group of musicians whose only claim to fame was for being deported from San Marino for defacing a motoring journalist. These were heady days in the music business, and Stephen hoped to hop on the slow-moving bandwagon of success, to not have to wait for another boat or miss out on gravy-filled rolling stock, to coin a phrase. At about the same time, Stephen also bought a very useful guitar and plectrum, which he planned to learn once his fingers were fully grown. He had an ear for listening and a painful wrist, which meant at times the guitar would sit gathering dust. Damian and Paul, who thought guitars were only for the rich and famous, longed to twang the strings and hum those country tunes that were so popular to country tune fans. Whenever an opportunity arose, the two brothers would hide away in the attic hole until Stephen had gone to work or sleep, and they would then creep out to experiment with the plectrum. They had to be careful, as the guitar was next to Stephen's bed, and if he was asleep, they could only pretend strum, rather like the artists who appeared on Top of the Pops.

Janine was a very reclusive child during these long hot summer days, and she would spend hours alone with only a word search and a Jackie magazine for company. Lacking any basic culinary skills, she opted to avoid the kitchen on most days, only leaving her room when all the words had been safely found. Her relationship with her parents was excellent, and she had a soft spot, but was receiving treatment from a local quack. Both Anne and Janine had book worms, a disease that was little understood in the 70s. Perched in their local library, the pair would spend hours scratching at books until they were asked to leave. Unable to afford to purchase books from legitimate sellers, they resorted to the black market, where poor quality copies of bestselling novels could be bought for pennies. Janine preferred the high-octane novels of Lawrence and Orwell, whereas Anne loved the works of Swift, Stern and Defoe. The eighteenth century was a time that resonated with Anne, and she would often lose herself — terrible fucking sense of direction. Those illicit copies would often be highly altered to avoid the excessive word tax that the Labour government had imposed on writing. Titles were changed to protect the foolish, whilst plotlines were adjusted to provide a more stimulating response from the reader, who might not fully appreciate nuance. Janine spent days ploughing through 'Buns and Brothers', a gripping tale set in the Nottinghamshire coalfields, charting the loves and doves of dull men and women, who might or might not have children. Anne read 'Two Lonely Men on an Island with very Little Chance of Rescue' seventeen times, thanks to its loose pages which were not numbered. Damian would often sit on his mother's arm, listening to tales from the high seas, or wonderful adventures in fantastical places. Who knew reading could be so enthralling?

# Juvenile behaviour

'Whimsical', 'sensitive', 'repressed', or even 'obtuse' — these are adjectives that are not often associated with eyebrows, but Damian was on the cusp of something, and when he first noticed the hairy lines above his eyes, he was filled with a sense of dread. He had seen eyebrows on other people, mainly adults, but was unsure how to broach the subject with his very reticent parents. When Thomas came home with a second-hand mirror one January day, few in the family could have predicted the impact it would have on the whole Carter household. Mirrors were familiar items to many people in the country at that time, but few people in Damian's circle had a mirror in the house, and even fewer dared to investigate one for fear of witchcraft and ugliness. A walk down any street in 70s Bradford would make it apparent why mirrors were a dangerous invention that if freely available, could lead to social upheaval and wardrobe mishaps. The sight of so many misshapen and ugly people in a built-up area presented a real problem to the authorities. If people, whose lives were already very ugly, had access to reflective technology, then who knows what level of civic unrest would follow. When mirrors become available at the start of the year, few people fully understood or appreciated how this would transform society.

One of the first effects of so many ugly people seeing their hideous selves for the first time was the urgent need to improve personal hygiene and hairstyles. Up until then, people of both sexes had simply grown their hair with no attention to style or colour. Looking back to those pre-mirror years, it is obvious that not many people owned a brush, understood shampoo or planned to get married. With the introduction of the mirror, it was hoped that people would take a little more pride in their head coverings and rely less on hats. However, one surprising and seismic aspect of freely available mirror technology was punk rock. Prior to 1977, music was all about long hair, ill-fitting denim and platform shoes. So many teenagers in the early part of the decade hid in dark corners, with high-waisted trousers, a tartan scarf and the expression of a constipated mammoth. Punk rock was to change so many aspects of everyday life, and Damian, if not at the actual forefront, but not at the very back, was swept along with this prickly new style of music, appearance and attitudes.

Anne was known for her large collection of haberdashery supplies, from zips to buttons and thread to safety pins, which meant that Damian had immediate access to punk rock fashion without having to spend a fortune. Damian threw himself into this wave of nausea and was soon sporting ill-fitting monkey boots, a mismatched cardigan with a slight tear below the armpit and a pair of jeans which were, if not totally bleached, in need of some bleach. With his new identity, Damian and his chum Mark were often seen around the local area in their new garb, drawing derision from all those who saw them. Of course, boys of that age are independent spirits and very stupid, so the catcalls and stones merely encouraged the pair to more outlandish clothing choices. Damian wore what could only be described as a hideous orange anorak, which was visible for several miles. To others he looked a twat, but in his own mind he was making a stand against the elite old guard who had dominated every facet of life in post-war Britain. Mark let his hair grow to the point where he was often confused by his own lack of visible face. On two occasions he was stopped by the police for having an out-of-control fringe which presented a serious threat to public decency.

It was during this explosion of rebellion and rejection of authority that Damian and his good friend Mark fell under the influence of a local criminal mastermind who had been courting Janine. Janine had been an average teenage girl for some years now, but when she met and not taken an immediate dislike to a boy, it could be a semi-serious situation. The boy/teen in question, Marcus Thrushbold, wore denim. Denim socks, underpants, vest, indeed anything that could be fashioned into an item of clothing, he would wear if it had overtones of denim. His long, greasy hair, flat cap and thick glasses made him appear an imposing figure. Coupled with a debilitating speech impediment, Thrushbold was a revolting, if not intimidating figure in the small area at the end of Damian's street. He had a Raleigh Chopper and could often be seen riding around the local council estate without bicycle clips, greasy hair flapping in the wind, like an overcooked piece of fried bread. The girls in the area all referred to him as Dickhead Thrushbold, but beneath that pathetic façade sat a rather underdeveloped sense of self-worth and chronic body odour. He was a collector of many things, something that had first piqued Janine's interest, and when he turned to collecting car badges, he found two willing fools in Damian and Mark to do the collecting. The proposition was quite simple; Damian and Mark would scour the streets for unattended cars, remove any badges, and then sell them at a reduced price to Thrushbold, who would then dispose of them via a Chinese chap who worked at the local takeaway. It was the perfect crime. Obviously, tools were needed to carry out this heinous crime, so Damian and Mark borrowed screwdrivers from their respective fathers, and with malice in their hearts, went searching for badges. Their first few attempts seemed too easy, snaffling badges from a VW Scratch, a hub cap from a Datsun Bloodspot, and some chrome trim from a nearly new Austin Sty. Thrushbold was pleased with the returns and seeing that these two idiots were willing to take the risk, asked for more, demanding that they focus on the more luxurious cars. This appealed to Damian and Mark's stupidity, and they soon became more brazen, more daring, in their quest to curry favour with Thrushbold. During the actual lifting of the chrome work, one would be look out, or both, and the other would remove the chrome work, or both. With hindsight, this system was inherently flawed, and so it was to prove one near fateful day in late July. The two idiots had identified a feast of chrome at the back of a local factory, and after staking out the area for five minutes, carefully planning possible places to spend their ill-gotten gains, and removing their socks so as to not leave fingerprints, they went in to snatch the loot. Mark had hidden his oversized screwdriver down his anorak sleeve, meaning he was unable to bend his elbow. With some help from Damian, the screwdriver was introduced to the light of day, and whilst Damian busily daydreamed about what he would do with his stash, Mark hacked away at a rather fetching Mercedes Goldflap, attempting to prize away a rather ornate badge depicting a mountain scene in Bavaria. Unbeknown to both idiots, the owner of the said car had watched this tragic drama unfold and was soon stepping into the scene with angry thoughts in his head and aggressive intent in his fists. Damian raised the alarm halfway down the road, and it was only Mark's slippery legs and innate sense of survival that enabled him to make good his escape, but not before the angry owner had given him a severe tongue lashing. Damian was by this time over a mile away, daydreaming prison visits and court. Fortunately, with the luck of the stupid, the pair managed to avoid detection and lay low for half a day until the heat was off.

Their next target was at a second-hand car garage near to their school. Again, with careful planning and preparation, the job looked easy enough. However, Damian and Mark were born idiots, and on the night of the intended snatch, were almost caught red-handed by a passing motorist who displayed far too much civic responsibility, chasing them for over twenty minutes in a clapped-out Honda Broccoli, a green machine before climate change was even conceived. Again, the pair evaded capture and hid in a disused Chinese takeaway for several minutes until they realised that it was not disused, just very quiet. This brush with death left indelible scars on the fragile minds of those two idiots, which would have serious side effects in years to come. Returning to Thrushbold empty handed was not an option, so the two idiots stole a door handle from a disability scooter and swore blind that it was from a Rolls Royce Silverbirch. Thrushbold paid the two off, saying that he was worried that they were drawing too much heat from the fuzz, to which Mark replied that he was willing to have a haircut.

The two criminal masterminds then turned their attention to another victimless crime: stealing trees to order. This audacious crime was the brainchild of Mark, who longed for a garden pond with suitable vegetation around its fringes. In those times, garden centres were the preserve of the rich and pointless, so the idea of buying garden plants was never a realistic option. Instead, the two idiots spent some time casing the gardens of the area, in search of anything that looked remotely tree-like, or green. With shovel and trowel in hand, the two fools would swoop and decimate some carefully manicured front garden for a dwarf conifer. The pain they caused could not be measured, but the rewards were immense. The garden pond looked fantastic, with an array of greenery taken from the front gardens of the neighbouring private housing estate. Those rich bastards really suffered during that herbaceous crime wave. Mugshots went up, locals locked their doors in fear of houseplant thefts, and lawns went uncut. They had the run of every garden within a half-mile radius and were able to despoil lawns with abandon. They were even given a name by local gardeners: The Green-fingered Fuckers. On completion of the pond, their desire to steal vegetation waned somewhat, and the gardeners of the area were able at last to plant again, without fear. A truly terrible crime wave.

Anne and Thomas were unaware of their youngest son's involvement in this crime wave, and it is fair to say that Damian's shame in later years was tinged with sadness, as he never stole any bushes or plants for his mother. Anne loved the dirt, with its endless possibilities, and the opportunity to fill her garden with stolen vegetation was surely an opportunity that she would have grabbed with both hands, but it was not to be.

As the year ended, Thrushbold moved away to pursue an apprenticeship in spot erosion somewhere in the north east. Janine waxed lyrically for hours about the denim possibilities, but by Christmas, Thrushbold was nothing more than a greasy memory, a future filled with spots and pus. Mark and Damian, along with many boys of that time, continued to scour the ether for new fashion items and ideas, but the pinnacle of their year was the donning of the donkey jacket. This truly hideous garment was the preferred choice of the roadside labourer but was to become the number one choice for fashion-conscious fools.

# Nice day for a ride in a hearse

Thomas was a man who dwelt on his own mortality at great length, often escaping to crowded crematoriums to inhale the life as it dissipated into the ether. He understood the fine lines and narrow margins but was a little rusty on boundaries and red lines. His need to be straddling the two worlds of life and death drew him to those who might well have the answers to the bigger questions that had vexed clerics, philosophers and great thinkers throughout time; how could he make more money?

In January of the year, he came up with a sure-fire way to make more money for his ever-demanding brood, and Anne's pipe habit wouldn't pay for itself. Scanning the obituaries in the Yorkshire Host (the foremost newspaper in the West Riding), he was struck by how many people were dying, on a regular basis, and it was forecast that the trend would continue. Disposing of the remnants of loved ones was an expensive business, but perhaps he had a way to make it a whole lot cheaper: part worn and nearly new coffins! His original idea had been to break into a funeral director's premises and borrow some of the caskets, selling them on via the small ads or down at the local working men's club. He realised though, that many coffins were bespoke, built for a specific individual. He remembered a friend he went to school with, Fat Leonard, whose coffin had been shaped a little like a humpback bridge, and a woman he courted in his twenties, Beanpole Brenda, whose coffin required sixteen pall bearers and a low loader. Therefore, he decided to target crematoriums, knowing that they often used off the shelf, one-size-fits-all caskets. At the time he had an acquaintance, Dee Seized, who was a folk singer who played at the local working men's club. Her act was mainly funeral-based tunes and ballads, and she had an intimate knowledge of all the workings of coffins, urns and other such paraphernalia. Dee was a very popular character in and around the toilets of the clubs, regaling the regulars with her woeful ballads, often until three in the morning. Some of her more memorable ballads are available on vinyl, and some can be seen on lino. Below are two of her most haunted efforts, kindly reproduced with absolutely no one's consent.

## The Ballad of Ernie Ashe

Ernie was a tiresome man, his habits really vile,
His eyes so small, his nose a point, he never used to smile.
He sat at home, alone and sad,
A wife he never had.
But in each drawer, and cupboard space, in his grotty little home,
Were funerals plans, and coffin guides, for death he had to plan.
The price of this, the price of that, was he often heard to moan,
Can I afford a fancy urn, oh yes I fucking can, I can,
Oh yes I fucking can.
Ernie's health was pretty good; he only had the piles,
That kept him up, half the night, to take away his smiles.
A cream of sorts would do the trick, to rid him of this bane,
Alleviate, remove forthwith this fucking awful pain.
But in each drawer, and cupboard space, he hid his secret life,
To send away, to some far place, to buy himself a wife.
So she could mourn, her grief so great, the cost was way too high,
Could she afford a fancy urn, oh yes she fucking can, she can,
Oh yes she fucking can.
As Ernie aged, as time went by, a wife still he did not,
But funeral plans, and coffin guides, he had a bloody lot.
In oak, in larch, what wood to choose, for his final resting place?
With silver handles, golden screws and lots of pretty lace.
But in each drawer, and cupboard space, were drawings, designs and sketches,
Of funeral plots, and tombs galore, and grieving bleeding wretches.
Who would come, to see him leave, just who would cry the most?
They'd give a speech and raise a glass, a gloriously rousing toast.

*Could he afford to die alone, could he afford to die?*
*He asked himself, alone at night, oh why, oh why, oh why?*

My Forever Home

*I'm in a box, I know not why,*
*I really don't want to die.*
*It's very small, it has no door,*
*A wooden box, on the floor.*
*It's leather-lined, warm as toast,*
*Although I'm not, one to boast.*
*It is quite cramped, so very small,*
*I'm five foot nine so not so tall.*
*I hear a noise, a switch is turned,*
*Am I about to get me burned?*
*I start to move, the box gets hot,*
*Goodbye from me, you've had your lot.*
*RIP*

Thomas could often be heard singing these doleful tunes as he drove from working men's club to working men's club, hawking his part-worn caskets to the unsuspecting heart attack and cancer victims who populated these clubs. If not a captive market, they were certainly keen to spend a couple of quid and pick up a nice gift for the wife, or so the line went. Thomas became known as Carter the Casket, and with Dee's assistance was able to identify those who, if not at death's door, certainly were due to make an appointment in the not-too-distant future. His caskets and after sales service meant that soon he was drawing unwanted attention from the bigger boys. They wanted a slice of the action pie, and Thomas wasn't prepared to forego his pie meal ticket. Dee urged Thomas to perhaps move into the decorative urn business, but caskets were Thomas's bread and butter (food idioms were very common in the late 70s) and he was loath to roll over and take any form of medicine. A meeting was arranged with the local casket clan committee, where Thomas was required to inform the head of the committee why he should be allowed to stay in business.

It was a take-it-or-fuck-off type of meeting, so Thomas decided to move on to greener pastures, and was able to secure a driving position at a down-market funeral director, 'Dig & Dropp'. He was responsible for driving the hearse and the upkeep of the warmer coffins.

Damian was keen to accompany his dad to work, when school permitted, as he was eager to understand the workings of low budget dying and spend some quality time with his dad. Thomas, who had very little faith in the schooling that Damian was receiving, rang the school and informed them that Damian would be unable to attend school due to bereavement. Damian was elated to be joining Thomas in the family hearse, and asked Anne to knit him something in black that would be suitable for a hearse driver's assistant. Anne, pipe at the ready, managed to quickly throw together a one-piece mourning suit in cobalt. On his first morning, sat in the coffin seat, Damian felt so proud as Thomas slowly reversed the hearse out of its hearse garage. First job on the agenda at 'Dig & Dropp' was to mop down the back of the hearse for any embalming or bodily fluids. Damian was able to remove most of the stains and with a squirt of fly spray, most of the nastier smells were masked. Next was rifling through the coffins for discarded trinkets and small denomination coins. This was how most hearse drivers managed to take home a living wage. On a good day there would be shillings, farthings and the odd threepenny bit; some of the coffins were over thirty years old. The final task before the first corpse collection was possibly the most important and could be the difference between a happy mourner, who might well invite you to the wake, and a wailing mob planning a fresh funeral. Thomas and Damian had to load up copious bundles of heavy-duty twine, gaffer tape and weights to ensure that the casket didn't bounce around too much en route to the burial site. Apparently, there was nothing worse than a battered corpse. Corpses could be very slippery, so Thomas would always nail twice, tie once, to ensure that the body remained immobile on its final trip, a sort of non-moving moving last journey. The time spent with his dad taught Damian the importance of discretion and a well-pressed suit. No one wanted their loved one carted towards the flames of finality by an undertaker unable to press his or her best black trousers. Many of the funerals and rituals burnings were deeply emotional, often as a result of a weighty casket, but on many occasions the whole rigmarole was routine, with bland words, bland mourners and nothing to bring cheer to the passing of a loved one. Damian decided to write his own eulogy to ensure that when his time for roasting arrived, at least the mourners could have a bit of a giggle. This moving celebration of Damian's fictitious life and achievements is reproduced below:

<u>*Damian – Husband, Dad and Son.*</u>

*Few get through life without fate's mischievous hand making a mockery of plans and ambitions. Damian was well versed in mistakes and mischief and spent much of his life sweeping the wreckage to the corner of life's room in an attempt to carry on despite himself.*

*Those gathered here today in the banqueting suite of the Bradford Pie Makers' Lodge will appreciate the irony of holding Damian's funeral inside a giant mock pie, made entirely from shortcrust pastry. His passing will leave a huge hole in the pie takings of pie-makers and retailers across the land, but like his father Thomas, he would cross the road for a decent pie.*

*Seeing most of his family here, along with the odd friend (thanks for coming, Mark) would amuse Damian no end. He enjoyed some of the funerals he attended over the years, and he hopes you remembered the whoopee cushions and the nodding dog for the hearse.*

*His distinguished career as an undertaker/ spy/sailor/cabinet maker/ski instructor, meant that he was always on call, ready to deliver an emergency skiing lesson, or knock up a cabinet for a spying colleague. He was a people person, spending much of his life conversing with people. He loved nature and would eat most things.*

*Pies were his passion, and thanks to his efforts, pies are now available on street corners, buses and at most good DIY stores. He was seldom without a pie, often keeping a slimline pie down his sock for an emergency nibble. He was honoured by the queen for his services to pie, but never referred to himself as Sir Damian; he was always just plain old Sir.*

*To his beautiful wife (she is surely short sighted) and his illustrious children he would say he loved you before, he loved you when he was breathing, and his love will continue to worry you.*

*Damian, dearly loved idiot, friend, father and husband. May his body burn brightly.*

After completing his eulogy, Damian locked it away in the hope that it would be read by a tearful child (his own, hopefully) at a very emotional pie-themed venue.

# I need to learn how much?

The Winter of Discontent, considered by many to be Shakespeare's greatest play, was also a great description of the tragedy that was unfolding in Britain during the first few months of the year. As the prime minister, James Carrierbag, wrestled with Denis Fealy's eyebrows, piles of rubbish built up in the streets, leading to outbreaks of stupidity, litter and tropical madness. Binmen, the perennial whipping boys of the era, refused to handle rubbish that was dirty, and the dispute escalated into what was the one hundred and fifty-fifth longest running industrial dispute of the year. Pedestrians, usually so good at voting with their feet, resorted to other modes of voting, whilst Scratcher, now a fledgling leader, had only insults and bile to throw at the prime minister.

In Damian's small part of the world, where rubbish was an everyday occurrence, few people noticed when the binmen went on strike. Damian was at secondary school, having completed firstary school. His new school, Tongue Reprehensible, was a sprawling blot of education on the scarred landscape of urban Bradford. Adjacent to Damian's pitiful school were two further schools, dedicated to religious boys and girls who believed in salvation and natural selection. Damian didn't understand either concept, so settled for the lowest common denominator, a non-religious school.

The first thing that struck Damian on his first day at the school was the P.E. teacher's plimsolls, casually discarded from a Fiat Loafer — the choice of all athletic types. The walk to the school was approximately short, and Mark and Damian would often vary their route to avoid the local tough guys who lay in wait with hardened knuckles and shiny boots. There were many tough guys in the area, and they could often be found near off-licences, railway bridges and in well-tended orchards. Nicotine-stained fingers and aggressive hair meant that eye contact would lead to a beating of sorts, depending on the weather. Fortunately for Damian and Mark, they deployed a range of ruses to avoid a pummelling. Mark, in what was the high point of his school career, suggested parka coats, as the fur lined hood offered more protection and was soft on his skin. The two fools could be seen each morning, hoods up, gently avoiding painful confrontations, intent only on abuse from a distance with hoods pulled firmly over their sweaty teenage heads.

What Damian disliked most about school were the teachers, a collection of social misfits whose only obvious positive characteristic was relatively good personal hygiene, which for Bradford was akin to showing off. His form teacher that year was Miss Hollowlegs, a tin-like woman who would often rattle when shaken hard or pushed over. Her feather-like hair meant that high winds could pose a real danger of flight, so most of the lessons she taught were indoors, despite her being head of horticulture and outdoor activities. Her ability to prune almost anything had seen her rise meteorically through the ranks of the Navy, but she had been discharged after only two weeks due to a perforated footprint and flat ears, so she turned to the only other thing she could do with any confidence: outside stuff. That year with Hollowlegs was a roller coaster ride of dismal under-teaching and protracted register taking. His first proper lesson of the week was double maths, or as Thomas called it, numbers. Damian had a natural flair, which at times flared up, but during maths lessons, he was able to control the debilitating condition. The maths teacher, Mr Stone, was a rock of a man, whose bulbous nose and pointed words marked him out as a pixie. A very strict disciplinarian, he would often beat his chest with a set square to intimidate the other teachers. In class, Damian studied small and large numbers, some shapes, some more shapes, some letters and numbers, and some other stuff. Memorable!

His history teacher, Mr Apples, was a twin (his sister, Mrs Pears, taught Homely Awareness) and would often immerse.

Unfortunately, not in history, and his grasp on facts was minimal. Damian spent the first four months of the year studying the impact Rapunzel had on medieval architecture. Mr Apple's lessons were always light on fact and heavy on fantasy. He loved the medieval period, and maintained that Robin Hood invented the arrow, Long John Silver was a crusader and Charles De Gaulle the inventor of the printing press. Little wonder that he was dismissed for incompetence the following year, but not before running bare-arsed across the playing fields shouting, "Yo ho ho and a bottle of rum."

Damian also had Mr Shears, a rather rotund history scholar whose predilection for Brylcreem meant that his hair could never be ruffled. His slacks, always slipping below his abundant waistline, were tea-stained and soiled and his shoes squeaked when he ran. He too had a slim grip on facts, and Damian was mistaught the French Revolution, the Dutch Revolution and The Scottish Revolution. Mr Shears loved revolutions, and in his spare time collected tyres and wheels. Shears was the son of a Welsh wheel maker, and his preoccupation with all things wheeled meant that Damian's view of European history was skewed somewhat. Shears insisted that the wheel was at the heart of most wars and civic unrest yet was also the solution to many of society's social injustices. During a rather tepid lesson on the War of the Spanish Succession, he spouted forth on the causes of flatulence at Versailles, scurvy in the British Navy, and the lack of moral fibre in the youth of today. The man was a fucking moron. He rode to work on a bike, and each morning, his Brylcreem mop flapping as one, he would arrive at work with a tale of some imaginary road accident that had befallen him the previous day. On one occasion he justified the lateness of his arrival at school by claiming that he had been assailed by a roaming gang of wheel thieves on the lookout for wheels.

Damian had Mrs Pears on a Thursday afternoon, where he would be taught how to prepare a cushion, about curtains and their pitfalls, and — scented candles, good value or a fucking waste of time? Mrs Pears was a vibrant-flavoured woman, whose claim to fame had been appearing on 'That's Life' in 1976 with a cushion in the shape of Edward Teath's rectum. Despite her obvious mental instability, she was kind and very generous. She would often make small fancies for her students, including butterfly flan, rose water puddings and treacle surprise. Her dress sense reflected her inability to co-ordinate, and she would often wear at least three cardigans, of differing fabrics, on top of her lime green anorak. Her shoes were made of leather and piss, meaning they were cheap to buy but horrible to smell. Those Thursday afternoons were a joy, and it is no wonder that in the future Damian adopted a very open door to interior design and tom-tittery.

Wednesday afternoon was spent with Mr Irons, the woodwork teacher and Mr Wood, the metalwork teacher. Three hours of banging and sawing meant that by the end of the afternoon, Damian had injured himself at least once, quite often needing first aid, or at least a little sympathy. The workshop, if that is what you wanted to call it, was a small hut set some way from the main building, with benches for banging sessions and vices for sawing sessions. The two materials, Mr Wood and Mr Irons never saw eye to eye, both having severe squints, and this led to many disagreements as to who would fill the kettle, turn the lights on, or use the chalk. Damian had a gift for shapes and fashioned many shapes during those cold afternoons in the hut. Indeed, even now, DIY is one of his least favourite activities, and he will throw himself into most small household projects with apathy and disgust.

Tuesdays involved modern foreign language, and Damian, keen to be understood somewhere, decided to learn French and German. The French master, Mrs Humanoid, was not dissimilar to a prison guard from some Weimar Republic institution, intent only on belittling her charges and wearing too much leather. Her grasp of French was whimsical, and she spent most of the lesson patrolling between the rows of desks, beret in hand and garlic at the ready. Damian took to French like a fish to batter and was soon able to mispronounce many words. His innate inability to roll his arse meant that some words were problematic, but he didn't let that stop him from making a tit of himself. Soon he was conversing with his parents like a natural born Parisian. His German master, Mr Humanoid, looked like something from a Fritz Lang film, with a dystopian view of his pupils. He would seldom frown, in fear of creasing his extremely smooth forehead, and occasionally brought magnets into class to try and make himself feel more attractive. German was Double Dutch to Damian, and he struggled to grasp the need for spittle when speaking this Teutonic language. The unnatural fluency that was required to be a linguist or coherent was something Damian had no hope of possessing, learning or buying via a fluency salesman in a very fluid marketplace.

His parents, who worried that Damian might be turning European, refused to engage with him when he attempted to speak in either French or English, so he spent most of his time practising on the family dog, Brussels, so called because his tail was a sprout. Stephen and Paul, who also spoke language, would often whisper silent curses to help Damian along, but he just didn't have an ear for any language.

The P.E. department was staffed with a motley collection of dilapidated halfwits, whose only obvious ability was never that obvious. Mr Stique, Mr Baul and Mr Larynx had a collective age of one hundred and sixty-five, which resulted in a total lack of physical activity on their part. P.E. took place twice a week, and Damian's natural physical attributes were very difficult to identify. He could co-ordinate his arse and his elbow, but his hand and his eye were always out of tune. The one talent he did possess was speed, or least feet and legs, which meant he was an obvious choice for the running team. Donning his pre-war running shoes, which were a gift from his great uncle John, he quickly developed a running style all his own. Choosing to eschew the advice of Mark and other well-wishers, he quickly became hopeless at sport. That would have been the end of his athletic career but for an untimely intervention by Mr Larynx, who suggested Damian try fucking off and jumping in a lake. That inspired Damian to try swimming, something that most fish do well, so how hard could it be? The facilities at the school were on a par, second to some, and without doubt appalling. With inadequate drainage, rampant verrucae and termites in the changing rooms, Damian soon learnt that the best place for swimming was in the water. Over the course of the year, Damian learnt to crawl, splash and fall, and when he came to the end of year assessment, he was the only one in his class who didn't come down with a severe rash and was, therefore, top of the class. The other two students are still undergoing treatment for a severe waterborne infection that can lead to complete apathy.

Science was something that showed little interest in Damian, and the mutuality of feelings led to Damian avoiding test tubes, photosynthesis and any form of reactions, and instead he chose to study technical drawing, a subject so obscure that Damian assumed that the lessons would be cancelled due to lack of knowledge, teacher or interest. However, the teacher of the subject, Miss Crosshatch, was an angular woman with a very cylindrical head and tubular legs. Despite her hideous appearance, she proved to be a brilliant disappointment. Unable to communicate even the simplest of ideas, Crosshatch would drone on like a bilious bee. The students sat in silence, poking their arms sporadically with sharpened pencils in order to stay awake. Yards and yards of pristine paper were wasted by the students as they attempted to draw side views of various industrial components. Damian's skill with an HB pencil brought him to Miss Crosshatch's attention. Despite her name, she wasn't always cross, nor did she like eggs, but she soon began to nurture Damian, and before long he was able to open his pencil case with ease, moving onto sharpening pencils and folding paper. Maybe one day he would design a sprocket for a machine; the possibilities were limited.

Damian loved reading, and would spend hours on the toilet, studying old Haynes manuals, never fully understanding the plot but loving the pictures. He moved onto to the Reader's Digest and believed with all his heart that laughter was the best medicine. His

English teachers, Miss Moore and Miss Less, were little known outside the English department, and their bookish demeanour meant that they were often mistaken for librarians. Moore, whose nasal cavities were filled with misfortune, struggled to be heard, whilst Miss Less was much diminished following an emergency removal of her torso, which left her lacking in depth. She loved Bronte and Austen and would dress as a neo-Georgian lady to get a real understanding of the nuances of the texts. Shakespeare dominated the teachers' talk, with oblique references to stanzas, iambic pentameter and quadrilateral verse. Damian was required to study Macbeth, a truly daunting proposition for a boy had only ever been to Dumfries as a small child and had little or no appreciation of dynastic infighting. Banquo was a posh dinner and MacDuff a Scottish dessert. Once again, Damian faced an uphill struggle and contemplated not reading ever again, or at least confining his reading to Readers' Digest. Literature was taught in a draughty room on the second floor of the sports hall, and every Monday afternoon he had Moore, and Thursday afternoon he had Less (a bit like maths). Their teaching styles reflected their lack of technique, and Moore would say very little, resorting to grunts and mime in order to convey the simpler concepts. Less, who incidentally was very short, had a towering opinion of her own abilities, and would strut in front of the blackboard, waffle in hand and chalk in mouth, quoting snippets from Macbeth, MacDuff and McDonald's.

The English timetables were extremely fluid, and at times Damian would not know if he was getting Moore or Less. This resulted in him missing lessons on some occasions, and on other occasions turning up for Moore when he wanted Less, or believing he was going to have Less but ending up with Moore. His teenage brain struggled to cope with this tom-tittery, and he started reading more experimental texts. He loved the works of Ambler and Greene, for their evocative, atmospheric portrayal of the mundane, yet also appreciated the high-octane novels of Bagley and Flushing. Dutch author Flushing's greatest work, 'The Surgeon', a rip-roaring tale of international surgery behind the

Iron Curtain, was a multi-million blockbusting, runaway jamboree of a novel, subsequently turned into a very disappointing franchise, flopping at every possible opportunity. Moore or Less tried to encourage Damian to focus on the course texts, but when he asked which texts he should specifically read, the teachers just gave him a rough approximation of possible books.

Damian's time at school would only get worse as he realised that the book learning nullified his natural curiosity. He dreamt of a future as a script writer, or a train driver, or a merchant seaman, or as a script-writing train merchant. He longed for adventure and beef fat on his toast. He yearned to be something, with a sparkle in his foot and a barely visible twinkle in his eye. Reality was very disappointing, and he would often escape in his own fantasy world, in his head writing scripts on a sea-going train, for stars such as Roger Sufficient (he couldn't get enough of him) and Ernest Intentions, Hollywood's biggest box office draw. At home, Damian had been given an old black and white typewriter on which he planned to write his brilliant script for an action movie. The typewriter, a Follies Mk11, had integral keys, disposable words and large print functionality, allowing him to cater for the short of sight, a key demographic for his action movie. Each evening, weather permitting, Damian would adopt a sitting position, Basildon Bond at the ready, and tap away at the Follies, gazing from time to time through the hole in the wall at the broken neighbours, burnt-out lawnmowers and gazelle, hoping for inspiration. The working title for his script was an amalgamation of possible titles, drawn from the bowels of his imagination. He had considered a short punchy title like Shithead or Turdwars, but was currently veering towards a more thoughtful, introspective title, like 'Are Turdwars Necessary? — Part One', or 'Shithead and Grim Expose some very Dangerous Things but Everything Works out Okay in the End'. The main theme of the script was love, redemption, romance, retribution and some fighting. Based loosely, its central protagonist was a maverick rule maker, and it used exotic locations with lots of car chases and beaches; Damian was confident that he could hammer out a halfway shit script, providing he had enough Basildon Bond.

# Part Three —
## I ain't wearing no fucking shoulder pads!
## The world is your shrimp!

Curly hair and sweat bands were the look of that year, and Damian was on the cusp of stupidity as he donned his new tennis pumps, stroked his velvety hair and put on a rather outrageous striped headband. He was going to play tennis with Stephen and Paul. Stephen knew a range of exotic sports, and when Damian saw John McNcheese shouting with a racquet, he knew he had to try his hand. The brothers had managed to fashion together three racquets using only twine, twigs and spittle. The ball they had stolen from their uncle who had a drawer full of the little yellow bastards. On paying the one-pound fee to access the court, it was decided by Stephen that he would rotate partners, so it was always going to be two against one. What followed was a masterclass in sibling manipulation, and unsurprisingly, Stephen won every game. Damian, who still had twinges from his Morton's toe, loved these sporting days, and when they couldn't play tennis, they would head down to the local pitch and putt and throw balls at old players. Realising they could probably spend their time more productively, the next time they went to the pitch and putt, they hired the requisite equipment and headed out towards the first tee. Stephen teed off first, deciding that he would demonstrate the correct fidgeting stance to his younger brothers. Both Paul and Damian proved to have potential in this exciting new pastime, and soon they were hitting balls here there and every fucking where. Rules seemed to evolve depending on the time of day and on who was winning. Quite often Stephen would introduce new rules that at first glance, appeared to give him a slight advantage over his two brothers, but Damian and Paul were just happy to be hitting things.

During this period of sporting magnificence, Damian began to think about future career choices. As a non-smoker, he felt that he would be judged by the careers officer on the cleanliness of his fingers. Nicotine stains had held Thomas back for years, until he started to wear thick gloves. Mr Glaze, the careers officer, was a tall and boring man with a very unreadable face. At times he appeared in pain, but quite often he would be smiling inanely whilst scribbling notes onto his hand. Damian was perceived at times as a stupid and selfish teenager, whereas he was just very stupid. He dreamt of dream jobs but struggled to find the vocation that would keep him away from a life of pies. He had decided to write a list of potential careers, listing the pros and cons of each job, in the vain hope that it would make his simple life simpler.

*Possible Jobs:*

*1/ Armed Guerrilla/ Insurgent:*

*Pros: Always fancied wearing a bandana, charcoaled up and chewing on a grainy cigarette or pipe. The struggle and eventual victory seemed less important than the image portrayed in the media. I've even thought of a nom de guerre: El-Charco. The insurgent was not necessarily everyone's cup of tea, and there was the danger of death, but high in the mountains or jungles, depending on where you were fighting, the guerrilla was free to set up camp and start fires as and when necessary.*

*Cons: 'Danger of being shot, wounded, or locked up in a dirty, shit-infested jail. No laundry facilities and the other insurgents may be a group of unscrupulous bastards. Not many opportunities for career progression and few perks (apart from frequent unfettered fires). Discipline would not be an issue, but some fucker always wants to be in charge. May have to buy my own insurgent uniform which could prove expensive although we always seem to have a lot of charcoal knocking about. Will speak to Dad about dangers.'*

*2/ Musician/Backing Singer*

*Pros: the chance to play the recorder in front of thousands of cheering fans was every schoolboy's dream. 'Three Blind Mice' played live at some packed out arena, with thumping bass and outlandish costumes was a prospect that sounded almost exciting. Would need a private jet and headband, along with a team of parasitical hangers on, but the upside would be free stuff, such a sweets and drinks, meaning a huge saving on the weekly shopping bill.*

*Cons: Not many people associate the recorder with rock, so openings in the business may be limited. My recorder playing was never brilliant, but I could do a passable recorder solo if pushed. 'Not sure about all the hangers on, pinching my fucking free stuff. That could increase my weekly shopping bill.'*

## 3/ Actor/Conman

*Pros: Everyone loves a clown, and many people are quite fond of actors and warm-hearted conmen. I have a natural ability to be distrusted but appear fairly honest. I can slip into a character with effort, fooling those who didn't know me into thinking I was actually somebody else. Put to good use I could see myself starring in low-budget foreign language films, or in front of a magistrate, depending on the roles I selected.*

*Cons: 'Don't speak many low-budget languages, and I have never been animated, so perhaps I would struggle to find roles. Costume dramas make me feel slightly bilious, and sci-fi films are the stuff of fantasy. May end up as an extra, working with a crowd of low life losers looking for fame with a large lack of talent. Acne could be the biggest hurdle. Have no outbreaks at the moment but do not want to be remembered as the face of spots in a low-budget teenage coming of age drama. Maybe I could do it weekends only, weather permitting.'*

## 4/ Undertaker

*Pros: 'Death, the final frontier. Love black clothes and might suit a hat. I have carried some pretty heavy things and can adopt a serious demeanour if required. Keen to meet new people and experience death second-hand. Get to ride in a hearse again. Rich pickings of the freshly* packaged corpse which could supplement the income. Availability of discount for friends and family. Urns are a wonderful addition to any household; could get mum one for future use.'

Cons: 'Mourners can be a bit miserable and don't always tip well. Don't fancy carrying a really heavy corpse due to weak elbows (Dad's fault), and rainy funerals can be so depressing. No opportunity to dress down and bring a little fashion flair. Would like a range of hats, perhaps flat, bowler and peaked, but unsure if this is possible. Will speak to Dad.'

### 5/ Horse or Dog trainer

Pros: 'Dogs are the canine version of cats, and as such, represent the pinnacle of the athletic animal. I could take a poodle or dachshund and soon have it running a marathon or the 110m hurdles. Horses are dogs with longer legs, and if they could bark would be the perfect accompaniment to any kennel. Imagine a horse doing the pole vault, or high jump. The Olympics would be better for such a spectacle.'

Cons: 'Allergic to dogs and horses. Was once bitten by an angry horse in Halifax, and on another occasion chased 7 miles by a rabid pony intent on kicking me. Dogs shit a lot and smell of piss. Not sure if dogs can eat pies but know for a fact that you can get horse pie from Gruesome's Butchers in Pudsey. Cannot talk with animals as I lack empathy. Nor do I have any inclination to race a dog.'

### 6/ Freelance Hairdresser/taxi driver

Pros: Still belong to a head of hair and understand the basics of brushing, washing and backcombing. Like the wind in my hair as it makes me feel alive. Often have things to do at the weekend, so I could engage in witty banter. Last weekend I cleaned the hubcaps on Dad's Austin Hairspray. Mum lets me use the non-serrated scissors so could be trusted not to do too much harm. Taxi-driving would not require a driving licence or spatial awareness, ideal for a clumsy fucker. Idle chit-chat appeals to the idiot in me, along with long waits outside grimy pubs late at night.

Cons: Hair brings me out in hives. Hate talking to the back of heads, which would make cutting the rear hair difficult unless I used a rotating *mirror. Tendency to slip when using sharp tools and spoons; could be problematic. Allergic to inane chitter-chatter, making this job a nightmare, and cleaning hubcaps is not everyone's cup of tea. Taxi driving would require me to buy a car, but I would need money to buy a car; I have no money. Ability to read a map may put me at a disadvantage.*

The writing of the list seemed to placate the urgency nestling within Damian's career advisor, but Damian was still unsure of what his particular set of skills would be seen as desirable for by any employer. He decided to speak to Thomas in order to clarify a few issues. Thomas and Anne got together and discussed their youngest son's dilemma, and it was decided that a trip to the Bradford Maritime, Aquatic and Pottery Heritage Centre would shed light on the infinite possibilities that fish and pottery offered a young man. The short drive in Thomas's new Austin Mackerel, a fish of a car with semi-aquatic features, which gave the car all-weather capabilities, was just long enough for Anne to give her new trout-shaped pipe a run out. Arriving at the centre's impressive car park, located between a bankrupt glass merchants and an automated car wash, Thomas parked close to the security hut to ensure the guard could keep an eye on his Mackerel. The admission to the centre was free, as they were trying desperately to encourage a younger generation to explore the wonders of pottery-based aquatics, and aquatic-based pottery. Thomas had a lifetime pass, which meant he could visit any time on a Friday with family or friends. He also received a monthly newsletter, 'The Ceramic Eel', full of fishy pottery facts and interesting articles about pottery, boats and fish. Thomas had always loved the sea, and when he had been demobbed from the navy, he signed up as a deep-sea fisherman in Hull. Joining the crew of the Red Herring, a one-hundred-foot boat with a crew of ten, Thomas had fished far and wide in the wild seas. His shipmates were a meddlesome collection of ex U-boat commanders, dissatisfied pirates and barnacle-encrusted bachelors. Thomas fitted in like a well-filleted mackerel in a tin full of fishy goodness. He had wondered about the possibility of his youngest son joining a similarly well-equipped rust bucket and trawling the high seas for sprats and high jinks. All the world loves a sailor, or so the saying went, so perhaps Damian could be catapulted into the glamorous world of fish quotas, net size and squalls. From port to port he would get the opportunity to meet salty mariners with little hope of matrimony, cutthroat sprat dealers ready to double-cross at the drop of a windcheater, and experience weather that would shatter any hope of ever being warm again.

Thomas hoped that the centre's many attractions and informative posters, some hand-written, would inspire Damian. The main space at the centre was dedicated to all things aquatic. There was a large fish tank with some small drawings of the fish that would be going in the tank once funding was released. There was an array of ropes used in the capture of fish, but unfortunately the curious visitor could not touch or experiment with the twine. In the corner there was an interactive fish-gutting display, giving the less squeamish the chance to gut a live mackerel using a selection of tools. Damian was keen to try his hand, but Thomas didn't want his Mackerel smelling of fish, so they just watched as a party of school children eviscerated a twenty-pound mackerel. Upstairs was the pottery section, which included a large pot/vase with some primitive fish etchings, along with a cabinet featuring a selection of famous cups, vases and plates. There was the teapot used by Wallis Simpson the day before she met Edward VIII, a plate which Buffalo Bill had shot at and missed, and a very fetching vase which was rumoured to have belonged to a friend of Joseph Stalin. Anne spent at least five minutes gazing at the glazed pottery pipes, transfixed by their sheer beauty and the intricacy of the designs. On one pipe there was a beautiful depiction of the Battle of The Nile, and another featured a life-sized depiction of a ladybird; it was genius. Anne would have remained there but for Thomas drawing her attention to the interactive pottery display, where feeble fools could try their hand at throwing a pot. Damian of course stepped up and was soon escorted from the building for throwing one too many pots at the over-zealous security guards. Whilst Thomas and Anne spent a further twenty minutes strolling around the exhibits and displays, Damian made his way to the Mackerel and contemplated his future. Seaman, potter or international man of destiny? Thomas and Anne returned to the car with a selection of gift shop tat to complement their already extensive collection.

The drive home was uneventful, and Thomas understood his son's frustration, so as a treat they stopped off at the local pie shop and spent like it was 1999, with two pies each and a tin of mushy peas to share. Every cloud! As for his future, Thomas suggested that perhaps the Doris Day approach would better suit Damian: que sera sera. Returning to school the following week, Damian informed his career advisor that he intended to underachieve for several years so as to not burn out too soon. Damian's star would burn brighter later in life, so for now he contented himself with low sights and missed targets, believing that in the fullness of time his ship would surely be somewhere close to land, if not specifically coming into port.

# Bloody liars

Like most households in Scratcher's Britain, toilet roll was a luxury to be used on special occasions. Damian, who had recently become older, worked long hours in the evenings at Morrison's, the local supermarket for downtrodden folk. One night Damian hatched a master plan that would see the Carter family finally step out of the dark ages. Damian would take between two and three of his father's turtleneck jumpers and wear them under his Morrison's uniform. When the store closed, having disgorged the hungry hordes, Damian would remove the jumpers and then, the crowning glory of his plan, he would wrap roll after roll of toilet paper around his torso. On some nights he could make off with up to fifteen rolls of the puppy's finest without anyone being the wiser. As he walked home with his friend Mark, who also had a very soft spot for toilet roll, Damian would turn into Cordial Street and there, perched on the bonnet of the Ford Bowel, was his father. Thomas, with binoculars in hand, would immediately discern whether Damian had successfully managed to smuggle the lucrative loo roll, and his face would light up with a childlike glow, knowing that they were the only family on the street who could look forward to streak-free visits to the toilet. Heady days for a family who seldom washed. Thomas would store the contraband in a specially designed cupboard in the attic. The cupboard could only be reached by going into the attic, and Thomas being a very cautious man, put a handle on the door to warn off nosey relatives. He used toilet paper every day, often risking arrest or embarrassment, and he made a pact with Damian; you bring it and they will use it. Of course, there was a price to pay for this abundance of bog roll, and as Thomas's wardrobe became more depleted it soon became obvious that Thomas could no longer wear turtleneck sweaters. This was a lesson that stayed with Damian throughout his adulthood, and even today, he always has his neck on display for all to see. This inevitably means that he is stopped more at supermarkets, but his father would be smiling up at him safe in the knowledge that his family had a plentiful supply of the puppy's finest.

Gary the Gable was a regular site in the area, up a ladder checking out the guttering of Bradford. He was an acquaintance of Thomas and had also served in the navy during World War Two. He was in a top-secret archery unit that had been charged with shooting down Heinkel bombers using only bow and arrow. It was of course destined for failure, and in 1941 he had changed his name to Basil Chantrell and enlisted in the OCS, or Overseas Charm Squad. Basil's missions were often behind closed doors, where he would be indoctrinated in the latest wooing and smooching techniques. The plan was to drop these volunteers into occupied rooms and charm the Nazis into surrendering. The War Department knew nothing of this hare-brained scheme, and after only one very unsuccessful mission, the unit was confined to barracks for the duration of the war, where Gary reverted to his given name and underwent training in all things guttering. He was now approaching sixty-seven, and felt he needed a guttering assistant to hold the ladder on blustery days, carry the ladder on dry days, and general ladder-related duties. Thomas suggested Damian, who was desperate to earn some easy money and had seen ladders in action. The fickle thumbs of serendipity had once again waved their enchanted wand.

Guttering, conduits and any form of overflow were Gary's bread and butter. He lived and breathed water relocation and would spend hours studying the methods used throughout the world to move water safely from one location to another without danger or hazard. Such dedication was rare in the 70s in the guttering sector, so it was surprising when his business closed suddenly. Damian later learnt that Garry had been implicated in a rather unsavoury food scandal, involving Russian sweets and bribery. Gary was last sighted fleeing Yorkshire on board a National Express coach heading for Accrington. He made a brief appearance on a pilot episode of 'DIY WTF' but died of water retention in his mid-eighties. Guttering's loss was felt throughout the free world.

This meant Damian had to find alternative work to supplement his £4.25 pocket money. Serendipity was soon hammering at the door of opportunity, when his uncle John offered him part-time work at his small engineering factory. The factory fabricated lies and untruths for the foreign market at knock-down prices. John had trained and was willing to teach Damian some of what he knew on a Saturday, from nine to five. His first day at the factory was an eye-opener; the factory floor was covered in lies and half-truths. Immediately Damian was put to work sweeping the half-truths under a carefully placed carpet, and then separating the white lies from the downright fucking whoppers. At first, he struggled to distinguish between little lies and misinformation, but after an hour he felt he was getting the hang of things; or was he? His uncle had told him that he would get a massive pay packet each week, along with complimentary compliments, which went well with Damian's ideas of remuneration. The products were fabricated on a small typewriter located on the factory floor and were separated into different categories depending on the market they were destined for. European lies were John's stock-in-trade, and he could churn out at least seventeen whoppers on a good day. The type of lie could be tailor-made for a specific client, or a mass-market lie intended for a larger audience. John's lies were such that Damian wasn't sure if the whole experience was some massive attempt to fuck with his head, but when he was able to view some of the fabricated lies before they were packaged up ready for dispatch, he was awestruck. Memorable lies included a simple but devious little invention which stated that British birds were now being forced to fly on the right side of the sky to conform to new regulations issued by the European Space Agency. There the lie concerning the origin of the Alps, which stated that the mountain range had been named in honour of a well-known muesli-based breakfast product. John was able to craft his lies so well that

Damian would often refer to his pocket encyclopaedia to check the veracity of some of John's statements. On one occasion, Damian had to take a longer tea break in order to fully digest a real whopper that had sold extremely well in Eastern Europe. Pigeons, so often the Cinderella of the bird kingdom, the tofu in a bowl of giblets, the scrawny-beaked buffoons in an aviary of cockatoos, were in fact part man-made. The thrust of the lie was that pigeons had faced extinction shortly after the building of the Iron Curtain, due to a lack of breadcrumbs in the Soviet Bloc. Scientists and other like-minded boffins had decided to redesign the bird with mechanical parts to reduce the need for breadcrumbs and implant low-grade surveillance equipment in the birds' beaks. The upgraded birds had wires and pulleys to control their movements and would follow humans with a determination bordering on psychotic. The only problem was that the new pigeons had a rather ungainly gait and their coos were slightly mechanical in their tone. John was understandably proud of this lie, and Damian went on to use it on his eldest daughter, who believed it to be true right into her twenties.

Soon Damian was churning out lies like a philandering bigamist and could knock off several in a day. The pay was still not forthcoming, but he had grown to love the inventive nature of the work. This sparked off his creativity, and he soon turned his attention to poetry and words. Damian loved words, not all of them of course, but quite a few, and some of his favourite words were in a dictionary. He had seen a poorly written limerick on a toilet door and been inspired to craft some of his own words into lyrical verse for the mass market, perhaps in conjunction with John, who had a typewriter. His first attempts were shit, but after a visit to a poetry repair workshop, he soon realised that his style was not Keats or Wordsworth, but more akin to the works of Cyril Wretched or William Flake. Flake was widely known as a twat in poetry circles, but his early work had hints of mediocrity, and Damian's favourite Flake poem, 'The Toilet', simply underscored the sheer majesty of his work. Set in a toilet in anywhere, the poem charts the daily indignity suffered by a toilet: (kindly reproduced with absolutely no one's permission)

## The Toilet

*Toilet, toilet, with your seat,*
*What a great human feat.*
*Receptacle for piss and shit,*
*For the arse the perfect fit.*
*Toilet, toilet, bowl so true,*
*Soil it not with piss or poo.*
*Flush the bowl, yank the chain,*
*The whooshing sound is just the same.*
*Toilet, toilet, splash of bleach,*
*Drop a phone, in they reach.*
*Smells and odours, you do keep,*
*Be careful what the bum does reap.*
*Toilet, toilet, new or old,*
*Silver, iron or even gold.*
*Ample tissue, you may need,*
*If the toilet you do feed.*

This poem was received badly by the critics, one observing that it belonged in its own subject matter. Of course, true art is subjective, and Flake went on to have a glittering career in the glitter ball industry. Wretched was a tortured soul, whose themes of loss and forgetfulness still ring true today. Possibly his most forgettable poem, 'What Did You Say?' is still misquoted to this day.

## What Did You Say?

*I thought I heard your dulcet tone,*
*As I sat upon my phone.*
*Did you call me, or I call you,*

*The line was busy, what could I do?*
*My ears, my ears, they hear so much,*
*It sounds like Dutch, or butch or hutch.*
*The lips do move, the words they climb,*
*But could you say them one more time.*
*My mind is full of things forgotten,*
*Oh dear oh dear I feel so rotten.*
*If you to me, do wish to speak,*
*For a notebook, you must seek.*
*Write it down, not once but twice,*
*Thank you darling, you're so nice.*

Wretched suffered from chronic malnutrition in his later years, possibly due to a lack of food, and this is reflected in some of the shit he churned out. For Damian, Flake and Wretched were poets who both inspired and distilled a sense of misplaced hope in the power of words. He would spend minutes banging away at the typewriter, trying to make the bastard pile of shit work. On the last Saturday of June in that year, he inadvertently smashed the typewriter with a sledgehammer, meaning John was unable to produce his lies any time soon. Regrettably, John had to let Damian go as he hung onto to the sledgehammer, and with a small pay-off for lies produced to date, Damian was on the part-time job market again.

He still had his part-time position at Morrison's, but the hours meant he had to work for sixty minutes per hour for what was, even in the early 80s, a very low wage. As he scoured the pans in the family kitchen, Anne, busy puffing away on her tweed pipe, suggested that maybe he could get a job in a bar or discotheque, collecting glasses and being a general dogsbody. Damian opted to do all three, and failed miserably, realising very quickly that the people he worked with could well be idiots, perverts or thieves. He was content to be an idiot for the moment, so never had his innate brilliance recognised, even when he collected glasses in a rundown pub. His ability to not drop glasses and maintain a modicum of sobriety was not considered anything out of the ordinary, and the manager sacked him for being too efficient, or for some other trumped-up reason.

# Greetings!

Mark, Damian's good friend, had not long passed his driving test and had been looking for a suitable set of wheels to reflect his glowing hair and sporting prowess. He would scan the local newspaper, often in the dark whilst combing his flowing locks. Damian, drawing on his extensive knowledge of clapped-out bangers, suggested a Fiat Grunt, a small city car with a powerful one litre engine, two complete doors and wing mirrors. Mark was at first reluctant to commit to such a powerful motor, but with the help of several pints of cider he decided that that would be the perfect car to cruise the mean streets of Bradford. He managed, after many hours of negotiation with his good sense, to purchase a beautiful ten-year-old Fiat Grunt, in canary yellow, for an amazing price. Getting it home was a bit of a problem as it wouldn't start, but he managed to push it for three quarters of a mile (it was a very light car) before three pensioners took pity on him and helped him with the final half mile.

Damian was immediately impressed with the wheels and roof, and the pair decided to clean up the pile of shite. The interior had a strong smell of animal, so Mark decided to get some cherry-scented air fresheners so that the Grunt would smell sweet, a Bakewell tart on wheels. The hub caps, a speciality of Damian's, were in fact four paper doilies stuck on to rust, with the tread barely visible. The wing mirrors were held on using congealed lard and hope, as were the quarter lights. It would take an eternity to make the Grunt road legal, but Mark, taking a very mature and pragmatic approach to the Grunt's many faults, said "Fuck it," and decided to go for a spin to get the wind in his hair. All this fun and high jinks, wouldn't help Damian in his quest for work, but it passed the time.

Thomas had secured part-time work at a greeting card factory, or more accurately, a factory that manufactured greeting cards and associated accessories, such as mugs, gift bags and novelty pens, for the European market. Thomas considered himself to be both cosmopolitan but also extremely insular, and the opportunity to be a small part in a global business exporting British-made greetings and paraphernalia to Germans, Swedes and Greeks filled him with hope and opportunity. Thomas fancied himself as something of a wordsmith, having written many offensive letters to various local dignitaries over the years, and he decided to pen some European-style greetings and slip them in with those produced by the more gifted greeting card gurus.

His first effort, for the Swedish bereavement market, was a simple little twenty-line verse:

*Flat packed*

*Inga, Sven, one has died,*
*One the husband, one the bride.*
*Bought a table, took it home,*
*Tried to make it all alone.*
*Started reading, had a snack,*
*Read the booklet, front to back.*
*Screw it, tap it, push it hard,*
*Lubricate with Swedish lard.*
*Now it's done, it looks okay,*
*But Sven or Inga had to pay.*
*They'd rushed; they'd pushed a bit too hard,*
*They'd oiled and greased, they'd used the lard.*
*So at the table, they did sit,*
*A Swedish couple, the perfect fit.*
*The chairs were nice, the table square,*
*But on the table, it was so bare.*
*He turned to Inga, his loving wife,*
*And stabbed her with a carving knife.*
*The table that they bought together,*

*Would stay with him for now, forever.*
*RIP*

Thomas also wrote several other nation-based verses, which have been reproduced thanks to the kind permission of 'Bradford & Berlin Greetings Card Company'.


### A Dutch Bride

*Marry me, marry me, in Rotterdam,*
*Marry me, marry me, I'm your man.*
*We'll take a boat; we'll cross the sea,*
*We'll have some cake; we'll have high tea.*
*Marry me, marry me, I have a ring,*
*Marry me, marry me, my love doth sing.*
*We'll buy a dress; we'll buy a veil,*
*We'll buy two hats; we'll find a sale.*
*Marry me, marry me, so we can dance,*
*Marry me, marry me, you're my last chance.*
*We'd be so happy, my little bleeda,*
*We'd buy a house and live in Breda.*
*SWALK*


### A Greek Tragedy

*Olive Green, her suitcase packed,*
*Her house so clean, she had it vacked.*
*She'd booked a break, a holiday,*
*Not a week, a fortnight stay.*
*Creams and lotions, bikini too,*
*Some sandals and a training shoe.*
*Off to Greece, to see the sights,*
*Scorching days and sultry nights.*
*She'd meet a man, the waiting kind,*
*At home in Bury, so hard to find.*

*The hotel was great, working loo,*
*Some soap, a sponge, some cheap shampoo.*
*She settled in, unpacked her bags,*
*Her clothes, her shoes, her travel mags.*
*But as she went to find the bar,*
*The waiter said it wasn't far,*
*She slipped, or tripped and broke her head,*
*Poor Olive Green lay lifeless, dead.*

Thomas was proud of his time at the factory and believed he made a real difference in the way bereavement was celebrated. Rather than viewing death and loss as the end of something or a time of sadness, Thomas took the view that it was a time of opportunity, and a chance to riffle through forgotten belongings and send crappy cards. His prose and poetry were soon in demand in and around the factory, and he was freelancing, setting himself up as the Thomas Carter Sentiment Centre, where no insincere sentiment was considered too crass or inappropriate. Soon he had a list of clients demanding cards for all manner of socially awkward situations where a card could express their feelings in a light-hearted yet touching manner. His range expanded, and soon his menu of mendacity ran to two A4 pages. He catered for loved ones, hated ones, indifferent ones, those whose name was long forgotten and those whose name was never written down in a safe place. He had sentiments for cousins, bigamists, car thieves, half-sisters, half-wits, dimwits and bastards. Some sentiments were short and pithy, such as the resignation: *Fuck you, I'm leaving*, whereas others would try to offer some solace in a time of distress and misery: *Pull yourself together, you timid git*. Many could be used for a range of circumstances, like the Superficial Range, a best seller, whose opening line was: *Sorry, but shit happens, and you'll find someone else, and just remember, every cloud has a silver lining*. This was popular with divorcees, the emotionally needy and serial killers on the path to rehabilitation and employment. His style of writing was compared to that of an emotionally stunted pygmy with all the empathy of a banana, but Thomas himself argued that he offered a service that idiots were prepared to pay for, and his niche filled a void, which was also an opening line in his lonely-hearts range. Damian would often sit with Thomas in a braingusting session, each trying to produce the card for the inappropriate romantic loser. Beginning with the 'Forlorn Fool', they moved onto the 'Wittering Worrier' and the 'Rampant Romantic' and the pair produced verse that would wither even the most retarded of romantics.

*The Forlorn Fool*

*I saw her by the apple sauce,*
*Near the ketchup, red of course.*
*Her eyes were open, she was surprised,*
*My shirt selection, ill-advised.*
*To say hello, or walk on by,*
*To stare at her, she'd wonder why,*
*The foolish hope, the foolish fool,*
*He looks a dick, the fucking fool.*

*Wittering Worrier*

*I've combed my hair; I've locked the door,*
*I've got the bog roll but need some more.*
*I've turned the lights off, windows shut,*
*The cat is dead, but I have a mutt.*
*I'll get the bus, no wait I'll walk,*
*But on the bus, to strangers talk.*
*I'll get the bus, but sit downstairs,*
*Avoid the muggers with evil stares.*
*I'll see a girl, with flowing locks,*
*Trainers on, she likes to box.*
*I'll say hello, she'll slap my face,*
*And in her bag, a can of mace.*

*Rampant Romantic*

*Girls and boys went out to play,*
*All the night and all the day.*
*Roses are red and I feel blue,*
*Until the day that I met you.*
*I've said it once, so many times,*
*To speak of love, in verse and rhymes.*
*To find a true one, love me do,*
*Or stalking habits from me to you.*

Thomas and Damian clearly had many issues, but their ability to produce low quality greeting was unrivalled, and this little hobby contented the pair on warm winter evenings.

# Adulthood

Scratcher and talcum powder were the words that echoed round many a street corner at the start of the year. With rising coal and slumps in mines, a new form of extremism was evolving, and its effects were felt far and wide. Damian, a semi-amateur academic with a nose for sniffing, was in the final year of his 'A' level studies. His choices had been limited due to a lack of choice, so he had plumped for English, History and a new subject, Eco-nomics. Damian loved the environment, long before it became popular with people, and anything with eco at the start must have been a good thing. He wasn't sure what nomics were, but with his large enquiring mind, he was eager to soak up as many nomics as he could. He applied himself with an indifference which was admirable, and soon was riding a wave of mediocrity. His teachers recognised the innate gas in him, and with encouragement and patience he was able to hope for a year of successful underachievement.

Meanwhile, Thomas, ever the eye for a business opportunity to keep a roof over the starving mouths of his bread-ridden family, realised very quickly that if the miners were to declare all-out war on Scratcher's army, then a new source of energy would be needed to keep the coal fires burning. January had been a very cold month, all things considered, and Thomas had recently come into possession of a large amount of talcum powder, along with three hundred kilos of table salt. Thomas had read in the Reader's Digest that talcum powder, when mixed with table salt, went through a chemical change which resulted in a material that gave off heat and had excellent adhesive qualities. Immediately realising the potential for this product, Thomas set to work in his basement cellar, mixing and screaming through the night. When the sun finally rose, Thomas had one thousand and twenty-one bags of his wonder product Saltac — good for food: great for warmth. Priced at a rather excessive five pounds per bag, Thomas immediately set about building a distribution network, using his contacts in the distribution world. His mate Derek had a 1974 Ford Cacophony with a trailer, and with a cover draped over the valuable bags of wonder talc, Thomas stepped out to make a very small pittance.

Damian was busy underachieving, and along with his friend Mark, spent a lot of time honing his dart-playing skills in the local pub, The Old Micoat. Mark was also focused on his darts skills, and many a lunchtime was spent in the pub, nursing a teacher and mingling with their lager. Those carefree lunchtimes were a period of Damian's life that was both extremely wasteful but also highly unproductive. Arrows in hand, fag in mouth, Damian would launch the projectiles more in hope than expectation, often hitting the landlord, Jeff, whose bullseye-like head made him a far easier target. Jeff was a mild-mannered type of chap, with luscious sideburns and a manly toupee. He never asked for proof of age, and it is rather funny that in later years the pub was converted into a nursery, as many of the drinkers were, if not pre-school, certainly pre-adult. Jeff's blind eye and need for customers meant he would not turn away anybody who looked vaguely like a customer or alcoholic.

Inevitably, these visits to the pub at lunchtime had a knock-on effect on both Damian and Mark's studies. From being rather hopeful of underachieving, they soon were categorised as immature buffoons. Their peers, who had little time, were often dismissive and offhand with the two misshapen misfits, and soon the teachers started to treat them like the fools they hoped to be. Both studied history, a subject that has been around for a long time, and their teacher, Mrs Baywatch, was a very lithe and athletic woman, even though she was approaching retirement. Her lessons were a mixture of lavender and facts, sometimes with a twist of tedium. Royalists and Roundheads were merely terms of abuse as far as the two misfits were concerned, and their inability to focus meant they never really saw anything clearly.

Mrs Baywatch had the measure of them, and would often be quite cross, raising her thrush-like voice to admonish the pair for loafing around or disrupting a tedious monologue. Soon the boys lost interest in the Royalist cause and fell in with the rebel cause. They were intent on making Baywatch suffer, and became even more disruptive during those long afternoon classes. Damian, who by this time was wearing a rather smart pair of prescription glasses, which meant he could focus as well as could be expected for a boy with his IQ, would often flip his glasses upside-down in a juvenile attempt to look interesting. Mark, ever ready with a pointing finger, would explore the inner reaches of his nose with a Vicks nasal inhaler, guaranteed to cleanse the mucus. This really was disruption at warp speed ten, and the pair were confident that Baywatch would explode, old limbs flailing, and lavender pouring forth from her unguarded orifices. It really was a high stakes game that the two fools were playing... and there could only be two losers.

Meanwhile, Thomas was quickly becoming disillusioned with his wonder product when he realised that all it was useful for was as a substitute for grit on icy or snow-covered roads, and even then, its effects were minimal. The skids would look a little hotter and smell wonderful. Trying to convince the motorists of Yorkshire that this material could be used in the kitchen, bathroom or front parlour was an uphill struggle one step beyond what Thomas felt like doing... his venture was doomed to fail, but not before one final push.

Thomas had a friend, or acquaintance, called Turkish Dave, who had served in the Romanian Navy during the Second World War. Turkish Dave had a metal plate in his head, which therefore meant he could not see the colours blue, red or white, making him appear a little unpatriotic. He was, however, a capitalist through and through, and loved the work of Scratcher. Initially he had suggested privatising the Highways Department, a route that would be fraught with difficulties. He then shifted emphasis onto publicising the privatising of the Highways Department. His idea was very simple, but he needed someone who had access to talcum powder and table salt for his venture to be successful: Thomas was that man. Turkish Dave intended to drive along as many untreated roads in and around the Leeds area as he could, in the hope that he would lose control of his Ford Avocado and damage his head. Obviously, his metal plate would offer some protection, as would his extensive fat barrier, located where his stomach should have been. Due to too many pies, his stomach was now occupied by flab. Once the crash had taken place, Thomas would approach the Highways Department with his new wonder product, and privatisation would follow. The plan appeared to be riddled with fools, and soon the whole idea was shelved thanks to a shift in naked ambition. Turkish Dave landed a high-powered position as an electrical current consultant, and Thomas flogged his Saltac to a travelling troupe of illusionists who had become disillusioned with contemporary norms and were intent on alternative therapies. With this in mind, the Saltac was to be the base product in a series of alternative therapies designed to alleviate apathy. Thomas was happy to sell low and aim even lower and was soon in search of another way to raise his income above any sort of threshold. He kept several tonnes back for personal use, but the rest was sold.

Shopping was all the rage in those pre-internet days, and people could often be seen on the grimy high streets of Yorkshire, picking up tat as unwanted gifts, and generally wasting their coinage on shit that was freely available at Dewsbury's rather impressive flea market. Scratcher was known for her free market views, and she quickly saw an opportunity to privatise consumers, giving back control, to the man or woman in the street, over who they shopped with and when. This simple yet totally ridiculous idea soon took flight with a gullible and stupid public, who were quick to jump on the bandwagon of freedom and choice, although other bandwagons were available at lower prices. Now idiots across the land snapped up shares in shoppers, and were soon sharing their questionable intelligence; had they been conned? No… this was the free market in which nothing was free. People could be seen wandering the streets looking for a shopper to shop with, and large groups of shoppers mingled on street corners, sharing their witless experiences. Thomas, ardent labour man and scourge of the idiotype, saw an opportunity to peddle what remained of his talcum powder. Knowing that most people, if offered the choice, would wish to smell of lavender, Thomas repackaged his all-purpose gritting material into small handheld pouches, called bags, relabelled as Lavender Discovery — the universal remedy to poor personal hygiene. He set up a small stall at the end of his street and was quickly chased off by a passing lavender salesman from a large multi-national lavender cartel. Undeterred, Thomas took to the streets and highways, dispensing lavender with a cheery smile and a whiff of deceit. The old ladies loved it, and soon he was up in court for unpaid lavender taxes.

Damian was in the final year of school, and he managed to get himself suspended for being offhand with the head of sixth form, the head of the school, and the head man from a tribe of head-hunters. He spent nigh on five months under house arrest, only being allowed in school to collect badly written homework, have a crafty fag and then bugger off for another week. This idyllic break from reality enabled him to spend time with Thomas, who was no cheerleader of organised education, and despite his best efforts, Damian actually did some studying, without the distraction of his peers and teachers. Only time would tell if this application to learning would be fruitful, but the time was memorable.

# All they do is moan

Damian was forever short of money, so when Thomas offered him some freelance work in his new business venture, The Carter Complaint Centre, a home-based moaning service, where Thomas would craft obnoxious and fatuous letters for illiterate customers, he jumped at the opportunity. Damian recognised the genius in the idea, and Thomas was a master of the witty phrase. He had a long track record of writing pointless letters to pointless people for entertainment, and Damian was keen to learn the tricks of the trade. Thomas kept a huge portfolio of letters and such under lock and key, by his bed next to his Victorian potty. Inside there were letters to celebrities, politicians, strangers, captains of industry, judges and one even addressed to the deposed King of Iceland, King Christian the tenth, written in 1977. Scanning the letters, he realised his father was a hidden menace, and wanted to learn as much about this illicit trade in words as was possible. Below are some of Thomas's finest pieces:

Kindly repossessed thanks to the Country Estate of Thomas Carter.

*Dear King Christian, Ruler of the Ice lands, lover of snow, benign leader of the hot spring,*

*It is with deep regret that I write to inform you of a very unsavoury incident that took place outside your Oswestry branch last Wednesday, pertaining to several frozen food products and their pricing.*

*I love ice lollies as much as the next man and will pay as much as ten pence (either pre-decimal gothic coinage, or decimal coinage based on the position of the moon) for a quality product. However, my father would often say, never eat a banana that has passed through the hands of a cleric, and for very good reason.*

*It has come to my attention that many members of the staff who are employed on a part-time basis at your Oswestry branch have dealings with clerics. I am partial to a frozen banana and will often eat two or three before the sun has risen, but when I heard a rumour that clerics were being used to handle frozen produce, it set alarm bells ringing in my burdensome head. Surely, as head of Iceland, your recruitment procedures would vet staff to ensure clerics are not infiltrating the ranks to soil the beautiful banana. Image my disgust knowing that my yellow skin of loveliness has been sullied by the sacred hands of semi-professional sermon writers. It makes me sick to the very essence and centre of my sensible sensibilities to think that a fallen dove of a cleric has even been within one mile of my fruit-based yellowness.*

*I am not a religious man, and this sort of religious indoctrination of frozen produce is plain wicked. If you want to sell hot cross buns, clearly label them; if you want to sell frozen crucifix shaped nuggets, clearly label them; but do not let clerics near my bananas, and if they do get near them, label it so I can make an informed choice.*

*I hope to never have to write to you again and expect to see a surfeit of labels in your Oswestry branch.*

*Yours sincerely,*
*Carlos Zinc.*


Another letter, which was written for a client with very sweet teeth, was addressed to the Sugar Cane Cartel. It is a masterpiece in understatement and tom-tittery:

*Dear Sugar Barons,*

*Sugar, morphine for the sweet addict, giver of decay, and bringer of obesity to the fat and feckless. Sugar, oh tool of the wicked, controller of the drool and millions of users. Your evil trade has led to senseless decay, loathsome stretchmarks and millions of wobbly bits.*

*I write as someone who has never visited a dentist nor needed a girdle to hold in place wobbly rolls of sugar ingested out of self-loathing. I merely write as a concerned dentist and addict. I currently use grade A refined white sugar, which is great for day-to-day rushes, but what I require is something stronger, something that will leave my teeth aching* to leave my mouth for good; something that will ooze through my already distended frame and cause further damage to my essential organs; I need a new sugar-based drug.

A colleague has told me of a mythical product, available in certain well-to-do areas, that is so powerful it can cure stupidity and increase the sheen on a man's brow. If this is true, can you please forward samples in discreet packaging, and in return I will forward money in equally discreet packaging.

I work for no law enforcement agency, am not affiliated to any political party, and have no plans to write a tell-all exposé of sugar abuse.

Please do something to fill the voids that exist in my heart and my gut,

and send me some sweet sugar.

Yours in hope,

Declan D'kay


Thomas's job applications were by far and away his finest work. No job was too menial to apply for, nor was his ability to fabricate intricate backstories ever curtailed by the nature of the job he was applying for. Below are three of his most memorable applications, kindly reproduced thanks to two injunctions being recently lifted.

Dear Recruitment Jonnie,

I recently gave up a very well-paid job as a travelling bird salesman, supplying chaffinch and warblers to the hotel industry. Thanks to a misunderstanding with a well-known hotel chain and an order for 50,000 starlings, I was asked rather forcefully to fuck off. That I have done. For the last two weeks I have worked freelance, supplying highly suspect ideas to a well-regarded pie retailer. My speciality is thinking outside the crust.

I possess a range of undervalued skills and qualities, which if harnessed and forced to focus, could reinvigorate any medium-sized business in need of a giggle. I can walk, talk and smoke, all without taking a breath. I work well alone and hate the company of those who have risen up the promotional pole with little or no effort.

*I need to work as little as possible due to my black mood swings, which often leave me on the verge of arrest or restraint. Despite this, I have yet to bankrupt any of my previous employers, and I half-heartedly believe that I would be a reasonable asset if you are willing to overlook my propensity to steal small value stock and rifle though my co-workers' possessions.*

*I can start any time in the spring, once I have sacrificed a small woodland creature and paid homage to the spirits of the dead rodents that lie rotting in the boot of my Austin Tremble.*

*I am available for interview most days, weather permitting, and look forward to taking up my new role as a freelance rubbish relocation consultant.*

*Yours faithfully,*
*Thomas Carter*


*Dear Recruitment Jenny,*

*Thanks to an upturn in my free time, I am now in a position to take on the role that was recently advertised in 'The Squirrel', the magazine for all rodent lovers. Recently unemployed, I am determined to bounce back and get back on the slippery pole-shaped ladder of a saddle. I was let go from my last position due to a misunderstanding with a broom and my supervisor's head.*

*But enough of him; what about me? I am in my late 50s, yet despite this, I still have some of my own teeth, dribble infrequently, and rarely shout at dogs. When not at home, I am usually out. This allows me to see things that I haven't got in my home, such as squirrels and hope.*

*I was trained in the navy to shoot mines, and I believe my ability to hit at least one out of every fifteen shaped the outcome of that dreadful conflict. By dreadful, I mean that there have been some better conflicts. I am never comfortable with people and prefer the company of my large family album. However, in view of your need and my desperation, I am willing to break a rule of a lifetime and work alongside living, breathing things.*

*I have spent some time outdoors, and could be persuaded to climb trees, but I draw the line at wearing a company hat. Alone I reckon I* could kill maybe 150 squirrels per day, meaning by the end of the week you could use the pelts to make a lovely blanket or scarf.

I am not available until late March, due to my bail conditions, but once I start in this exciting role of conservation, or is it conversation officer, you won't regret much.

I can be contacted via the other side most days, and I see a great future for some of your staff.

Yours faithfully,
Thomas Carter


Dear Recruitment Pete,

In a world where too many squirrels are shot needlessly, what we need now is some type of squirrel protection unit. I am not saying it should be based on the lines of the SAS, but armed men patrolling squirrel haunts would certainly scare off some of the squirrel hunters.

Let me introduce myself; the names Tommy, but you must call me Thomas, and I am the answer to someone's prayers. Thanks to my inhibited mental stability, I fear no squirrel, army or pacifist. My unique set of ingrained prejudices allows me to see bad in most people. I can detect insecurities and undermine at will, and if called up, would shout abuse.

Thanks to three years shooting squirrels, I am ideally placed to understand the weaknesses of the squirrel, and in doing so, protect them from unscrupulous hat retailers. I work well up or down trees and can supply my own ladder at a push. In a previous role I ate many pies, so understand the need for tight deadlines. Pies sometimes need to be eaten in a hurry. What isn't eaten today is often wasted tomorrow as the old saying goes.

I am not available until next August, due to a very serious skin condition, but if the ointment works, then I could do a few days per month, flakiness permitting. I can be contacted via most well-known methods, and look forward, as it is painful to dwell on the past.

Yours faithfully,
Thomas Carter

Thomas's genius was lost on many, but to Damian, his ability to not care about most things marked him out as a one in a million. Damian cherished those hours with Thomas, when all of time would stop, and Thomas would impart some nonsense to his son. A cake amongst biscuits.

# Water Works

The world of work had been calling Damian, and when he secured a position at a water authority in Birmingham, he was ready to be thrown in the deep end, sink or swim if you like, and surge ahead on the tidal wave of successful water administration. The offices were located on a street, and his first day was a mixture of misunderstanding combined with overt body odour. Damian's calm, repressed demeanour, his possession of a functioning tongue and his inane ability to follow very simple instructions, meant he was the ideal fit for the cut and thrust of water administration. Water was the life blood of the people, and high-pressure water administration had seen many office jockeys burn out. Damian took to it like a duck to water-based services. The office itself was deep underground, slightly below the water table, and was reached via a chute located behind a telephone box. Getting into work was never a problem, but Damian found it a struggle sometimes to navigate his way up a greased-up chute wearing a three-piece ensemble. His desk was adjacent to the water cooler of all things, where the O.J.s (office jockeys) would congregate during times of stress and laziness. His manager, Mr Slurry, was a distant figure who kept himself in the corner of his corner office, like a cornered animal in a tight corner. He only ever left his office to go home; toilet breaks were done in-house and lunch was usually liquid. Damian's immediate superiors were many, but his supervisor, Miss Blunt, was a keen-eyed witch of a woman who spent her time watching the clock on behalf of her colleagues. She used a stick, had a pronounced lisp and was unable to engage in idle chatter. Her only saving grace was her forty — a-day habit, which resulted in a nicotine haze trailing her like a lovesick puppy looking for scraps. Her coughing fits would last for hours, but thankfully she had copious amounts of part-used cotton handkerchiefs to mop up the worst of the spittle and nose fluid. Damian was taken under her wing and despite his obvious ineptness, she identified in him as a willing partner in smoking oblivion.

Quickly learning the ropes, Damian was soon put in charge of his own telephone, and once it was connected, he would be allowed to answer it. His desk was sparse, with only his Fisher Price phone, a picture of Walter Mitty and an oversized ashtray. He was given three pens (one for each day of the week he would be required to scratch on a piece of paper) and put to work counting paper clips. It was dirty work, and on some days, Damian wouldn't eat lunch or dinner, busily stacking the paper clips into piles of a hundred and then placing them in the paperclip cupboard. Opposite him was the elder of the team, Betty Smokestack, a large woman with ample eyebrows and an extremely sharp tongue, which she used to skewer pickled olives. Next to Betty was Gavin Splurge, a flamboyant heterosexual with a tendency to exaggerate. Prior to working in water, Gavin had been a semi—professional spy, a vegetarian scientist, a mole hunter, test pilot and a stunt double for Cilla Black. Gavin was the eyes and ears for Miss Blunt and was always the first to know useless water-based gossip, the drips and spillages of office-based bitching.

At the end of the working day, Damian would occasionally go for a drink with Betty and Gavin at The Gilded Teabag, a rather low market hostelry with low slung bar staff and piss-poor lighting. The talk would inevitably turn to work and the rigours of paperclip stacking, and as the drinks flowed, the conversation would turn to office romances, Blunt's softer side, and the need for more staff toilets. Sewage was often discussed at length, as was the need for bigger water for larger people, the shortage of sturdy toilet roll, and other water-related topics. The evenings would drag, and sometimes Damian didn't get home until well past six forty-five p.m. His claustrophobic flat was situated in a hole below the ground floor of a terraced house in north Birmingham. His landlord, a shifty fellow with narrow eyes, had thrown in a bed and a window to make the flat seem more attractive, and for Damian, it was the ideal place for self-loathing and inner turmoil — his bumhole of a bolthole. The rent was a piddling thirteen pounds twenty-five per week, but that didn't include doors, kitchen or running toilets, which were an extra forty-five pounds. He needed to move!

Damian's work-life balance was out of kilter, and he yearned for something more than paper clips to stimulate his loathsome mind. Serendipity soon came running at his desk when he was offered a secondment at a top-secret water facility hidden away in the suburbs of Solihull. Mr Slurry was tight-lipped about its location, but Miss Blunt was eager to show him pictures of the place, advising him that the opportunity was too good to miss; he would be a clandestine water administrator.

Taking the bus from his low-grade hovel, he travelled many miles before finally arriving at the top-secret establishment, known by those in the know as the Cistern. He was greeted at reception by a rather tepid looking man, Mr Luke Warm, head of P section at the Cistern. Warm was responsible for producing cutting edge final demands, supply interruption notices and general feel-good stationery for the consumers in the Birmingham area. Deep in the bowels of the building was a tiny cubicle containing Damian's new tools: scissors, craft knife, glue and many letters. Bundled into the cubicle by Warm, Damian was asked to sign a leaving card for one of the office jockeys, and then instructed to make himself not too familiar with the layout of the building.

Over the next three weeks he underwent intense training to get up to speed on the intricacies of the job. First there was instruction in how to apply correction fluid in the dark and the dangers of sniffing it too much, followed by a masterclass in snipping and cutting by a very severe-looking fellow with too many eyebrows. Next was hand to hand gluing, which Damian excelled at, meaning he couldn't clap too well. Finally, he was introduced to the letters, twenty-six in total, which were used to send threatening demands to reluctant payees. Damian had seen some of these letters before, but collectively they looked like an overindulgent anagram: U, B, and T were familiar, but he didn't know Y. With the help of Warm, he was able to master the water-based alphabet, and within weeks could write his name in a variety of fonts. Soon he was producing a wide range of obnoxious demands, designed to put pressure on water consumers. The taps were open, and he became more and more creative in his methods, resorting to name calling, lies, and music-based demands.

The music of the 80s had been a constant source of disappointment for Damian, and he drew on this deflated sense of wonder to craft subliminal messages, all taken from well-known tunes, to convince consumers to stump up and pay. He had no boundaries and would use any song that would wreak the most annoyance on the unsuspecting customer. His favourite technique was to put the lyrics of a well-known tune into the past tense — time travelling music. Examples of his work include:

*Woke me up before I went, went,*
*We were the Champions,*
*Helped, I needed somebody,*
*Did they know it was Christmas,*
*Tried a little tenderness.*

This list was endless, and soon the water board saw an incredible twelve per cent increase in payments, possibly as a result of Damian's subliminal messages. Warm was pleased and offered Damian a cigarette. As always, Damian's restless nature and lack of vision meant he wasn't able to recognise the signs, which were everywhere in the building. This would lead to his dismissal and resignation in one rolled-up ball of career suicide. His boots, if not too big, were certainly larger than they should have been, and he was taking more and more risks with his messages. It came to a head when his subliminal messages became non-subliminal, telling one customer to fucking pay up now, and two further customers that there wasn't enough water in the world to make

166

them clean. When Warm got wind of this, he boiled over, with an outpouring of steam and anger. Damian was his monster, yet he could not allow him to continue in this offensive vein; action was needed and needed fast if P section wasn't to become the laughing stock of the Cistern. Rivals were queuing up to knock Warm off his perch, so Damian was thrown before he was pushed, but not before one final act of rebellion against water conformity. On his last day at the Cistern, Damian set in motion a chain of events that had very little effect on anyone. The final notice he had been working on was for an overdue cesspit inspection at a local beauty salon. He had decided to include the lyrics of as many water-based songs in the cesspit notice as he could. It was sent to the salon on Damian's last day at the Cistern, and is reproduced below with the consent of some adults:

*Splash, ha-ha, he sprayed every one of us, (Queen)*
*Waterloo, couldn't escape to do a pooh, (Abba)*
*Splish splash I was taking a bath, (Bobby Darin)*
*Pay up you fucker or die (Hardnosed Jack & the Thumb Screws).*

He was out of work yet felt remarkably upbeat about his time working in water. Dried up he wasn't, but he did need a fresh challenge. In the meantime, he decided to take some time out to visit Thomas and Anne. Thomas had missed Damian and would write every week, keeping Damian abreast of the activities of his siblings, his mum and current weather conditions.

Thomas was the owner of an antiquated static caravan on the outskirts of Scarborough, bought for three thousand pounds in 1981 from a travelling static caravan salesman. It couldn't be described as bottom of the range, but it was certainly moving in that direction. What it lacked in modern comforts, it made up for with its roof and door. There were three windows, only visible from the inside, along with a two-ring hob, a basin that doubled up as a spittoon, and some beautiful chipboard panelling, giving it the feel of a rather down-market Swiss chalet. Time permitting, Thomas and Anne would jump into the Austin Beaver and hit the

A54367 to the coast. The journey usually took approximately seven hours, due to the piss-poor acceleration of the Beaver, but its winding twists and breathtaking traffic lights made the whole journey a second honeymoon for Thomas and Anne. Anne, pipe on full power, would spend the time knitting recipes, whilst Thomas, who often dozed at the wheel, would catch up on his reading. Thomas only ever read one book, Treasure Island, but over the course of his life he had reread it many times, backwards and forwards, to fully understand the Kafkaesque plot twists. In the boot of the Beaver was a weekend valise, plus sandwiches to last the weekend, fifteen Kevin Stickies and two tomatoes, for variety.

On arrival at the caravan, Thomas would remove the hubcaps from the Beaver (hubcaps in the 80s were a prime target for opportunist chrome thieves) and then decamp to the outside sitting area. Located in the far corner of Scabby and District Static Caravan Park, Thomas was incredibly envious of some of the more upmarket, high end models on view. To the left of his there was a static that belonged to a Swedish couple, the Bloomqvists, who had spent thousands on making their static stand out from the rest. It had interior seating, marvellous views of the neighbouring car park, and a revolutionary plumbing system, which flushed the shit directly into the neighbouring field. On the right there was a family of window cleaners who had been unable to get on the property ladder, so had made the park their permanent home. Stan and Steph were diehard chamois leather enthusiasts, both having grown up during the lean years, when both ladders and leathers were outlawed in certain parts of the country. Their children, Bucket, Jerkin and Sponge, were always at their parents' side, listening out for nuggets of window wisdom.

As Anne pottered away preparing a tomato, Thomas would take his binoculars and observe Scarborough's unique wildlife. The area was awash with native fleas, ticks and head lice, making it a botanist's paradise. Thomas suffered from irritable skin and would apply a homemade ointment to keep the worst of the little bastards at bay. He had a little notebook and would meticulously catalogue every itch, scratch and irritation.

Of course Damian would sometimes join his parents on these getaways to the barmy outskirts of Scarborough. The car journey was his favourite part, as he loved to see his parents so content with their surroundings. In the evenings, they would make the short journey across the sewage works for an evening meal in The Itchy Inn, where a cheery welcome was never guaranteed. The innkeeper, Harold Slope, had served in some capacity during the Korean War, where his face had been hideously disfigured by some overly spicy chicken wings which had sent his left cheek into uncontrollable spasms. The spasms could only be controlled using powerful electrical impulses from a fifty-watt battery. Although it minimised the spasms, it also meant that over time the whole left side of his face loosened, resulting in a sloping effect on his face. Despite this, Harold was a miserable bastard who despised most of his customers. He did, however, have a soft spot for Thomas and Anne, whose uncluttered expectations of food meant that most slop was greeted with thanks and a handsome tip, often in pennies. Damian would sit with his parents, spicy chicken wing at the ready, and listen to Harold's turgid stories of communist infiltration and duplicity. For a boy who understood a few of the longer words, duplicity and infiltration were the preserve of history books, a clear sign that Harold wasn't only a far-fetched fucker of a fellow but also the sort of shit who would look words up in a dictionary to impress customers at a flea-hole of a pub. Thomas, elbows twinging, would never mention his own wartime experience, letting his eloquent silence do the talking. Anne, buried beneath a sheet of pipe smoke, would give the occasional unseen nod and the evening would continue.

Eventually the static had to go due to flooding and the lack of walls, and Thomas, if not distraught, was a little perturbed. He had invested very little in the upkeep of the caravan, and would often curse its very existence, yet he had spent many a happy weekend there, over joyous summers. What remained of the caravan was packed into tea crates and sent to a municipal dump in Hartlepool. Thomas managed to salvage the portable toilet and sold it to a travelling incontinence salesman from Bury St Edmunds. He made £12.82 on the transaction and invested the whole lot in a huge mega pie to celebrate the end of an era. There was nothing that a pie couldn't improve, and when Thomas ruefully reflected on the build quality of the caravan, he wondered if it would have lasted longer if it had been constructed using good quality pie crust.

# Romance?

Damian wasn't the best-looking boy, with his dysfunctional nose and misplaced hair, but somehow, he had managed to find a girlfriend. What was even more surprising for those who had seen Damian was that the girlfriend was still alive, and not a corpse he visited at the weekend. Her name was Claudette and she was a Londoner. They had met whilst studying business, and to say it was love at first sight would be an overstatement, but they didn't hate each other and had a shared love of cigarettes, especially the more expensive brands like Lung Sap, Phlegm and Smog. They quickly decided that the worst thing to do was to move in together, and so that is exactly what they did, sharing a small one-bedroomed terraced house thirty yards from a very popular fish and chip shop, the Hopeful Haddock. They immediately set about making the hovel into a semi-home, with curtains and candles — the basics if you like.

Claudette's parents were not at all eager to meet Damian, but Claudette insisted, so Damian packed his Russian horse doctor's valise, jumped on the coach, and headed for the shining smoke and big lights of London. He felt nervous, sophisticated and a little bit travel sick. He had never been further south than Dunstable before, but had seen black and white pictures of the queen, black cabs and cockneys. It was a whole new world for the gauche boy from Yorkshire, whose flat vowels and turgid dress sense marked him out as a northerner. Arriving at Victoria coach station, he was immediately hit by a cyclist — fucking eco-warriors! Claudette was at home in this urban zoo, with its towering noise and shimmering fashionistas. He had never seen such sophistication in his life, and he was a little overwhelmed with the shops, shoes and shirts. Damian loved a good shirt, and would often wear one, but down in the capital, shirts were of a different order. In

Yorkshire, shirts only came in two varieties, clean and short-sleeved, but on show in London were colours that Damian had only dreamt about: vivid blues, yellows and even striped shirts with two colours. London was so far ahead in the shirt stakes that Damian wanted to experience all the shirts.

First, he had to meet Claudette's family, John and Cynthia, and her brothers Rory and Ralph. Damian had never met anyone's parents before, apart from his own, but that didn't count, so he was unsure how to behave, believing small talk was something toddlers did. On the train ride to south east London, Damian was coached by Claudette in what not to say. He mustn't mention Arthur Scargill, Norris McWhirter or any fat-based food group. Nor should he indulge in speaking with his eyes closed, farting with a whistle in his mouth, or clapping along to the national anthem. As they alighted the train in the leafy suburb that Claudette called home, Damian was struck by the naked affluence on show. Up until then he was under the illusion that affluence was a posh word for shit, but when he saw the carefully manicured gardens, driveways, and curtains in every window, he knew he was stepping into the gilded world of suburbia.

As they approached the front door of number 56, Molehill Avenue, Damian noticed that none of the windows had net curtains, and even more of a revelation, the windows were all double-glazed. How could these people afford such luxuries? In Yorkshire, net curtains were a badge of honour, and the greyer they were, the better. Double glazing was having two windows in a house, so as he stepped through the front door, he was feeling light-headed and gormless. Immediately Cynthia darted down the hallway, not noticing the northern git standing awkwardly, Russian valise in one hand and a three-month-old copy of the Reader's Digest in the other, to greet her disappointing daughter. John was nowhere to be seen, but young Rory, a sprightly boy with academic teeth, bounded down the stairs and hugged his sister. Ralph, the elder brother, was upstairs in the bathroom practising his front crawl; he had ambitions to be a world class swimmer. Once the hugging and fawning had finished, Cynthia turned to Damian, glass eye in hand, and inspected the sorry-looking fledgling, his hair fragrantly poised with hair wax and his best shirt eagerly tucked into his bleached jeans. He looked a complete twat. The welcome was suburban, unlike something that could be expected in Yorkshire, where a thrown dog turd was a sign of affection. A handshake was overblown gushing, hugs were reserved for visiting mystics and dead relatives, so when Cynthia lunged toward Damian to hug him, he immediately lashed out with his rolled-up copy of the Reader's Digest. Cynthia ducked, revealing incredible agility for a post-fifty woman, and Rory was hit square in the face. This was not a good start to a relationship that would be fraught with hatred, disdain and mistrust. Damian was quickly given the cold shoulder as Claudette and her mother caught up on family affairs.

When John returned from work some hours later, Damian had been shown to his quarters, and they really were quarters, as there wasn't much space in there for half of a single bed. He had unpacked his valise, carefully throwing his two shirts into the corner, when there had been a knock on the door. It was John. This was the moment when father met future ex-boyfriend, and everything needed to be uncomfortable. John was a lecturer in Sanctimonious Outpourings at a diminished polytechnic in south London, which gave his brain a thin veneer of conceit. He took an instant dislike to most people, but Damian represented everything he resented about northern people.

With pleasantries complete, the two made their way to the dining room, where Rory was busy laying the table for dinner. For Damian, unaccustomed to eating dinner at teatime, the idea of sitting at a dining table to nosh on three courses was the height of gluttony. Back home, a dessert for Damian was either a cold Yorkshire pudding with treacle, half a bowl of strawberry Angel Delight or a vast expanse of sand. The meal after teatime was supper or pudding, or both, and Weetabix. To John and Cynthia, who shopped at M&S, dessert was cheesecake, soufflé or a rather crusty pudding, crème brûlée. Bloody stuck-up bastards. They even had napkins, not serviettes. Damian felt out of his depth, unable to cope with all the cutlery — a northern Eliza Do-nothing with no chance of becoming anybody's fair lady. The first dinner felt more like the last supper for Damian, and Claudette was his Judas, betraying his simplicity and exposing him to sophisticated small talk that left him confused and diminished. He was due to stay in London for the week, but it became obvious that this would be unacceptable to Cynthia, John, Rory, Ralph and Claudette. He had to think of a way to escape this aristocratic nightmare, but before he could do that Claudette had made plans for him to meet some of her London chums. He didn't sleep well that night, partly due to nerves but also because the shed was incredibly cold and the lawnmower incredibly large.

The following morning, with a fresh pair of eyes, he felt back to his usual self, and was ready for whatever London could throw at him — pure northern grit. Claudette had arranged to meet her friend from school, Claudine, along with an ex-boyfriend, Claude, at a swanky West End bar called The Wanker's Hole. Overpriced cocktails and cherries were not Damian's cup of tea, and he only had £27.76 on him, so one round of drinks would wipe him out. Claudette maintained that it would be fun, and insisted that her friends were normal, just like her. On the way to The Wanker's Hole, Damian realised that the relationship was doomed; he was the duckling in a world full of peacocks. What he should have done was end the relationship as soon as he returned to Yorkshire; that was the grown-up course of action. When they finally split-up twelve months later, the London trip was the high point of the relationship.

Damian had been living in Birmingham for several months now, and to say the loneliness was crippling would be a gross overstatement, but he did need to find something to do in the evenings. He had always loved the roar of the greasepaint and the smell of the crowd, believing that if people smiled at you, they probably wanted to be your best friend for life. Fragile egos and low self-esteem are the watchwords for many a performer, and Damian certainly had brittle self-esteem. He decided to find a hobby that would allow him to meet new people and express his nascent creativity in a safe environment. He had tried boxing but that was painful on a physical and emotional level, and after the disaster at the Birmingham indoor bowls club, which Damian believed to be a group of like-minded washing up enthusiasts, he thought perhaps he needed to try the stage. Performing was in his blood, or so he thought, and he soon joined a very amateur dramatic society around the corner from his one-bedroomed hovel. It was close to a Chinese takeaway and a pub that sold the best chilli con carne in a two-mile radius. Perfect for thespians, who he had heard loved Mexican food and noodles.

On his first visit to the theatre, he was shown around by Margot, a very peculiar lady with a strong aftertaste of lavender. Her husband was something big in the talcum powder world, but she had always wanted to perform, charmed by the fantasy and fairy tales of theatre. A broken imagination had left her dull, so she had been unable to fail in her ambitions professionally. Settling for second best wasn't an option, as she lacked talent, so she finally arrived at the theatre in 1939 where she was put in charge of some wardrobes. Her domain was a world of crinoline and silk; top hats and wigs; long capes and sweat. Locked away in a very small room at the back of the theatre, Margot spent her time sprinkled in lavender, stitching and sewing costumes for the fat and the faulty.

Margot advised Damian to come back on the following Monday when there would be a casting for an Irish play, The Shaughraun, and they needed a handsome lead. Over the weekend Damian swept his hair back, to the side, parted it, combed it forward, shaved it and then re-grew it, all in search of the right look. Stood in front of his broken mirror, he practised his Irish accent, based on Frank Carson. He practised his look: smouldering, angry, hurt, confused and passionate; he was ready.

On the Monday at the allotted time and place, he entered via the stage door at the side of the building which led to a small rehearsal room underneath the stage. On entering he was greeted with resentful looks and warm smiles. He had been told to ask for Edward, the director and elder brother of Margot. In the corner of the room was a rather sheepish-looking fellow with a lovely corduroy three-piece suit. His bright ginger hair, abundance of freckles and Clarks shoes marked him out as a potential rival to Damian in the leading man stakes. Sitting near corduroy was a rather large lady with a mop of ginger hair, obviously very drunk and with a bluebottle sitting on her shoulder. She was demolishing a French fancy whilst reading a copy of The Lady. Without doubt the heroine, or in need of a warm place to indulge in her love of Bacardi and cake. In the far corner was an elderly gentleman with a severe stance, ramrod straight moustache that had been combed to the left, green slacks and a rather fetching neckerchief. He had obviously served in the guards, or the lancers, or some other regiment where a stiff moustache was a mark of achievement. This was Edward, and as he turned to look at Damian, it was apparent to Damian that Edward didn't like the look of this wretched northern-looking fellow with a disastrous hairstyle. Edward ran his military eye over Damian, explaining that acting is like being in the army: fear, discipline and lots of lines. He said the most important thing was to enunciate. Damian, stupid as ever, thought he heard 'a nun sea state', and immediately his mind began to wander. He pictured a mother superior at the head of a religious fleet of fisherwomen, out to trawl the souls of their foes. A mother superior whose seafaring people took to the high seas in search of adventure and regular routines; a mother superior who demanded clean habits and sensible shoes; a mother superior who never had to learn her lines. Edward realised that Damian, although a little gormless and very northern, might be the perfect fit for the role of Robert, a Fenian and a very dull romantic lead. Without even giving Damian a script, he told Damian to go away and work on his Irish accent. Edward wanted a Dublin accent, similar to Terry Wogan's. Edward's ability to bark orders in such a clipped and precise manner left Damian feeling weak and inadequate; he had always wanted a dog.

All week Damian watched recordings of 'Blankety Blank', listened to Radio Two, and watched 'One Man and his Dog'. By the following Monday, Damian felt he had a very slim grasp on his character's accent but was a little closer to investing in an Irish Wolfhound.

At the first formal rehearsal, Damian was introduced to the rest of the cast, who appeared to be old hands and familiar with Edward's idiosyncratic ways. Opposite Damian, playing the heroine, was Vera, the ginger-haired cake eater, whose broad Dudley accent marked her out as someone slightly more obtuse than Damian. Then there were Sheila and her husband Vincent, who both worked for a well-known car manufacturer and loved to go for long walks with their two dogs, Rusty and Scraps. Sheila would take on any role as long as it didn't require a beard or singing, whilst Vincent preferred to play fast and loose with his erratic eyebrows, which were legendary in the theatre. He had worked as a butcher, baker and a candlestick maker — very much a master of nothing but willing to do anything that allowed him to raise eyebrows. Vincent also sang in a barber shop to soothe the worried customers. Then there was a very rotund gentleman sporting a flamboyant waistcoat and an elegant pair of spats, who looked like the archetypal villain. With rolls of fat hurrying away from his body, it was obvious that this luvvie loved a cream cake. Raymond Monkfish had acted professionally as a child, appearing in 'Puss in Boots' at the Chichester Theatre alongside Sir Jonny Hills. He later went on to be a mildly successful settee designer, designing settees for several early morning breakfast shows. He had contacts in showbiz and wanted everyone to know. Damian was drawn to Raymond's aura; he oozed charisma and used a silk handkerchief to wipe it off his forehead. If anyone could give Damian tips on how not to make too much of a tit of himself, Raymond was that man. Edward and Raymond did not see eye to eye on creative matters; Edward believed his military background allowed him to marshal his cast ready to counterattack at any moment, whereas Raymond, who was also something of a director, believed in giving the actors freedom to explore their character's motivations. Raymond was Patton to Edward's Monty. It was a creative stand-off that would lead to many disputes during rehearsals.

As rehearsal progressed, Damian felt the need to adopt some type of thespian affectation. He had toyed with the idea of sporting a fez, or a smoking jacket, but his budget was limited. Finally, he managed to pick up a cigarette holder from a junk shop which when modelled in front of his mirror, gave him a Dirk Bogardesque look. He had also taken to drinking vinegar in the hope that it would sharpen up his performance and give him an edge. All actors drank strong spirits, and as he couldn't afford Crème de Menthe, Sarson's seemed like the next best thing. He did notice an improvement in his skin, but his odour was slightly pickled. The rehearsals were physically and mentally demanding, and Damian's work had suffered. He no longer focused on water and would often wake in the night in a cold bath. He was struggling to learn his lines, barely able to get past his opening line. Edward could see that Damian was a very unnatural actor but persisted as no other fucker wanted the part. As the dress rehearsal approached, Damian suffered a loss of confidence in his talent, believing he would make a complete arse of himself. He had invited hundreds of people to come on the opening night, but he was beginning to regret his bravado. Like most actors, he was racked with doubts and fears, along with some chafing on warm days. To try and cope with the chafing, he borrowed some strong talcum powder from Margot. The doubts and fears remained. He had tried on his costume and was unimpressed. Ill-fitting ankle danglers, a moth-eaten cloak and a straw hat worn at a jaunty angle hardly made him look like a Fenian hero — more like a wicker salesman in a storm.

Every evening, following rehearsals, he would pace his room looking for his character, delving within to try and find the spark that was so obvious in Raymond. What was his character's motivation? Was Robert a tortured soul in need of forgiveness, or was he a forgiving soul in need of tortured forgiveness? What was a Fenian? All these questions and the constant chafing of his mind had drained Damian, and it was reflected in his pitiful accent, wooden acting and pickled odour. Yet Edward, who had his faults, had been kind to Damian, only calling him a useless fucker seventeen times. In Damian, Edward saw a young man fresh from the mean streets of Yorkshire who could bring an energy and vibrancy to the after-show party. Most of the cast were over fifty-five and were usually in bed by ten p.m. Edward had no problem with ginger cast members, but Damian was the only one with non-ginger locks. Diversity was in short supply, so when you're scraping the barrel you really have to get your nails dirty. Damian was the grime in Edward's manicured nail.

Damian resolved to plod on regardless and break many legs as the show must go on. The bug had bitten and becoming an actor meant so much to him now, even if he was shit. Thomas and Anne were unable to come due to lack of interest, and the remaining members of his family were inexplicably unavailable for the whole two-week run of the show. His colleagues at work, who viewed Damian as something of a social turd, had promised to come, but a series of family disasters/tragedies meant that none actually attended. Damian was alone and tormented by a huge moth in the dressing room. As he applied his greasy make-up, smearing moth wings on his furrowed brow, he reflected on the lonely journey every performer had to make in order to achieve success; then he had a piss and waited for the curtain to go up.

The performance was a blur, in part due to Damian forgetting his glasses, but also as a result of the adrenalin that hit Damian like a hammer, forcing him to slur his words and remember very little of that first night. Maybe it was the nerves, maybe it was the vinegar or maybe it was none of these things. Whatever it turned out to be, Damian had experienced a new type of failure and loved it. His lines and performance were secondary. What mattered were the free drinks available in the bar and the wide selection of nibbles laid on by Margot, who was actually a decent cook. Her vol-au-vents were superb and the onion flan went down a treat. If this was theatre, then Damian could eat his fill of free food. The run went really badly, and all who saw were unimpressed by Damian's feeble machinations and verbal acrobatics. The review, which featured in the local voluntary newspaper was damming of all the cast members and is reproduced below:

# The Hutton Herald

*The Shaughraun- no stars*

*If ever you're at a loose end and want a cheap night out and a few laughs, then I recommended you take yourself down to Hutton Amateur Dramatics Society where acting is in short supply, but the laughs keep on coming. From start to finish it was obvious that this shower of shite hadn't any understanding of staging, lighting, and possibly most importantly of all, acting. The director, Edward von Butterball, is a stalwart of the military dramatic scene, with many sub-standard productions under his leather-look belt. His ability to miscast is beyond compare, and his obsession with ginger-haired actors is strange bordering on ridiculous. The one non-ginger in this sorry shambles of shite, was a young northern slack-jaw, Damian Carter, whose hacking cough and pseudo-Dublin accent was akin to Terry Wogan on helium in a room full of ginger-haired cake eaters. This is truly a dreadful production with no obvious saving traits. I would you suggest a bag full of dog turds could put on a more coherent and enjoyable evening's entertainment. Do not waste your money on this bilge.*

Damian went on to his next show, which was a musical. Having been tortured by Anne as a child into sitting through 'West Side Story', 'Seven Brides for Seven Brothers' and 'The King and I', Damian hated musicals, so was reluctant to take a part in the next show. Raymond was directing and he had promised a show to rival anything seen in the West End. Raymond could be very persuasive and when he offered Damian two solos and complimentary vol-au-vents it was too much for Damian to say no.

# The theatre

Rampant incoherence would often possess Thomas as his mind battled with the invisible echoes of sins of the past. The voices that reverberated around his sordid mind would leave him quivering and foetus-like. He was tormented by visions of villains and vagrants, all intent on upsetting his carefully arranged collection of chrome hubcaps or stealing away with his prized trilby. At night, walking stick in hand, he would stalk the hall of his ground floor flat, searching for intruders who were intent on despoiling Anne's marmalade collection. These lapses into mental fragility came and went like the wind, and Anne, whose wits had ended many years earlier, was at a loss as to how to comfort her husband. The voices would often wake her, so loud was Thomas's reaction to the invisible menace that filled his mind with confusion and trepidation. Anne would boil a kettle and fill several mugs with boiling water, leaving them by the door as a first line of defence against potential intruders, real or otherwise. Of course, after half an hour, a face full of tepid water presented little threat, but it gave Thomas some relief from his anxiety. He also made elaborate twine defences, stringing length after length of twine from bookcase to chair, from chair to table. These homemade trip wires made moving around the flat a challenge, and with Anne having developed weak ankles, her ability to hop was somewhat limited, so she would often send ornaments crashing in her attempt to clear the trip wires.

When Damian spoke with Thomas, he witnessed a father whose faculties had left and were not due back any time soon. His ramblings consisted of tales of horrendous misfortune, egg mayonnaise and soiled carpets. Heaven knows what sins he had committed in an earlier life, but Damian could only offer a forgiving ear and strong tea to assuage the guilt that Thomas felt.

On one occasion, Thomas recalled an episode in 1940s Bradford involving a disgruntled fish salesman and some shoddy paint work on an Austin Rationcard, the transport of choice for the aspiring villain. Thomas was neither a mover nor a shaker, preferring to stay in the shadows and avoid detection. His early criminal experiments were the stuff of legend in his head, consisting of theft on a small scale. He would take home the odd kipper or haddock when on shore leave from the SS Briny or borrow disused harpoons and resell them to vigilantes in and around his neighbourhood. With his father, Thomas Senior, he would roam the dirt-ridden streets of Bradford, borrowing milk and associated dairy products and sell them on at under-inflated prices to wanton wives wanting whey. It was harmless thievery that left an indelible scar on Thomas's young brain.

Mental instability ran in the family and had haunted the Carter line for generations. Thomas Senior spent three months in the brig in 1916 following a failed mutiny. He had attempted to corral several horses and lead them on a march to general headquarters, confront Haig and demand better fodder for all equines. His mutiny lasted three minutes, as two of the horses were spooked by a rather loud trombone and the authorities were able to suppress this potentially war-changing episode. Thomas Senior's experiences in the brig though, were inhuman. Forced to eat food and given blankets and far away from the constant shelling, he became calm and focused on things he enjoyed. He was a very talented artist and drew on his experiences with horses to make brushes. The army psychiatrist, Doctor Harpoon, recognised in Thomas Senior a very rare condition: saddle shock. The smell of leather is at the best of times a heady mix of danger and unpredictability, but at the time, little was known of the effects that leather sniffing could have on the human mind. Thomas Senior had obviously been exposed to dangerous levels of saddles, and this in turn had led to a fixation with horses, reins and saddlery. His mind was unable to focus on non-leather-based items, meaning he was likely to suffer boils, chafing, and in his more lucid moments, outbursts of neighing. A course of treatment

182

was prescribed by Doctor Harpoon that was considered reckless bordering on outrageous. Thomas Senior was given unguents, morning and evening, which were believed to repel horses and any thoughts of horses. Whilst the short-term results were amazing, in the long term it actually encouraged horseplay and tom-tittery. On release from the brig and readmitted into the specialist horse and stable unit somewhere near Arras, Thomas was the model trooper, but later in life his mental instability somehow seeped into his son Thomas.

Damian had seen horses, but even in the 80s, there was still a great deal of ignorance surrounding this type of mental fragility. Seeing his father neighing at the moon was a distressing image, yet Damian would often join in with this bizarre behaviour. As a child, Damian would watch all the great horse-based TV shows, from 'Fiona the Frolicking Foal', a hit cartoon in the early 70s, to 'Horses and Homes', which showcased the stables of the rich and famous. Nowadays, the innocence of those shows is lost on cynical viewers who cannot truly appreciate a well-kept stable, but in the 70s people had an appreciation of straw, hay and saddles, indeed in some schools, children were taught by real horses. Damian would try and comfort his father as and when he was able to, and Anne was always on hand with a pipe and a knowing wink, but the equine echoes would continue to haunt him day and night.

Damian continued his acting efforts and was cast in several topical plays during the year. His first big challenge was to play the butler in George Bernard Straw's 'The Ideal Stable Hand'. Set in Edwardian England, Finshaw was a stable hand like no other. His ungainly appearance and total lack of grace and charm meant that he was forever looking for work in the cloistered households of well-to-do families, with little success. Damian threw himself into the part, spending several weeks working on a voluntary basis as a stable hand at a rundown equine centre in Sutton Coldfield. Polishing silver, serving tea and generally looking at horses enabled Damian to really live the part. This dedication was not reflected in his performance, which was likened to watching shit slowly slide off a slippery shovel. The cast were very supportive, offering to give Damian a two-week break during the run of the show, and even insisting that he stay away from rehearsals to protect his talent. The director of the show, Barry Guffaw, was enthusiasm on legs, with a jaunty arse and very small fingers. He couldn't point and often this led to confusion and anger, as the cast were never sure of whom he was directing his directional demands at. Sonia Slopop, the heroine of the piece, would often leave rehearsals in tears, in part due to debilitating haemorrhoids, but also in part because of Barry's pointless pointing. The local theatre critic, Daphne Dowell, was far from forgiving in her review, comparing Damian's performance to that of tarnished spoon in a drawer of shiny knives, lacking polish and very obviously in the wrong place.

Damian's next show was an uplifting pantomime to cheer the heart and generally uplift the spirit. Again, Barry was directing, reuniting his fingers with a cast who failed to get his point, and casting Damian as the villain in the children's favourite, 'The Incredible Mr Toad Stole a Car and Attacked some Stoats'. This classic of talking creatures is dismissed as unsuitable for public consumption by many, but Barry was adamant that this time it would convert the unconvertable — the reluctant soft-tops, as Barry referred to them. Damian was to play a badger/stoat/weasel, as his costume was an amalgamation of roadkill, and Barry was all for innovation. Rehearsals were spent in the local park in an attempt to capture the wilderness and replicate the conditions that many animals might well experience. On cold November evenings, astride a dirty bench, Barry would sit, pointing stick in hand, demanding his cast come out from underneath the trees and stop fucking around. Damian, half badger, half roadkill, attempted to bring life to a character that was fast on the way to being lifeless. Playing alongside Damian was Gwenda-Lou Philips as a dormant dormouse, Danny Gutter as a maverick reptile and Sylvia Cereal as the myopic mole with self-esteem issues. Part musical, part Greek tragedy, the play focused on the enduring bond between roadkill and driver. Several acts of the play were cut, and the running time of twenty-five minutes meant the audience could leave without having to sit through too much of the shit. There were songs a-plenty, and Damian really enjoyed this aspect of the production. His favourite, which he can still be heard to hum to this day, was 'Don't Squash Me With Your Motor, Mister', reproduced below with absolutely no one's permission:

*Don't Squash Me With Your Motor, Mister*
*Driving down the road one day, I spy a little mole,*
*Its little snout poking up, from its grubby hole.*
*It looks to the left, it peers to the right, it seems to be all clear,*
*So foot to the floor, close my eyes, to the mole towards I steer.*
*Driving down the road at speed, I spot a massive toad,*
*It doesn't know of safety or the Highway Code.*
*Foot down hard, my toady friend, it's time to meet your end,*
*I'll finish you and continue you on, around the hairpin bend.*
*Driving down the road at speed, from nowhere comes a stoat,*
*With shiny teeth and scabby furry coat.*
*So peddle down, ignore the brakes, and aim dead straight and true,*
*I'll bundle off this little thing then get myself a shrew.*
*Roadkill, roadkill, nature's euthanasia,*
*Roadkill, roadkill, in Europe or in Asia.*
*Roadkill, roadkill, a game for day and night,*
*Roadkill, roadkill, drive with hate and spite.*
*So when you think of driving, think of this advice,*
*Drive too fast, drive too wild, and try and get the mice.*

The audiences were morbidly fascinated with the lack of talent on show and thanks to an abundance of no emotional intelligence, the cast assumed that audience members were laughing because they enjoyed the performance. Building on this misguided belief, Damian decided to try his hand at directing, and put himself forward to direct the next scheduled production, a thriller written by a local man who had experienced some thrills in the early 60s. Set in a disused costume hire shop, 'The Fancy Dresser' was a tale of greed, gluttony and ill-fitting fancy dress. Damian, acting alone with no encouragement, decided to deconstruct the original play, bringing a harder edge to the action and dialogue. Casting would require skill and a delicate balance between upsetting most of the established actors and encouraging younger actors, whose enthusiasm and raw stupidity would generate energy and excitement. Any lighting as such was decided against; the action would take place at night, and going against conventional wisdom, the cast would be required to sell at least ten tickets apiece or risk being kicked off the production. The lead role of Sirus, the owner of the fancy dress shop, was given to a young fellow named Eric Strap, part-time postman and budding athlete. He had dreams of acting at the Olympic games, and what he lacked in talent he made up in sheer stupidity, enabling Damian to fill his head with shit and nonsense. Opposite Eric was a young woman who worked at the local chip shop on a Friday and Saturday evening, Sheena Shine. Her abrupt customer service skills and inability to communicate effectively made her ideal for the role of Sharon, a shy and awkward woman who had lost her innocence in a revolving door of relationships. The opening scene was incredibly tedious, yet essential in lowering the expectations of the audience. As the curtains opened, Sirus was sweeping the remains of another day into the sack he called his memory sack, reflecting on the vagaries of fancy dress and costume hire, when Sharon, who had been sleeping in the corner, woke up with a start, realising she was wearing a grubby gorilla costume. She had attended the annual 'Chippie' awards believing it to be fancy dress, only to discover that she had misread the invitation, which actually read no fancy dress. Leaving the event early, she makes her way back to the fancy dress shop, her emotions fried like a well-cooked piece of haddock, only to discover the shop unattended, so decides to take a nap in the corner, the effects of too much rum and coke kicking in. When Sirus sees this vision of gorilla gorgeousness, he is smitten, but does not recognise the costume as one of his. He only hires orangutan and chimp costumes, avoiding gorilla like the plague. Sharon had returned to the wrong shop. The two fancy dress lovers soon embark on an ill-disguised relationship, dressing up to impress, and as each costume becomes more elaborate, so their relationship becomes fraught with anxiety, bitterness and jealousy. Sirus is forever dressed as a clown of sorts, while Sharon prefers the more sophisticated costumes, like the 'Hotdog' or 'Battered Sausage'. It is obvious that the play is going nowhere, and soon. In what can only be described as the final act, the two protagonists return from a night at a themed sausage and clown event realising that they fucking hate each other. They go their separate ways and never speak to each other again.

The play was a violent flop, with many of the audience members moved to lobbing small denomination coins at Damian and the cast. They wanted to hurt Damian, but not too badly. Following a break from the theatre, Damian decided to find alternative ways to make a tit of himself, but still feels that if he had been talented, he might well have succeeded in something.

# Nappies and a cranium

This was a momentous year for Damian's pitiful journey into adulthood. He became a father in very early June, and it was everything and more of what he hadn't expected. Fatherhood had never been on his radar, due to a lack of perception and forethought, but when it arrived screaming that June morning, his emotions were a tangled box of weblike ventricles — whatever the fuck that might be. His first born, Sarah, was an iridescent bundle of words and bubbles, whose disproportionate cranium heaved with words and social ability. She was a tiny baby, with all the requisite parts and a cranium that both frightened and delighted in equal measure. After much protracted negotiation, a name was chosen: Sarah Nicole. The joy of becoming a failing father was tempered with the knowledge that responsibility was something that stuck to him like tear gas, painful and unwanted. He needed to find a job to support his indifferent partner and baby daughter, and yet again, the fickle fat finger of fucking fate pointed him in a direction which would see him waste nine years of his life in a shit job.

A fellow at the theatre ran a mildly successful mobile wrestling ring franchise and needed staff to assist with the general upkeep of the rings, the only requirement being that the candidate must know the inner workings of a mop. Damian had used a mop in the late 70s so felt well equipped to carry out this arduous yet very unrewarding role. Turning up for the interview dressed as Giant Haystacks (a good first impression can really make a difference) Damian faced a gruelling interview from the two owners of the business, Mr Half-Pike and Mr Pirouette. Half-Pike was in his early twenties and wore ill-fitting overalls and a large bonnet, whilst Pirouette wore tight shorts whatever the weather. Their questions were rigorous, intended to stretch Damian and explore his motivation and propensity for hard work. The first question, what does wrestling mean to you? was intended to knock Damian off balance, but he was able to fire straight back with a pithy yet long-winded exposition on the social value of excessive sweat in the larger man, suggesting wool with a hint of nylon would increase the sweat quotient by a factor of ten. He then expounded on the benefits of open-air wrestling schools and their impact on inner-city children. Damian really could talk shit, and after a marathon (some might know it as Snickers) the interview continued. The questions were quick fire; the answers quicker fired. How many corners has a seven-sided wrestling ring? Four too many. How do you remove overbearing sweat stains from the canvas? Strong bleach and elbow grease. Who is your favourite wrestler? This was a trick question which Damian refused to answer on religious grounds. There then followed a series of physical tasks intended to see if Damian's back was firm enough. He was given a large bag of onions and asked to peel them without shedding a tear. This he did. Then he was required to run on the spot with a savoy cabbage balanced in each hand. This he did. Finally, once he had recovered the cabbages, he was asked, "Who is your role model?". The answer was easy: Thomas. The two gentlemen said they would be in touch. Damian faced an agonising wait, and as this was a time before mobile phones and Wi-Fi, he would have to wait for possibly days before he knew if he had got the job. As the minutes turned to hours, and so to days, Damian spent his time biting his knuckles and oiling his palms to make them appear sweaty. Right then and there, all he wanted was the truth. Was he good enough to be second assistant in a mobile wrestling ring business?

When the letter arrived, he couldn't bear to open it, but braving paper cuts, he ripped open the envelope. Success! He was to start the following week on a wage, working plentiful hours and supporting his family. His career was still to begin.

Those first few months in the job were a whirlwind of grease, sweat and discarded leotards. Long days and even longer lunch breaks meant that at times Damian rarely got to see his young parasite, Sarah. With an angry mouth and a hungry stomach, the child needed her dad, but his commitment to feeding her occasionally meant that he had to go where the work demanded. His employers were understanding and would often loan him a wrestling ring at weekends to entertain himself and his child, but food is what they really wanted. Day to day, he performed a variety of tasks, and having been shown the ropes, he was shown the canvas and the ornamental bell.

Each morning started with a roll call of the staff. Along with Damian, there was Stevo the Weirdo, a squat man of about fifty who was unemployable, Chris the tool, so called because his head resembled a piano, and finally a trainee, Brad the keyboard, so called because of his overindulgent teeth. Stevo had been in a successful band in the early 70s, *Xavier and the Xylophones,* but had left to join *Gary and the Glockenspiels* due to musical instrument differences. After the *Glockenspiels* split in the early 80s, he fell into a pit. Turning his back on society, Stevo vacuum-packed his feet and laminated his hands in an effort to weather the storm that was the 80s. As a result of this misguided attempt at insulation, Stevo's feet had never fully ripened, and it meant he suffered from inefficient feet and hands. Damian felt no sympathy whatsoever and thought him an annoying twat. Brad had the worst teeth that Damian had ever seen, row after row after row after row of mouldy molars and insipid incisors. Brad was a medical rarity and had never visited a dentist in his life, believing he would catch gum disease if he did. As a result, his teeth had run amuck, almost as if his teeth had reproduced but none were willing to leave. His saliva was incredible, a perfumed mix of mould and decay.

The crew, as they were known, would then load the 1970s Ford Truss and head off to the first customer. On arriving at the customers', it was Damian's responsibility to ensure everything ran like clockwork. He was a natural with wrestling rings and could use his good eye to check for curvature of the canvas, wonky ropes or a dysfunctional bell. Fortunately, his inefficient feet did not impede his day-to-day work, although he was unable to hop with any joy. He spent many a happy hour testing the ring for safety, going through a series of safety tests to ensure no lardy bastard fell out of the ring due to poor assembly. No lardy was going to suffer broken blubber on Damian's watch.

Some events were memorable, but one that has remained with Damian to this day is the 1988 Inter-Church Wrestling Tournament, between several different denominations. It took place over the Easter weekend and was very well attended. There were Methodists, Baptists, Catholics, Anti-Baptists, Presbyterians, Calvinists, Lutherans, Seventh Day Adventists and several atheists who had no place there. The event was designed to give these god-botherers the opportunity to wrestle with weighty theological issues in a safe environment. The opening rounds saw the clerics and theologians dancing around the ring, tossing out platitudes and sermonising on sweat and honest toil. The Catholics would often breach the unwritten rules, but they would then ask for forgiveness. The Baptists seemed to produce an unholy amount of sweat, and the Calvinists were considering rebranding to something more modern that reflected their austere outlook. Weightier issues were thrown into the mix, and a tussle between a very angry Presbyterian and a laid-back lay preacher from a Methodist church in Leytonstone turned very nasty. They were discussing eternal damnation and the meaning of the afterlife when the preacher was floored by a theological uppercut; the lay preacher lay there motionless, but his towel man, who happened to be a Baptist, inadvertently tripped, sending a bucket of holy water everywhere. The air turned blue, as the Presbyterian threatened to excommunicate someone, and it was only the timely intervention of the Seventh Day Adventist that prevented a very unholy war breaking out. Defrocking was mentioned, but that was unrelated to the issues at hand. The final bout took place on Easter Sunday, when it was a free-for-all, last-man-standing-type affair. The Catholics started well, but when the reformation and counter-reformation were thrown into the ring, all hell let loose. Blaspheming as if it was judgement day, the clerics certainly worked up a sweat, so when the bout finally came to a very unsatisfactory conclusion (they agreed to disagree) the ring was awash with holy sweat. Damian, using only a squeegee and a bucket, managed to bottle the sweat and sell it on to his spiritual friends as sweaty holy water. He made £4.87 per bottle. Damian continued at this job but knew that wrestling rings were not his future. He needed to find something that would stretch his limited mind. As yet he was still trawling his life for inspiration.

Thomas had always been afflicted with health, with misshapen elbows, a tendency to be rather bilious and many heart palpitations. He was also struck by crippling in-growing ears, making the voices in his head seem even louder and more strident. He would spend days alone, listening to half-hidden messages that haunted his waking hours. Damian, unlike Thomas, had sympathetic ears and was known as a good listener, or at least someone who if he was ignoring you, it wasn't that obvious. Damian would sit with his father, who by now had adopted an array of walking sticks and listen as Thomas regaled him with tales from inside his head. Thomas desperately believed that people were out to pinch his highly undesirable collection of tat. He resorted to a range of tactics to avoid losing his least prized possessions, including mugs of boiling water, left adjacent to the front door of his single rise sheltered flat; scratching messages onto lampposts and purchasing a dog whistle to terrify the local hounds. He was obviously a desperate man in need of diazepam. His collection of long johns was put to good use when he decided to wear all fifteen pairs at once, in the hope that it would make him invincible. His actions worried Anne, whose pipe-smoking had gone through the roof, and she was soon on twenty-eight pipes a day. As Damian listened to his father, he slowly drew out the inner demons that so bedevilled his ageing role model. Thomas had always been an active man, his mind alive with ideas and tom-tittery. Seeing him disabled by his inner demons touched Damian, who would try to understand why his dad was a fucking fruit cake. He suggested that perhaps a week away at a retreat would help Thomas eliminate some of the more active voices and bore some of the less threatening voices. Thomas agreed, and soon he was packing his humble belongings for a week away at the

'Mary Mason Making Nutters Better Sanctuary', located in a leafy car park/DIY distribution centre several miles outside Bradford. Mary Mason had served as an auxiliary fire marshal at a paint factory for many years, and her experience with chemicals and fumes meant she had a rudimentary understanding of the workings of the human anatomy.

On arrival, Thomas was greeted by Hector, who was the supervisor/head guard at the facility and shown to his sumptuously sparse cabin/cell/room. Equipped with a single bed, two sinks and a window, it had all the home comforts needed if you needed very little. The ethos of the facility was calm and tranquillity, where the inmates could reconnect with reality and touch base with sanity. Thomas had always been in touch with sanity and was a realist through and through; it was this that made him hear voices as he believed everybody else was a fucking nutter. But he had an open mind (part of the problem), so quickly unpacked his three pies, a month's supply of cigarettes and a copy of the 'Readers' Digest'. He was then given a very brief tour of the facility by Hector, whose many scars and bruises suggested he was a clumsy type. On the ground floor was the disused forklift truck parking point, which was now used for yoga sessions. Inmates could use a forklift, but only when they had successfully completed three full sessions of yoga and were able to do the discarded lettuce, a crippling yoga manoeuvre. He was then shown the shared toilets (shared with the distribution centre) and given a quick glance at the dining room, which also doubled up as a makeshift infirmary should treatment go wrong. Outside was the car park, where on warmer days, local trolleys were dumped, so the inmates had something to get off on. The three trees and assortment of weeds made the car park a semi-tranquil space, home to some quite tame wildlife.

Upstairs were the rooms for the more serious cases, and it was here that the staff spent most of their time, baiting and cajoling the more aggressive inmates into breaking down and rediscovering their inner tranquillity. Paint fumes were often used to give the illusion of fresh starts and newness. At the far end of the first floor was Mary Mason's inner sanctum, where Ms Mason, or Mary, or the Head Honcho, would routinely humiliate inmates and staff alike, with the intention of strengthening their inner core. Quite often this would leave the poor individual dribbling with lack of esteem, but statistics could be used to prove that this method was effective some of the time, in conjunction with strong hallucinogens. Thomas returned to his room on that first evening knowing that he had wasted his hard-earned cash on a fraud but decided to stick it out to see if it might be an enjoyable break. The next day he was due to have a one-to-one with Mary, so he spent the evening planning his responses. The transcript of the meeting is reproduced below and is still referred to in several psychiatric journals.

*Mary Mason v Thomas Carter*
*MM: Thomas, tell me, do you hear voices and if so, are they talking to you now?*
*TC: Well, Mary, they are currently talking with my alto ego, and as I have no truck with my alto ego, I no longer eavesdrop on conversation that don't concern me.*
*MM: So your alto ego is currently chatting, or is it more of a listening exercise?*
*TC: Nodding along with what appears to be a discussion about potted plants. I'm not much of a gardener, so it may well be potted shrimps.*
*MM: Do you like shrimps, Thomas?*
*TC: I had some during the war, and they left me feeling bilious. I once potted the cue ball.*
*MM: When your voices speak to you, what do they talk about? Is it general chit-chat, or is it more specific?*
*TC: I have a silver-plated cane that I use to berate the voices. They threaten my bookcase most days.*
*MM: Your bookcase — do you enjoy reading?*
*TC: I have fifty-six copies of Treasure Island, arranged alphabetically. It means I never read the same one twice. I like order.*
*MM: Do you feel like a prisoner inside your own mind?*

*TC: More like a paying inmate. I pay with anguish. My wife Anne has catamarans in her eye, but she has never sailed. She went to the Isle of Wight once, but that was by sea plane.*

*MM: When the voices become too loud, what do you do, Thomas?*

*TC: I retire to my imaginary garage and count the pies that I have eaten, mentally cataloguing each one. It gives me some peace, plus I like counting pies as it makes me feel drowsy.*

*MM: Thank you for being so candid, Thomas. I think we will finish for the time being. Would you like to come back later in the week?*

*TC: If I come every day could I have a cranium shaped thermometer to measure the temperature of my head? I read in the 'Readers' Digest' that an overly warm brain can result in disturbed brainwaves and irritability. Plus, it would be a nice addition to my thermometer collection.*

*MM: We can discuss that tomorrow. Thank you, Thomas.*

Thomas met Mary one more time, but remembering his naval training, refused to give any details that might reveal his unit or current location. He spent the following day in the infirmary looking for interesting thermometers and discharged himself early due to an urgent issue with his bookcase. The voices continued, but Damian realised that his dad was not troubled, just different at times. He loved him all the more.

# Thomas the Younger

Thomas had been bedevilled with health problems throughout his life, suffering a ruptured armpit in 1937, a perforated oesophagus in 1954, an ulcerated bunion whilst working as a wool counter in 1960 and a series of heart problems. Thomas had a fantastic heart, full of love and warmth, and this meant that it sometimes got too warm, precipitating irregular moods and heart attacks. Damian witnessed his father having an attention seeking heart attack back in the late 70s. It was a shocking moment as he was trying to watch 'Scooby Doo' with Stephen. Once the ambulance arrived and Anne got over the shock, they were able to continue to watch a particularly gripping episode of that classic cartoon series. Thomas didn't die that time, but it did give Damian a new appreciation of TV, so when as an adult his father was unwell, he adopted a very blasé approach in order to ward off the pain and sympathy that he was emotionally ill-equipped to process. He would retreat into his bucket of clichés when asked about his feelings, resorting to such lines as 'it is what he would have wanted if time had waited', 'what does kill you leaves behind a victim' and his go-to cliché, 'it's fucking character-building'. Thomas had been diagnosed with a chronic heart, meaning he needed to have some new arteries rebuilt and diversions put in place. This complex surgery required an incredible team of microsurgeons who were able to perform amazing things using only fine twine, a sharp knife and some powerful reading glasses. Anne was understandably upset as she had lost her pipe, and the night before the big operation by the microsurgeons, she had made an emergency dash to buy a replacement pipe. Made entirely of laminated tweed, the pipe was both sleek and environmentally friendly. With her pipe Anne could cope with most things that life's bastard children threw in her direction. Her backbone was twice the usual girth of a woman of her age, resulting in a need for powerful girdles, but that is for another day.

On the day of the operation, Damian paced up and down outside his house, desperate to hear news on the whereabouts of his stolen car, without which he could not visit Thomas. The operation was due to last some time, and when this ran over, the whole family looked for better timekeeping instruments. When they were finally allowed to see Thomas, he was hooked up to a host of medical paraphernalia, with lights and bells and a spinning wheel for decoration. He looked peaceful, resplendent in bandages and fine twine. His chest had been carefully stitched back together, and with his new plastic arteries, the prognosis was average; ten years max was the educated guess given by some of the better-informed medics. The family, Anne, all those who remotely cared, had been to Warrington and back, to use a cliché from the bucket of clichés. Sucking hard on her pipe, she hugged her children and swore never to lose her pipe again.

Damian had been living in Birmingham for some years and found its people to be progressive, yet at the same time oppressed and slightly awkward in matters of speech and social interaction. Birmingham at the time was going through tremendous changes to bid for the 1997 Running and Jumping Games. The council had spared no expense on installing new pedestrian crossings, road signs and high wattage street lighting. The city was buzzing with possibilities, and it was possible that the council were pissing in the wind. The big city was a very scary place to be, and when Damian had first moved to Birmingham he had been intoxicated by its bright fumes and heady mixture of buildings and streets. He had been told that Brummies, as they were known, were a dour bunch, but he found them to be as dour as Yorkshire folk without the mean-spirited edge and flat vowels. Quickly becoming accustomed to the vernacular, he was able to buy cigarettes, bread and milk from a range of shops. He was integrating and felt at one with the people. What also helped was the birth of his eldest son, Thomas (the younger), a bubbly and effervescent ball of shit and piss who has brought immeasurable happiness to Damian's life. Thomas the younger was born in July, and with his elder sister Sarah, presented Damian with a host of changes in his life. As a young man he believed that only fathers had kids, but now here he was with two children and a partner who was not too fond of him: progress. Fatherhood was the making of Damian; a role that was both daunting but also unbelievably rewarding. In those first years as a father, he would often turn to Thomas for advice, guidance and the occasional cigarette. Thomas was a caring father, writing long rambling letters to his son in Birmingham, with sage advice and quick tips on changing an alternator on a Ford Bathtub. Damian had bought a car three months earlier to ferry around his growing self-esteem and children. The big question that haunted Damian's waking hours was "how should I be a father?" He had a fantastic role model in Thomas but felt that he couldn't just copy his dad; he needed to find his own way, be that a strict disciplinarian, a slack-jaw with no boundaries, or something completely different. He was drawn to the idea of experimental fatherhood, where consistency was less important than fun and an easy life. Of course, it had its pitfalls, as the kids would grow up to be annoying little fuckers, and as he thought over this apparent problem, he had an epiphany. ''Be yourself' was the mantra of Thomas, so Damian just had to be himself (not a particularly exciting prospect) and parenting would become easier. He wasn't a hands-on father in the sense that he didn't want to do everything, but he did want to enjoy his parasites as much as possible. To this end, he started to write down his thoughts, which he eventually put into the form of a letter, to be sent to his parasites if they ever had the misfortune to have children. It is reproduced below:

Dear Parasites,

If you are reading this, I am either dead or you are being very fucking nosey. Or, you may be expecting a parasite of your own. Parasites are a breed unlike any other. They are there to frustrate, annoy and generally be loved. You fuckers deserve all the love I can give you, but being a parent is never easy. I recall Anne, your gran, a woman who feared spinsterhood, with its icy loneliness and desperate days of sitting alone at railway stations, pondering on the unquantifiable beauty of a well- crafted pipe and parenthood. Spinsterhood had stalked her as a teenager, and she had avoided floral frocks, extolled the virtues of libraries, and would often perch in the back garden on Mother's Day with a new woollen pipe, hiding from isolation and cats. As a wife, she had feared widowhood, its tentacles spreading indiscriminately. Thomas's mental and physical instability had left Anne walking a brittle line, never knowing if it was a cry for help or a cry of despair, with dry runs to the doctors, the hospital or morgue a weekly occurrence. Thomas, your loving grandfather, once decided to have a very unnecessary heart attack during a gripping episode of Scooby Doo in the late 70s. Standing in the front room, possibly to inspect the bitter net curtains, he decided that it would be a good time for his heart to have a short break. As both Stephen and I were engrossed in Scooby Doo, it was left to Thomas to call Anne to come down and call the ambulance or taxi. Whilst waiting for the ambulance/taxi, Thomas sat down with his sons, a little ashen-faced and in some obvious discomfort, where he remained incredibly calm as he puffed on a calming cigarette. Damian was fascinated by the possibilities of a day off school, either for hospital visiting or a funeral, so mentally encouraged Thomas to feel unwell but not too unwell. Of course, this was not your grandfather's first attempt at heart failure, and his continued existence was a bloody miracle. His first attempt at heart failure had been when he was in his early '40s, so obviously he felt he needed more practice. Throughout that period of illness and random hospital visits, he was always a father. So children, when you decide to have kids or accidentally come across your own children hidden in some car park or DIY superstore, cherish and love them, regardless of the circumstances, and know that I will always endeavour to avoid heart attacks during Saturday TV, and will love you always.

Yours with love,
Dad


Damian placed the letter in a safe place, and for many years was unable to recall ever writing such a pile of shit, but when he eventually came across it during a house move, he decided to keep it, for no obvious reason.

Damian's children were a constant source of inspiration, love and bewilderment to him, and he would often spend hours sitting in the dark, wishing he had paid the electricity bill. What kept him going then was the adoration and futile hope his two young children gave him, without question. Sarah, with a head like an experiment and Thomas the younger, who was breaking in his tear ducts, would always have a smile or tantrum at the ready when Damian arrived home from a soul-destroying day's work to spend a soul-destroying evening in his bile-infested two-bedroom maisonette. With bitterness dripping from every cornice and curtain rail, the maisonette was not a warm and inviting place to dwell. This period of Damian's existence was heaped with guilt, disappointment and futility. With no obvious parachute to optimism, it was a series of days that became weeks that became months, all the time never understanding how or why he ended up in a two-bedroom maisonette with two kids and a partner who was desperate for him to be somewhere else. Of course, every cloud has a silver lining, and for Damian, that silver lining was the world of books and history.

During those fossilised weeks and months, Damian would immerse himself in book after book, devouring history as if his calcium-deficient bones depended on it. He would switch from reading a thoroughly rubbish account of the War of the Roses to a thoroughly forgettable retelling of the Pheasants' Revolt. Several books that he read and reread during that period remain on Damian's bookcase to date. His favourite of the time was a social history of the cream industry, written by a disgruntled milkman, entitled 'The Stomach-Churning Diary of a Dairy Slave', written at a time when few milkmen had enough calcium to see them through the week. The author and retired milky, Pat Urised, gives a gripping and no-bars-held account of life in a 1950s dairy, when dried milk and sterile hope was the diet of many a Briton following the defeat of the Nazi hordes. Below is a short passage which has been kindly reproduced thanks to no one giving a fuck about copyright.

*Monday 15th: Bloody cold morning. Hate cows. Filled the float with cows. If only someone, somewhere, could think of a better way of transporting cows and their by-products. Lost two good milkers on a hump-backed bridge last week, crushing a pensioner and ruining a beautiful tulip arrangement.*

*Thursday 18th: high speed chase with traffic police. Apparently, I had loaded too many cows on the float. Forgot my milking stool so a quick dash back to the depot resulted in a four-cow pile-up and milk spilt everywhere. Cows can be so leaky.*

*Monday 22nd: Children should be taught that every time a cow is milked, a calcium-deficient bull dies somewhere — that would make them drink the bastard stuff.*

*Thursday 25th: Saw three cows walking down the street this morning with umbrellas up. It wasn't even raining so suspect they may be mad cows. Took to wearing a beret to deliver yoghurt as I feel a little more sophisticated when I deliver in a beret.*

*Friday 26th: had three hundred pots of yoghurt stolen from the dairy last night. Obviously been targeted by some well-to-do thieves, intent on exporting the yoghurt or selling it on to wealthy yoghurt collectors.*

The diary continued in this vein for many weeks until the final entry, which suggests the milkman came to a very sticky end.

*Thursday 15th: Woken by milk-curdling screams in the night. Out of bed like a flash and down to the float to see if the precious liquid was still there. Took my powerful torch and some tweezers in case there were armed yoghurt thieves up to no good.*

This was of course the start of the infamous Lactose Wars, a clash between intolerant vegans and intolerant milk drinkers. What started as a dispute between two rival café owners in a quirkier part of Bradford developed into a bitter and violent dispute between two diets. The aftershock can still be felt today in certain parts of the more lucid imaginations. Frank Osolate, an indecisive vegan with tendencies, was a violent opponent of cows. Rumour had it that his mother Iris had preferred cows to her son and spent too many hours in the pastures with the milkers and not enough time with her fledgling son. Frank had opened a vegan café, the first of its kind in Bradford, after being demobbed from the Special Food Corps. He was an expert in brown rice, and his years of training meant he could subsist on rice and water for hours. His café had been in danger of going under due to rampant distrust of fancy new ideas, so when a milk bar for intolerant milk drinkers opened next door, it pushed this volatile man to, if not exactly onto, the edge. The Lucid Lactose Lounge offered milk, milk and more milk to lovers of non-dairy milk: milk from plants, bees and crops. The owner and intolerant milk drinker was Sirus Suckle; a withered excuse of a man who had spent the last fifteen years incarcerated in a dairy farm in Lothian. This left him with a bitter aftertaste and hives, and he had sworn off milk as a point of principle. He was, however, in direct competition with Frank. It was only a matter of time before this milky simmering rivalry boiled over and tears were shed.

What started off as a simple comment on the lack of customers in The Vague Vegan became a soufflé of curds and whey, or was it words and khey? The vitriol was real, the anger intense, and the non-dairy milk, off white. Like a bad pair of 70s jeans, tempers were soon flared, and when Frank suggested that Sirus go stick his head up a cow's arse, all-out war broke out.

On the streets of Bradford, no milkman (or woman) was safe. Floats were sunk, eggs were cracked and tea was left unbrewed. Each morning, milk floats were upended as the two rival cafés took their war to a wider audience. Who could have their morning brew if the milk was not delivered? Was milking a cow to become a crime? Would Frank and Sirus bury their intolerances and open a vegan milk bar? These questions were soon answered when Frank disappeared for a period of weeks, allowing the people of a small part of Bradford to inhale the fumes of milk in peace. When he finally resurfaced, he closed his vegan café and re-opened it as a trendy greasy spoon café, serving all manner of milks and tolerating all intolerances.

History is a cruel and deceptive mistress, but Damian continued to read stolen library books whilst searching for his own future history.

# Part Four — The wasted years
## Cushions

Cushions and curtains were used to calm Thomas when his violent head voices overcrowded his weary cranium. His wartime experiences would haunt his days, with images of German cars with unpronounceable names driving toward him at breakneck speed, German fish flapping menacingly as he swam for safety in Lowestoft harbour and mackerel and cod bedecked in Nazi uniforms, wrapped in yesterday's Daily Panic. When Thomas heard the voices, they were either in a strong Bavarian accent or Welsh, and this apparent paradox would send him spiralling into a vortex of self-loathing and panic. Often, in the early hours of the morning, he would creep into the back garden and plant ugly flowers to deter theft or run to the local supermarket and demand to see a spiritual healer. It was this last demand that piqued Damian's interest in his father's mental issues. Damian had read in 'The Journal of Cushions and Cures' that cushions could be used to calm the neurotic and unstable. Damian had no interest in alternative therapies, but whilst at the dentist he had flicked through a copy of the journal and found the contents both amusing and alarming. Below, kindly reproduced for those who may have a passing interesting in tom-tittery, are several of the articles featured in that very issue.

### Does Your Cat Flap Give You Nightmares?

*Hi, I am Doctor Frank Exchange, expert in cat flaps and cat psychiatry, and long-standing practitioner of cat flap therapy. My good friend and colleague, Doctor Cindy McFluff, recently spent several weeks surrounded by cats, in our purpose-built cat facility, to study the ways in which cats and their flaps affect human well-being. Our findings may* strike you as shit, but I assure you that I wrote them all down and can vouch for their accuracy.

The facility is located three miles outside Santa Fe and occupies an old ice cream factory. The faint smell of vanilla is still a reminder of the building's history, along with piles and piles of wafers. Cindy, on seeing the building, had to suppress her desire to hit me full on in the nose, but following a brief fist fight, we agreed that there was no alternative available. A suitable control room was identified, which apparently used to be the gents' toilets, and with some modifications and the removal of the urinals, it proved to be an ideal nerve centre. Cindy worked away installing cat flaps, and soon, with the help of several local cats, we were ready to start the experiment. Cindy would inject herself with cat hormones and prowl the corridors in search of mice and solace. When it became apparent that neither was at hand, she would curl up in a corner, usually close to a beautifully embroidered cushion and gently clean her whiskers. Over the course of several weeks, the change in Cindy was remarkable, and as long as the cat hormones kept coming, she was able to find some comfort in the cushions.

Reviewing the grainy video I made of the study, it appears to me that Cindy really let herself go; her hair was matted, her coat had lost much of its natural lustre, and she would often shit in the most inconvenient locations. The only thing that seemed to regulate her moods and bowels was the introduction of a cushion. From this I can claim, without further studies needed, that cat lovers love cushions.

## Walking Sticks: Why I replaced my stick for a cushion!

I recently lost the use of one of my hips and half my sense, so I had to use a stick to get out and about, and of course gesticulate in a threatening manner. Day after day I would wander the streets, pointing at far-off buildings and buses. My stick, Wanda, was my constant companion; a third arm in a world of duality. I wasn't born with a stick, and as a child believed sticks and canes to be a wicked affectation of the rich and idle. It was only when I lost half a hip in a dance hall hip-hop hopping competition in Watford that I demanded to be taken to a stick shop to prop up my unsupported legs and fragile dance skills. I immediately bonded with Wanda, and soon we were inseparable, enjoying short walks and days indoors. I took Wanda to the cemetery where my parents were scattered, and two of my close friends agreed to have a group photo with Wanda. I felt complete, but when half of my sense drained away following an overly long nap, I began to distrust Wanda. I felt she no longer wanted to support me, and she would often leave herself on buses or park benches. Pretty soon we were at each other's throats. It all came to a head when I repeatedly struck myself with Wanda, giving myself an unwanted stay in a secure unit and a nasty scar on my left buttock. Whilst recuperating, I was offered a cushion by a kindly cushion salesman who would often hawk his wares at the secure unit. It was a pretty innocuous looking cushion, with a simple puppy print on both sides, but I was instantly taken in by its beguiling softness and beauty. Soon Wanda was so much kindling, fit only for dog walkers and draconian schoolteachers. Clara the cushion was my constant companion, and we could be seen most days smothering small animals or swatting cats away in the local park. Clara was robust yet soft, so squirrels could be swatted without any pangs of guilt.

I am currently suspended from a tree with Clara strapped to my head to avoid any pain when I inevitably fall from the tree. Wanda could never protect me in the same way. It was always Wanda this and Wanda that, but with Clara, the voices tell me that she really is a cushion for life.

<u>Shock Findings in Herbalist — The Alternatives.</u>

Rock legends, The Herbalists, recently performed an impromptu gig at Herbie's Herbalist Shop to enthusiastic hypochondriacs dissatisfied with conventional remedies. The Herbalists were the UK's greatest alternative medicine rock combo, renowned for their smooth herbal sounds and syncopating lyrics. Who could forget their seminal song, 'Crystal for my Ruby', the lyrics of which were written on the back of a herbal remedy for sore throats. They are reproduced below with no apology needed.

Crystal for my Ruby

It was late July and the moon began to shine,

*Ruby said she loved me but needed some more thyme.*
*Basil said to garlic, my green and scented friend,*
*Ruby looks a little red, her head we need to mend.*
*Ruby used to shimmer, shine and twinkle bright,*
*Now she's dull and glimmer-free, an echo of the night.*
*Linseed had its uses, as did pumpkin seeds,*
*Useful for snacking, the intermittent feeds.*
*Ruby looks so tarnished, Ruby looks so glum,*
*A remedy is needed to make her number one.*
*Crystals are the answer, a friend of mine was told,*
*A brave, exciting answer, it's got to be so bold.*
*Sprinkle, hum and polish, herbs and seeds and oil,*
*Put it in a pan 'til the substance starts to boil.*
*Crystals give us hope, energy and life,*
*But if your need is surgery, you need a fucking knife.*

This song was an alternative anthem for a generation of herbalists who yearned for cures that were both cheap and ineffective. *The Herbalists* toured the West Country, spreading the message of oils and unguents, in the hope that they could sell more albums and cure the sick. Lead singer, Dave Margarine, left the band in the early 80s to pursue a career as an acupuncturist in Batley, West Yorkshire, whilst also running a small double-glazing business. Now he was ready to hit the road again with a new line-up and a new name for the band. The band now perform as '*The Pointless Heralds*', singing a mix of glazing-based songs with a nod to acupuncture. So if your existing glazing was a little condensation heavy, and you suffered from a bad back, then possibly a night with '*The Pointless Heralds*' could be the cure for two of your problems.

Thomas enjoyed a very narrow range of music, and certainly wouldn't normally listen to any alternative crap, but following a long and distressing conversation with a glazing advisor from Manchester, decided to pop along and visit Mr Margarine's studio/showroom/surgery in Batley to see if this alternative really was an alternative.

Damian decided to accompany his dad, not through any sincere fear for his father's mental health, but because he wanted to meet the margarine man. Was he really an unhealthy fraud, or could he cure Thomas's internal struggles? On arriving at the showroom/surgery/studio, Damian was taken aback by the sheer shabbiness of the premises. Located next to a disused funeral parlour, the salesroom/studio/surgery was in desperate need of light, heat and furniture, but undeterred, Thomas parked his new Triumph Gizzard and entered the premises, Damian in tow.

They were greeted by the margarine man, who was dressed in surgeon's scrubs, along with a baseball cap emblazoned with the legend 'Spread the Word — Margarine Saves Lives'. They were handed a questionnaire along with a disclaimer and a brochure for budget conservatories. Thomas completed the questionnaire in no time, and whilst Damian browsed the extensive collection of downmarket conservatories, Thomas was asked to remove his shirt so that Mr Margarine could assess his back. On the wall was a guide to the human back, with key pressure points highlighted, alongside some hand-drawn images of conservatories. Thomas was diagnosed with having disc problems, and thankfully, Mr Margarine could offer Thomas a very enticing package of acupuncture with a free fitting of any conservatory bought today from the 'Shatter' range. Thomas needed time to think about the need for a conservatory at his ground floor sheltered accommodation, so Mr Margarine began to select suitable needles that would help identify pain and pressure points in Thomas's back. Two of the needles were very similar to Anne's knitting needles, but Damian decided not to tell his dad. As Thomas lay there, Mr Margarine gently prodded and poked, but never quite inserted any of the needles into Thomas. Mr Margarine was a bag of small talk, recounting his years with *The Herbalists*, his time on the road as a double-glazing consultant and his experiences on the three-week acupuncturist course. He believed that all of Thomas's physical ailments were connected to his body, and if they could be cured then his mental health would stand isolated and cure itself. This really was alternative medicine.

Damian watched how Mr Margarine worked with minimal effort — in fact it was if he was doing nothing — and was surprised that Thomas hadn't walked out in disgust. He knew his dad didn't want a conservatory, nor did Thomas care for rock music, so maybe, just maybe, the needles were working. After what seemed like ten minutes, Mr Margarine asked Damian if he had any need for a conservatory or acupuncture. Mr Margarine was a fucking fraud. Driving home from Batley, Thomas was particularly downbeat, having splashed out on a celebration pie that would have to wait until his brain felt better.

Thomas's alto ego, the not-so-silent voice in a very acoustic head, was called Albert, after his great-grandmother, Albert. Thomas believed that Albert was responsible for most of the voices in his head, along with a retired admiral who occasionally barked orders from the poop deck of Thomas's mind. According to Thomas, Albert was born sideways, meaning his feet were always pointing to port. This might be fine in a sailor, but Albert had land legs and was not at all nautical like Thomas. This conflict had led to some very heated disagreements within Thomas's cramped mind. A sideways birth can traumatise both child and mother, not to mention the midwife, so it was no wonder that Albert was forever pecking at Thomas over seafaring issues and childbirth. Sideways-born alto egos are known to be overly aggressive and desperate for approval. Many sideways-born children have very soft legs and an inability to grasp seafaring terminology. Thomas would spend hours explaining nautical terms and traditions to Albert, often sitting by a river in his Austin Splash, deep in conversation with his own mind. Nautical terms and traditions, like pies and his children, were close to Thomas's heart, and he could explain in great detail the meanings and origins of hundreds of nautical terms and traditions. As a boy, Damian remembered sitting on his father's knee as he explained in significant detail the workings of the poop deck and how it came to be known as the 'gentleman's deck'.

209

Years before ships were used for traversing the oceans, a poop deck was so called because of its resemblance to a poop, a small mammal-like fish found only in the rivers and puddles of northern Norway. When Vikings and other bearded invaders brought their wares and fish south, along came the poop. It was often eaten at midday by ravenous Vikings who had finished pillaging and were in need of a non-calorific yet healthy bite to eat. The poop, about the same size as a healthy dog turd, was green in colour and tasted a little like rabbit-flavoured chicken. Served on a bed of soiled grass, it was recognised as a cure for dropsy, slippage and that perennial bugbear of the avid sailor, soiled trousers. As time passed, the poop fell out of favour, replaced by the more exotic and healthy sardine. It was only in the late eighteenth century, when the poop was added to the menus of Nelson's fleet, and gentlemen began to fully appreciate the nutty, bitter, vole-like flavour of poop that it came back into fashion. George IV would often eat poop whilst choosing a dandy hat or frock coat. Queen Victoria loved a poop, often before and after breakfast, and it was decided that sailors should eat this unusual and distasteful fish only on the deck of a ship; hence the poop deck became the place for poop.

'Shiver me timbers' was a phrase often on Thomas's placid lips, and it was no coincidence that he often felt like his brain was very cold. A timber, or timbre if the French pronunciation was adopted, is a tiny part of the brain that is responsible for regulating balance and levels of anxiety. Discovered by famed anthropologist Serge Bervoir, the timbre is understood to assist balance and allows most normally developed brains to remain on an even keel. Albert was constantly, with complete disregard for Thomas, adjusting the mental thermometer that regulated Thomas's anxiety. This meant that Thomas would frequently wake up with a cold brain and feel very anxious. He always wore long johns, regardless of the weather, so when his anxiety levels became dangerously hot, it led to episodes of excessive hat wearing coupled with bouts of falling over. Thomas displayed all the symptoms of an undiagnosed pirate with a severe case of cold timbers. It cannot be cured, but with patients such as Thomas, it can be ignored. Thomas would often sit in his second favourite armchair and sing tunes from sea-based musicals, periodically shouting out "Shiver me timbers,' which for Anne was upsetting and amusing in equal measure. One of Damian's abiding memories of this period is the sight of his father, plastic sword and eye patch suitably placed, singing the haunting melody 'Bubbles in my Brain'.

Bubbles in my Brain
Switch them off, switch them on,
Where have all the voices gone?
Albert, Albert, help me hear,
Stop my pain and stop my fear.
Bubbles, bubbles, in my brain,
I feel the heat; I feel the pain.
Bubbles, bubbles, in my brain,
When will they come back again?
I saw a ship; its mast was tall,
I'm at the top, about to fall.
I scan the deck, I look, I weep,
The fucking water is so deep.
Bubbles, bubbles, in my brain,
I feel the heat; I feel the pain.
Bubbles, bubbles, in my brain,
When will they come back again?
Rolling waves crash on the deck,
I feel his hands around my neck.
Albert lurches, the timbers chill,
I need a drink, a fucking pill.
Bubbles, bubbles, in my brain,
I feel the heat; I feel the pain.
Bubbles, bubbles, in my brain,
When will they come back again?
Falling fast I'm falling down,
A splash, a scream, about to drown.

*Save me, Albert, I'm getting old,*
*Save me, Albert, from the cold.*
*Shiver me timbers, bubbles be gone,*
*Shiver me timbers, it won't be long.*

Of course Damian hadn't a fucking clue what the song was about, but he was sure that Thomas was desperate to release the oppressive bubbles that were chilling his brain, or he was completely off his fucking rocker.

Thomas turned to strong drugs to silence the ever-present sound of Albert's pea-shaped voice. Doctor after doctor prescribed stronger drugs that sent Thomas into a spiral of weirdness that saw him slip in and out of sanity. He still loved his pork pies, his random tat and of course his cars, but at times he would seem distant. This could be because Damian lived in Birmingham, but Anne was also aware of these apparent lapses into madness, pushing Thomas to do stranger and stranger things. He never harmed himself or others, but he could present Anne with issues that at times were beyond her realms of understanding. Damian would speak with his father on the phone, several times a week, and each time Thomas would recount strange happenings, adopting a range of accents and personas. There was nothing that Damian could do, so he did nothing.

# Food, glorious food

Road trips and new vistas were never far away now that Damian had access to a working car and the ability to steer in a straight line. Thanks to a small loan, Damian had purchased, on the recommendation of Thomas, a Ford Catflap, a small family car with many hidden doors and no obvious place to have a shit whilst on the move. Resplendent in a blueish hue, the Catflap was nowhere near the pinnacle of motoring comfort. It didn't even purr. What he needed was somewhere to go.

He set his heart on a gastronomic tour of the local area to fully experience the delights the local culinary scene had to offer. He packed a small notebook, a road map and several pencils, and then started the Catflap and hit the open road. His first destination was a small eatery he had noticed several weeks ago as he was returning from a long evening at the wart clinic, poring over several troublesome warts that had flared up on an old running injury. Just around the corner from the clinic was Hilda's All-day Bistro, a slum of an establishment, resplendent with period features on display in the window. There was a life-size drawing of a Victorian goose egg, partially boiled, along with a gas lamp dangling precariously from a rusty bracket above the door. On entering the establishment, Damian was greeted by an urchin with cherub-like cheeks, scuffed knees and a Victorian gait. At the far end of the bistro was a small serving hatch, behind which stood Hilda, ladle in hand, scooping beans from a large tin into a rusty pan, ready for frying. Hilda had probably been attractive in her younger years, but she looked a little drawn and haggard as she wiped bean juice from her cigarette, careful not to knock the ash into the yummy beans. The aroma of cheap pork fat wafted across the seating area, sparsely populated with degenerates and vitamin-D-deficient customers. The lighting was pallid, giving the whole interior an eerie, undead ambience. Damian ordered the breakfast surprise, cheap at only £ 1.39 including a pot of tea and two slices of unspecified bread product. Taking his seat by the window, Damian took out his road map, planning out his route to the next eatery. A couple of hours on the road would give him enough time to digest Hilda's finest, and the Catflap always worked better with the wind in his hair, ears back and roaring down the byways of nowhere land.

After a short wait, Hilda arrived at Damian's table with an array of fried pork products, possibly some eggs and a huge pan of beans, for flavour. Devouring the meal wasn't a possibility, as Hilda had no cutlery to speak of, so rudimentary spoons and old knitting needles served as knife and fork. Skewering beans proved an enjoyable way to take away the pain of digesting the indigestible. Hilda might have offered quantity, with copious amounts of meaty gristle, but cooking was certainly not a priority at the Bistro. Damian quickly visited the toilets, made a brief deposit and left. It could only get better, or so he thought.

Next up was Pete's Pie, Pork and Pea Emporium, a celebration of all things pie, pastry and pulse related. Set in the sumptuous grounds of Bradford's third oldest abattoir, Pete's was a glorious monument to sloth and inactivity. Bedecked with period pastry and peas from across the globe, the establishment reeked of festering flavours intent on entering the gut. Pete's was the sort of institution that was far too often overlooked or closed down due to hygiene standards, but scrape off the thick veneer of grime, and underneath the inquisitive diner could experience a truly riotous mix of meat, crust and percolated peas. A cacophony of enjoyment hit Damian as he entered Pete's, with happy diners in the adjacent fast-food outlet greedily eating fried burgers and saturated chips. Meanwhile, the diners inside Pete's were a more sedentary crowd, who preferred the slow approach to service and food. If a pea needed twenty-four hours to steep, then so be it. If a pie crust needed to ferment, then those twenty-four hours were hours of valuable flavour time. If you preferred your pork served the old way, with the harder bits of the animal included, then Pete's was the place. Pete's had been serving pie-based products for nearly half a century, and some of the fillings were bordering on foetid, giving them a historic taste, and would not be out of place in a morgue or care home. The prices had risen over the years, but quality had been sacrificed to maximise profits, so quite often pie crust would be nothing more than crisp newspaper cuttings mixed with a ladle of lard. Despite this, customers continued to flock to the beacon of bacon. Aficionados of pies would hold meetings in its cramped dining area, and it was a must-see for any pie lover. Damian was keen to sample a Pete's Platter, which was a selection of pies served swimming in peas. Amongst the pies served with the platter was a 'Rudolph Mess', made entirely of antlers; the 'Slain', so called because many things were sacrificed to fill it; and the 'Bruiser', which was so dense that it could bruise the stomach if eaten too quickly. Another feature of Pete's was the in-house radio station, which broadcast pie melodies all day, every day. Pete was known to take to the decks from time to time, picking out pie-themed songs for tuneless diners. Classics such as...

*Why my Pie, Delilah... Frank Fillet and the Fins*
*I cooked it Pie way... Jose Del Pont & and his Band*
*Show me Pies, show me Sweet little Pies... Heysham and the Coattails*
*Pie – This can't be love...? Von Helan*
*Lucy ate my Pie with diamonds... The Heffers*

There was a poem, written by Pete, which is a beautiful lament for the pie and the lost world of pie production. It is produced below:

## Merciful Pie!

*Merciful pie, oh pie of the north,*
*Bringer of comfort, as I sally forth.*
*Rich with your blessings, sumptuous you,*
*So many fillings, and health-giving too.*

*Merciful pie, slay thee my hunger,*
*Make me look lithe and forty years younger.*
*Bountiful crust, so rich and so crumbly,*
*You lead me; I serve thee, ever so humbly.*

*Merciful pie, oh friend of the pea,*
*Perfect with beer, or a fresh pot of tea.*
*Content is the one, who savours your taste,*
*Eat every morsel, not a crumb must we waste.*

*Ring all the doorbells, knock on the doors,*
*Come get your pie, crawl on all fours.*
*A pie that can save, that can lift up your soul,*
*A meal in itself, all served in a bowl.*

*Save me, protect me, cherish my gut,*
*A pie in the morning, no if nor no but.*
*Facing the world, with lard in my heart,*
*The day is complete, right from the start.*

*Merciful pie, oh merciful pie,*
*Stay with me now, 'til the day that I die.*
*Merciful pie, oh merciful pie,*
*Don't ever leave, for sure I will cry.*

Damian loved a good lament and was moved to clear the way for the paramedics whose defibrillator was kept under the counter due to its regular use. The platter was a mountain of meat and crust, swimming in peas and awash with prehistoric aromas, producing a smell reminiscent of cardiologists. Ploughing his way through the eminent crust, Damian soon came to the conclusion that his good eye was way too big for his worried stomach, and he only managed two bites of the 'Slain' and a slosh of tepid peas before he began to get pie sweats. Deciding that discretion was the better part of valour, he asked for a doggy bag (which was also a pie filling) and left Pete's place somewhat sturdier.

His next stop in this journey into gluttony was a recently opened vegetarian restaurant which offered meat-free dishes to first-timers. If, like Damian, you considered vegetarianism a weird cult but did not want to appear too judgemental, the next eatery offered virgin veggies the opportunity to experience hunger at reasonable prices.

Jumping in the Catflap, he took the short drive to the local allotment, where a group of enterprising gardeners had pooled their love of vegetables and their knowledge of the catering scene to open the Bean and Scone, a wholefood establishment with only half the calories. Designed to look ramshackle and grubby, the Bean and Scone was the brainchild of budding poet and lover of most things green, Samson O'Grady, retired paratrooper and green-fingered hero. Using his knowledge of armed combat, stealth and camouflage, Samson had created a wonderfully esoteric venue, with stuffed vegetables mounted on the walls, pictures hung depicting scenes of a wonderfully bucolic vegetarian wonderland and a 'no meat' sign hanging above the toilet door. It was obvious to Damian that his taste buds were entering a war zone, with items on the menu that echoed a wartime battle report. At the top of the menu, which was actually referred to as the casualty list, was the 'Missing in Action', a diced vegetable dish served on a mini hospital bed, with a rich blood-red sauce that could well have been blood, or beetroot juice. The next item was the 'Take no prisoners — Give no Quarter', a two-pound hunk of patty, infused with spices and chilli that was sure to encourage a rapid retreat to the toilet. There were several items all with references to shrapnel, wounds and festering blisters, but the items at the very bottom, under the specials, were a 'Critical but Stable', and a 'Missing in Traction'. Both dishes intrigued Damian, so in the spirit of adventure and sadism, he decided to order both, reasoning that if the worst did actually come to the worst, he was only two miles from Thomas and Anne's house, so decamping the dishes would be quite rapid and not too painful. He took a seat by the bust of Percy Thrower and waited for his gourmet selection of green goodness. After what seemed like just over ten minutes, a waitress headed towards him, steering a heavily laden hostess trolley. Atop the wheeled chariot were two domed platters, their contents hidden from prying eyes and hygiene inspectors. The waitress arrived at Damian's table and began to regale him with a detailed explanation of the ingredients and cooking process of each dish. The 'Critical but Stable' was a melange of overripe vegetable, stewed for just under a month, and then fricasseed with abandon. The caramelisation gave the whole dish a sweet/sickly undertone, and if you were able to see past the smell, the flavour was not too horrendous. The 'Missing in Traction' was an elaborate sculpture of root vegetables depicting a dying soldier, with hideous carrot-inflicted injuries. The tableau was impressive, if a little on the raw side, and once Damian had swallowed down the bile that was waiting to leave, he tucked in with as much enthusiasm as a man who has already eaten two very large meals since the start of the day. He soon realised that vegetarians, if not misguided, were not all ex-paratroopers and might well produce better dishes that would appeal to a wider market. Leaving the establishment, his stomach advised his brain that maybe no more nourishment was needed, so he guided the Catflap to his parent's house and spent a very satisfying thirty minutes recycling the digested and reflecting on the current state of food outlets in and around Bradford. In the late '40s, Bradford had been a hotbed, but after several severe winters and a decline in taste, the current situation was depressing. It was almost impossible to get a cheap, tasty and nutritious meal without running the gauntlet of listeria, salmonella or the shits. Thankfully, Anne always had a ready supply of turnips, pies and cupcakes, so Damian wouldn't starve any time soon.

# Pilot episode

Thomas's ailments and hypochondria were well documented, and his efforts to cure insignificant niggles and alike had occupied too much of his time. From an attack of loose earwax that left him unbalanced, to a weekend bout of hysterical hiccups which interrupted his chain-smoking, Thomas had visited a range of quacks, hypnotic acupuncturists and misguided charlatans. Anne had lived with this rolling rollercoaster of illness, and pipe in hand, refused to be drawn on the seriousness of each complaint unless Thomas was at death's door, in which case she might have called an ambulance if the mood for a quiet life took her fancy.

It was the golden era of TV game shows, so when Thomas noticed a small advert for a new TV game show, his interest was piqued when health and illness were mentioned. The game show had the working title of 'You Name It, I've Got It', a medical/sickness-based game show where the winner would possibly extend their existence by as much as three months, thanks to a range of glamorous healthcare prizes on offer. The basic premise of the show was for contestants to compete to see who had the most outrageous, incurable and downright disgusting health issues that medical science has turned its back on. Prizes were promoted as mildly beneficial to positively wasteful.

Remarkably, Thomas got through the first two stages of the selection process thanks to a very bad head cold and an ingrowing, fungal-based rash, which appeared from nowhere one Saturday afternoon (Anne put it down to anxiety and too many pies the previous Tuesday). He had also sent in an x-ray of a walrus to demonstrate his bilious stomach. He was invited to a large disused office suite in central Leeds to meet the producers, where they would see if he really was living a miserable existence

— a prisoner to ailments that most people would shrug off as just being unfortunate by-products of a diabolical diet and lifestyle choices.

The producers were very impressed with Thomas's ability to speak confidently about a range of ailments that were, quite frankly, fucking ridiculous. Thomas was able to produce photographic evidence of an abrasive personality which had resulted in a violent outbreak of hives on his left ankle, written confirmation that his toes were in the wrong order thanks to an innumerate foot surgeon who operated on his club foot when he was still a babe in arms and testimony from Anne and two of her children that his eyes would change colour during periods of high temperature, removing his ability to distinguish between right and wrong and leaving him tired and drawn. He also possessed, wrapped in greaseproof paper, samples from previous infections that had resulted in immediate dismissal from a position in a pie shop. One of the specimens was a greenish, flesh-like material which had an uncanny resemblance to a half-chewed midget gem. The clincher for the producers was Thomas's availability; he was on call day and night and could muster an illness with as little as thirty minutes notice. He was duly signed up and recording of the show would start in two weeks' time. In the meantime, Thomas was given £3.48 towards transport costs and asked to dress like a sick person on the day of filming. He was overjoyed.

The night before filming was due to start, Thomas had a serious attack of cold feet, which he believed could be attributed to erratic circulation in the ankle area — another ailment to add to a very long list. Anne calmed his already outwitted nerves with a restful cup of strong tea and a soothing pork pie. Thomas had spent all afternoon trying to strike the right note when it came to his appearance. He wanted to look mildly sick but not quite knocking on death's door. He wanted to exude an air of stoic indifference to a baffling array of unexplainable illnesses. Thomas was confident that a smart pair of grey slacks would suggest he was a man in command of his own waterworks but expected to be taken with a stomach ulcer or a bilious episode at any moment.

His choice of oversized jumper was intended to demonstrate weight loss, whilst two days growth of beard offered a sneak preview of a man who knew his end was near and so had resigned himself to looking like a careworn vagrant.

On the day of the filming, Thomas and Anne set off in the new car, a Ford Hippo (roomy, not too quick but able to ford shallow rivers), hoping to snaffle some of the free grub that would be available. Thomas was under the impression that all of the complimentary food would be high in fat and low in life-enhancing qualities. He was keen to sample a deep-fried pork pie and rammed the Hippo into fourth gear as he accelerated his way to medical mayhem.

At the studios/disused abattoir, Thomas and Anne were greeted by a flunky who introduced himself as Graham Sore-Point, a dogsbody who was there to ensure that Thomas didn't eat too much or make himself too ill. There were some disclaimers and waivers to sign without reading, and introductions to the other contestants. There were five other unstable types all vying for the top prize, and Thomas eyed his competitors with a mixture of contempt, envy and desperation; some of these fuckers looked at death's door. Thomas and Anne were introduced to Selma Sole, a cheap-looking health hazard with open sores on her arms, flaky skin either side of her miniscule eyes and a limp that left her unable to easily navigate sharp left turns. Selma was a lifelong smoker who had inhaled her first fag as a five-year-old whilst employed as a proxy smoker for pregnant ladies. She had gone on to work as a human guinea pig for the animal pharmaceutical industry. She was immune to most bovine and equine illnesses and had spent the last ten years living in a stable-cum-shed, shared with two old nags and a Friesian called Meg. She also claimed that she had fifty mouth ulcers that made biscuit consumption a living hell and three in-growing hairs on her back that were in danger of piercing her very fragile heart. She was thirty years old and had a full head of hair.

Thomas and Anne were then introduced to two supposedly conjoined twins, Frank and Earnest Fibb, who had quite obviously used strong horse glue to stick their forearms together; it was obvious as they still had their jumpers on. The 'twins' maintained that their lives had been one long roller-coasting carousel of misery and ill-health. Frank had suffered from outrageous warts from a young age which had spread onto Earnest, who had then developed an allergy to concerted effort or action. Their lives had been overtaken by inertia, and as a result their ankles had ceased to function, hence the reinforced roller blades which gave them limited mobility. Earnest also claimed to have an overwhelming desire to eat too much, and it was only thanks to Frank that his weight had remained at a constant thirty-one stone. Frank was stick thin and was liable to snap if Earnest fell the wrong way. Frank had very unique dietary requirements, refusing to eat anything which wasn't red. He had spent the last five months eating only tomatoes and the occasional scotch bonnet, ruining any hope of a toilet-free day.

As Thomas enjoyed his fourth deep-fried pie, he was approached by a short fellow wearing what appeared to be a tin foil bowler hat and wetsuit. This was Owen Tocircumstances, a pallid excuse for life who immediately began to cough as if his lungs were desperate to see the light of day. After what seemed like five minutes, Owen explained that he suffered from unexplainable bouts of coughing and had a limp tongue. This had prevented him from enjoying the delights of ice cream, and he had visited several misinformed alternative therapists who had applied unguents and a brace to his tongue in the belief that it would somehow resolve the many deeper issues he was facing. When asked to explain the wetsuit, Owen maintained that water was a silent killer that had limited his life to sporadic bathing and dry climates. He lived in a makeshift cave just off the M62 near Leeds and could often be seen in his local supermarket purchasing roll after roll of tin foil to protect his fragile brain from toxic radio waves. Another fucking nutter!

As Anne availed herself of complimentary pipe tobacco, Thomas was hijacked at the tea urn by Walter Grope, a man who possessed very long arms. Walter wore ill-fitting shirts that only covered a third of his extensive arms. He was uncomfortable with his arms and adopted a tree-like stance to try and alleviate the pain from having arms longer than his legs. He was adept at swinging and reaching but found running a drag. He had worked as a part-time shelf stacker for many years and was eager to find some relief from the constant infamy of having arms ill-suited to most clothing. Thomas found Walter a tragic figure and assured him that he would be clapping on his behalf if Walter got through to the final round, or 'Death's Door Face-Off'.

The format of the show was very simple; each contestant had to perform everyday tasks and explain how the ailment/imagined sickness impeded their life. Points would be given for frowns, grimaces and groans. Bonus points would be awarded for collapsing and remaining conscious. If any contestant collapsed and slipped into a coma, they would be carted off and treated by a registered nurse who was loitering in the wings. Round one was all about staying upright and conscious, but round two really was designed to push the medical oddities to the limit. Each contestant had to perform a vigorous workout, and rather than points, tablets and unguents were awarded. So it was vital for each contestant to really push their bodies to the limit. On completion of the workout, the contestant with the least interventions would be carted off and treated by a registered psychiatrist for delusion and given some strong antidepressants. Round three was the quick-fire round, where against the clock, each contestant had to list the symptoms, real or imagined, of their most debilitating ailment. Only the top two would go onto the final round. The final deathmatch was a head-to-head between the strongest (or weakest, depending on how you looked at it) contestants. Each contestant was required to re-enact a serious medical episode, using real doctors, and the audience voted to see who deserved treatment and who should be left on a gurney waiting for an elusive specialist.

Thomas breezed through the first round, demonstrating frowns and grimaces that were all too real to Anne, who had lived with this nonsense for years. His ill-fitting elbows made his attempt at closing curtains a painful exhibition of ineffectiveness coupled with real groans has he grunted and groaned with the Dralons. Thomas collapsed twice, once when his pick-and-mix toes caused him to overbalance as he emptied a washing machine. Fortunately, he remained conscious, even managing to sort the smalls from the whites, so received maximum points. The twins, Frank and Earnest, fell at the first hurdle when the glue binding them gave way and they decided that there must be a better way to get their fifteen minutes. Walter made a strong start, deliberately attempting to thread a needle with his arms fully extended, knowing that without his glasses it was bloody impossible. The audience lapped up his contorted expressions and whimsical groans; he was a top class sicknote. Selma scored highly as she attempted to sweep a patch of linoleum floor, all the while flakes of who knows what making her job a never-ending cycle of scratching, sweeping and weeping. She was a hardcore sicko who seemed to revel in discomfort. Owen spent the first round coughing, as he attempted, with little success, to make a cup of tea. Germs, spittle and phlegm all made it a horrendous spectacle, and as he tried to add the milk, a huge ball of lung appeared to land in the cup, leading to a disconcerting cry and some very pitiful whimpering.

Round two was a challenge for Thomas as he was used to being stoical in the face of hypochondria. Thomas, after a quick pep talk with Anne, immediately asked for a cocktail of tablets that might well have given temporary relief to his elbows, but he also insisted that he be given a brace for his elbows and round-the-clock bandages. He then produced swabs which seemed to resemble congealed fat, maintaining that he needed an urgent wax transplant otherwise his ears would dry out. He then fell over, requiring a sticking plaster for a grazed eyebrow, and omitted a constant hum that he attributed to the bees nesting in his sub-conscious. Despite his worries before the start of the round, he scored highly and was safely through to the next round. Walter really shone in this round, with a masterful minute of bumps, bangs and abrasions that left him a bloody mess in need of some sort of evaluation. It took the nurse five minutes to stop Walter's nosebleed, brought on by a careless flick of his left arm, and when he accidentally tripped himself with his right arm, he twisted his ankle and needed two pairs of strong socks to remain upright. Selma made a strong showing as she desperately scratched at already oozing sores and needed the nurse to apply mittens so as to avoid any blood-borne viruses. She complained as she walked, demanding a minimum of three different walking sticks and medical insoles to alleviate the pain from the blisters on her soul. Owen, who seemed to have coughed his last, was rushed to hospital after he inexplicably died. It transpired that he was suffering from a debilitating case of near-death coughing, but doctors had misdiagnosed.

The quickfire round was a blur, as Thomas reeled off an endless stream of symptoms for his ill-fitting elbows. He was able to bamboozle his opponents with his knowledge of the workings of his elbows and his detailed research into the side effects of strong painkillers. His delivery was flawless as he mentioned light-headedness, distorted reality, myopia, vertigo, agoraphobia, irritating bowels, over-anxious eating, odorous earwax and the one symptom that seemed to really wow the audience — the inability to wave with enthusiasm: a life-changing life sentence.

He was through to the final and was to be joined by Walter, who had a very clear grasp of his long arms. Walter wrapped his opponent in knots with his arms, giving details of the common symptoms of overly long arms, which to the laymen would appear to be common sense. He rattled on about a pain that started at one end of his arm and would last until it went away at the end of his other arm. He mentioned cold hands, unbrushed teeth, oral hygiene in general, and his lack of a life partner. He was a wizard with an encyclopaedic understanding of limb-related pains, discomforts and assorted arm impediments. The audience applauded for a full thirty seconds, rousing recognition of a man in control of his faculties, if not his arms.

Selma seemed to wilt under scrutiny, showing a weakness for gibberish which she attributed to a childhood smoking accident, and was unable to stay focused. She blamed her lack of coherence on ingrowing stupidity which she had first contracted whilst working as a filing clerk at the Home Office. She had hit a wall, but thankfully she was okay, although she did flake more skin, losing an incredible thirteen pounds during the recording. The skin was swept and given to a local charity for redistribution to the needy. She had fought the good fight, but had fallen at the final hurdle, mainly due to her club foot and lazy eye. She was last seen scratching a living as a part-time manicurist at a working men's club in Wakefield, infecting others with her disdain for personal hygiene.

Thomas and Walter were through to the final, and as Anne watched from the wings, she could see that Thomas was seventy-three per cent focused, intent on leaving with nothing less than a modicum of dignity and the knowledge that in medical circles at least, he would be held up as an example. Thomas had thought long and hard about ailments and incidents of medical calamity, some might say too much, but it was his moment under the spotlight, and he was determined to glimmer brightly and fade a little. His focus would be on his elbows, a lifelong sentence that had left him a shell of a husk of a man. His re-enactment was from an incident that had happened whilst serving in the navy during the war.

It had been a calm sea that greeted the crew of his ship, HMS Flotsam, as they patrolled and swept the channels for mines. Thomas was on the stern near the front of the ship, wistfully wondering when the war would end, when he heard what sounded like an engine. Scanning the sky, he thought he saw that dreadful beast, the Stuka dive-bomber. He had to warn his crew, who for some reason were at the other end of the ship looking at newspapers, fish, each other, but not the sky. Thomas had to catch their attention, and the only way possible was a strong, powerful wave. The sort of wave that would make people stop and stare; the sort of wave that would wake a sleeping giant, the sort of wave that would etch itself onto the retinas of all those who witnessed it. As Thomas went to wave, it became apparent that his elbows were misbehaving. Try as he might, he couldn't wave. He flapped, he slapped, he even shouted, but no wave was forthcoming. Desperate and afraid for his comrades, Thomas writhed around on the deck, unable to summon a wave, his elbows firmly glued to his midriff. The plane drew closer, its engines roaring, yet still the crew were oblivious, focused on the fish and newspapers. Time would judge if Thomas could have acted differently, but as he ran along the ship, desperately hoping his elbows would see sense, he was aware of a flash and a thunderous noise and then nothing. When he was rescued from the brine, he was told that he only survived thanks to a life jacket, the bomb being a dud, and the quick thinking of the crew, who managed to stop him from falling off the ship. Unfortunately, during the mayhem, the ship had hit a British mine and had been destroyed. Oh, the pain. If only his elbows had functioned like they should, none of this would have happened. That non-wave haunted him, and it was a brave person who didn't wipe away a smirk when they witnessed three partially-clothed doctors, a vet, two nurses and a border collie attempting to recreate the pain that Thomas felt that day. It nearly brought the house down.

Walter had a lot to do, but he was a man who could stretch and twist the truth to fit the emotions of others. His tale had begun at the Wakefield and District 'Under 29s' amateur swimming gala, a righteous affair of swimming and splashing. Walter had been entered into the relay race. He assumed it was because of his graceful butterfly, which had drawn admiring glances from those who knew a thing or two about butterfly. He had purchased some new trunks, invested in a towel, and even gone to the trouble of having a bath. He was as excited as a man with long arms could be, finally being accepted into the cloistered world of swimming and galas. On the day of the gala, Walter arrived early so as to iron his trunks and practise his splash off or start. His was an unconventional style, and he had never raced before, preferring instead to swim alone in the canals of West Yorkshire. As the start approached, Walter felt the butterflies in his stomach (how appropriate) and was having second thoughts about competing;

maybe he should stick to the canals and mill pools. He remembered the words of his swimming coach, and these seemed to inspire and strengthen his resolve. His swimming coach, Willy Drown, had always said to Walter that it wasn't the length of the stroke but the length he would go to in order to win. Walter had an incredibly long butterfly stroke and was determined to finish in the top four places. It was now or never. As he waited for the starting gun, he became aware of the eyes burning into the back of his head. Someone approached him and demanded to see his arms. Walter obliged and he was then frog-marched (which is a non-regulation stroke) into the referee's tent where he was told in no uncertain terms that his arms were nonstandard and therefore, he would not be able to compete. Walter was crestfallen, his spirit broken, his heart weeping. As he dragged his arms away from the gala, he swore he would never swim competitively again. The pain that day was sharp and bitter, and Walter was hoping to tap into the audience's love for a plucky long-armed loser. For his re-enactment he had asked for a swimming pool, and when he was told this was out of the question, he had to make do with a children's paddling pool and two nurses as his competitors. It lost some of its impact, in part due to neither of the nurses being able to swim, but he still got a very warm reception, and it was difficult to decide who deserved to win top spot.

As Anne and Thomas waited for the votes to be counted, Thomas was sure that whatever the result, he could walk away with his head held high, thanks to the free neck brace that was given to all the contestants at the start of the day. The sense of anticipation was akin to waiting to hear if you are going to be overcharged for a dodgy haircut. Thomas gnawed on a lucky pie, and Walter flapped nervously, omitting a low hum, trance-like. The host bounded on to the rickety stage and the lights went down. The winner would walk away with a top of the range first aid kit, a year's subscription to 'Hypochondria Monthly' and the knowledge that their ailments were truly jaw-dropping. The loser would receive three months' supply of bandages, a six-month subscription to 'Get Back to Work You Shirker', and the knowledge that their shirking, although good, wasn't good enough.

The silence wrapped itself around the audience, and not even a pitiful cough could be heard. When Walter's name was called out there was genuine apathy, and the audience sat in silence, stunned by the stupidity of the show. Walter was jubilant and his face was covered with something that resembled a smile. Thomas, gracious in defeat, threw his lucky pie to the ground and demanded to see a doctor as he felt unnatural spasms in his elbows. As Walter collected his glittering prizes, Thomas was whisked away by a flunky and given his prize, a note for his doctor, and the taxi fare to get him home.

Walter went on to gain minor celebrity as the face (and arms) of Bryant's Patented Elbow Pads. He toured the country extolling the benefits of strong elbow pads and associated arm support, never realising that it was Thomas who really needed the elbow support. Walter, single for most of his life, married Linda Apron, Britain's premier health visitor, and they settled down but never had kids. Walter died in 2011 in a freak arm-wrestling incident, suffering distended bones and flapping that proved to be fatal. Thomas felt no ill-will toward Walter and used the bandages to fashion a very nice shirt and trouser set. The magazines went unread as he was too ill to think. Damian was extremely proud of Thomas, believing that yet again Thomas had excelled in underachieving.

# Thought he would be dead by now

Hard as it was to believe, Thomas was now seventy, and the family wanted to give a suitable surprise to demonstrate their love of pies and tat. Anne was unsure as to what would be a suitable location for such a celebration, so came up with the idea of sealed bids from Stephen, Janine, Paul and Damian as to how they believed Thomas would like to spend his birthday and any special or original ideas to nullify any possibility of Thomas falling asleep. Anne laid down specific guidelines to ensure that the bidding process was fair and above board, and she gave the children ten days to produce their bids. Thankfully, due to Anne never throwing anything away, not even rubbish, those bids still exist, and are reproduced below to demonstrate how not to win a father's love.

## Sealed Bid 1 – Stephen

*It is my intention to make this day truly regrettable, not for Dad, but for all those who aren't invited. With this in mind, my first decision was to choose a venue that would not only reflect Dad's idiosyncratic nature, but also be very cheap. Dad's love of tat has sustained him through illness, a world war, several near misses in his Austin Claxton, and of course his ongoing battle with ill-fitting elbows. As a boy I was unaware of the need for tat, believing it to be cheap crap that satisfied the avarice of tasteless idiots, but I now realise that tat has a deeper significance, and if a love of tat is nurtured in a child it will sustain a mind regardless of life's adversities. It is also, it has to be said, readily available and bloody cheap. Therefore, I believe that a tat-themed birthday celebration would answer several questions.*

*1/ Will the present be expensive? No, it will be cheap tat. No one wants to fork out a fortune for something that will be both useful and* possess sentimental value. Is it not better to buy some cheap tat, such as a part-worn iron, that if is unwanted or shit, does not represent a huge outlay?

2/ Does Dad like parties? No, but if he can be persuaded that his party is being held in a rundown second-hand emporium, where he is free to browse that tat whilst still enjoying the delights of a pork pie and a strong cup of tea he will be more willing to don those festive long johns and party like it's 1899.

3/ Is our budget minuscule? Well, if we each throw in a tenner, we could buy a good selection of tat, wrap it in Dad's favourite newspaper and then have a slap-up fish supper from the corner chippy near to where Dad was born, the Rancid Fat.

These are my suggestions and I hope you look at them with a non-judgemental eye, and I sincerely hope that whoever's bid is successful, chips play some part in the catering.

Your loving son
Stephen


## Sealed Bid 2 — Janine

As you know only too well, Dad has suffered many health scares, and I believe any celebration should be as low key as possible. The last thing we want is the old fucker to die on his 70th birthday with pork pie in one hand and tea dripping from his still warm corpse. This may sound heartless and cruel, but I genuinely believe that a sedate and almost non-celebration is the right choice for a man whose heart is as rickety as a house built from three-day old ice cream wafers.

It is my hope that Dad could have a quiet morning in bed, perhaps until midday, then on rising he could perhaps have a lukewarm tea with some low-fat dripping on toast, just so as to break him into to what lay ahead. Following another four-hour nap, perhaps we could present him with a cheap card and the promise that if he survives the year we might, and I must stress might, buy him some sort of gift for under ten quid. I would rather not invite any of his friends as they are mostly dead, presenting a logistical nightmare. I understand that grandchildren should be invited, but as they are so young it is probably safe to say that they will not remember the event in a week's time, let alone twenty years' time.

In the evening, weather permitting, Dad could stare from the window vacantly, perhaps with his favourite wireless tuned into the shipping forecast. He would retire at seven thirty p.m. and rise the following day, a little older but not suffering from the aftershocks of an ill-thought-out birthday celebration. Let us not forget that surprise parties for the over 70s are the third biggest killer in the UK according to 'Grump', the magazine for the miserable old bastard. I know my siblings will offer more exciting possibilities but let us not forget that those three men are turgid wastrels.

Your loving daughter,
Janine

## Sealed Bid 3 – Paul

Smiling and wood; that's what would make Dad the perfect day. I know a man who knows a man who met a man who had a birthday at Yorkshire's premier wood museum, and he hasn't stopped smiling since. Wood is the glue that joins us as a family. We came from wood and when we die we return to the soil as wood, or in wood, or near wood, or at least we may well have seen some wood. I took the liberty of visiting the wood museum, just to get a feel for the place and enquire as to how much a premium museum would charge for a 70th birthday party for a man who loves pies and has an affinity with most wood-based furniture. The chap there, Elmore Birch, a sprightly twig of man was as helpful as a sprightly twig of a man could be, offering wood-based answers to all my wood-based questions. They have a forest of exhibits that truly are wooden, and inside the event centre, located in the car park near the gents' toilet, there is ample room for thirteen fully grown adults or saplings to celebrate any significant birthday. Catering is done off site as there is no power supply (as yet, although they do have a wood powered generator), and they offer a range of wood-themed pies, from the Oak 'n' Acorn, an ancient pie made from wood shavings and leaves, to the sophisticated Ebony and Ivory pie, filled with all manner of things that costs lots of money. Dad will love the venue, and as it is only 20 minutes from his doctors, if he were to have an unfortunate turn, or get a twig stuck in his throat, then help is not too far away. On leaving, the happy birthday man or woman (not many women usually celebrate their birthday here) can have their portrait painted by the resident artist, Phil Stroke, which is then photographed and framed for the lucky recipient, all for a very reasonable £32.97. Dad has never really expressed a dislike of wood, so I think this offers an affordable way to celebrate what is, by any measure (imperial or metric) a fantastic achievement in reaching 70, when his diet and lifestyle is taken into consideration.

Your loving son,
Paul


## Sealed Bid 4 – Damian

Anne: can I call you Anne? Thomas, or Dad, as always been a man of three halves and several quarters. A jigsaw in search of a solution. A water slide with no obvious incline. A bike with a reluctant saddle. Knowing that he shies away from social gatherings where there is a chance of meeting fools and arseholes, I think the celebration should be a small family gathering, with invitations sent to a select few and plans only disclosed on a need-to-know basis.

I have thought long and hard about what would truly be a perfect setting for a man who has never had everything, and I have reached the conclusion that The Yorkshire Transport Centre would not only be the perfect venue, but also the perfect place to pick the perfect gift for a man who wants for many things. Established in 1971, the museum is an eclectic mix of cars that no rational person would buy unless they were picking at the holes of desperation in their life or were wanting in cash. Dad has faced adversity with his cars, and despite only having a rudimentary understanding of the combustion engine, he has strived to make a succession of shit cars work. What better way to celebrate that sacrifice than a day at the museum. Dad will be able to gawk at the inept designs of such vehicles as the Austin Frampton, one of only two cars ever to have the driving position as optional, and the Ford Flotsam, a car so light that when it was first launched it floated four miles before engineers were able to secure it to a very large shire horse. Dad marvels at such design, their names evoking a time when functionality was less important than a good name or round steering wheel.

The museum offers a range of packages to suit the most frugal of families, and with that in mind, I took the liberty of putting a £1.00 deposit (non-refundable) to secure their 'Wilderness Room', a beautiful room with a tiny mural of all the places that people could break down and possibly die through starvation. This would appeal to Dad's can't do attitude and also mean that we can really splurge on the choice of food. They offer a selection of menus, all located in poor design and unreliability. There's the cheap but cheerful 'Fucking Exhaust Special', which includes complimentary cutlery, the 'You Wanted a Bastard Tow bar', which can be vegetarian if the meat is removed, and my personal favourite, the 'We'll Have to Turn Back', a vomit-inducing smorgasbord of various offcuts of meat with some brown gravy. All menus come with a wipe clean option, and if we wanted to bring the odd pork pie to supplement their pitiful offerings, they are willing to turn a blind eye.

Dad can be an awkward bugger at times, but I hope my suggestion is treated with the same level of contempt afforded to my siblings' bids.

Your loving son,
Damian

Anne was a Guardian-reading, pipe-smoking, free-thinking cake woman, and on reading her children's suggestions, immediately discarded them, opting for her own plan. Anne always knew that Thomas would like to return to the restaurant where they had shared their first romantic meal. The Haunted Pie Bistro, three hundred yards from junction 29 of the M62, was originally an undertaker's overflow premises for the bodies that would not quite fit into their allotted coffin. Thomas was amused by this apparent reluctance to be buried, and when it was converted to a mid-market pie emporium in the late '50s, Thomas used a coupon to take Anne for a sumptuous meal of pie and peas. The staff, the food, the ambience — all represented everything that wasn't quite right with British catering in the '50s and 60s, and Thomas yearned for the days when gristle was a staple, when tepid peas were arranged in order of rawness on a plate and when a service charge was a fucking insult. He longed for the cut and thrust with an overweight waitress who exuded sweat and distemper. A return to such a restaurant would complete Thomas's culinary journey. Anne duly made the arrangements and booked a four-seater booth for the eleven guests who were expected to attend. Although the seating would be cramped, it would ensure that everybody got the opportunity to sit near the birthday boy.

On the allotted day, sometime in early October, Thomas and Anne drove there in his new car, a Ford Griddle, famed for its air conditioning and four functioning wheels. Damian was driving up from the Midlands, and his children were excited to see the old man. They had even gone to the trouble of drawing a very poor birthday card and buying £3.76 worth of vouchers for a pie shop of Thomas's choice. As the family assembled in the booth, it was obvious that some had been a little heavy-handed with the deodorant, and the dress code, not strictly enforced, meant that it was difficult to tell whether it was fancy dress or funeral attire. Thomas wore his customary blazer and tie, whilst Anne opted for a tweed three-piece, which set off her pipe beautifully. The menu was resplendent in grease and a forlorn search for flavour. As he scanned the menu, it was obvious that Thomas had forgotten his reading glasses, but fortunately Anne had remembered Thomas's magnifying glass, so he was able to inspect the restaurant for clues. Damian was eager to taste the delights of a café that had mythical status in the Carter household, and years later he still has flashbacks of that memorable menu. It is reproduced below for all those gourmets and social historians who might be eager to understand primitive food substances.

### The Haunted Pie Bistro- Bring your own napkin

#### Starters
*Drizzle of pea on a slice of bread with knife and fork*
*Pea soup with spoon*
*Melon & Pork Pate with knife (bread is extra)*
*Selection of savoury pie crumbs (use your hands)*

*Mains*
*Melange of Pie with a decadent Gravy (spoon provided)*
*Deep-Fried Peas with a crusty Pie of your choice (Pork)*
*Vegetable and Pork Pie Surprise (suitable for partial vegetarians)*
*Scales & Trotters (Fish Fingers and a Pie)*

*Dessert*
*Pie Souffle with Pork Ice cream*
*Jelly and Peas (straw provided)*
*Sweat Tea with a hint of pork*
*Some cheesy stuff*

Whilst Thomas was excited by the elaborate dishes on offer, some members of the family opted for the bread-and-butter option. Thomas ate like a king and was even given a doggy bag containing a souvenir, dog-shaped pork treat, and a pint of frozen mushy peas. It really was his birthday to end all birthdays.

# The enigma

Katie, or parasite three, or the Enigma, was Damian's youngest daughter, born on a windy March night when most sensible babies would have at least waited until the rain had stopped and the wind died down. Her bluish-green eyes, auburn hair and blank expression meant that it was very difficult to read exactly what she might be thinking. Later in life the Enigma would have part of her brain removed by a surgeon, part of her nose removed by a dog, and be the butt of all piss-taking, yet she was able to remain calm and enigmatic throughout. As an adult she would travel the world serving high altitude food to incontinent minds on many continents. Damian adored her as she could get him cheap fags.

Travel was in the Carter blood, a rich vein of passports and borders. Damian had toyed briefly with the idea of being a part-time, self-employed tour rep, offering wonderful breaks to woeful idiots whose lack of culture and geographical insight meant they would go anywhere if it was packaged. He had, with the help of Thomas, drawn up a list of destinations that would appeal to a range of travellers, with prices to suit all.

*Possible Destinations for Carter's Cartography: Re-drawing Travel.*

*1/ Boston: With its tree-lined fields and extensive turnip industry, Boston really is the destination for the budding vegetarian on a tight budgie. The locals, or Turnips, are a hardy breed, surviving on root vegetables and hope, welcoming tourists with a warmth that is hardly recognisable. Famed for their dour intolerance and rampant insularity, Turnips have a wonderfully blinkered view on life. Visitors to this hotspot of despair can expect to see houses, partially finished retail centres and general disrepair. A range of local tours may well be available* but priced to deter purchase. Getting to Boston is an arduous struggle, and many have died in the process. An international airport was mooted but deemed fucking stupid by those who had a slim grasp on reality. The busy hotel scene belies a torpid desolation that is unrivalled for miles, and the weekly pig hunt offers a glimpse of the sub-culture that anthropologists are desperate to study.

*Best time to go: Wednesday*

*Top attractions: life-sized statue of Sir Terrence Turnip, inventor of the turnip dicer.*

*Food and Drink: Harry's off-licence offers a range of cheap plonk and cider, along with cigarettes. There is also a very reasonably priced Belarusian takeaway on the Grantham Road.*

*Top Tip: take a shot gun for the pig hunt.*

*2/ Hastings: This bustling market town is only thirty miles from the sea, so is the ideal destination for sun worshippers and sand collectors. Brimming with people, it has been called the Venice of the south coast, with over three miles of river and brooks. The locals, better known as the 'Battles', love nothing better than welcoming bewildered visitors to their overcrowded town. In the '50s, many great Hollywood stars would spend their vacations lost in its baffling maze of streets, which were designed to confuse the Germans during World War Two. Hastings has seen many changes, and now has a fully functioning cash machine, a supermarket and a state-of-the-art bus stop. Famously, it was the scene of the Battle of Hastings, which, even three hundred years later, is remembered by locals as being bloody noisy.*

*Best time to go: after dark.*

*Top attractions: Sir Dave Belly's Sand Park and Museum. This magnificent world of sand will bring tears to anyone who has ever owned a bucket and spade. With interactive sand displays, an hourly sandstorm and a bouncy castle for the over 70s, it really is an hour wasted.*

*Food and Drink: the locals love nothing better than a 'Battle Bap', brimming with meaty bits and things; it's guaranteed to fill even the fattest. There is also a reasonably priced Peruvian takeaway on the Brighton Road.*

*Top tip: take a helmet.*

3/ *Malvern: Located on the east coast, Malvern really is the small jewel in a very poorly made ring that is probably fake. Famed for its healing waters and rolling competition, Malvern was the birthplace of eighteenth-century composer and artist, Sir Belton Braces. His seminal work, 'Ode to a Trouser Salesman', is still sung in the streets of Malvern most Friday evenings. The gothic town hall, rebuilt two years ago, is really nothing more than a building with doors and windows, and many visitors will feel short-changed. Located near a disused mortuary, Malvern's Museum of Modern Make-up is a real eye opener. Rammed to the rafters with obsolete eye pencils and mascara, it charts Malvern's role in the development of down-market make-up. During the English Civil war, Malvern famously supplied mascara to the Royalists, who as we all know, always wanted to look good.*

*Best time to go: when the mood takes you.*

*Top attractions: Malvern is awash with sewage, so why not spend an afternoon at the nearby Museum of Sewage. This small urinal of a museum offers visitors the chance to study shit up close. There are some rides for the kids, including the heart stopping 'Tunnel of Shit', guaranteed to bring a tear to your eye.*

*Food and drink: try one of Malvern's marvellous melon pies. Grown locally in Europe, the melons are prepared and then served. Locals go wild for these mushy meals. There is also a jerk chicken shack on the Leamington Road.*

*Top tips: wear oily undergarments for ease of use.*

4/ *Stockport: Built on the ruins of an Aztec burial ground, Stockport's main cemetery is about five miles from the town centre. Stockport has a very large Aztec community, so be sure to visit one of the many Aztec-themed shops, selling a range of Aztec-themed gifts and shite. Stockport is now a semi-retired town, with many people leaving the town due to lack of hope and road maps. An influx of Eskimos has seen a gentrification of parts of the industrial estates, but not many locals will eat seal or whale meat. There is a fascinating furniture shop on the outskirts of town, and anyone who loves sitting down can spend at least some time sitting down in Stockport.*

*Best time to go: during the rainy season.*

*Top attractions: Ronny Rollmop's Rug Shop is a magnet for those who like rugs, have bought a rug in the past, or may be considering buying a rug in the future. Whilst there, visitors can buy fish-based gifts from the extensive gift shop at prices that will make your eyes bleed. On the outskirts of town there is an Eskimo village, adjacent to an Aztec village, and both are worth visiting as you leave, if for no other reason than you will never return.*

*Food and drink: seal and whale are high on the menu in most of the restaurants, and diners can enjoy seal pie, seal taco and even seal pizza. Locals love the affectionately named 'Seal Pup Pie' rammed to the lid with fresh seal and sardines. There is a reasonably priced Alaskan bakery on the Sheffield Road.*

*Top tips: Dress to impress; wear a hat.*

*5/ Glastonbury: birthplace of music and mud, Glastonbury is about seventy-eight miles from Manchester, and can be reached by pony, horse or by foot. Situated at the confluence of the rivers Glass and Bury, it is often many feet under water. Locals are often very competent swimmers and may have webbed feet. The local honeybee also swims, and is the emblem used on 'Glastonbury Wine', a heady mixture of meths and alcohol that is manufactured by bees. The locals can often be seen sucking on a bee to get a taste of the intoxicating liqueur.*

*Best time to go: sometime in the past.*

*Top attractions: the Museum of Water, built at the confluence of the rivers, is often closed due to flooding, but when open, offers some water-based attractions that would moisten most appetites. On the outskirts of town there is a large jug factory, which is well worth avoiding if you suffer from a ceramic allergy.*

*Food and drink: the local speciality, is the Bee kebab, a mouth-watering mixture of bee and kebab. Eaten with a spicy sauce, the kebab is often eaten at lunchtime or other special occasions. There is a very reasonably priced Nigerian Noodle Bar on the Bristol Road.*

*Top tip: don't scratch when suffering from eczema.*

The guide was an instant talking point amongst the well-oiled and travelled, and soon Thomas and Damian were inundated with enquiries. Deciding to expand the venture, Thomas and Damian went on a road trip to research other possible destinations. Using Thomas's newly cleaned Austin Visor, so called because of its restricted view and dark green windows, they decided to travel further afield. There was a whole world out there, and both wanted to visit as many places as possible. First stop on this road trip of a half-life time: North Wales. The lakes and pastures of Wales had always fascinated Damian as a child, and the opportunity to experience this little corner of Wales was a gift-wrapped treat of travel. Arriving in the pretty seaside town of Rhyl, the two set about exploring its wide rolling cul-de-sacs, myriad dark alleys and herring museum. Rhyl, often referred to as the dead end of Wales, was originally the home of a very reclusive order of monks, led by the infamous Widebody the Unwitting, a devious and mendacious man who would often steal prayers from unsuspecting worshipers. Now all that remains of the order and its medieval monastery is a small retail park: The Wing and Prayer Retail Centre. Here unsuspecting shoppers can purchase monk-themed tat, cat food and ironmongery. Thomas and Damian were particular impressed with the architecture of Rhyl, and the 70s municipal advice bureau was a model of a dirge in concrete. The cuisine was underwhelming, mainly a mix of pungent pies, downtrodden fried food and a moth-eaten ice cream bar. Deciding that Rhyl was a bit of a shithole, the pair jumped in the Visor and headed north; Scotland the brave awaited.

Braving Scotland was a formidable enterprise for Thomas and Damian. Thomas did the bulk of the driving, but his ill-fitting elbows were a constant thistle in his ability to steer, and his muffled cries at the wheel were heart wrenching, reminiscent of a rutting stag. Arriving at the border, the formalities took longer than expected as Damian was unwilling to try shortbread without tea. A kindly police officer pointed out that there was no actual border, so the pair continued on to their destination: Loch Macanism. Described by the nineteenth century French poet, Antoine DuSpray, as the gateway to wilderness, the loch is the smallest in Scotland. Only half a mile long and less than two hundred yards wide, it is home to few fish and even fewer attractions. Lined by stunted shrubs and goats, it was often fly infested in summer and bleak beyond belief in a blizzard. Legend has it that an aquatic goat haunts the banks in search of solace, chewing up those visitors who are averse to hardship. Thomas and Damian were accustomed to hardship and decided to spend the night at the one hotel on its banks, The Goat and Loch.

Owner and part-time historian, Owen Tanothing, offered to give the pair a tour of the hotel, a wreck of a ruin with very little of note. On the ground floor was the old scullery, which had served as a catacomb in the last century, along with a milk churn that Bonnie Prince Charles reputably pissed in. Thomas lapped up the history, like a starving cat in search of a creamery; he was thirsty for facts to add to his travel guides. Taking the back stairs, they arrived at the master's chamber, or the Wee Willy Winkie suite, bedecked with tartan from every corner of Scotland. It was trial by colour, and soon Damian felt lightheaded with all the plaid. Along the corridor was the one working lavatory for ten miles, and it was only flushed twice a year and on Kenny Dalglish's birthday, the fourth of March, referred to locally as 'King Kenny's Day'. As they made their way up the winding staircase that also doubled up as a fireman's pole to the servants' quarters, Owen explained the significance of the roof, which until recently was partially open, due to funding issues, hence the indoor garden and moss growing in the corner. Legend had it that a fair maiden had been locked away in the attic, separated from her true love by a harsh uncle intent on locking away nieces. Even to this day, Owen refuses to contemplate marriage due to his appalling hygiene and rank odour. The guest accommodation, or annex, was situated five miles away in Owen's comfortable bungalow. With hot double glazing and running heat, the bungalow offered somewhere to rest their frazzled heads before they headed towards the Highlands in search of ruined hopes and dreams.

The Highlands: a wonderful and exotic place to visit. When Thomas crested Mount Meup in the Visor, the view that hit the pair was astonishing, even for a pair of travellers who had already seen the unbridled beauty of Rhyl. The Burden and Hope Distillery and Quaint Old Smokery was Scotland's oldest thrice bankrupted whisky and kipper producer, and as such had a partially stocked gift shop, and also offered an inexpensive tour to visitors and staff alike. Pulling up in the empty car park, it was obvious to them that the tour should be completed first before spending several minutes in the gift shop. Dennis Killmostthings had worked at the distillery for fifty-nine years, man and bairn, and what he didn't know about the business, the manager did. The heady smell of stale alcohol and wet fish lingered like an old relative left for dead in an armchair. The huge casks of semi-decomposing salmon offered a fleeting nasal clue as to what lay ahead. Cask after cask, after cask, after cask — each smellier than the previous. The whisky, which was actually produced in Japan, was shipped over in huge wooden bottles and then decanted into plastic barrels to be sold to wealthy Americans looking for a cheap hangover. Chief whisky taster and semi-retired lush, Dougie Stumble, knew very little of the intricacies of whisky, but was able to recommend several cheap hangover cures. His motley-faced and alcohol-infused head meant that at times he appeared incoherent and pissed, but his manner was that of a friendly drunk, not a punchy-punchy fighty drunk, which meant the tour was uneventful. Arriving at the gift shop, Thomas and Damian decided to splurge on goodies to take back to the parasites waiting on their return. Damian chose a decidedly dodgy pair of salmon-shaped slippers. Thomas spotted a salmon-shaped pipe which would fit well with Anne's drive to smoke more healthily. For the kiddies, Damian bought a selection of strong liqueurs in the belief that it would harden them to alcohol, plus they were very cheap, and two kilogrammes of slightly off salmon was thrown in at half price. Thomas bought a 'Guide to Alcohol and the Fishing Industry' for some light bedtime reading. The following day they were heading to some islands to experience knitting close up, so a leisurely drive awaited.

Thomas had been driving for many years, and his elbows had taken the brunt of sharp left turns and abrupt halts outside pie shops. The twisty and winding roads of Scotland were doing his elbows no favours, and they were forced to pull over at a knitwear outlet three miles from Oban. Thomas's aversion to wool and its minions is well documented, but Damian was keen for his father to see this misunderstood crop through fresh eyes. Maybe a tour of the production facilities would refresh in Thomas his love of wool and suppress his desire for nylon and rayon. Greeted by wool harvester in chief, Tammy Scratch, the pair were quickly shown some shoddy slides explaining how wool was grown in the olden days. Farmers, often knee-deep in shit, would plant baby sheep in the hope that lambs would grow, bringing hope and warmth. Quite often the crops would fail, many believing the bastard English had somehow despoiled the fertile ground. With developments in education and progress made in the battle against stupidity, the farmers were soon using hot houses to fast-track the wool harvest. Quite often sheep would be overcooked, or burnt, ruining the precious wool in the process. By the turn of the twentieth century, wool farming had made incredible progress, and when inventor Cleft McScrote developed the wool scrubber, it seemed that wool would once again be produced in quantities that few would care to dream of. Unfortunately, heavy bleeding and death meant many of the sheep died before wool could be taken from their blood-sodden carcasses. Nowadays, wool is virtually produced using synthetic computers and algorithms, meaning the production operative never has to leave their bed, and fresh wool is made and ready at the breakfast table each morning. Cleft likened it to egg production but without the chickens.

The outlet itself was dingy and had an all-pervading aroma of arrowroot. Cleft explained that a lamb had recently defecated in the stock room, and that it was a bugger to get rid of the smell. It was part and parcel of wool farming, and as the saying went, you can't make a turtleneck without a defecating lamb. Damian was drawn to the quirkier designs on offer to wool wearers, including a tumbler-shaped woollen hat for the impulsive yet cold whisky drinker; the goose-shaped foot warmer and his personal favourite, a woollen pipe, making it an ideal gift for Anne. Thomas enjoyed the interactive nature of the whole day, and he only sneezed the seventeen times, suggesting that his aversion/allergy was on the mend. He did, however, buy a beautiful woollen fresco, depicting monks mining wool, knitted by the famed knitter, Ivan Stitch, costing a mere £7.21. Thomas loved his tat.

The pair were soon back in the Visor, heading west in search of bleak horizons and foaming seas. The ferry crossing to the Isle of Brute was scheduled to leave in two hours' time, so Thomas had to stifle his cries and slip the Visor into fifth gear. They caught the ferry without incident, and as they disembarked on the tiny Isle of Brute, an overwhelming scent of aftershave poisoned their nasal cavities and tore at their eyes. They were in the land of masculine aftershave! The only hotel on the island, The Astringent Arms, used to be an aftershave factory, and was brimming to the rafters with cologne memorabilia. Thomas and Damian checked in and were given the Henry Hooper Suite, a twin-bedded room with a view over the disused aftershave vats. Aftershave, which can be used at any time of day, was an innovation designed to mask the smell of despair and shit. The stronger and more pungent the smell, the pricier the aftershave. Traditional methods of farming aftershave had been employed by generations of Brutes, as the locals were known, and even today, some families still went smell-picking in the hills of Brute to find the aftershave bulbs. Dogs could be used, but purists preferred a strong hint of masculinity to hunt down the elusive smellberry. Crushed and crushed again, the spirit of these smell farmers was a wonder to behold, and Thomas and Damian watched with the slackest of jaws as the old boys dragged their scented sacks of smell into the harbour for export to the mainland and non-Brutes. Nowadays, South American migrant workers flock to the island between the months of September and November to earn incredibly pitiful wages for backbreaking work. Many of these migrant workers would stay and develop a love of smell that was simply beyond their worst nightmare, marry a Brute and live a Brutish existence. The price of smellberry had dropped significantly in recent years, so many of the Brutes had headed to the mainland to become itinerate door supervisors or private security guards. Their haunted and gaunt expressions belie a life of smell and fragrance that for many is the true meaning of masculinity.

The hotel itself was everything you would expect for £9.97 per night, including a warm breakfast. Scented pillows, scented toilets and scented soap were all optional extras, so Thomas and Damian opted to have a scented breakfast instead. This consisted of smellberry pancakes, smellberry smoked bacon and fifteen eggs. The hotel's bars were to keep people out, so when Thomas and Damian enquired after the local tipple, Fay Grant, the proprietor, nipped upstairs and produced a bottle of her finest brew, Masculinity, a potent mix of smell and alcohol. Three shots of this heady brew would peel the varnish of most feet, and Thomas suffered from moist feet for the rest of the trip.

Deciding that a ferry to Larne would be problematic due to shortage of enthusiasm, the pair drove to Fleetwood and sat on the seafront. Armed with a broken pair of binoculars, Thomas scanned the horizon in the hope of at least spotting some part of Ireland, or if not, The Isle of Man. Thomas loved to look at the waves as they lapped up the trash encrusted shingle, recalling his time in the navy when he varnished his feet to keep them dry.

This probably explains the Enigma's love of travel.

# Storming up a cook

Damian had always fancied himself as a bit of a cook, creating exotic dishes from only the finest of ingredients. Anne, whose taste buds had been removed so as to accommodate her pipe-smoking, encouraged this idiotic notion, as did Thomas, whose input would be vital if Damian was to produce fantastic dishes. He thought it would be great if he could write a cookery book for like-minded people whose taste buds had been dulled by years of animal fat and grease. In discussions with Anne and Thomas, who would act as technical advisers, it was decided to produce a book celebrating traditional dishes that had slipped into obscurity due to lack of taste, fashion or digestibility. Too often, culinary fashions had ignored the humbler dishes, preferring instead the fancy explosions from the continent, with fricasseed this, and flambéed that. Damian was determined to reverse this slide into taste and restore a little indigestion to the nation, whose taste buds were crying out for grease and fat. He planned to tour West Yorkshire to research the hidden gems which were lying dormant, in need of resuscitation and fat.

Starting in Batley, birthplace of batter and many things fried, Damian visited the famous Batley Batter Museum, a cornucopia of batter, crispiness and cholesterol. The museum was housed in an old fish and chip shop and was run by volunteers who had very little else to do during their waking day. Director of the museum, Clive Frazzle, rose to prominence in the early 60s as a pioneer of the deep-fried egg, a truly awful concoction which never really broke through into the mainstream. He worked for many years as an adviser to the Fried Food Marketing Board, introducing initiatives to encourage school kids to eat more fried food and avoid fruit at all costs. He was known for his pallid complexion and grubby hands and spent several years as the poster boy for the Lard is Lovely campaign, which promoted a range of lard-based products. His wife Deidre was a stalwart of the Suet Appreciation Society and memorably stated that suet should be added to the local water supply to encourage growth in rickety children. She was also responsible for Make Suet Global, an initiative that intended to see British suet on dining tables across the globe. Following a short spell in prison for suet theft, she was now working at the museum, on a purely suet-advisory basis, and wore a tag constantly.

Walking around the museum, it was obvious that it bore very little resemblance to a tourist attraction, and many of its exhibits looked on the wrong side of shit. Frazzle was eager to point out that due to funding cuts and no visitors, the museum faced imminent closure, so Damian's visit could well spark a revival in fried food and associated memorabilia. Strolling towards some of the more grotesque exhibits, Damian was drawn to the section on 'Fried Food Through History' a rip-roaring tale of war, betrayal and lard, or so the blurb promised. Starting in the late seventeenth century, it attempted to draw parallels between historical events and breakthroughs in frying technology. The Glorious Revolution is attributed to a disgruntled chef who preferred to use lard when cooking and insisted on battering everything so as to kill any residual germs. With the support of William of Orange, and the chef, Gerald Grunt, lard was enshrined into the Bill of Rights and oranges became the mascot of all fryers. To this day, professional fryers avoid oranges, fried or not, and the little ball of vitamin C is viewed as sacrosanct. Chips were originally made from oranges and the frying bible, 'The Fat' mentions oranges three times, suggesting it has significance somewhere in nutrition. Later in the timeline, during the reign of George III, it was suggested that the king's madness could have been prevented if he had eaten more lard-infused fruit, along with the occasional battered sausage. The madness was attributed to a deficiency of lard in the king's diet, leading to fury, bloody fury and finally bloody madness. With hindsight, it is clear that anyone would have gone mad having been denied fried food for so long. The exhibit was a very degrading attempt to entertain those whose limbs were not fully functioning due to an excess of lard. One small exhibit displayed frying implements as used in earlier times. There was a stone wok, a wooden basket used for frying primitive sausages, and a bust of Lenny the Lard, Yorkshire's premier frying exponent who had died suddenly three years before following an accident with his head and some scolding lard. Frying's loss! The only high point of the visit was an old recipe book from which Damian was able to steal some very interesting ideas for rehashed fried stuff.

Returning home, he experimented with these fascinating old recipes and below is a sample of some of the more creative ideas.

*Deep-Fried Grapes with Battered Tripe*
*For the Grapes:*

*Ingredients:*
*1/ Grapes — a child's handful*
*2/ 476 g of lard*
*3/a spoonful of sherbet (any flavour barring lemon)*
*4/ 7kg of very strong, robust flour*
*5/ A pinch of tweed*
*6/ 1 bottle of vinegar*

*For the Tripe*

*Ingredients:*
*1/ A large bucket of tripe (rinsed and deloused)*
*2/ Nasal clippings*
*3/ A shrill scream*
*4/ Batter (available from most good batter outlets — not to be mistaken for butter)*

*Method — Grapes*
*Take the child and remove the grapes from the child's hand. Wash in cold water for five minutes until you are thoroughly drenched. Leave to dry in a cool room or in the back of a taxi. (At this point the child can*

return to playing or holding more grapes.) Take the lard and place in a large copper-bottomed pot, heat and then boil. Once the fire has been brought under control, drop the by now dried grapes into the hot lard and hope for the best. Meanwhile, sit back and watch something on the portable TV in your lovely kitchen. After five minutes, remove the grapes, place to one side and turn your attention to more pressing matters.

## Method – Tripe

Take the bucket and using only your left hand, remove the least smelly piece and place on some clean velvet. Take a pair of scissors (an adult could do this if you are afraid) and trim the tripe to bite-size portions or into fifteen cm pieces, depending on the size of your mouth. Avoid cutting yourself, but if you do, use the shrill scream and nasal clippings to signal your pain and disgust. Toss the tripe into the lard-infused batter, rest awhile, then toss into a large pan and hope that you will know when it is cooked. It usually takes minutes, but can, depending on the season and prevailing winds, take up to two hours to be sure that the tripe is dead. Put your feet up and if necessary, have a strong drink. Once you are satisfied that your life cannot get any worse, take the tripe and place on a china plate and decorate with the grapes.

Serve with a strong drink.

## Carrot and Banana Confit (Fried in lard)

### Ingredients:

1/ 7 bananas, thinly sliced and left to fester
2/ 7 carrots, thinly sliced and left to dry out
3/ 1kg of meat (any meat will do, the fattier the better)
4/ A bottle of cheap red wine
5/ Salt, pinch of
6/ Cheese and onion crisps
7/ Lard- as much as you can get your hands on.

*Carefully throw the meat in a large bucket and beat it with a rolling pin. This is to stimulate any remaining taste in the meat and is a good way of reducing stress. Add the bananas and carrots, along with a tiny, tiny, tiny pinch of salt. Open the wine and have a glass, or two. Pour any remaining wine into the bucket and marinate for two minutes, allowing the flavours little time to do anything. Meanwhile, in a separate bucket, pour the crisps in and leave to rest.*

*Take a very hot pan and some very cold lard and mix until the kitchen is full of acrid lardiness, then add the by now marinated meat and have a crisp as a reward. Whilst the meat is being cremated, enjoy the remaining wine with a crisp. After several glasses of wine, you may feel drowsy, so remember to take the meat off the heat and leave to confit overnight.*

*In the morning, remove the meat from the congealed lard and fry in a further vat of lard until thoroughly crispy. Serve with a hint of trepidation.*

Damian wanted to find more recipes to stimulate the leaden palettes of the nation and turned to Anne and Thomas for inspiration. Anne was heavily into tweed-based recipes, which had been the staple diet in her childhood. Thomas was a pie man, and had some ridiculous ideas for wedding pies, celebration pies and pies for busy people. Together they worked to create some of the most experimental dishes ever seen, and below are some of the more memorable dishes to whet the appetite and dull the taste buds.

### *Tweed wrapped in a beery batter*
*Tweed is considered a delicacy in many parts of the world but has fallen foul of food standards thanks to its clothy taste and texture. For many years in the early '40s, young children in parts of West Yorkshire would feed on discarded tweed, often served with warm milk and a little hope. The vitamins found in tweed have no health benefit but do offer some protection from strong winds.*

*Tweed wrapped in batter offers a warming and indigestible delight for those who feel the cold:*

*Ingredients*
*1/ 7 bottles of very strong beer*
*2/ 1 tweed jacket or 2 tweed gloves and 1 tweed sock*
*3/ Some batter*

*Method*
*Take one bottle of beer and settle those nerves; it's been a long day and you deserve it. Shred the tweed using a pair of shears or teeth, whichever is easier. Toss into the batter and thoroughly soak until all the tweed looks like it might be edible. Open another beer and think of happier times, or the last time you had a decent meal. Soak the battered tweed in boiling lard for three minutes until crisp and burnt. Sprinkle on a sprig of mint and garnish with rose petals or cabbage. Take the stock and pour down the drain. Have another beer and look forward to a mild hangover.*

*Commuter Pie or Pie a-go-go*
*Pies have littered history's hospitals and waiting rooms, leaving behind a trail of half-eaten pork or cherry with a crust that once bitten is then discarded. Too often the pie is left on the metaphorical shelf when the eater is required to move or perform at least one other task. Pies have never been truly portable, suitable for eating on the go or whilst playing sport. Sporting events would be far more appealing to spectators and participants if pies could be designed to fit in with the action at hand. To this end, two new portable pies have been created that in time will revolutionise the way we eat pies whilst living our busy lives.*

*Ingredients:*
*1/ Chunks of meat, either chicken or animal.*
*2/ Lard for taste*
*3/ Short fuse pastry mix — shop-bought will suffice*
*4/ A degree of mobility and flexibility*

*Method*

Take the meat/chicken and douse in lard until thoroughly coated. Fry for a while until you can fry no more. Meanwhile, in a separate room, prepare the short fuse pastry and leave to stand for ten minutes or until you are tired. Roll out the pastry into two rectangles, tie into a bow and place in an arrow-shaped pie mould. Allow the lard-encrusted meat to cool and bring it to the mould. Fill the mould with meat and anything small you can get your hands on. Egg wash and place in a preheated room to enable the lard to evaporate. Take a long walk and reflect on your shortcomings.

When you return from your walk, cook the pie for some time or until golden. Enjoy indoors or at a sport event with friends and extended family.

### Wedding Pie or Fiancée's Fancy Pie

Wedding: what better way to get married and enjoy a pie. Centuries-old tradition dictates that a pie can really make a wedding go off with a bang, and a good pie can really decrease the chances of infidelity and an early divorce. A special wedding pie is easy to digest and can be knocked up by even the clumsiest halfwit. It can be decorated and given layers in an attempt to make it look more appetising.

### Ingredients:
1/ 1 tabloid newspaper
2/ Meat or fish, depending on the season
3/ Cabbage or a plump cauliflower
4/ Icing- any colour but not grey
5/ Lard

### Method
Take the newspaper and enjoy half an hour catching up on the news and sport. Roll up the newspaper and set to one side. Mix the meat/fish with the cabbage/cauliflower until all that remains of your dignity is dripping from your sweaty brow. When you feel up to it, take the mix and cram into a pie dish and grate lard onto the mix to ensure maximum fattage. Cook for a considerable amount of time. Take the rolled-up newspaper and track down that bastard fly that has been buzzing around

253

*all fucking day. Squash if possible and then remove the pie from the oven. If not burnt, allow to cool away from flies. Take the icing and make a half-arsed attempt to decorate the fatty pie, avoiding the congealed fat if possible. Sprinkle with a selection of marriage-based clichés and serve with sincerity.*

Damian was eager to include some of his gran's recipes in the book, and Anne was able to remember, between pipes, some of the tastier dishes that had been slopped in front of her as a child. These represent not only the pinnacle of frugal cooking, but also a glimpse inside the arteries of the pre-war citizen. Ida, Damian's maternal grandmother, lived a full and long life, and this was in part due to her never eating what she cooked. Her favourite concoction for her brood was boiled liver with a sprig of lard and dried aphids. This dish required hours of diligent eating as it tasted rank but was full of lard-based nutrients and minerals that would ensure her children could stand up to Mr Hitler.

*War Winning Liver*

*Ingredients:*
*1/ Lard — half a medium-sized bucket should be enough for a family of nine*
*2/ Liver — assume that no one likes it so nine is more than enough*
*3/ Aphids — best picked in the picking season or can be bought at specialist shops*
*4/ A tiny pinch of essence of elderberry — too much will make the dish unpalatable*

*Method*
*Take the lard and heat until there is a small possibility of a kitchen fire — lower the heat and thank your lucky stars you have a fire blanket. Chop the liver into heart shaped pieces and toss with abandon into the cooling lard. Simmer with rage at the state of your life. Once the liver appears dead, carefully add the essence, mindful that too much could cause vomiting. Leave to putrefy overnight and just before serving,*

*sprinkle with the aphids. If you have no aphids, then apricots will suffice. Serve with warm milk and crusty flakes of lard.*

The war years had stripped the country of many of its natural resources, but lard was in plentiful supply, and Anne recalled a pudding that was often served during blackout that would leave her family constipated for days — lard sponge with a rich and creamy lard custard. As Hitler's bombs rained down on the streets and towns of West Yorkshire, Anne's family would be tucked away safely on the outside toilet, confident that any explosion sent by Hitler could be equalled in their bijou outside toilet.

*Lard Sponge with lard custard*

*Ingredients*
*1/ Large bucket of lard*
*2/ Two family-sized bathroom sponges, without scouring pad*
*3/ Some flour for bulk*
*4/ A tiny pinch of nutmeg*
*5/ Milk — 4 litres*
*6/ Hairspray — strong to super strong*

*Method*
*In a bucket, mix the flour and lard with vigour and enthusiasm until you feel drained and ready to give up this charade. Check your hair and apply hairspray if needed. Continue to stir and then carefully add the nutmeg and walk away. Decant into a large pudding basin and steam for hours. Check hair and apply hairspray. In a cold pan, pour in milk and boil for two hours until the heat becomes unbearable. Remove from the heat and whisk yourself off to the bathroom to freshen up. Once the milk has cooled, add the lard and nutmeg and mix. The custard should be runny — thick enough to stick to a mirror if thrown with some force. When everything appears to be going tits up, serve the pudding with a shovel of custard and sit back and watch. Remember to ensure the hairspray is used only under adult supervision as it can lead to bad hair.*

Damian was more than happy with the contents of his book, and whilst he understood that there would be some resistance to his more outrageous lard-based recipes, he hoped that with clever marketing and lies, people would embrace a lard diet. Thomas had eaten lard most of his life, and whilst it had severely affected his heart and arteries, he had lived a full and lardy life. Anne, who was a dyed-in-the-wool lard fiend, stocked up her fridge with lard to such an extent that it was impossible to fit anything else in, despite frantic heaving and shoving.

# Tat

When Thomas first heard of car boot sales, he was like a puppy with three tails. He imagined a magical place full of boots for every make of obscure car. A land of shimmering boots for Austins, Fords and Rovers, or indeed any other model of car that had lost its boot. A world where the customer could wander through fields of boots, wind in their hair, and have a wonderful selection of rust-encrusted rubbish at pitiful prices. When Damian told him that it wasn't a literal name, and the boots were used for carrying tat to be sold, Thomas once again resembled a dog with many tails. Thomas wanted to treat Anne to a day of tat browsing, so he quickly brushed his luxurious hair, changed his shirt and whisked Anne off to the Dewsbury Saturday Boot Sale, a monumental mess of tat, crap and fried food. On arriving at what could only be described as a field, it became apparent to Thomas and Anne that there was an abundance of tat to be had and time was against them. Parking the Ford Shoehorn (great for parking), Thomas and Anne headed off into the jungle of junk to scavenge for shit. Their noses were drawn to the wonderful smells of burnt fat and onions, peas and pie, and blancmange and custard. Feeling peckish and with a wallet full of coins, Thomas approached Pete's Pie and Pea Shed, an oily excuse for a food outlet that smelt of boiled peas and pork. The menu offered a range of pork-based pies, served with a ladle of peas and a sprig of mint. The prices looked reasonable, and Thomas ordered for Anne and himself, hoping to fuel up on stodge in readiness for the tat hunt that beckoned. Anne devoured the meal without blinking, puffing on her pipe all the while. She was as keen as Thomas to find that chipped vase, that collection of wine glasses with hairline cracks, or the print of the Rialto Bridge which would look beautiful hung in the bathroom. Thomas was on the hunt for a spanner of any size, possibly an electric fan heater (with or without a plug), and a road map of northern Norway (Thomas believed that Ford made most of its cars in Norway). When Anne immediately came across a vast collection of 'Pipe Smoker's Digest', a veritable vault of pipe-smoking trivia, she immersed herself in the hidden world of pipes. She had read as a child that fertility was directly linked to the number of pipes a person smoked in a calendar month. The explorer Sir David 'Oatflake' Weevil was an avid pipe smoker and often wrote witty and interesting pieces for the digest, and Anne was a big fan of exploration, porridge and pipes, so she was keen to see if she could find any of these vintage articles. Whilst she puffed and browsed, Thomas made his way along the rows of tat. Touching, sniffing and generally getting a feel for the quality of tat, he spied what could only be described as a universal multi-headed utility spanner, the nirvana of spanners. He had heard tales of a spanner that could be used for any ridiculous job, be it unscrewing a stiff ballcock, to loosening a reluctant nut on a Triumph Oxtail. Caressing the spanner, it was obvious to Thomas that it was the real thing, and perhaps even more surprising, it was being sold for under £1.27. This was the bargain of the century! So far so good; the boot sale had proven to be a rich pasture of pure piss, but soon things would turn for the worse.

As the happy pair of tat hunters wandered amongst tables laden down with unused plastic items, repackaged rubbish and books that would never be read, Thomas noticed what appeared to be a three-bar electric fire, with fake oak veneer and a very long flex. This was an ideal gift for anyone who longed to ward off winter with the warm glow of electric heat. Cherished by pensioners across the land, the three-bar electric fire represented the cutting edge in heating systems. Thomas recognised that to find such a pristine example of 70s technology was a once in a lifetime chance — serendipity made real. Carefully packing his utility spanner into Anne's bulging carrier bag, Thomas swiftly darted through a throng of tat collectors and offered to buy the fire, untested, for an astonishing £2.73. He was serious and was prepared to go up to £2.98 if that meant he could be the proud owner of such a wonderful example. The stallholder, a stumpy lady with huge hair and brows that could furrow most things, wrapped the fire in foil (to retain its heat) and assured Thomas that if there were any problems with the fire, then she could be contacted via a series of bells and whistles. Returning to the Shoehorn laden with tat, the next stop for the pair was a wonderful afternoon of browsing charity shops, possibly to buy tat, but more often than not, Thomas and Anne would merely dream of owning their own charity tat shop — a place rammed to the rafters with useless and worn household items. Thomas had even gone so far as to come up with a name for the imaginary shop: 'The Patricia Hiss Benevolent Association — Helping the Needy Acquire Self-Esteem'.

Patricia Hiss was a creation of Thomas's imagination, but loosely based on a guest house landlady he had once met whilst spending an enjoyable half hour gazing at the world-renowned Tower of Blackpool. As children, Stephen, Janine, Paul and Damian would spend hours sitting by their father's armchair, enraptured by tales of Blackpool, Morecambe and the infamous Patricia Hiss. In the early '50s Thomas would often drive to the west coast in his Austin Rollercoaster, a car predominantly built with parts from a rollercoaster, and spend hours sat by the seafront, staring out to sea, remembering his time in the navy. He would also wander the streets of these seaside towns in search of a tea and a pie, wistfully whistling nautical tunes. It was on such a day that he first met Patricia Hiss outside the Tower of Blackpool.

Patricia Hiss was one the foremost charlatans operating in the North West, usually at seaside resorts where she would expect to pick up a lot of business due to the large number of happy tourists looking for a good time and the opportunity to speak to their late mother/father/dog, via the other side. Patricia advertised her services discreetly, usually in the small ads or in fish and chip shops, where many of her potential customers could be found. At her sessions, going under the mystical moniker of A Moment with Miss Hiss, she stated that she could read palms, tell the time, converse with living and dead and foretell the future. Her career trajectory had been flaccid, but she had earned enough to buy a reasonably sized crystal ball, a deck of tarot cards and several fetching outfits, all with snake motifs. She drove an old Ford Spiritual, a car that would often veer over to the other side of the road, had intermittent contact with comfort, and an extremely large windscreen for seeing into the night. It also came with a complimentary crystal ball holder, and a handy pocket for tarot cards. Weaving her way across the palms and dreams of the gullible, she would park the Spiritual outside the nearest church in the hope that it wouldn't be possessed, and make her way on foot to clients' houses, armed with all her charlatan tools. She would often fall into trances, or at least potholes, and recall vague details of families at war, at lunch or generally at home. "Eric has something to tell you, Nora," was one of her most common lines, which would inevitably lead into a deeply disturbing conversation regarding unfurnished houses or unfinished houses; the messages could get confused during transmission.

Thomas had first encountered Miss Hiss on Morecambe seafront when he was looking for somewhere to park his Austin Falsehood. Seeing what looked like a small police hut, Thomas entered and asked where he could find a suitable space for his Falsehood. Miss Hiss immediately grasped his pie-encrusted hand and began a ten-minute reading. Miss Hiss was skilled in reading most pastries and was soon weaving her charlatan madness over Thomas's half-eaten pork pie. Apparently, the road ahead had many turns, and there was a good chance that his cholesterol levels could fluctuate. He was warned to avoid pasties and sausages rolls, and as it was his first visit, he was given a coupon for a free palm and crystal special, including three fairly sane predictions for his future. Thomas was sceptical about most things, but when it came to the supernatural and alien abductions, he displayed complete apathy. However, Miss Hiss promised revelations and insight that would destabilise his mind, if not blow it, so Thomas agreed to return the next time he was looking for a space for his Falsehood. This he did and over the course of many years, he learnt of Miss Hiss's benevolent work for down and out mediums, palmists and Tarot readers. Miss Hiss was one of the lucky ones as she had convinced enough people to cross her threshold of disbelief, but many mediums and alike spent most of their days as filing clerks or retail advisors, so often lived on the breadline. Her hope was to give something back to these underperforming mediums, so that they could face the derision with a meal in their rumbling stomachs.

During the Second World War, Hiss had worked at a top-secret facility somewhere off the A72, producing toxic stories and improper propaganda for home consumption to boost morale and make a few bob. She was a master of the twisted and could weave and fabricate with such fluency that after the end of hostilities she was awarded the Queen's Medal for Fibs, Second Class. Some of her more memorable work was reproduced in a small booklet distributed to the wholesome to stiffen resolve and shift a few copies. At three and six a copy, Hiss made a small fortune from her fibs, and in memory of her war service, some of her classics are reproduced below.

*Hissteria – the Truth never Looked so Bad!*
*Issue No. 1 – 20th July 1944*
*Organised Panic!*
*People frantically walking for a runny egg is an all-too-common sight on the streets of Britain, with scant regard for the frail-minded, egg-loving patriot who may well have served King and country but can't get a bloody egg anywhere. Dried toilet paper and desiccated hope is no way to win a war. Grocers across the land have been rushed off their flat feet trying to source goods that have been hoarded by selfish profiteers and numbskulls. Greedily snapping up all the available spam, corned beef and masticated oatmeal has left many a citizen making do with perishable hopes and a rumbling stomach. No one needs four hundred and fifty-six tins of sardines, nor can they possibly wash themselves with scented lavender without drawing a curious crowd of envious neighbours. It's time to pull together, and Mr Churchill should introduce communal*

breakfasts for the poor, pan-fried bananas for the well-oiled, and three weeks in the brig for profiteers.

We can beat this tom-tittery if we remember that we are in this together when it suits us, careless dribble is dangerous, and loose hips cost wives. Mr Hitler may well like the odd liverwurst with his morning schnapps, but here in Blighty we are made of sterner stuff. Remember, hardship is an adjective used to describe a boat, not a state of poverty. We can all dip a toe in the runny egg of hope if we pool our collective eggs and make breakfast a meal to remember.

Never in the field of human cornflakes, has so much been riven with fear, by so many, for so little. It is a far better thing that we did yesterday than we shall ever do tomorrow, and you have to crack an egg to make an omelette. This is not the end of the beginning, nor is it the beginning of the end, it is somewhere in between, so ask not what we can do for your country, but what can you get from your country.

Keep digging and march on for a breakfast we can all enjoy!

### Fiendish Enemy

With our boys busily burning bridges on the march to Berlin, news has just come in that Mr Hitler has a cold. Secret reports, that have only been seen by two sets of eyes and a cat, suggest that in his hidden bunker deep underground in a hole in Bavaria, Hitler has spent the last three weeks sneezing without any chance of a handkerchief to catch those pesky germs. Rumour has it that a plot to infect Herr Adolf with a severe head cold was first mooted several months ago by a disgruntled group of generals, intent on bringing an end to the war. Germs were planted in his treetop hideaway, inside what can only be described as a shabby briefcase. On opening the ticking time bomb of sneezes and sniffles, his remote offshore hideaway was infected by germs that could cause a cough, a sore head and some discomfort. He was advised by his personal tissue dispenser, Herr Gesundheit, to avoid loud noises and shouting.

The despicable little man is currently convalescing in his secret helium-filled head until such time as a cure for sneezing can be developed. Top boffins at the Ministry of Sneezes and Coughs predicted that he would be better in a few weeks — just enough time to win the war and march right into his floating hideaway on the River Danube.

## New Wonder Weapon on the Horizon

*Poleaxed by the onset of victory, Herr Moustache was seen quivering in his secret mountaintop hideaway, staring into the distance and wishing he had better binoculars. Meanwhile, boffins at the Ministry of Long-Distance Vision have developed new and crazy things to baffle the enemy and wrap up this war by the start of May next year. Using high precision hands and cutting-edge tools, a new wonder pair of all-seeing binoculars has been developed by small-eyed boffins who had been working around a very clock-like table.*

*The binoculars, or Utility Crystal Ball Binoculars, were the brainchild of Professor Franklin Myopia, and he predicts that they will shorten the war and extend the peace. Using top secret, premium grade crystal, Myopia has managed to harness the ability to see beyond reality, meaning he can now see the sunlit uplands and hope all at once. The binoculars allow him to turn a blind eye to many things that could be distressing, and they come complete with free rose-tinting. Early tests have shown that if the binoculars are used in the right circumstances, all pessimism can be overlooked, and most reasonable clouds will have a silver lining.*

*Production has started to produce the fifteen pairs needed, and it is hoped that soon we will all be looking forward to victory and papering over any dissent. Professor Myopia, whose grandfather invented the spoon, is currently working on a very uncomfortable chair, and he hopes that after hostilities have ended, he will be recognised by the king and given some meaningless award and a new chair. When asked if he was a hero, he nodded and stated that his hearing was fine.*

## Cows to be Dropped on Berlin

*Top chiefs in charge of metal flying machines have developed a new wonder weapon to cow the nasty Herr Spitler and end the war before St. David's Day. Working alone and often in pairs, boffins at the Ministry* of Farm Animals have been experimenting with dropping unpasteurised cows directly onto Herr Spitler's sterile bunker deep in Saxony. The plan, first hatched in a barn in Wiltshire by renowned milk drinker and fan of dairy, Doctor Hugh Haychtee, sounds fucking crazy, but after a Lactose Heavy Bomber inadvertently dropped two Friesian calves onto a perfumery in Cologne, soaking the fräuleins with unpasteurised cow juice, the good Doctor Haychtee was quick to see the potential for this extraordinary animal.

Loading three fully bloated, milk heavy cows onto a twin-engine Udder, top notch pilots headed out from their secret base in the hills of Lincolnshire, heading towards Herr Spitler's half-hidden, top-notch cow shelter. When the bombers reached a certain height, the cows were released, and as they descended let out a gentle mooing sound, reminiscent of cows falling from altitude.

Aerial photographs taken by a keen amateur have produced some lovely pictures of the cows just before they were dropped, and given the conditions that the photographer had to work in, the pictures were bloody brilliant. The Ministry also plans to drop ewes, goats and tons of fermented soya in the coming months, drenching Herr Spitler in lactose and washing away any hope of a fragrant funeral.

## King to Dress the Nation

In times of peril and occasionally late on summer evenings, it is traditional for the monarch to address his subjects with fine words and flattery. Now that the horizon is clear, and victory is making its way to a corner near hope, the king will make an address to the nation, outlining what needs to be worn when the war is finally won. The king is expected to make several suggestions as to what would be the appropriate dress for celebrating the end of a conflict.

Insiders have hinted that several fashion tips will be forthcoming from the king of haute couture, revealing a deep understanding of how to look good during a victory celebration. Strong sherry drinkers are recommended to avoid vivid floral prints and excessive hats, whilst robust-chinned types should aim to hit the high notes with an off-the-shoulder pullover or cardigan.

*Those with spindly legs who may struggle to stay upright could do worse than wearing leather trousers with strong twine to support those wafer-thin thighs; no one wants to topple to the ground underneath some celebratory bunting with a scotch egg half eaten. For those who enjoy a bracing breeze, the king recommends strong adhesive trousers and robust underpinning of flyaway garments, such as a tent or tarpaulin, which if left unchecked will look so 1942. Obviously, it is a victory celebration, so the king would like to see vivid browns and greys, with splashes of black and crimson to jolly along the near dead.*

# Fashion icons

Thomas had always maintained that if a job is worth doing, then there will be a competent person to do that job; for all the other jobs, an idiot would suffice. DIY, as it is affectionately known, has long been the merry widow of hobbies, practised as it is by young and old alike, with an abandon that verges on the reckless. Thomas was known to possess a sturdy pair of pliers and a half-broken hacksaw. He had instilled in Damian a distrust of perfection and detail, preferring instead to focus on the vagaries of a bigger picture. As time elapsed, Damian appreciated the Thomas approach to DIY; if all else fails, botch and ignore. Taking this as a starting point, Damian decided to start up a small DIY business, performing household jobs for those whose DIY abilities were even worse than his. No job would be too large to quote for; no job would be too small to underestimate. Damian needed to do some research before his enterprise could be launched onto an unwitting public, so he headed to the local library and borrowed 'An Idiots Guide to DIY', along with a Deacon Blue album and a Desmond Bagley novel. The guide proved to be an indispensable reference, offering shortcuts, which if they were any shorter, would not exist. Damian rapidly understood that if not out of his depth, he was not a strong swimmer in the DIY pool, so pitched himself as the 'odd' odd job man — cheap, cheerful and with half a toolbox.

A flyer was produced to promote Damian's limited services, and soon he was spending hours by the phone waiting for his first big job. He dreamt of rebuilding a listed building or repainting a disused public toilet; the possibilities seemed finite. Of course, as the old saying went, beggars can fuck off, so Damian had to be very loose with the truth when it came to quoting for jobs. His experience was limited to wallpapering Thomas's Austin Gloss to windproof the draughty auto, and on one occasion, varnishing Thomas's legs to stop the rot. Finally, after what seemed like three months and seven days, he got his first proper odd job. The client, or cheapskate, was a retired vicar who wished to freshen up the hall in his sinful rectory.

As Damian made his way to the consecrated hall, he thought of a suitable pitch to ensure that he didn't lose the job to Blind Bill, his main competitor. Bill had been pinching business from Damian, offering lower prices and fewer breakages, and Damian was determined to snap the rectory up before his paint brushes became museum pieces. Arriving at the dilapidated vicar's house, Damian was struck by the size and endless possibilities of screwing this opportunity up. Before he had the chance to ring the knocker, the door opened and standing before Damian was the Right Reverend Doug Magraive, never defrocked but threatened many times. Probably in his late '50s, with Methodist hair, he wore a very thick pair of glasses, a green cardigan and an 'I love Worshipping on a Wednesday' badge. It was obvious to Damian that he was not a local, as his accent sounded a little too cultivated; he was educated to a level that enabled him to understand road signs. He welcomed Damian into his hall and explained that he wished to freshen up and demystify his consecrated entrance hall, as it had become a little musty and off-putting to his worshippers. Damian quickly surveyed the walls and suggested that a hundred and fifty-five pounds would be a reasonable price for wallpapering, plus a further fifty-seven if he required any painting. The reverend appeared to flinch at such an unholy sum, but it turned out he was suffering from a devilish bout of sciatica. Damian was keen to do as little damage as possible, so promised that he could have the whole job done in two days. The reverend had already chosen a very satanic floral print, in an attempt to bring the outside in, and he had also snapped up two tins of discontinued 'Beelzebub Blue Matt Vinyl' paint, so if Damian was able to, the job could begin the next day.

Damian pulled up the next day prepared for the worse. He had been unable to source a set of step ladders, so had instead packed in an old milking stool that Anne had used as a child, along with a couple of chairs and two broom handles for the tricky corners. His Ford Bracket was rammed with dust sheets, white spirit and crusty paint brushes, along with a spirit level (it was always advisable to have level spirits) and a strong pair of scissors. The reverend was due to meet the bishop later so was busy with churchy business, meaning Damian could crack on and start measuring the walls in readiness to cut the strips to the appropriate length. Fortunately, he had remembered his twine and was soon up and down the milking stool, twine in hand, confident in his own ineptitude. For a paste bucket he had brought a wide mouthed vase, and his paste table was the bonnet of the Bracket. It wasn't ideal and meant on the drive home he could well have leaves plastered all across the bonnet — a price worth paying if Damian wanted to be a success. His next problem was to transport the strips of pasted wallpaper from the bonnet of the Bracket to the hallway without tearing the delicate floral pattern. It was a very windy day, so Damian struggled to maintain the integrity of the intertwined tulips and devils that the reverend had chosen to adorn his hallowed hallway. His worry was that matching the design up once on the wall would be impossible, but deciding that he really didn't care, opted to freestyle, and put the paper up in a random fashion, in the hope that the reverend would be overwhelmed with the overall devil/tulip effect. He made rapid progress and after his fourth tea break decided to turn his attention to the painting. Searching the boot of the Bracket, he quickly identified a brush that would leave the least number of streaks and bristles. Popping off the lid of the tin of paint, he was partially blinded by the sheer ugliness of the colour. It was hard to imagine in which abattoir this paint would look better than the rows of carcasses and pools of congealed blood. It really was a vile colour, but as the reverend had bought it, who was Damian to argue about its aesthetic qualities? Sloshing on the paint with abandon, all the time wearing a very loose-fitting bandana, meant that some spillage did occur, but thankfully, only onto the newly applied wallpaper, which also had hints of Beelzebub blue in it.

The completed look, when Damian had smeared, wiped and touched up, was a blend of tulip, evil cherubs and blue, perfect for any rectory or newly renovated font. When the reverend returned from several hours of spiritual administration with the bishop, he entered the hallway expecting a half-finished job, as Damian didn't look too efficient, but what greeted him was a completely transformed space that would have not looked out of place in a kaleidoscope, so confusing were the colours. The reverend was stunned, and he immediately fell to his knees and let out a small prayer or sigh, thanking the Lord for his chronic myopia. He was aware of the overall mush of a mess that Damian had produced, but it did look fresher than before, so he was prepared to stump up and pay for the onerous results.

It was around this time that Anne set up a small family business — Carters' Cardigans of Distinction, producing bespoke cardigans for the carsick and elderly. Carter's Cardigans was the brainchild of Anne, who had been fortunate to have experienced vomit leakage on long car journeys. Most of the younger ones, but Damian in particular, had suffered from debilitating car sickness, and would vomit if speeds went over the legal limit for a Ford or Austin motor car. What she was looking for was a robust cardigan that could hide some of the smells associated with vomit and also mask some of the obvious pieces of semi-digested turnip, pie or pea. Nothing would have a greater adverse effect on social interactions than a vomit-stained cardigan with visible vomit protruding from a casually rolled up sleeve, or semi-liquefied crust falling to the floor as Anne attempted to explain the finer points of pipe-smoking.

Using only a powerful pair of knitting needles, Anne experimented with various wools and methods to try and discover which would have the best vomit saturation properties. She trawled the wool shops of northern England in search of a fabric that was both robust yet absorbent. Thomas would spend hours in his Vauxhall Vomit, so called because it would make most drivers physically sick, waiting for Anne as she browsed the wool selection in some obscure wool retailers round the back of a cement factory. She approached several disreputable sheep farmers in an attempt to convince them to rear a super sheep with a fleece that was somehow resistant to vapours of vomit. Thomas quite enjoyed these jaunts out into the wilderness, observing that country folk appreciated pie in a different manner. Anne searched and scoured for the elusive wool, and she eventually found a farmer who was willing to mutate his lambs to make motor journeys less irksome. Of course it was not cheap, and Anne got into considerable debt in order to start her cardigan empire.

Like most pipe smokers, she had little experience in high finance or marketing, so she was learning from the ground up whilst all the time trying to hit the very same ground running. Long nights huddled by an open oven door meant that after three months of countless prototypes and singed sleeves, she finally had a product to take to market. Deciding that she needed a marketing strategy, she asked Thomas to produce a leaflet that could be thrust into the hands of unsuspecting motorists who had smears of vomit on or around their person.

## Carter's Cardigans of Distinction

*Are you tired of overalls? Do wake up sweating due to overuse of a jumper? Are your arms symmetrical? Few, if any, realise the importance of a good cardigan. Sitting on a bench near a playground can be a chilly business, as can walking to the local toffee factory for a guided tour. A cardigan can make those chilly days a little warmer. Can you imagine a world where vomit would not be seen as a sign of oral diarrhoea? Vomit, or puke as it is referred to in medical circles, can ruin any long car journey or woollen garment.*

*Now, thanks to hours of arduous knitting and a dedication that borders on reckless, Carter's Cardigans of Distinction bring a whole new world of woollen joy to satisfy even the most demanding arms and journeys. Carefully made in a dimly lit kitchen, the Carter range offers something for every loose-stomached vomit aficionado. Below are details of our exciting new range, which if you order soon, could be dispatched.*

- *The Lake District: a sumptuous blend of colour that will easily hide any Thai green curry or chicken tikka masala- perfect for outdoor types who have a small car. Complete with detachable sleeves and instructions.*

- *The Urban Myth: Cool cats and hipsters will love the outrageous use of sleeves in this slick attempt at knitting. Collar and back are optional, but you are guaranteed a vomit-reducing garment on that short commute to the juice bar or therapist.*

*The Fragment: Lovers of explosions will love this deconstructed expression of futility, with ample room for instructions and unnecessary fat. Complete with sewing kit and twine, this is ideal for the weekend warrior who loves the comfort of the uncomfortable, rough type.*

The leaflet was rammed through forty-two letter boxes within the first week, and soon the orders were waiting to flood in. In the first month alone, Anne sold just over two and a half cardigans, and it was obvious that Thomas's leaflet was convincing the unsuspecting public that a novelty cardigan that had vomit-resistant qualities was a desirable fashion accessory. The dispatch department was overtired but managed to get both orders out without too much effort, and systems were put in place to ensure there was always enough tea, sugar and milk for the quieter times. Thomas also installed a pie dispenser in the cellar, but thanks to faulty wiring it only dispensed mini pies, which would not be sufficient once the business hit peak business in summer. On the back of the success of the cardigans, Thomas invested in a new pair of binoculars and Anne treated herself to a woollen pipe warmer, for colder days.

However, just as everything was pointing to a place on the rich list, tragedy struck. Thomas and Anne had been dealing directly with a lamb dealer from Yorkshire, whose animal husbandry practices bordered on the insane. When a local animal welfare charity got wind of these outrageous incidents of shepherding, the farmer was immediately sent on an animal welfare awareness course and given two years' community service working in a sheep sanctuary. Animal charities are often seen as the black sheep in a room full of runts, but in this case, their swift action put Anne out of business. From that day on, Anne swore off lamb and avoided overly woollen garments. At the time, once the initial shock had subsided, she tried to find an alternative farmer/pervert, but in a global market, prices were too high, so she threw in the towel (man-made) and reverted to weaving cotton spoon holders for hikers and wandering salesmen. Thomas continued to write leaflets, which were not only effective, but also slightly offensive. Below is one of his finest:

## Carter's Cardigans of Distinction — Closing down Event!

*What better way to celebrate a promotion or bereavement than a new cardigan? Here at Carter's Cardigans, we specialise in cardigans for special occasions or every day, run-of-the-mill, hum-drum shit, and we are confident we have the right cardigan for your arms. You may be the lucky owner of asymmetric arms, or have withered elbows, or even too many arms. Whatever the case, we have a garment waiting for your expectant arms. Why not browse our intimate collection and then get your grubby little digits dialling our dedicated order line.*

*The Bell Ringer: made from pure iron and cast in the foundries of the historic Carter Foundry, this cardigan represents the very heaviest cardigan available legally. Available in rustic red and rusty red, the cardigan would be the perfect choice for any body building bell ringer.*
*The Cardiac Cardigan: If your heart is slow, too quick or misshapen, then this could be the lifesaving choice, with built in defibrillator and quick dial to A&E. Ideal for the heavy smoker in your life, or the morbidly obese. Complete with lard storage capacity and comb so as to look good if the ticker plays up.*

*The Multi-Button: Not enough buttons in your life? Tired of idle fingers and easy access clothing? Then the multi-button is the obvious choice. Depending on the girth of your fingers, you can choose between the 500 button, the 750 deluxe, or the luxurious 1000 button. All the buttons* function and come complete with working holes. Treat yourself and look like the archetypal button fanatic.

_Fowl or Fare_: Are you a bus-driving chicken? Perhaps you goose-step on the way to the train station? Whatever your choice of transport, there's a bird-themed cardigan for you. Feathers adorn this piece of artistry, and Anne, our chief designer, knitted the feathers by hand close to a working oven. What's more, the cardigan is pre-soaked in meat stock to give it a great birdy aroma. Perfect Christmas gift!

_The Pie Crust_: Imagine a cardigan so crusty that it would take a fleet of highly skilled chefs to produce. A cardigan so impossibly tasty that even the biggest pie hater could not resist its enticing crustiness. A wondrous garment so magnificent that armies would march miles to marvel at its meaty innards. The Pie Crust is such a beast. Using only the finest wool and shortcrust pastry, Anne, our chief chef, has accomplished the improbable. Working long hours near a fully working oven, Anne has crafted a truly delicious cardigan that could easily feed a family of six. It comes with complimentary spoons, napkins, and a large tin of mushy peas.

Now that you've seen what Carter's can bring to your wardrobe, why not gives us a call and snap up a cardigan.

Call within the next three hours and get a free scarf or reusable spoon!

# All quiet at the front

As the wrestling ring hire business became more competitive, Damian began to tire of the constant bouts with boredom that dominated his waking day. He needed new challenges but was unsure as to what to do. The business had recently been sold to an investor from Essex who had radical plans for wrestling rings and was keen to meet his new workforce. His desire to be liked by his staff meant that Ruben Le Roux bought individual pizzas as a golden hello for his new employees. Ruben was of the school of business that demanded enthusiasm and commitment from its employees. Dressed in highly camouflaged trousers, his legs at times were impossible to see. His headgear, a green beret, suggested a military background, and he liked to be referred to as the bombardier. Marching on to the premises on the first morning, pizza in hand, he struck a pathetically comic figure, barking like a dog on a mobile phone that was so big it came with its own trolley to complete its mobility. Ruben scanned his staff, and realising that most of the enthusiasm and commitment had arrived late, attempted to be chummy. Enthusiasm, the watchword of the idiot and the confused, was something that Damian could never get excited about. His whole life was built on expecting disappointment and tom-tittery, so when Ruben suggested a team-building day to forge bonds between people who really wanted to break the shackles of boredom, Damian felt nothing but trepidation. Ruben, referring to himself as the Bombardier, said that paintballing would be an excellent activity, and that he was more than willing to supply the army fatigues as he had a job lot which he had bought from a retired legionnaire from Dulwich. A suitable paintballing site was located, and the crew started to prepare.

The Bombardier suggested a series of manoeuvres and skirmishes to prepare for the impending battle of the paint. Using only some of his wit, he decided to deck out the warehouse in camo netting, complete with sandbags, bunkers and a portable toilet that had been manufactured in 1941. Code words were to be used and he was to be the Big B, on account of the size of his arse, or at least that is what Damian believed. The first manoeuvre involved a search and rescue mission, involving two rolls of toilet tissue and an upset stomach. The Big B had installed a mess tent in the warehouse, and very kindly prepared a breakfast of bully beef, hard tack biscuits and hot, steaming tea. He had secreted laxative into one of the teas, and then hidden the toilet tissue. The mission was to locate the tissue before the explosion of bully beef occurred. The crew was split into two search teams, Foxtrot Dancer and Easy Peasy, with Damian co-ordinating communication using a series of whoops and whistles, something that he had practised as a child with Thomas. The Big B was to monitor progress using a large relief map of northern Belgium, with Antwerp representing the toilet tissue. Foxtrot Dancer headed off in the direction of the portable toilet in the hope that the tissue would be hidden in plain sight, whilst Easy Peasy went on a flanking manoeuvre and headed for the fire escape. The tissue, which The Big B had hidden in one of his extensive pockets, looked like it would never be found as Foxtrot and Easy stumbled around the warehouse in camo gear, with Damian whistling and whooping with no real purpose. As the bully beef bomb ticked away, desperate to evacuate the stomach of the unfortunate who had no nose for laxative, it became obvious to Damian that The Big B was a complete tit. Eight grown men searching for two rolls of toilet tissue was hardly the intense preparation needed for a whole day's paintballing. Whistling and whooping, whilst a pleasant enough activity, was no way to communicate when the rest of your team had no idea what those whistles and whoops actually meant. The Big B was thrilled with their progress, happy that they hadn't told him to fuck off and having eaten all the pizzas. As the search continued, Damian made the decision to leave the wrestling business and try and find employment where he wouldn't be exposed to such tom—tittery, but not before enjoying a day of paintballing at someone else's expense. Plus, he liked to whistle and whoop. From a distant corner of the warehouse, he heard a rasping sound followed by some guttural screams, which he deduced to be the bully beef making its way to freedom. The toilet tissue wouldn't be needed.

On the day of the jolly to the paintballing venue, Damian arrived at the rendezvous bright and early, ready to shoot friend or foe. He had no qualms about being a complete bastard and shooting at his own side, remembering the advice Thomas had given him: 'Neat brush strokes never won a war.'

Decked out in their 1950s legionnaire costumes, like a 'Beau Geste' cloning club, they headed off into the wilds of Shropshire, knowing that they might not be back, or at least that they would be back, but it could be quite late. Casualties would be taken, paint would be smeared, and stories of heroism and fortitude would be fabricated. On arrival at Grunt Ridge Paintball Centre, the crew disembarked from their trucks and headed for the makeshift mess tent, desperate for tea and bacon — the grunts' lifeblood. There was to be a safety briefing in ten minutes, so quickly finishing their rations, the crew headed for the briefing tent, where they were met by a bulk of a fellow with a mad eyebrow and huge ears. This was Nuts McNulty, the head honcho, whose word was law when it came to paintballing on his fields. No head shots, no screaming, no friendly fire and strictly no improvised paintballs. If shot, retreat to the safe zone, brush off paint and return when instructed. Masks should remain on at all times, and do not shoot at the wildlife. Just like the SAS, Damian had spent the previous evening writing a marching song in an attempt to stifle the boredom, and it is still sung by those who were there that day as a reminder of the suffering that all paintballing participants experience, reminiscent of 'Lili Marlene'.

*Ode to Jackson Pollock*

*Marching into to battle, buddy by my side,*
*Fighting for our freedom, ain't no easy ride.*
*Squelching through the woodland, paint gun in my hand,*
*Knowing that my buddy may not make it back.*
*My buddy of the paint gun, my brave paint gun buddy guy.*
*Marching into darkness, dangers everywhere,*
*Fighting for our future, shoot me if you dare.*
*And there 'neath the bow of the old oak tree,*
*My buddy of the paint gun, my brave paint gun buddy guy.*
*Dodging all the Dulux, goggles raised up high,*
*Crawling through the long grass, I hear my buddy cry.*
*And there 'neath the oak tree, I watch my buddy die,*
*My buddy of the paint gun, my brave paint gun buddy guy.*

The crew were as ready as they would ever be and as Nuts McNulty explained that the first round was a flag-capturing task, the Big B gathered his troops and produced a piece of paper. He had prepared a Churchillian speech, to rouse his troops and send them off to battle with hope in their hearts and pride in their uniform. The speech is reproduced below and is still used at Sandhurst as a training tool.

*Into the woods we must go!*

*"Gentlemen, ask not what your finest hour will be, but make every hour your finest. Scorched earth has no place without a seared heart; let those who have fought before never forget your sacrifice. The dark before the dawn, as the enemy prepares to attack, will see many men turn and run, but you, my band of brothers, you will march forth and vanquish all those who point paint and destruction at the heart of the brave warrior. And if we fail, think only of yourself, and that there is a legionnaire in a far-off field, who may have washed by a river on his way home. We should fumble ecstatically and trudge through fatigue and drink. We shall be victorious, for never, in any field, as so much been paid, by so many, for*

*so much. We shall reach journey's end, with hope in our hearts, to go home and wash off the paint. Go forth, and for England, for me, be victorious!"*

Damian was underwhelmed and reflected on the stupidity of the Big B. As he trudged towards the start point for the first activity, he studied the faces of the enemy. Danger lurked on their shoulders, and each one looked like a trained painter, ready to Pollock at any moment. All looked as if they had stared paint in the face and come out undecorated. Turning to his comrades in paint he became aware of the deficiencies in their preparation. Whilst toilet roll is a daily essential for most people, finding a hidden roll in a warehouse will never truly prepare anyone for paintballing. The Big B was obviously hoping that what his platoon lacked in training they would make up in enthusiasm and raw courage. Damian planned to lie low and avoid getting painted. As Nuts McNulty explained the rules of the game, Damian checked his weapon, adjusted his glasses and prepared to hide. As the whistle sounded, two groups of fully-grown adults ran in opposite directions to plan their strategies for capturing a flag — a truly monumental waste of energy. The Big B called his platoon into a huddle and explained his tactics. We were to split into two squads, one taking the left flank, the other creating a diversion on the right flank. He would lead squad A, and Damian was put in charge of squad B, the diversion. Damian had taken many diversions in his life, not always whilst driving, and understood the concept of diversionary tactics, but as for actually creating a diversion, he had no idea whatsoever. Thinking on his feet, he decided to lead from the rear, and ordered his squad forward at the double. Deciding that the best form of attack is done by others, he quickly dropped back and started to take pot shots at trees, flowers and his squad. The Big B was one of those fellas who would walk into a room full of squints not knowing who he was looking for and be found by squints who weren't looking for him — clueless and completely adrift in his own camo trousers.

Damian drifted back to the safe zone and sat out the remaining activities, using a brief but painful outbreak of sciatica as his ticket back home. It was clear to Damian that his future lay elsewhere, and the following day he would resign, leaving behind the Big B and wrestling rings, and search for new employment.

# No!

Tragedy used the phone to shatter Damian's splintered existence, piercing his diminished heart and leaving a void that could never be plugged. The world fell out of his bottom, but that would have to wait: Thomas had died. A hammer blow could be felt but not heard. Damian climbed down from the garage roof to fully take in his handiwork and absorb the news of his father's death. It was coming; we all die, but Damian wanted to know why and how. Was it the elbows that finally caught up with him, or the ingrowing armpit? Or maybe his heart finally gave way. Damian had to break the news to the kids, so he decided the best way to tell them that their long-distance grandfather was in a better place was through the medium of verse.

*Where's Long-Distance Granddad?*
*Driving up the motorway, no time for drinks, or have a piss,*
*Driving up the motorway, long-distance granddad we do miss.*
*Greying hair, wild tattoos,*
*His walking stick he did lose.*
*Sat in chair, half asleep,*
*No snoring here, not one peep.*
*Driving up the motorway, no time for drinks, or have a piss,*
*Driving up the motorway, long-distance granddad we do miss.*
*Smiling gums, where are his teeth?*
*See the paper, they're underneath.*
*Read the small ads, bought a car,*
*Go and buy it, not too far.*
*Driving up the motorway, no time for drinks, or have a piss,*
*Driving up the motorway, long-distance granddad we do miss.*
*Granddad's dead, he's gone and died,*
*Anne, the kids they cried and cried,*
*Granddad's dead, he is no more,*

*They found him slumped on the floor.*
*Driving up the motorway, no time for drinks, or have a piss,*
*Driving up the motorway, long-distance granddad we do miss.*
*We'll bury him, in a deep, deep hole,*
*Along with all the things he stole.*
*A starter motor, some hub caps too,*
*We miss you, granddad, we do, we do.*

The children loved poetry and took the news very well. The next task was to travel up to Yorkshire to riffle through his belongings for anything of value. Grief is a difficult mistress and can manifest itself in many ways. Damian, who possessed no real quantifiable emotions, supressed his feelings and maintained a rigid façade of disinterest.

Arriving at the Carter country retreat on the outskirts of Wibsey in Bradford, Damian was greeted by Anne in her ceremonial garb. Tweed was the order of the day, and Anne, lover of tweed and smoker of pipe, was determined to adopt a llama, but that would have to wait as she had more pressing matters to attend to. Consulting her children, she agreed that they should follow Thomas's wishes and given him the send-off that a man of his dignity and stature deserved. Many things could be said of Thomas: lover of chrome, driver of cars, awkward waver, but no one could deny him one last ride in his favourite car, the hearse. At times he was compared to a cocktail stick, sharp and to the point, and on other occasions to a banana, ripe and often peeling. He was a giant of a man in a world of smaller giants, giver of pies, father, son and husband.

Thomas had been living all his life for the day he died and had made meticulous preparations. His first request was that all the food at his wake should be pork pie-themed. He wanted pork pie trifle, pork pie sandwiches and pork pies in a range of sizes. He had specified that he wanted a mushy pea fountain for mourners to dip their pies in as and when the fancy took them. Tea was to be pumped in via a huge vat that Thomas had secretly installed as a thirtieth wedding anniversary gift for Anne. It was located in the cellar of his first floor flat and was very unpopular with the residents on the ground floor. Anne was to wear tweed and the children could choose between woollen garments adorned with chrome or chrome garments adorned with wool, depending on the weather. The hearse was to be decorated with mini pork pies and a huge arrangement of ornamental pork pies should sit atop his coffin and then be shared with the mourners on conclusion of the ceremony. He wanted his children to drag his coffin into the chapel, symbolically suggesting that not even death could take him away from his children, whilst Anne was to stand on the coffin, like Boudicca, proud and only a little defeated. There were to be readings by Stephen and one by a distant acquaintance that Thomas hadn't seen since his time in the navy during World War Two. Thomas wanted someone to give a detached and disinterested view of his life. Frank Cavity had been a very petty petty officer on Thomas's first ship, HMS Cavity. He had shown Thomas the ropes, the guns and the portholes, seeing in Thomas the potential to get shot, bombed or drowned.

On the day of the funeral, the mourners arrived looking fairly sad. Anne, resplendent in tweed, sat on the pie-encrusted coffin (her bad hip was playing up) whilst the children dragged and heaved it. The mourners gently arrived, hushed, and Frank Cavity strode to the front to give his disinterested eulogy:

"Thomas once asked me if fish had ears, and I turned to him and could see that he had been thinking on this problem for some time. As he looked at me that day, the wind gently rocking his beard, I knew this man would make a great sailor. His innate ability to tell up from down, wet from dry, night from day, meant there was very little danger of him drowning in the foreseeable future. His love of the piano accordion made him a very unpopular member of that tight-knit band of brigands we called the crew.

"He served his country well, and when a German flying submarine dropped a huge bomb onto HMS Cavity, it was Thomas who flailed around in the water, shrapnel burrowing its way into his body. It was Thomas who hoped that the fish would hear his cries and rescue him from this watery torment. Fortunately, Thomas was spotted by a passing whim, and spent the following three months under lock and key. He was considered to be too valuable an asset to risk being captured, on top of which he was planning to go AWOL to be with a very pretty WAAF from Sidcup. A broken heart and a shattered back meant that when he left the navy, he only received two medals: the AWOL medal, and the Shrapnel medal.

"I never saw Thomas after the war and was surprised when I was invited to the funeral. The pies are lovely and thanks for the tea.

"Happy New Year."

Thomas had died on the second of January, so the final sentiment was a nice touch. Stephen then rose and made his way to the front to deliver a very difficult eulogy, as it was written in gibberish. Stephen held his emotions in his left hand and delivered a very moving piece that brought the assembled half-wits to tears. It is paraphrased below:

"'Never leave home with a dirty shoe, son' was a piece of advice that has stayed with me throughout my life. 'Don't drive on the left in Barrow and avoid buying cars from clerics'. Dad, Thomas, Mr Pie, The Hearseman — he had so many names, but to me he was just plain old Dad, with a pocket full of crumbs and a world of wisdom to share with his children. He never played sport due to his misaligned elbow, nor did he ever partake in hunting with hounds at the weekend. He led a simple life, devoted to his wife Anne and his four children, and maybe even their children; it was difficult to tell. His inscrutable manner could often be mistaken for insolence. His unusual gait and jaunty smile were the mark of the man — a man who was unable to smile fully thanks to life's bitter twists — a man whose feet, rather like Janus, faced both ways, ready for anything. Shoes were his secret passion, and he had two, one for each cardinal point.

"It is a mark of the man that he never swore in front of the television, for fear of upsetting the BBC. He never sang unless sodden and would often write ambiguous letters to inappropriate people to keep himself fit in the head. He inspired a generation of his children and will be missed at the job centre and doctors' surgery.

"Thanks, Dad, and Happy New Year."

Stephen captured the essence of Thomas to a degree, and all those who heard the eulogy couldn't remember much of it three weeks later.

Thomas left no will, so his estate was shared equally between the children. The contents are listed below:

A collection of hats bought from a second-hand shop in Cleckheaton,
Three all-weather walking sticks,
A woollen coat, pair of riding boots (size 12),
Some chrome polish which had been left under the kitchen sink,
Fifteen pristine copies of Reader's Digest circa 1974,
A red pair of electric pliers,
Several walnuts (uneaten),
A road map of southern Belgium,
A disused potty,
Three porcelain figurines eating pork pies.

The children all took something, more for its sentimental value than its intrinsic value, and Anne was left £173.89 to spend on herself.

Life must go on, but without his beloved dad, Damian was adrift, and found focusing difficult thanks to the loss of his glasses, and Thomas.

Damian was working as a self-employed courier, delivering meaningless packages to meaningless people. It was a soul-destroying job, but Damian had very little soul left to be destroyed. His natural sense of direction meant he was often in the right place at the wrong time, and soon he was marked out for demotion. Parcels and packages were never an ambition, and to occupy himself Damian took to writing short letters to disgruntled shopkeepers, businesses and politicians, as he had often done with Thomas. He found it very therapeutic to complain in writing, inventing problems that needed no resolution. He kept many of these letters to prove to his parasites that he was literate, and the best are reproduced below.

1/ The Sugar Cube Issue
*Dear Sugar and Son,*

*I recently drank some tea and was shocked when I discovered it contained little or no sugar product. I quickly ran to my nearest sugar outlet to buy a suitable sugary product. The cubes, as they were called, were in fact a variety of shapes and sizes. I am a small-minded individual with too much time on my hands. When I checked each cube, which took me an incredibly quick fifty-seven minutes, I was devastated to find that there were only three cubes in the box, the rest being a mish-mash of shapes. One of the cubes resembled the head of the Church of England, whilst another looked like David Hasselhoff. I have no issue with Baywatch, Knight Rider or God, but I expect my cubes to be cubes, not spiritual leaders or Hollywood superstars. Is that too much to ask?*

*As a consequence of this unfortunate and relatively upsetting issue, I have now resolved to watch Baywatch and pray at least once a year. From you I require an apology and a solemn promise that you will ensure that no cube is disfigured. A child could be really frightened.*

*I hope you do not discard my letter and look forward to any response.*
*Yours faithfully,*

2/ The Litter Issue
*Dear Mr Blair,*

*I appreciate that you are a very busy man, what with running the country and bringing up John Prescott, but I felt compelled to write to you regarding an issue that has burnt a hole in my soul: LITTER!*

*I live in a very crowded cul-de-sac, where space is a privilege few of the residents fully embrace. My pokey one-room hovel has only one* window, a door for emergencies and a chute for any waste products. Unfortunately, the chute is a communal chute, meaning that all manner of litter and shit passes my hovel on an hourly basis. When I am engrossed in a very engrossing episode of Quincy, how in God's name am I expected to keep up with the subtle plot twists if all I can hear is shit and litter whizzing past my kitchen?

Mr Blair, you seem like a clean man, the sort of chap who might wash his hands when leaving the lavatory, so you will understand my worries. The last thing I want to happen is to break out in hives during a re-run of Kojak or The Sweeney.

Would it be possible to set up a task force, or appoint a Shitty Tsar to take control of this shitty chute situation? I have paid income tax on two occasions and feel that my contribution to society is minimal. I have also, I would like to remind you, voted Labour ever since I was old enough to write a cross. Do something, Mr Blair, or the stains of shit will be on your hands.

Yours with love,

3/ The Neighbour Issue
Dear Housing Team,

My hovel is very draughty, and at night I am often woken by the strong breezes that seem to dominate my waking hours. Sometimes the breezes are so strong that they ruffle my carefully coiffured barnet, leaving me feeling dishevelled and downhearted. When I mentioned this to my neighbour, Mrs Twig, a branch of a woman with trunks for legs and roots that have long since died, she happened to mention the communal door, which is shared by me and the seven other hovels in my block. Mrs Twig suffers from night terrors and will often wake in the night screaming 'timber' at the top of her voice. The only thing that seems to assuage her fears of being chopped down in her prime is having the communal door open at all times to allow the evil within to escape. She is obviously a fucking fruit cake (excuse my language, but needs must and all that shit) and has not been herself since her husband Seth left her for another man.

I don't expect you to persuade Seth to return to his estranged wife, which seems to be asking a little too much, but I would hope that you appreciate my dilemma and install a scream screen to baffle some of the more hair-raising screams. Mrs Twig is destined to ruin my hair and my sleep, and I think as a responsible housing department, you should pull your finger out and either surgically install ear plugs in me or remove Twig and rehouse her somewhere remote.

Once again, apologies for the fruity language, and I hope to get a good night's sleep in the near future.

Yours lovingly,


## 4/ My Car Issue

*Dear Mr Car Salesman,*

I have a history of mistakes and misfortune when it comes to modes of transport. I have ridden in cars, buses, a hearse, and on one occasion, a horse-drawn milk float. Never have I felt truly at ease with the speeds achieved by these vicious modes of transport. I have in-growing armpits and inefficient feet, making it difficult for me to be completely pedestrianised. Therefore, I am always on the lookout for alternative methods of transport — something that is inexpensive yet stylish.

I recently visited your business with the intention of browsing your extensive stock of vehicles and alternative transport solutions. Your manager, or at least that is how she introduced herself, explained that my budget was insufficient, and the only thing I could possibly purchase was a one-way railway ticket to Keighley. This sort of offhand attitude is the cause of the UK's ills. Granted, I hardly look like the sort of fellow who would be interested in alternative transport, and my facial tics can appear very aggressive, but that doesn't excuse the offhand treatment I received.

I have many lycra suits and have peddled my wares far and wide, so when I requested a test ride of the new Speedo-Bike, I was a little surprised to be rebuffed in such an offhand manner. I may not appear to know a pedal from a saddle, but I have spent my life studying horses and bikes. I understand the subtle differences between a well-made cycle and an oversized crock of shit. My budget, as I may have mentioned, was minuscule, a meagre £13.32, and I was hoping to lavish this on something that would enable me to speed my way around the winding lanes of the West Riding. Leather helmet on head, skin-tight socks *hugging my ankles, I would travel betwixt and between small cafés like a flash of wholesome fresh air. Saving the planet in the process, I was an environmental warrior before the environment was even considered a viable entity to destroy. Suffice to say, I didn't get that Speedo-Bike, and the environment is now on its proverbial last knees, having bypassed the calves completely. I hold your company wholly responsible for this turn of events, on account of your unwillingness to even consider dropping the price of the Speedo-Bike by £200. Greedy businesses like yours are killing the free market and destroying the planet along the way. I hope you suffocate in a bag of overripe tomatoes.*

*Yours with a bitter taste,*

The final days of 1999 were bittersweet. It was not only the end of the millennium, but also the end of Thomas, and Damian was determined to somehow make a better life for himself and his parasites. The new century would offer new hope and opportunities, and with new glasses and a sleek beard, Damian would step forth with a confident glow, and not a trace of ringworm.

# Part Five — Events, dear boy
## Spy

Following Thomas's death, many skeletons crept closer to the cupboard door, not quite stepping out, but certainly having a sneaky peek. As Damian went through what was left of Thomas's private papers with Anne, it became apparent that Thomas had led a very colourful secret life as a spy of sorts in the mid-70s. Working deep undercover, so deep that he wasn't aware of his own cover, he was tasked with touring the working men's clubs of West Yorkshire on the lookout for Soviet spies and new talent. Anne had been aware of his many visits to the grimy clubs of West Yorkshire, but the papers he had kept revealed a trail of failed artists all under observation by Thomas. His usual disguise when in the clubs was that of a well-dressed lorry driver out for a fag and a pint with fellow working men. Smart blazer, dark red tie and a suitably ironed shirt all gave him the look of a well-scrubbed driver in search of a destination. He carried his notebook with him at all times, with copious scribbles on various half-soaked singers, magicians and comedians he had seen throughout the year. His attention to detail was minimal, as many of his notes were made under the influence of powerful alcohol and strong, unfiltered cigarettes. The trail of surveillance and subterfuge began in 1974 at Slack Hope Underworked and Affable Men's Club, a pit of a piss hole at the back end of Keighley. That first foray into foreign intelligence saw Thomas exposed to a contortionist from Wigan, a juggling pianist with a glass eye and a comedian with out-of-control alopecia. Thomas was particularly interested in the contortionist, and his notes are reproduced for the first time below:

*Friday 16th March:*

*Windy with heavy drizzle, causing my hair to frizz – not happy with choice of tie – will change.*

*Approached bar and suspect Dave is in the pay of the Soviets, drinks too much vodka for my liking and very fond of his Skoda.*

*Red Reg walks in looking smug. Think he is in the pay of the emulsion magnets. Very red cheeks – should stop drinking so much port.*

*Contortionist, the Fantastically Elastically Stretching Steve, was very good. He started off with a few powerful lunges and a mistimed back flip and then spent ten minutes inside a medium-sized fish tank (fuck knows why). Performed a few stunts inside a sack and fell off a stool, twisting his ankle. Might be okay but a little over ambitious for a twenty-five stone man.*

*Red Reg slumped in corner with a copy of 'War and Peace'. Maybe he is a Soviet mole.*


*Saturday 24th March:*

*Wind finally died down although still beset with heavy drizzle. Contemplating buying a hat to protect the barnet.*

*Bar is busy with a shifty crowd in to see a magician who once appeared on a talent show in Lowestoft. Not sure if many are Soviets or members of the Magic Circle.*

*Red Reg slumped at the bar with a half pint of port and a copy of 'Anna Karenina' – looks more and more like a mole for the red menace. Will monitor and perhaps set up a covert surveillance operation if the Ford Espionage will start.*

*Magician came on at nine p.m., thirty minutes late, and the crowd were very aggressive. His rabbit was obviously a fake and only had the one ear. Several members of the audience shared their drinks with him very enthusiastically. Show paused to mop the stage. His card tricks would work better with playing cards, and his wand looks similar to a car aerial. I suspect he may be a talentless twat in the service of the Soviets. Will set up monitoring operation.*

Thomas then visited several other clubs in and around Bradford, one of which, The Haunted Wastrel, was known for its red toilets and garish lighting.

*17th April:*

*Drizzle still proving a problem for my hair. Decided on a stovepipe hat to blend in with the clientele of the club.*

*Jonny, the loose-lipped compère, has just left hospital following lip surgery, and he is in full flow, warming up both of the audience members with a torrent of incoherent grunts and clicks. Should have gone private for his lips.*

*Nice to see a variety of acts on tonight. Looking forward to the impressionist who once appeared in a Pedigree Chum commercial dressed as a bone.*

*Impressionist came on stage early to get it out of the way, in his words. Performs a passable Charlie Chaplin, without hat or cane. Spends five minutes trying to Velcro on his moustache for a quick Hitler/Groucho Marx. I think he might be short sighted as the moustache was stuck to his chin for most of his act.*

*Red Reg falls through the door with a copy of 'Crime and Punishment', observing that the fucking impressionist is a crime against entertainment. Followed Reg last week and spent three hours outside Oddbins.*

*18th May:*

*The Honolulu Cabaret and Cricket Club is on the outskirts of Leeds, sitting next to a disused horse rendering plant and a pipe factory. Famed for its grass toilets and spin bowlers, it often stages specials based on Hawaiian entertainment. Tonight, there is a surfboarding ventriloquist, a grass-skirted fire-eater and a Welsh male voice choir who can do a passable version of the 'Hawaii Five-O' theme tune.*

*Red Reg has his head buried in 'Doctor Zhivago' — too obvious to be a mole — perhaps he is working for the CIA as a double agent?*

*The ventriloquist, Lenny Lips, is oily, sweaty and has a dummy bedecked in a grass skirt with colourless garlands around its neck. He starts off by singing a few tunes from South Pacific, then has to nip off stage as the dummy needs a piss. Doesn't return.*

*The fire-eater has cancelled thanks to a severe bout of hay fever, so when the choir comes on, the audience are at fever pitch, drooling for some uplifting tunes with a Pacific theme.*

*Red Reg leaves the bar and is spotted smoking a cigar in the car park — suspect the red hand of Castro.*

Thomas was first approached to monitor talent and spies when he was working as a chauffeur for a wealthy needle magnate who was unable to drive due to extremely thin fingers and brittle eyes. The magnate, or 'Mr Pin', asked Thomas for some recommendations for a good night's entertainment in West Yorkshire. Immediately Thomas realised that he was being recruited to spy on the Soviets, and the rest, as they say, is hearsay. Lonely is the man who has no calling, no ambition or friends. Thomas had all of these packed away for a rainy day, so in the meantime he had been happy to play a small part in the downfall of 70s' chicken in a basket culture and the red menace. His work for 'Mr Pin' was neither dangerous nor arduous, but it did shine a very dim light on some very dim people.

Frequenting the clubs of West Yorkshire in the 70s was not just a lifestyle choice, it also offered an opportunity for a Desmond Morris-type examination of the human in its natural environment. The clubs, always dimly lit and reeking of a torrid mix of sweat, smoke and Bacardi, could be both dangerous and welcoming in equal measure. Thomas fell back on his naval training, remembering the motto of his skipper, Captain Dredge, which had resonated with Thomas, even as a young man. Dredge, who had a fake eye and several wooden teeth, had instilled in Thomas the importance of eyes, and the motto 'Better one good eye than a blind eye', had seen Thomas through the dangerous days at sea. It was thanks to his naval training that Thomas realised that 'Mr Pin' was in fact a retired river boat captain who once owned a party boat on the River Humber, sailing from Hessle once a week with Hull's glamorous party-going elite. Deciding that spying and talent-spotting were a little too mundane, Thomas returned to his first love, and continued in his quest to source as much tat as possible. Mr Pin took it well, observing that there wasn't much subterfuge worth monitoring, and with the onset of colour TV, talent was less in demand.

Also, among the many papers left by Thomas were clippings from the Naval Gazette and The Ceramic Eel. It was wonderful for Damian and Anne to find some old copies of The Ceramic Eel, a magazine that Thomas had read assiduously on long journeys to Hornsea. Packed with wonder, the magazine was a treasure trove of tips, trivia and topical articles that brought comfort to Thomas when tat was not readily available.

*The Ceramic Eel*
*How best to throw a fish-shaped vase.*
*By Valerie Claypot*
*Flowers are the land's fish — colourful and varied in shape. Splashing in the meadows and florists, flowers can also be served with chips at a push. Imagine though, if you can, a way of combining those two great icons of British life, fish and flowers, in a pottery marriage. Eels, the slippery appendage on a cockney's foot, but also the king of the freshwater pond. Electrifying in their sleekness, the eel was, and is, a staple of both the dining table and the florist's window display.*

*When I first decided to throw a fish-inspired vase, the obvious choice was our pious friend, the monkfish, followed by the sole and halibut, all fish that could swim alongside any monster of the ocean. My husband Vic, not usually a creative or talkative fellow, suggested I try the eel, as its shape is redolent of the stems of many a flower. It was a flash of sheer bloody brilliance that has inspired me to create a vase that could accommodate the longest of stems.*

*However, as with most things, pottery related, there was a catch. My pottery wheel, a Zumba 550, will only fit enough clay to throw a medium-sized kipper or a freshly hatched plaice. Innovation and flexibility would be needed if I was to achieve the eel-shaped floral receptacle. Using a discarded inner tube and some robust gloves, I decided to work the clay free hand, melding and moulding over a seven-*

day period to produce a vase that would be robust yet delicate — fine but not feeble. The resulting vase is both unique and versatile. I would suggest that it would not be out of place in any well-organised public toilet, or in the kitchen of a roadside café.

The next time you have the urge to throw an exotic shaped vase, think aquatic, think fresh water, and maybe adopt a more relaxed approach to the outcome.

Next week I will discuss the best pottery-based gift for an imminent divorce.

*Ask Meg Mouthful!*
*The Ceramic Eel Help Page- Pottery-based problems answered by Meg Mouthful*

Dear Meg,

My husband is riddled with small insects and refuses to wash. He smells to high heaven and hasn't worked for seventeen years. Can you help?

Dear Laura,

I was married to your husband once, and the only thing that really makes him happy is a well-turned milk jug. Of course, he may well have changed, so perhaps you could sketch a picture of a pitcher. Some men respond better to craft-based gifts, and my second husband Rory was always happy with a well-crafted liquid vessel.

Try it! Meg

Dear Meg,

I recently broke a very expensive pottery collection, and I am currently on the run. Is there any where you could suggest where I could lie low for a while until the crying and hatred stops?

Dear Betty,

What a fucking nightmare. I suggest you fuck off and be more careful next time. What were you thinking you clumsy fucking oaf. Fuck off.

Hope this helps,

*Meg*

*Dear Meg,*

*I am at my wits end! I recently discovered my husband was keeping fish in my best bone china. It was a wedding present, and I am worried that the fish will spoil the taste of my morning cuppa. Can you help?*

*Dear Frank,*

*I would imagine your husband is very lonely and this is a cry for help. Have you considered drinking a little less tea and perhaps trying coffee?*

*Yours, Meg*

*Top Trivia*

*1/ Clay was used by the early Romans to fashion false teeth and missing digits. Often, they would paint the teeth, hence the phrase, 'teeth like a centurion'.*

*2/ Pottery is fragile, and this is because it can break easily. In the old days, pottery was made from wood, making it more robust and woodier.*

*3/ Clay pigeons can't fly, but a breeding pair can produce a litter of thirty. If kept in a warm place, they tend to melt.*

*4/ Jugs are similar to vases, but quite often have handles and have a different use. Some jugs can be very big.*

*5/ Large pots are a great place to hide decomposing relatives, as are fridge freezers. Fridge freezers are not made using clay.*

Thomas loved The Ceramic Eel, and it was a very sad day in his head when it ceased to be published, due to lack of readers and a loss of advertising revenues. With the onset of virtual pottery, ceramics became mere ornaments collecting dust in the houses of the feeble and fragile.

# He's a wrong 'un!

The magistrate looked like her face had taken a severe beating from the weather. Her chin swung like a pendulum on a face that had seen too much time. Jowls and wrinkles jostled for space on her overcrowded face, and her eyes dripped contempt. Damian was up before the beak for drink-driving. He had been driving his Audi Thrust in a manner that was considered erratic, and when cornered by the police, he had hidden for ten minutes contemplating his stupidity. There was no excuse for his crime, the only bright note being his capture before he did serious damage to others. On the drive back to the police station, cuffed to a police dog, he had played his stupidity out in his head over and over. The dog, part of an elite undercover police dog team, sat impassively, occasionally licking its arse but otherwise saying very little.

Arriving at the station, Damian was led to the desk sergeant and told to remove anything of value and his belt. The sergeant, a burly fellow with a warm smile and a mischievous truncheon, explained the charge and then led him to a cell. He would remain there until the morning when he would be released on bail, pending a date before the beak. His solicitor, Mr Wheeze, was constantly on the look-out for his next breath and explained to Damian the possible consequences of his stupidity, all the while holding an inhaler and panting like a very thirsty dog. Wheeze was a month away from retirement and he was eager to go out with a win. By win he meant not too heavy a fine and disqualification. He advised Damian not to bend the truth and to be contrite. Damian could do that.

When the chief magistrate, whose face really was dire, rose to pass sentence, the hush that swam across the court room could be heard miles away. Damian had endangered his own life and that of innocent motorists and pedestrians. His reckless behaviour deserved a sound thrashing and several weeks in the stocks. However, it was not in her power to sentence Damian in this way, so he received a hefty fine and lost his licence for two years. He was also given eighty hours of community service. Cries from the public gallery rang out as an undercover police dog sunk its teeth into a wanted drug dealer's arse, and Damian slumped into his chair, fully appreciating that he would have to dispose of the Thrust and spend time doing something for nothing. Justice had been served.

He was told to report to the probation office in a dusky part of town to be given his community service duties. Arriving there with a sense of dread, he was met by a very friendly woman, Miss Clutch, who escorted him into her office and proceeded to explain how his community service would be administered. He was then given an A4 folder and asked to select his own community service. A menu of potential punishments lay before him, from sweeping old people to hand painting with geriatrics. As he flicked through the menu, he was desperate to find something that would enable him to pay for his crime. By chance, he spotted an opportunity to work in a charity shop, assisting the volunteers and generally being a dogsbody. It was perfect, and once the necessary paperwork was completed and a confirmatory phone call made, he was told to report to the charity shop the following Saturday for his induction.

Arriving outside 'Scream', a charity dedicated to people who shout too often, Damian swallowed hard and entered the premises. Behind the till was a woman who looked incapable of shouting, and in the corner another woman was busy wiping down some dusty clothes which were due to go on sale. Mrs Volumes, the manager of the shop, was a large lunged lady who had spent her whole life shouting at irregular intervals, and when she retired a few years ago, finally got the treatment she so obviously deserved. Her pent-up voice was, even after treatment, still very loud and had a slight northern twang to it. Damian was given a tour of the shop by Mrs Volumes, and she outlined his duties, hours of attendance and policies on raised voices and loud music.

His role was to steam donated clothes from nine in the morning until five in the evening, ensuring that they did not smell of death too much. It wasn't back-breaking work, just very tedious. Piles and piles of clothes littered the upstairs room which was to be Damian's cell for the forthcoming weeks and months (only Saturday; he was allowed home for the rest of the week). Mauves and mustards polluted the antique blouses and frocks that were the daily donations from the bereaved and colour-blind. Damian inspected his tools, a rather ancient looking steamer and a coat hanger, and realised he would have to try and see the positives. He wasn't dead and the staff were friendly.

As the Saturdays passed, Damian marked off the hours he had completed on a handy little sentence calendar that came free from the probation service. By late October he was nearly halfway through his term and was on the verge of selling his Thrust to a relative of someone he knew at work. A price had been agreed, and he had come to terms with using public transport. The buses in the area were mainly clean, and if he avoided eye contact, he very rarely had to speak to deranged pensioners on their way to buy random potions and eggs.

Damian had been working in recruitment for the last couple of years, and he had risen slowly to a position of meagre authority. He was though, in charge of his own day, and his main responsibility was to interview potential temps and produce monthly forecasts. He also was responsible for fabricating equality data which was needed to make the department look good; this he did with abandon, calculating that no one in their right mind would trawl through the guff that he produced, with pie charts, graphs and diagrams.

He had met his future wife, Sadia, via the agency, interviewing her for a position and instantly recognising the mother of his future son. Her beautiful eyes, ability to use Word and Excel and warm smile drew him to her, and he had asked her out for a drink. They would be married in 2004.

A normal day for Damian at the agency would involve reading through a heap of over-enthusiastic CVs and rejecting the vast majority, coupled with interviewing the few applicants who had slipped through his meticulous criteria, alive with fully functioning brain. Curricula Vitae are strange beasts, and even to this day, Damian finds the notion of selling yourself to secure employment a ludicrous circus of lies and insincerity. The flavour of the applications he received was usually bland with a hint of desperation. Below are a few sample personal statements that he had to endure.

*Personal Statement One:*

*I am a keen go-getting, results-driven dogsbody who can work well with or without my eyes open. I can build barriers and bridges, depending on my mood swings, and am noticeable in crowds due to my rather inflated opinion of myself. Training would be a problem as I know everything, but I am willing to condescend and belittle colleagues if I am given this fantastic opportunity.*

*Personal Statement Two:*

*Recently released from prison, where I was voted most likely to reoffend by my peers, I can garner support from unlikely quarters if it will make me look good. I have severe trust issues and would not cross the road to piss on you if you were on fire. My attributes include a modest approach to effort, poor hygiene, and a lacklustre mouth. By employing me you will ensure that I won't reoffend too much during working hours.*

*Personal Statement Three:*

*Without doubt, I am the nicest person you will ever want to meet. I have a huge heart, which can be heard beating in quieter situations, and a willingness to bend over backwards in order to be appreciated and loved. My insecurities are many, but mainly due to self-esteem issues and a cheating partner who left me for the local butcher. Kindness is a word I use to manipulate those who are too stupid to realise that I have no real feelings, and quite often my moods will swing faster than a baseball hitter's appliance. Happy I could be if you were to release me from this ever-increasing vacuum of love… please, please, please employ me!*

*Personal Statement Four:*

*When I am your boss, I will give it three months before I sack you. If you give me this job, I will try and get there sometimes, business commitments permitting, and I will not leave my dog parked by my desk in the afternoon. My wife fancies a cruise, and I would hate it if you disappointed her, without thinking about the consequences for your health. I would expect you to bank my wages in an offshore account and not use my real name when filing my details on your system. I will be available for interview once the extradition proceedings have been dismissed, and I know that will be a formality.*

The interviews themselves were an opportunity to find out more about the person behind the bullshit, and Damian had a series of questions designed to draw out the worst in each and every candidate. Below is a transcript from a memorable interview Damian had with a convicted necrophiliac.

*Damian: So, dead bodies are not something we see on a daily basis. What skills do you have to make a corpse feel welcome?*

*Clive: I am a go getter, so I would go get her.*

*Damian: Imagine a scenario where you are dealing with an angry corpse who is dissatisfied with the service offered. What would you say to the corpse?*

*Clive: I trained in the armed services, so if necessary, I would drop and roll, eluding the corpse and passing a message to my superiors.*

*Damian: You say that you were in the armed services; what exactly was your role?*

*Clive: I used to knit the body bags for the MOD. I was part of a rapid-response body bag knitting unit, operating out of a secret location in the Outer Hebrides, on a need-to-know basis of course.*

*Damian: You specify kite-flying as a previous hobby, stating that you gave it up due to fear of flying. Do you think this will affect your opportunities for advancement?*

*Clive: I spent three hours being pulled along by that bastard kite. It was me or the kite. I had to do it. I still get flash backs now.*

*Damian: Thank you, Clive. We'll be in touch.*

The mundane nature of his job meant that Damian took to drinking more, quite often in the boozer around the corner from his office. Most evenings he would retire to the bar of The Host and drink away the early evening with a collection of broken spirits and ex-military men reliving their non-service in some long-forgotten conflict. Regulars at The Host included Welsh Bob, a serial dognapper who always had at least three dogs in tow; Reckless Chris, a microbiologist who had been dismissed by his previous employers for allegedly being too tall and Derek Stifle, a retired journalist who had written a gardening column for the local rag but had been forced out of his job for suppressing gardening stories. It was rumoured in the bar that Derek was in the pocket of a local gardening magnate who had been attracted to the wife of a rival gardening magnate. Physics being physics, it would never end well, so when vandals allegedly pulled up several fruit trees outside the local council offices, the competing gardeners were eager to win the contract for replanting, with some estimates stating it was worth up to £1213.74. Derek was aware of the whole sordid affair, and when he was offered a Victoria plum tree to keep the story off the front pages, he was more than happy to bury the story on page thirty-three, next to the situations' vacant ads. His editor got wind of this journalistic replanting and swiftly repotted Derek into retirement. Derek was apt to reminisce about the old days in gardening, when a spade really could be called a spade, and not a soil relocation implement.

# Hippocampus

Katie was due to go under the knife in late March. She had been diagnosed with a strange brain, and the doctors were concerned that if they didn't operate soon then her brain would only become stranger. The procedure involved many saws, drills and hammers. They had to drill down deep into the core of Katie's afterthoughts, remove her ability to reminisce and scrape back on her frivolity. This procedure had been carried out only once before on a clown named Gerry, who was way too frivolous and apt to reminisce about the good old days of vaudeville. As the day of the operation approached, Damian prepared himself for the mental anguish by doing some lunges, which seemed to free up most of the anxiety.

On the day of the operation, Katie was injected with strong drugs and asked to recite her fifteen times tables, a task which was fucking impossible for an eight-year-old. After only a few seconds, she was away with the fairies; the same could not be said about Damian. Wracked with guilt, he reflected on his daughter's frivolity; is it possible to be too frivolous? Would strong bandages have reined in some of her strangeness? These questions were hypothetical, and as Damian wandered the streets of Birmingham looking for a lava lamp, the surgeons were shooting probes into Katie's rather thick crust, hoping to drill a hole large enough to extract some ideas. It was a nerve-wracking time.

After an impossible wait, Damian returned to the hospital with a rather fetching lava lamp and a 'Hope You Enjoy Your Retirement' balloon. Katie had been moved to the recovery ward to recover. As Damian entered, he noticed Katie parked in the corner, complete with brain drain and comedy bandages. He felt light-headed and a little queasy, so took a bite from a large pork scratching to settle his stomach. It was difficult to see his daughter as there was a crowd of surgeons with substantial clipboards gathered around her bed. The head neurosurgeon, so to speak, a Doctor Scrape, had qualified as a horse surgeon in New South Wales in the mid-70s, but had switched to humans when the market for horse surgeons dried up after the great drought of 1996. Damian approached his daughter, scratching in hand and asked Doctor Scrape for the prognosis. Doctor Scrape, a difficult communicator, simply put two thumbs up and smiled. The frivolity had been cured!

Doctor Scrape went on to mime Katie's long-term recovery, explaining that there might be brief outbursts of over-exuberance, but these were normal in such cases. He also prescribed some large bandages, several cotton buds and a bucket of pills, to be used whilst sitting in traffic or at family functions. The aftercare offered was world-classish, but beggars can't be choosers. The road to recovery for Katie would be winding with some potential hazards to be aware of in case she developed afterthoughts, which with hindsight, could impede recovery. She was also given five complimentary bandanas as a souvenir of her stay and to help her remember the holes in her head. Katie recovered rapidly, and she was soon skipping with not too much frivolity, had an ability to focus on the future and remembered very little.

Reckless was the watchword during this rolling news year in Damian's journey from the dark side. Having being made homeless thanks to his feckless behaviour, he spent several weeks camping on a Serbian sofa in a suburb of Birmingham. He was treated to Serbian dishes and warmth and was soon ready to find a hovel for himself and rebuild his dysfunctional life. Divorce is a cruel mistress, or is the cruel mistress the cause of the divorce? Damian wasn't sure, but the time spent rebuilding what little he had was difficult, especially without the guiding hand of Thomas.

He had managed to rent a small decomposing hovel close to the parasites, complete with wicker chair, inflatable bed and partially cleaned toilet. Damian never met the landlady as she lived in a remote part of Sheffield and was busy building up a corrugated iron business. This was fine by Damian, and he dutifully paid the rent each month, receiving only the occasional telephone call from the landlady during quiet times in the corrugated iron business.

It was around this time Damian met Sadia. Sadia was and is a strange woman, and this is what drew Damian to her in the first place. She enjoyed the company of budgies, made fantastic food, and was extremely beautiful. She was some years younger than Damian, and many people saw them as a bit of an oddity together. The pie-loving Yorkshireman and the budgie-loving young woman made an odd couple, but it worked, as they shared a distrust and dislike of many things. It was always good to have shared enemies and dislikes, and psychologists have proven that couples who hate together, stay together.

Sadia would often visit the hovel and attempt to make it less like a dead person's last resting place and more like a temporary home for a semi-functioning Damian. Gradually piecing his mind together following the death of Thomas, Damian would often find comfort in drink, spending too much time in the local pubs. Whilst there he would meet the most extraordinary characters who had for one reason or another had been rejected by the world of work. His favourite pub was the Overly Excited Locksmith, a hole of a pub not far from a hole. Quite often Damian would sit for hours nursing a conversation with a drunk or lonely customer, enraptured by the sheer wonder of humanity. Several of those characters would regale him with tales of heartbreak, loneliness and failure. Two or three actually went to the trouble of writing down their misfortune in the slim chance that one day someone somewhere would write about them. Damian never promised a thing, but below are a couple of short excerpts.

### Green Sleeves: a Tale of too much stout.

*Thackeray Mcbust loved gardening. Thackeray loved drinking. Thackeray loved drinking and gardening. He planted flowers, he planted drinks, and he would often drink his flowers and eat his drinks. He was a wreck of a gardener, and all those who knew him believed his downfall into drunken green fingery started at the regional horticultural show* several years earlier, when a run-in with a judge sent him into a spiral of self-loathing and despair. He was an ardent royalist and was devoted to his herbal medicines, of which he had hundreds. In the evenings, kitchen door ajar, Thackeray would sit on a recycled milking stool and grind away with his pestle and mortar, hoping to discover a remedy for loneliness. Humming country and western tunes and gently tapping his one working toe, he would concoct potions and unguents if drink hadn't worked its magic.

Peering over his herb-infested fence, pestle in hand, he would implore Damian or anyone else within earshot to try one of his wonder cures. Over time Damian tried at least two, and on reflection, he saw some improvement in his ability to stir tea, wipe his nose and shuffle a deck of cards. Thackeray put this down to his herbal healing potions, insisting that the herb was an untapped resource which would eventually save humankind.

Thackeray would take his valise, stuffed full of potions and unguents, and tour the pubs of the area, tossing out basil and thyme, lavender and sorrel, to all who looked in need of a cure. He called into the Rancid Butter, a converted creamery that now served only bitter customers with equally bitter drinks. The barman, Finty McQuail, had acute mucous and chronic misapprehension. Thackeray applied a lavender-infused poultice to Finty's ego, and before long Finty was over the bar and manhandling Thackeray with a punch wrapped in gratitude.

Thackeray then collected his dignity and made his way to the Lonesome Harlot, a stenchy bar frequented by loners in desperate need of a companion. Sweaters oozing with desperation, and eyes that would light up when they spotted a breathing female, the regulars needed curing of something. Thackeray had identified this yearning for acceptance by the clientele, whose contact with the opposite sex was limited to their deceased mother and grainy pictures of Isadora Duncan. Sprinkling essence of rosemary in what could only be described as a reckless bout of stupidity, he was able to soak most of the drinkers with a dash of the feminine herb. Halfway down the road, as the baying crowd realised that drinking bitter had diminished their running abilities, Thackeray reflected on the vagaries of doing good.

Thackeray's final stop on his herbal odyssey was to the Retired Belt Makers' Social Club, a wraparound sort of establishment that catered for the individual with trouser issues and no braces to speak of. Located in an ex-belt factory, the smell that assailed Thackeray's nose as he entered its strapping premises was a mixture of a bracing sea breeze fused with despondence. Many of the ex-belt makers had suffered from lapses in trouser etiquette, loose waistlines and an abundance of underwear seepage. Believing that a strong herb, such as sage or cumin, would provide enough support for any drooping waistline, Thackeray had prepared his patented Herbal Hold Up remedy, designed to be used in conjunction with strong twine and glue. The healing properties were as yet unknown, but the herbs would certainly improve the aroma given off by the smelly bastards inside the club.

As he strode forth, remedy at the ready, he could be heard singing The Herbals, a traditional bluegrass tune that could stir any alternative therapist into a frenzy of misplaced belief in the power of herbs. It was a truly haunting tune that Thackeray had learnt as a child. His one-thumbed father, a veteran of the Mint Wars, had lost his thumb following a dispute over acceptable gestures at the roadside. The lyrics are reproduced below.

The Herbals

Mace, mint, they make me malodorous,
Lavender, clove, the scent washes over us.
Thyme is so rare, dill very sparse,
Good for the spots on a cyclist's arse.
Borage is heady; too much makes you weep,
Fennel's a fucker, but ridiculously cheap.
Sage for the wise, your wisdom to grow,
Wasabi is hot, of this you must know.
Saffron the queen, so vital for life,
Garlic so pungent, like my ex-wife.
Chicory is slippery, hold on keep it close,
Pepper and parsley, you triple the dose.
Nutmeg for nutters, catnip for clergy,
Mustard for headaches, ginger for scurvy,

*Allspice for all sorts with or without hair*
*A bucket of mace, for families to share.*

*Thackeray was last seen leaving the Doleful Weaver with a sack of turmeric over his shoulder and a crowd of well-wishers hurling chairs at his fragile head. The Herbals was the tune he could be heard screaming over the cries of pain emanating from his withered mouth. God bless Thackeray.*

# Wedded again

Two things happened this year that transformed Damian's life. The first was his marriage to Sadia following a protracted courtship and many house moves. The second was Mark's double transplant, a feat of medical brilliance and innovation.

The wedding was to take place in a yet unidentified venue somewhere in the Bradford area. Their budget was to be frugal, preferring to focus on cheap sausage rolls rather than beef wellington. The transplant took place at an unspecified abattoir and was very low budget, Mark preferring the organs of wild animals to run-of-the-mill human organs. The wedding was a small affair with family and friends, numbering no more than twelve guests; the transplant was similarly a very intimate affair, with only a partially qualified surgeon, an apprentice butcher and a trainee vet in her third year of university. The reception went long into the night, with loud music and plentiful supplies of pork pies. The operation went long into the night, with screams and blood-curdling cries as the surgeon struggled with a very uppity calf. The morning after was a casual affair with pork pies served with hollandaise sauce. The recovery period was unknown as they had never tried such an operation before.

As Damian and Sadia settled into their marital home, Mark faced a gruelling recovery. He had lost the use of his ears, which was an unfortunate side-effect of the drugs he had to take and so had to remove his earrings. He was also confused by up and down and would spend hours wandering around cricket grounds dressed in some very fetching pyjamas, believing that he was the embodiment of umpires of old. Sticking one finger skyward, he would declare everybody to be out and then retire to the pavilion for some tea and cake. A cocktail of powerful drugs was needed to keep him coherent, and any exposure to bright lights and cement could jeopardise his sanity. Damian had been friends with Mark for many years, and the thought of his friend being nothing more than a dribbling headcase with the need to umpire events filled him with laughter.

Damian had been contemplating a career change for some time, believing that somewhere there was a job that would enable him to do as little as possible for a decent wage with excellent holidays and opportunities for early finishes. He had inherited his work ethic from Thomas, but subsequently lost it at a high stakes' poker game. Not wanting to work in the private sector, something which he had already had the misfortune to experience, he focused on public sector positions. Social work seemed way too committed and involved dealing with other people's issues and histories. Civil servants were way too civil, and Damian had an abrupt manner from time to time that could be misinterpreted as misanthropic, so that ruled out any customer-facing job. Prison officer was a fucking no, as were any of the emergency services because of Damian's dislike of anti-social hours and fragile blood tolerance. Whilst reading one evening, a rather racy novel by Lester La Doom, Damian hit on the idea of being an English teacher. How hard could it be? He could walk, talk, read and write, and was not unwilling to put a spoken sentence together from time to time. What's more, he fancied teaching adults, as he had a morbid dislike of children and their parents.

When he shared his idea with Sadia, she was very supportive and offered to buy him a pen and some paper. Damian scanned the internet and soon found a course and university that would accept his under achievements, and he was signed up to start his second round of higher education; what a doss!

Damian had no qualms about being the oldest student on the course, realising that what he lacked in youthful exuberance and enthusiasm, he made up in oodles of cynicism and a deplorable dislike of young people. Freshers' week was soon approaching, and with all the enthusiasm of a painter asked to touch up the Titanic, Damian crawled back into education, with his goal a degree of sorts and some vaguely recognisable teaching qualification. Deciding that English was the obvious choice, his timetable looked suitably native, with words that he was instantly able to read. Damian viewed this as a positive start to his re-education. His modules included 'English Literature in Times of Old', 'Basking in Grammar', and his personal favourite that first semester, 'Nurturing Words the Old Way', a blockbuster of a subject that explored the genetics of language and how a pigeon became a creole. Damian knew what a pigeon was, having driven over one a few years back, and Creole was the surname of that musical hipster, Kid, so the module would probably be a walk in the proverbial woods. Nurturing bitterness against the enthusiastic, he attended his lectures with a scowl and unseemly body odour to prevent friendships being created. Neediness is the mother of fuck-tittery, and Damian wanted to focus entirely on his studies and count words all day. He had no time for coffee and idle bullshit. Books were his new diet of choice, and he devoured all manner of writing like a fat kid in a pie shop. He found the routine of reading and then writing undemanding and was soon marked out as a swotty bastard. Trawling through obscure literature from the seventh and eighth centuries, written when pens were homes for chickens, Damian found a new love for early English poetry, and he would often cite his favourite poem, 'The Weaver', to Sadia in an attempt to make her drowsy.

*The Weaver*
*Anon*

*Frolicking, bollocking, woeful weaver,*
*Hath no faith, a non-believer.*
*His God the wool, his church the farm,*
*Summer winter, he's always warm.*
*Norseman cometh, with sword and shield,*
*To pillage wool, he will not yield.*
*Lambs are slaughtered, chickens taken,*
*They even took the bleeding bacon.*
*Weaver, weaver, weave a shield,*

*Take your army to the field.*
*Thrust your sword, do your worst,*
*The weaver's craft, the weaver's thirst.*
*Norsemen came, Norsemen fought,*
*Weaver wove, Weaver taught.*
*Weaver died, his fleece lives on,*
*Now that all the Norse have gone.*

This poem inspired a love of wool in Damian and brought back happy childhood memories spent with Thomas counting sheep and admiring woollen garments.

His next foray into literature was less successful; he had to study the works of Harbinger Crud, nineteenth century artist, author and good time Charlie. His most famous work, 'Brickworks', was a classic in Victorian drudge and doom. Below is a brief excerpt of the memorable opening paragraph.

## Brickworks

*Eustace Crumple strode into his office and took a seat; he had fifteen now, and very soon he would complete his collection of Georgian seats. A grim man, not too tall yet strangely giraffe-like, Eustace removed his dust ridden cap, tossed his walking stick into the corner, and proceeded to count his bricks. Equipped with two vicious eyes and a mouth that screamed to be punched, Eustace could never be described as handsome. His feet, of which he had two, were gifted with two extra digits, allowing him to count up to twenty-two with ease. It was a happy coincidence that he loved to count as he knew numerous numbers. Charged with such an onerous task of counting bricks, most men would buckle under the monotony, but not Eustace, whose love of bricks was borne out of a desperate attempt to have a solid foundation in all aspects of his life. Engaged to his withering fiancé Esme for over seventeen years, he did not want to rush into marriage without the surety of compatibility. A handsome woman she might be, but Eustace wanted to be sure that once wedded, he would not uncover a facet of her being that made him bilious. He had always prided himself on his bricks, spending his youth in a brickwork factory and learning the basic shapes. Not one for outward shows of emotion or humanity, he had a private collection of bricks that was estimated to be worth as much as two shillings. Such high-minded fastidiousness had cost him dearly with his nearest and dearest. His father, Jebediah, hated Eustace with a passion, and the pair had not spoken since Jebediah expressed a fondness for stone and half-timbered dwellings. A wall had been erected, figuratively speaking, and the only communication they had was via small notes attached to large pieces of masonry. His mother, also referred to as Esme, was a chunky-fingered lady with a secret love of preserves; she spent her days grubbing around in hedgerows in search of ingredients for a new jam or pickle. Her love of preserves had kept her looking young, but her personal hygiene was questionable. She too had no love for bricks.*

Damian failed to appreciate the underlying themes of destruction and futility which were Crud's signature. The subtle interplay between Esme and the bricks later in the book meant little to Damian. He preferred fiction that had real meaning and shorter words. He recalled a tale Thomas would tell him as a child.

After the war, Thomas had spent some months working in a noise factory. The factory, producing noises for the home and business, was located in a quieter part of Bradford and produced noises that would have been deemed impossible thirty years earlier. Thomas regaled Damian with fun facts and anecdotes about escaping noises, unintended noises and misplaced noises. The working day started with a bugle call and several cockerels celebrating the new day. This was followed by a gentle hum and a hush that would sweep over the factory. Several types of racket and two jars of bluster were the standard on Monday and Wednesday, and on Fridays a growing sense of urgency could often be heard.

Inside the cavernous factory there were several different departments responsible for a variety of noises. Thomas was assigned to the groaning department to begin with, but as a result of his ill-fitting elbows, his groan was seen as too vulgar and a little on the offensive side, so he was transferred to the animal division.

Animals were Thomas's bread and butter. He could produce bullocks and rams at the drop of a hat, and for a country starved of wildlife after a wartime edict by the Ministry of Farms, anything remotely reminiscent of the countryside was a welcome breath of farmyard air. He proved to be a natural, and his talent for noise was recognised by his peers and his superiors. Soon he was seconded to the specialist noise division, located in a disused wind tunnel. Ordered to create sounds that would lift the nation's spirits, Thomas quickly set to work with a grease gun and a tuba. At first his colleagues dismissed his noises as ludicrous and unachievable unless indulging in wrestling in an ill-fitting corset, but soon they came to appreciate his noises.

His first truly innovative noise was the 'Squirrel at a Wedding', designed to replicate the sound of a vicar crushing a bridesmaid's hopes. High-pitched and at times truly awful, it perfectly captured the despair so often felt by the more grotesque bridesmaids. He then came up with the brilliant 'What's That, Chum?', a cross between a snarl and a gruff response to a question from an acquaintance of some years. Gruff yet menacing, its intention was to startle the listener into mild shock and loosen the odd stool. The 'Happy, Clappy Evangelical' was a glorious celebration of blind faith, with a series of slaps, claps and whoops, all in time to a primitive chant. Thomas believed that in some it would inspire hope, in others pity. The perfect retort to travelling clergy who might come knocking at the door in the dead of night. Many of his experimental noises were locked away as they were felt to be too dangerous for a population whose ears were still operating at pre-war sound levels. He often spoke of the 'Vast Pit of Despair', something so horrid and dreadful that he only ever produced the noise after a large pie or an unsatisfactory meal at a roadside café. So distressing was it that it caused mild alarm in Whitehall and mandarins decided that it should be saved and only used when 'fuck off' wasn't sufficient.

Thomas loved a wedding, and he produced several wedding-related noises, from the 'Dishevelled Parson' to the 'Bigamist's Trombone'. Both noises were unisex, and any halfwit could use the noises without danger to the wider congregation. The 'Bigamist's Trombone', a cross between a rodent frying an egg and a large man applying talcum powder, fizzed with hope and opportunity, and anyone who heard it would immediately think of the bigamist in their family. The 'Dishevelled Parson' was a work of true beauty, designed to imitate the noises usually only found in a humid vestry. Rancid with hope and pity, the 'Dishevelled Parson' was compared to a large man in a small room trying to fit into a ludicrously small pair of leather trousers with only one good hand. Muffled grunts and the occasional yelp were mixed with discordant grunts and a whistling noise that was only discernible to hounds and children under four.

Possibly Thomas's greatest noise, and the one he is most remembered for, is the 'Heaving Tugboat Captain', a celebration of nautical weddings lost at sea. With Thomas's keen eye for all things moist, he crafted a noise so exquisite, so visceral, so magical, that any couple planning a wedding at sea on a tugboat would instantly choose it to accompany their walk down the briny aisle. Slippery and elusive, the 'Heaving Tugboat Captain' evokes a simpler time, when a foghorn was a musical instrument, when fish knew their place and when a seagull was perfectly acceptable food for a disorientated fisherman. Fusing guillemot calls and the easily identifiable sound of a cod having a shit, Thomas captured an age-old noise that would not be out of place at a land-based wedding.

Big things were expected of the noise, and as couples across the nation planned their nuptials, the 'Heaving Tugboat Captain' took centre stage. Tragedy struck Thomas on a personal level. The pressure of producing world-class noises on a daily basis had caused a very undramatic change in his mental state. He found himself isolated and alone, and longed for the simplicity of the whistle. Boffins burrowed around Thomas's lab trying to replicate his unique noises, and the unexpected consequence was complete silence. He was spent, a noise genius in a mute wasteland.

In the days and months that followed, Thomas tried to recapture the joy of noise, but despite strong inducements and the sympathy of colleagues, he knew that his noise-creating days were numbered. On the third of October 1948, Thomas created his last recognisable noise — the 'Gallic Shoehorn', a simple lament, combining the unmistakeable sound of tight shoes with just a hint of Parisian savoir faire, like a hiccup and fart combined.

Damian loved this part of his father's life, and was never quite sure if it was entirely true, but he imagined his father as a noise pioneer, breaking barriers quietly, with dignity and with a smile on his face.

Suffice to say, Damian completed his studies and took his love of literature to a dark place and never speaks of it before midday.

# Pearly whites

Teeth, the gateway to the stomach, the body's defence against pureed food and jelly. Damian had used his teeth most of his life, and he had become quite attached to several of the more enthusiastic ones. Following advice from Sadia, Damian joined a dentist society to try and encourage his teeth to hang around for longer. His dentist, a short man with no hair and very little grace, had no teeth, believing that teeth were an impediment to truly enjoying lollies, soup and mashed potatoes. He had small, stumpy fingers, a determination to manhandle Damian's mouth and too much spittle. Appraising Damian's mouth, the dentist, Mr Mund, suggested that Damian should label the teeth he wanted to keep and then the remaining teeth could be retired. Realising that Mr Mund intended to kidnap some of his teeth, Damian suggested a compromise. Mr Mund could take three teeth but must promise to use them for future research into unwanted tooth syndrome.

Damian was placed into a large cling film-covered chair and strapped in. He was then injected with a mixture of drugs that left him feeling euphoric. Slipping into the arms of Mr Mund, he realised that the dentist hadn't a clue what to do, and Damian would later recall hearing screaming and bitter cries of despair. It turned out, following a lengthy police investigation and sordid tales in local newspapers, that Mund was actually a leading member of a shadowy organisation, the Radical Front for the Liberation of Teeth. The Front, as it was later referred to by the media, was set on liberating teeth to free the mouth from unnecessary chewing. Funded by large jelly cartels, they had infiltrated dental surgeries both in the UK and more worryingly, the Scilly Isles. They produced a weekly pamphlet detailing the woes of teeth users, who had been mouth washed by a government intent on encouraging oral hygiene. Mund would print pamphlets in the back room of his surgery and then distribute them in the care homes and sweet shops of West Yorkshire, disseminating toothy lies and jaw-dropping threats to those users of toothpaste and brush. One such pamphlet, that was found in Damian's possession, read like a 'Who's Who' of dental infamy.

## Chew and be Damned!

*Cold is the man who brushes his mouth and munches peanuts! Foolish is the woman who flosses in the morning yet chews chocolate late into the evening! Stop this criminal misuse of the molars, this callous canine calamity! Act now and liberate your teeth. Free them from servitude and decay. Every day, somewhere in a mouth near you, a tooth dies. Every day, somewhere in a mouth not too far from a sink, teeth are being abused by brushes, floss and other instruments of torture.*

*The government peddles lies and falsehoods to keep you trapped in a cycle of cleaning. An oral odyssey with no end, only gum disease, fillings and sparkling smiles to look forward to. Fat cat dentists fill your mouth and their pockets, whilst you scrub and polish; to what end?*

*Liberate your teeth and embrace jelly. Too many teeth can be dangerous, and can lead to undue spittle, lengthy lips and gums that need shielding. Only by removing those wanton ridges of enamel and calcium will your mouth fully appreciate smooth peanut butter and jelly, trifle and jelly and jelly and jelly.*

*Act fast before your teeth become prisoners to your adoring mouth. Release them, emancipate the enamels and liberate your lips. As the great Greek philosopher Socrateethes was often heard to say, "A wise man with teeth can only envy a wise man with jelly."*

*This pamphlet is produced by the Radical Front for the Liberation of Teeth.*

*If you would like to donate, be it money, teeth or soiled clothes, then please write for more information to: The Front, Stability House, Rotten Road, Plymouth, or call 09876 876 876 and ask for Dave. Alternatively, visit our website, **www.Pullemhard.co.uk**, where a wealth of information on teeth, gums, pliers and jelly is available, along with tips on how to*

317

*extract your own teeth in a painful yet efficient manner. There are also jelly recipes, a fun games page for the kids, and an online shop selling jelly, jelly themed tee-shirts and socks, and a handy planner for jelly festivals around the UK.*

As Damian came around from the barely sufficient anaesthetic, minus three teeth, he noticed Mund sucking on a chunk of jelly, and realised that his mouth had been violated. Staggering from the chair, he went to leave the building, but was bundled to the ground by an officer from the Dental Crime Unit. Mund was being raided in what turned out to be a co-ordinated series of mid-afternoon raids on dental surgeries across the country. Damian was eventually released from custody once it became obvious that he was a feckless fool who had no idea of what had happened to his teeth. Mund was sentenced to some time behind bars, serving two weeks once good behaviour had been factored in, and he now runs a Tooth Rehabilitation Centre in Fife. The Front still operates, but following a clampdown by the authorities, teeth were taken off the political agenda when it was apparent that jelly's toxic ingredients were likely to lead to immaturity, baldness and impotence. A subsequent government enquiry went nowhere, and jelly is still freely available on the street, sold to unsuspecting kids. The dealers, who behind the scenes peddle their strawberry flavoured poison to a new generation, continue to evade prosecution, and Damian has had more teeth removed but only for cosmetic reasons.

Anne was sympathetic to Damian's teeth-related issues and believed an excellent way to avoid teeth troubles was to chew on a vegetable. She was familiar with some vegetables, having read a short article on carrots as a girl. Rumours about other vegetables had swirled around the shops of Bradford for years, but Anne had been reluctant to extend her vegetable vocabulary in a world where a woman was judged on the quality of her pie.

Thomas had first discovered carrots in a rancid Irish stew when he was training to be a sailor. The colour had sent him blind for a matter of seconds and he vowed never to touch a living vegetable for as long as he had his own teeth. This changed following a very interesting talk on the wireless by the Minister for Vegetables shortly before VE Day. The Minister referred to exotic vegetables with unpronounceable names like broccoli, courgette and aubergine. To Thomas, who believed in spies and loose lips costing lives, it seemed that this was some vile attempt by the Germans to poison the valiant sailors with foul tasting vegetables. The wireless was a very important source of food information for a population who had subsisted on dried meat and bread for the last six years, and Thomas was wary of trying any vegetable that wasn't orange. Years later, he would often visit Bradford's number one fruit and vegetable market with real fear, still afraid of poisonous aubergines and toxic courgettes.

Anne, whose mind was wide open and welcomed any new ideas when it came to feeding her parasitical children, appreciated the possibilities of feeding her thankless children cheap shit and dressing it up as nutritious. The children would be given, during breaks from lard-filled pies, a cabbage or courgette to chew on. It never did any obvious harm, and even though they protested, their teeth remained fairly clean. Following the death of Thomas, Anne was desperate to find a purpose in her life other than the weekly chair aerobics class. Vegetables became her raison d'être, and she was soon working alongside other like-minded strangers, campaigning for free vegetables on the NHS. She quickly found an ally in Janine, who by now had eaten many cabbages, and the two set up a not-for-profit organisation, Free Veggies, to push their radical agenda. In their bunker somewhere in a secret location in Wibsey, they drew up a ridiculous manifesto for vegetables. The very first thing they had to do was create a list of all the vegetables they knew and produce some placards for their planned march to Bradford city centre. They then produced their radical manifesto outlining their core objects, long term ambitions and favourite colours. This document was a turgid attempt at rationalising the irrational, with crackpot notions of nutrition, half-baked (like Anne's cakes) ideas, and vegetable-based recipes that could prove to be disastrous. Below it is reproduced with most of the shit redacted.

### Free Veggie – Unearthing the Impossible!

*Who hasn't spent hours watching a carrot slowly mature, or an onion gently turn from edible to mush? Who hasn't woken in the middle of the night, screaming like a deranged banshee, wishing for more turnip in their diet? What does a woman have to do to get her hands on carrots and cabbage without suffering the withering looks of a judgemental butcher?*

*Vegetables, or veggies as they are known on the street, have existed for decades, yet few people fully appreciate the benefits of eating carrots and cabbages, preferring instead a beautifully prepared steak and ale pie with a rich gravy. As a child I was denied aubergines and courgettes, dismissed as a witch when I bought pumpkin, and very nearly arrested when I stole a packet of dried peas as a young mother. Is this any way to treat a mildly respected member of any community?*

*As we race towards chronic meat saturation, surely, we must pause awhile and reflect on the benefits, both physically and emotionally, of eating a wide range of greens. If the so-called cardinal veggies were eaten by more people, then the nation's health would vastly improve. Take the carrot, so long reviled for its similarity to the parsnip – its fluorescent colour, its association with decaying snowmen; it is actually riddled with nutrients. If you take a sharp knife to a carrot in a very quiet room, you can actually hear the vitamins cry a little. Quite often it is possible to collect these escaping nutrients and use them in carrot-based recipes. My favourite is carrot soufflé, a rich and repugnant dish often served at night.*

*The cabbage, considered by many to be a ball of smell and gas, is in fact awash with minerals, making it the number one choice for athletes and plumbers alike. It is almost impossible to eat too much cabbage, and there's possibly nothing better on a warm summer afternoon than cabbage ice cream with fresh strawberries. It will leave you glowing for days. Ideally, cabbages should not be eaten on a full stomach or Wednesday, and for the squeamish, get your greengrocers to gut and fillet the cabbage, so you can spend more time with guests and family friends.*

*Aubergine, the bulbous cousin of the courgette, is viewed by many as a side show of a vegetable, suitable only for small animals and moussaka. In the 1940s, aubergines were used as soundproofing at the ministry of colour, a shady department responsible for shades of many things. It was only when aubergines were featured in the hit musical, The Eggplant and the Fly, that people began to sit up and take notice of this hideously misshapen vegetable. Possibly the best way to eat aubergines is in the dark, and the warm glow of smugness will illuminate the empty room as you sit alone enjoying the health benefits of the eggplant. In Victorian times the aubergine was seen as a cheap alternative to the egg, and many lesser educated idiots believed that purple chickens came before the eggplant.*

It was obvious to Damian that his mother and sister were off their fucking heads, but he decided to humour them as their intentions were good. Anne was a healthy woman, if her retarded lung and pipe-smoking was factored out of the equation, and Janine had very strong wrists, meaning she could grip a door handle for hours without any need for artificial stimulants. Both women would avoid robust exercise regimes, preferring instead the more sedate types of exercise, like looking, strolling and gawping.

Anne's lungs were a mixture of dark, runny ooze and dried pipe smoke, resulting in an intermittent rattling sound, often brought on by vigorous window cleaning or climbing ladders. Doctors were often surprised she was still alive, but she seldom complained. She took comfort from her low-emission pipe and wrapped herself in green credentials. Her ankles, often the Achilles heel of weaker pipe smokers, were in fact freakish in their strength. She was born with a semi-fossilised ankle, which had metallic properties, allowing her to play hockey with abandon and perform daring pirouettes. As a young woman, she had spent a few days as a bare heeled fighter, but her pipe-smoking and three children put an end to that. From time to time, she would reflect on past pipes, remembering a lost youth when pipes were a passport to wealth and exclusive clubs. She once entered a poetry competition, which had a top prize of three months' subscription to 'Pipe Monthly', but she only managed third place. Her poetic effort is reproduced below.

### My lungs

*Suckle and nourish, a pipe does it all,*
*Winter or summer, spring and the fall.*
*Lungs at the ready, fill them with smoke,*
*Cough and a splutter, ready to choke.*
*Beautiful lungs, bags full of air,*
*One is enough, but better a pair.*
*Pipe as a babe, at mother's knee,*
*Room full of smoke, bastard can't see.*
*Went to the doctor, lungs full of stuff,*
*Needed more oxygen, hadn't enough.*
*Gave me a bag, said breathe into that,*
*Lungs still not working, he looked like a twat.*
*Pipe is my friend, my one true confessor,*
*Smoked by the good, the great and the lesser.*
*Smoking my pipe, in wind, rain and snow,*
*Born with a pipe, to my grave it will go.*
*Lungs, lungs, oh beautiful things,*
*Sucking on pipe, they give me wings,*
*To soar above smoke, the pipe is sublime,*
*Get your hands off the pipe; it's not yours it's mine.*

Damian admired the fortitude shown by both Anne and Janine, but knew in his heart of hearts that socially, they were a lost cause.

# Night talker

Small talk was something Damian avoided at any opportunity. He considered small talk the property of those people whose tongues had very little else to do — people with too many teeth and no fucking sense. Small talk was the dog turd in a flowerbed of roses. He would cringe when asked how his weekend had been by someone who had little or no interest in the answer. His bowels would head south when quizzed about holiday plans by an over-curious hairdresser or dentist. It's not that Damian yearned for deep meaningful dialogue on weighty matters, but more the case that he loved bananas but hated banality.

When he accepted the role of night dispatcher at a Birmingham breakdown recovery company, he was to experience no small talk, just buckets of bullshit interspersed with straight talking aggression and tom-tittery. The business, 'Ratchet & Sprogg Recovery', was located in one of the shittier parts of Birmingham, adjacent to an abattoir and opposite Birmingham's premier fancy dress shop, 'Guess Who!'. The premises were dilapidated, with hot and cold mould, leaky urinals and a kettle that had been salvaged from the siege of Mafeking. The ponderous lighting was always unsure whether to be on or off, so was in a permanent flutter, whilst the windows, if not totally broken, were close to a breakdown. The owners of the business, Don Ratchet and Ron Sprogg, were old-school idiots, with too much money (earned through hard work and lies), no common sense and very little self-control. At the interview for the position, Damian had been grilled by Don whilst Ron sat impassively, smothering his face with a bacon, mushroom, cheese, sausage and tomato sandwich. Questions had ranged from 'Do you like confrontation?' to 'What's your favourite John Mills film?' They ran the business with a rod of lard, insisting that all employees did not cut their nails and cultivate grime at any opportunity. Fried sandwiches were a staff perk, with any combination possible as long as it included bacon, lard, bacon, saturated fats and more bacon. Having been shown the layout of the building, Damian had been introduced to the mechanics and drivers — a gaggle of grime and no-hopers, whose only saving grace was their ability to drive in a straight line and bamboozle mechanical dimwits. The manager, Den, was a shaking mass of nerves whose attachment to cigarettes meant that his smoking breaks spanned most of his working day; he was constantly in search of a light and a Regal to calm his overactive nerves. Den was the whipping boy of Don and Ron, and when they were off the premises, he acted as their eyes and ears — a glorified snitch without any of the glamour. Everyone liked Den but no one respected him, in part due to his habit of tucking his shirt into his underpants and making no effort to hide the fact. He was a man with a nervous arse, so kept it tucked up tight. His knowledge of cars and bacon was encyclopaedic, but his debilitating nasal condition meant that most of what he said sounded like snot escaping from a bad handkerchief party.

The mechanics were a breed apart, and Damian found them entertaining and helpful. As a child he had watched Thomas struggle with cars and their workings, on one occasion assisting Thomas in changing the engine on a Ford Squat. His father had many spanners, and Damian was sometimes trusted to degrease and count them. Thomas was a keen bodger and would never truly fix a problem on any of his cars. Damian took that ability to count spanners with him to this new role, and believed his numeracy made him the perfect person to monitor spanner usage. The mechanics at Ratchet and Sprogg were hard-eating, rabble-rousing spanner-monkeys, who loved the life on the road, with the smell of diesel fuelling their paranoia. Every job was always the hardest job or a piece of piss. If the stranded motorist was an attractive woman, then the mechanic usually had to 'fight her off'. They really were cowboys of the road. The drivers, who delivered and collected vehicles, were at the bottom of the food chain, employed because they had avoided driving penalties and death.

Damian was based at the heart of the operation in the control hub, a dimly lit hole secreted with grime and carpet. It had a small window and a tiny hatch, which was his window to the world and disgruntled customers. At his desk there was a computer, a primitive telephone with substantial deposits of earwax and a two-way radio for communicating jobs, instructions and sandwich orders to the mechanics and drivers. His first task was to learn the phonetic alphabet, as used by the emergency services and dickheads throughout the land. His next task was to learn the geography of the area and where they operated. These two activities did not require any steep learning curve. The hardest part when he first started was trying to understand what the idiots at the other end of the radio were saying. The mixture of accents and jargon left Damian confused, and to begin with he would often make up messages to get off the radio.

There were six mechanics employed at the business, and the most experienced of the lot was Gary, a toothless giant with low self-esteem and an endless waistline. He never chewed his sandwiches; he ground them with his effortless gums, which were on show whenever he smirked, smiled or farted. Gary had a thick Black Country accent, which meant Damian would often smile and nod without knowing what Gary was trying to communicate. Gary always had his ukulele in his van, and at quieter times would pen mechanical ballads to get him through the long nights when cars refused to break down. His wife had left him for a Nissan salesman from Darlington, so he refused point blank to repair any Nissan. One of his most haunting ballads was all about the tortured divorce of a mechanic with no teeth.

*Your Love Gave Me Something To Chew On*

*My gums are sore, I've done all I can,*
*You stole my wife, with a blue Nissan.*
*Your shiny suit and your greasy hair,*

*My wife and you make a Nissan pair.*
*Shiny, cheap and smelling of plastic,*
*Leaving me, darling, was so fucking drastic.*
*I'd buy you a car, German one too,*
*Twelve years old, I can't afford new.*
*The air is so foetid, my teeth they have gone,*
*You left me in Darlington, for a salesman called Ron.*
*You have all the gadgets, and shiny blue paint,*
*A fancy new motor, a Mercedes it ain't.*
*Shiny, cheap and smelling of plastic,*
*Leaving me, darling, was so fucking drastic.*
*I'd buy you a car, German one too,*
*Twelve years old, I can't afford new.*
*So now as I sit, alone in my car,*
*You travelled away, Darlington's far.*
*A Nissan, a Nissan, you fucking great fool,*
*You smell like a bull frog and look like a mule.*
*Shiny, cheap and smelling of plastic,*
*Leaving me, darling, was so fucking drastic.*
*I'd buy you a car, German one too,*
*Twelve years old, I can't afford new.*

Damian was often moved by this evocative lament to a love lost by a gummy mechanic, so much so that he moved further away from the radio.

One mechanic, Pete, was a turd of a man with oblong eyebrows, over-enthusiastic nasal hair and an extremely under-developed tongue. As a child, Pete had been diagnosed with 'Spitty Tongue' or 'Needle Tongue', a debilitating condition that resulted in several punctured cheeks, an inability to eat ice cream and a constant whistle when he spoke. He was despised by all the staff because of his penchant for detail and correctness. His underpants, or so it was said, were arranged alphabetically and colour coded to show when they should be worn. Blue nylon was for warm nights and cool summer days; yellow was for flamboyant Fridays and hot picnics north of Birmingham. He had a whole wardrobe full of socks, which were in his words 'the window into a man's desires'. He was a perfectionist who performed his tasks to the best of his abilities, which is why he was so hated by his colleagues. He would go that extra mile to solve a mechanical problem, whereas most of his fellow mechanics would barely go half a mile, and only then if there was a possibility of a sandwich stop. When he spoke, his words were accompanied by a low whistle that seemed to be his theme tune. Certain phrases would cause his whistle to grow louder, particularly 'Your wheels were ruined' and 'Your wiring, really is rotten'.

Bozzer was the rogue amongst the mechanics, always dodging and diving to earn more and maintain the vast collection of tropical fish that he kept in his studio flat. He also kept three monkey fish in a specially adapted tank in his cab, believing they brought him good fortune. Monkey fish are the hairiest of all fish, and their long hair makes them very slow swimmers but very nice to look at. Bozzer called his monkey fish Fed-up, Fucked-off and Blowback, after a 1960s folk band. His wife, Lisa, had left him after a massive row over 'too many fucking aquariums in the bathroom', something that Bozzer was at a loss to understand. He maintained that it was perfectly acceptable to bathe with tropical fish as most of them were disease-free. He had a scam for everything and would often take part of his wages in tropical fish, which he would then resell at inflated prices (especially blowfish). His dress sense was based on an early 70s TV detective, wide open shirt with hairy chest for all to see. This made him a very popular mechanic with single female pensioners, who could smell his love of high-speed tropical fish as soon as he pulled up at a job. He was often to be found in 'Guess Who!', the fancy dress shop opposite the business. The owner of 'Guess Who!', Gwenda Grunt, admired Bozzer's disregard for tropical fish hygiene. Gwenda had worked as a TV and film extra for many years, appearing in many popular 70s TV shows, including 'Ooops, that's my Shaving Foam, Neighbour', 'Living with Haemorrhoids', and that hugely unpopular classic, 'Racist Motherfucker'. She also played the part of second servant on the left in the 1972 box office blockbuster 'To Serve is to Arse-lick'.

The costumes to be found in 'Guess Who!' were an eclectic mix which reflected Gwenda's dysfunctional narrative. She had suffered many heartbreaks in her relationships, and she had sworn off men many times in the past, yet she still found Bozzer's animal musk and scaly skin attractive. Her costumes very much appealed to the bitter-middle-aged-woman-scorned market. Below is a flyer listing some of the more popular costumes:

*Dress Up by Guess Who!*

*For The Bitter Slim Divorcee:*
- *The Crumpled Mess — Similar to a Down and Out but with essence of despair and pigeon shit — £13.25 per hour*
- *The Disorderly Party Guest — Includes complimentary vomit pack and two tubes of tears — £7.54 per hour*
- *It's not you, it's me — a stunning backward facing costume that is completed with a two-faced mask — £1.79 per hour*
- *Where's my F...ing Drink? — a slimline costume, replete with beer stains and essence of cigarettes — £78.36 per hour*

*Costumes for those with low self-esteem:*
- *The Slimline- an industrial-strength corset that can withstand 400kg of pressure, complete with ribbon to give it that whimsical look — £91.31 per half-day*
- *The Sobbing Misfit — Gold Tuxedo with matching Moon Boots and spinning cummerbund — £43.31 per hour*
- *You Lookin' at me Darling? — Enjoy your reflection in a full-length mirror with this ill-fitting cat suit, complete with tail and dog whistle (available in blue) — £4.38 per day*
- *Buckle Up and Jump on My Bike — The lycra look has never looked so fetching, with cellulite inserts in all the wrong places — £17.37 per weekend*

*Special Offers!!!*

- *Dress Like a Monk, Live Like a Monk* — *Stunning one-piece sackcloth with tie for the more spiritual heavy drinker* — *£1.76 per week (Cleaning not included)*
- *Lord Thrush the Stamp Collector* — *an awesome retro costume for anyone who loves the aristocracy and stamps* — *£0.60 per week*
- *Deep in Space Mine- Perfect for star gazers and sci-fi nerds alike, with integral belt for quick toilet breaks* — *£3.98 per week*
- *Edwardian Dentist* — *Go back in time and grow a beard. Perfect for pulling teeth or the opposite sex* — *£5.37 per month*

*All costumes come free with a pack of sanitary wipes and surgical gloves. All costumes must be returned promptly, or we will sue the fucking pants off you.*

During the long evenings and nights spent at Ratchet and Sprogg, Damian would contemplate Bozzer and Gwenda, Gary's broken heart and teeth and Pete's meticulous sock wardrobe. He soon realised that to engage with these people in a rational way would be fruitless, but he was more than capable of being irrational as and when the mood took him. He also looked forward to the day when he could leave and focus on a career that didn't involve grease, earwax or saturated fat.

# Bricks and Mortar

Estate agents were the bitter taste in a bottle of cherry cough medicine — the unexpected aftertaste that left the patient feeling a little surprised at how bitter the taste was, even though they fully expected the bitterness. Damian had lived in many rented houses over the years, and he had met his fair share of bitter cherry cough medicine in that time. He had often thought of setting himself up as an independent, one-man house-selling machine, offering honest and clear selling to buyers who too often distrusted the very lips of estate agents. Deciding that boldness was the mother of disaster, Damian initially decided to set up a shadow estate agency, run from the back bedroom of Sadia's and his extensive two-bedroom terrace. He would draw up details of properties, estimate dimensions, import images from Google and then post the details randomly to non-existent clients who looked like they might want to move, ought to move or were nearing death. He would hope to garnish feedback and assess how effective his methods were.

The first thing to consider was a suitable name for his agency, and after very brief discussions with two well-placed pedestrians and a short consultation with Sadia, he arrived at a shortlist of three potential names. The first, 'Towers & Turrets', was an obvious attempt to appeal to the Rapunzel-loving knight of old on the lookout for a suitable property with kerb appeal and good schools. The second suggestion, ' Dross & Dregs', was aimed at the bottom end of the market for those buyers whose budget might just run to a bus or static caravan; shit on a shoestring was Damian's target demographic. The final name was 'Gutters and Gables', focusing on the nuts and bolts of property, and those people who would pick holes at every fucking available opportunity — the delusional arsewipes wanting something for next to nothing. Unable to choose a name, Damian decided to run the three names in tandem and see which received the most feedback/hate mail.

Damian scouted out several properties and quickly identified several possible properties that could be marketed without the knowledge of the unwitting owners. His rationale was that the owners, although settled and happy with their homes, may well be tempted if they could turn a profit on their bricks and mortar. His first choice was a stunning neo-Gothic terraced heap in rural Birmingham. Below are the particulars that Damian carefully crafted to appeal to discerning idiots with too much money and an obvious shortage of sense.

*Outstanding Period Property!*

*Birmingham, birthplace of the brick and architecture, home to many a jewel in a tarnished crown, and an ideal location if you yearn for easy access to motorways and roads.*

*Recently wallpapered, this four-walled property offers an ideal investment for the hard-hearted landlord or a magnificent family home for those who love small spaces and grandeur. Built as a plaything for a pampered Edwardian lady, this mid-placed house sits between two other houses and has rampant access to the adjacent pavement. Any discerning investor will appreciate the subtle nod to neo-Gothic details, which gives the accommodation a charming ramshackle feel. Complete with gargoyles, an array of flying buttresses and some beautiful roof tiles, this property is a true eyesore.*

*The accommodation comprises of three sturdy windows on the ground floor, with views across the road. The windows are encased in real bricks, giving the whole property an air of completeness. The internal dimensions of the ground floor accommodation are such that you will have some room to locate those precious knick-knacks that so cluttered your previous home. A kitchen was planned, but due to slippage and a chronic lack of mains water, the catering will be done off site. This obviously allows for more dining out for the discerning purchaser.*

*Climbing the hastily built ladders reveals that the upstairs has
everything one person would need to live, including a large door, four
walls and a hole for pissing in. Original features abound, and it is no
coincidence that the previous owner was loath to leave the property,
thanks to the rickety stairs and his untimely death due to too much
gravity.*

*Outside, there are two functioning abattoirs right on the doorstep,
giving any lucky buyer fresh meat day and night. Local schools are
planned, and it is hoped that in time mains gas will stop leaking from the
nearby gas works.*

*This property is a once in a lifetime chance to step onto the rickety
property ladder and rent out a hovel to some unfortunate fucker with
little hope and even less money.*

Damian ran off five hundred copies of the details, including its
full postal address, and posted them to random houses in the
greater Birmingham area. His second property was a fixer-upper,
chosen for its obvious potential and location.

*Deep in the Birmingham countryside there sits a wonderful nugget of
bricks and mortar. A find so rare that we at 'Gutters & Gable' can hardly
contain our piss due to excitement. Set in over an acre of built-up area,
this property offers every opportunity for the man or woman with the
picky eye and idle mind.*

*On approaching the property, what strikes the buyer is the
wonderful paint factory directly behind this beautiful semi-restored
fourth floor garden flat. Previously owned by a pharmaceutical salesman,
it has remained empty since he went to work for the government for
fifteen to twenty years. On approach to the front door via a concealed
tunnel, the aroma of fresh paint masks the unmistakeable smell of cat
piss. Who doesn't love animals? The sound of children playing is difficult
to discern thanks to the bottle factory, with its beautiful melody of
machines that can be enjoyed 24/7. The front door, reinforced to prevent
unwanted raids, is painted in a wonderful selection of street colours, and
the integral spyhole enables the den owner to screen unwanted callers.
Inside is a wonderful treasure trove of filth and garbage. The kitchen,*

with its mauves and browns, has a real earthy feel, complemented by the shrubs and mould that have taken root behind the washing machine. The open plan lounge affords wonderful views onto the staff car park of the local discount plumbing warehouse, with toilets of all varieties visible day and night. Along what can only be described as a dingy, ill-lit landing, is something that resembles a bathroom, without a bath, toilet or sink but otherwise ready to move into. The large rear bedroom has built-in ceilings and walls and could be used for growing herbs if a sofa bed was bought.

The vendor is currently away, so early viewing is recommended before he is released. The garden flat comes complete with neighbours, who we understand have some form of electronic tag system to record their movements, and are keen to continue good neighbourly relations, for a price.

The property may well be freehold or leasehold.

Damian sent several copies of the details to local church clubs, scout huts and fitness clubs in the hope that he could offload the property to sympathetic buyers. If not, he would target pathetic buyers. The third property, under the wing of 'Dross & Dregs' was a real humdinger, offering a fantastic opportunity for the half-hearted halfwit.

*Huge Pile Will Go This Week!*

*This could be the last chance to take ownership of an outstanding pile on the outskirts of credibility. The pile, which has yet to be built, could be perfect for the open-minded developer who really wants to part with unlaundered money and build a portfolio of sorts. Set in a remote quarry on the outskirts of a larger quarry, the pile is exactly that; three hundred thousand bricks arranged in a pile. They are in decent condition, and with the right person could be used to build something. The vendor has offered to transport the pile to anywhere within a ten-mile radius, weather permitting, and can access other building materials that could be useful when building property or buildings.*

*Recently dumped in a quarry, the pile was previously several run-down streets in Humberside and still retains the smell of the sea. Complete with graffiti, scraps of wallpaper and associated decorative features, the pile was hastily arranged into a neater pile to attract unhinged developers. The vendor is currently travelling incognito following a misunderstanding with the owners of a shotgun factory but swears blind that the pile is legit and above board.*

*Any prospective purchasers are welcome to view the pile, either in person or via a highly sophisticated drawing done by my seven-year-old daughter. She used a range of colours to reflect the diverse nature of the pile, but many of the bricks in the pile are not blue, it just happens to be her favourite colour. All parties in the sale would be expected to bring cash, in small denomination, unmarked notes, preferably in a dark brown attaché case.*

*The pile may well be freehold or stolen.*

Damian toured the local pubs and left copies of the details in both gents' and ladies' toilets, to widen the potential pool of fools.

His ambition was at least to give some unwitting tit a virtual tour of a property that was not in his gift to sell. He sat and waited for the first phone call, dressed in what he considered to be the standard uniform of any self-respecting estate agent: ill-fitting shoes, shirt, jacket and trousers, with hair suitably beaten down into remarkable compliant obedience, and a small wallet/folder for those all-important pointless documents. Nobody called!

# Not again

The year was bedevilled with death and heartache when first Stephen, Damian's eldest brother, and then a very close relative of Sadia's died suddenly. Death struck and for Damian, the loss of his eldest brother meant that he might be able to get his hands, on Stephen's golf clubs, unless Paul got there first. Happy hours spent thwacking golf balls in the cellar of Janine's house would be no more, but the clubs looked to be in a decent condition and the bag was virtually new. Stephen's wife was understandably heartbroken, as she had never had the chance to hit golf balls in the cellar with Stephen.

The funeral took place during the week, and Damian felt compelled to deliver a eulogy to his eldest brother, an inspirational man possessing such warmth and joy. Below it is kindly reprinted in English from its Japanese original:

*Dripping on toast and fish and chips,*
*Stephen's greatest foodie hits.*
*Bread and jam, cup of tea,*
*All this curry is for me.*
*In the car, driving fast,*
*All the memories of our past.*
*Playing footie, golf and tennis,*
*Hitting golf balls with such menace.*
*Long fur coat and platform shoes,*
*Cigarettes and cans of booze.*
*I'm mad tonight so go to sleep,*
*Stephen's gone, so I must weep.*
*Rest in peace*

Stephen had many gifts, from an ability to avoid choking at weddings to an innate sense of up and down. At no point during his too short life did he ever confuse up with down or consider himself gravity-free. His hair was his pride and joy. Indeed, as a teenager he was often stopped in the street by unemployed hairdressers and complimented on his useful locks. He cultivated small fungi in his fringe for a short period before suffering a catastrophic outbreak of acne, but he bounced back and later wrote a very moving essay on the dangers of excessive fringe growth. As a child, growing up in a period of black and white and suffering the loss of his one good milk tooth prematurely, he demonstrated amazing resilience. He would chew sweets, arrowroot and on occasions the fat, never displaying any satisfaction or dismay. His calculating walk allowed him to stay upright most of the time, and his sporting prowess was known far and quite wide in the vicinity of his house. He was an avid footballer, playing with both feet, at times competently, and when he rose to head a ball, quite often his fringe would give him superhuman strength, plunging him upwards and ensuring the ball knocked out whoever was in its trajectory. He had trials with several clubs and was universally recognised once he had been introduced repeatedly. He was a pioneer of roller skate tennis, a death-defying, ankle-breaking lottery of hand-eye coordination at breakneck speeds. He could top spin most balls, and his reverse sweep backhand-over-head chip would leave tennis aficionados in tears of laughter. He never played in any competitive capacity, for fear of injury and mockery, but in experimental games with Damian and Paul, the brothers were able to conclude that it was a feasible way for tennis to progress, providing adequate safety measure were written into the rules.

Stephen also had a very soft spot for table tennis, a game created for those who don't like strong winds, heavy rain and the great outdoors. He could play in the orthodox style, using a standard issue Piablo Paddle, or if circumstances demanded, the more experimental Panno Paddle, which was nothing more than a frying pan with a rubberised handle — perfect for ping pong, unsuitable for frying large eggs. Saturday and Sunday evenings were ping pong time, with Damian and Paul pitted against their Zen-like elder brother, whose agility and understanding of the rules meant that he always won. Ping pong balls were in short supply in the late 70s, thanks to an embargo on imported spherical objects, which brought many sport players to their knees. Stephen would often use putty, carefully rolled, as his preferred alternative, and although it was spherical, it refused to bounce and would often stick to the table. The net was usually an old pair of Anne's tights, strung between two twigs across the dining table. Games would often last up to five minutes, with furniture moved and the three remaining wine glasses moved into the back garden to avoid spillage and breakage. Thomas, Anne and Janine would take their seats in the yard and try and keep up with the action as the brothers crashed and thrashed around, putty splinters everywhere and no chance of a fried egg any time soon. Inevitably, as most parents would have done in similar circumstances, Anne and Thomas joined in and soon pans and putty were intertwined with limbs and teeth. Thomas, despite his advancing years and ill-fitting elbows, proved to be an exquisite exponent of the backhanded smash with twin pike and follow through. Anne, concerned as she was for the remaining crockery, would attempt to minimise the damage and salvage what little dignity she could. Janine, a passive sports person, would punch and kick for no other reason than to inflict pain on her stupid brothers.

Golf, often described as a bloody long walk with some sticks, was Stephen's other passion. Despite not being born with a club foot, he took to the game with ease, and would often practise his swing at inopportune moments: whilst driving, bathing, at urinals. This love of golf became infectious, so much so that he would often drag Damian and Paul, kicking and screaming, to some arse end of a course to hit grubby golf balls in driving rain. Damian took to golf and swinging his club immediately. Paul, whose enigmatic smile hid a range of emotions, proved to be a very competent hitter of things. The three brothers, armed with only three stolen golf balls and a shared love of the rain, would spend hours hitting and thwacking until Stephen decided it was time for a pie. Those days of sport and pie are long gone, but will never be forgotten.

# Harris-an experiment

Fatherhood came knocking on Damian's door again, after what seemed like just over fifteen years. He had opted to have a partial vasectomy several years earlier, believing that he was full up with fatherhood and never likely to meet a woman who would want to share the school run with him. Sadia had changed all that, but before the child could be delivered, it needed to be conceived. This involved many initials and a considerable amount of cash. The procedure that Damian and Sadia endured was intrusive, distressing and mildly irritating. Using cutting edge technology (what else?) and the latest laser guided needles, along with a pulley and some rope, the couple were delivered with some hope. In February Sadia bought seventeen pregnancy testing kits, and when they all returned a positive baby indication, Sadia went to the doctor to confirm the pregnancy and find out when the little cherub would be hand delivered. The suggested date was November the sixth, giving them ample time to redecorate their home, sweep some leaves and possibly buy some nappies. Over the course of the summer, the baby grew, and soon Sadia had to stop playing tennis and refrain from drinking carbonated water, and the high jump was out of the question. As summer rolled into autumn, the birth became more of a reality; each passing night was a reminder of what they would be giving up.

When the cherub didn't arrive on the due date, Damian was incensed, and wrote a very stern letter to the Ministry of Babies and Midwifery, which is reproduced (no pun intended) below:

*Dear Head Midwife,*
*I recently ordered a baby for my wife and myself, specifying that it would be convenient if it could be delivered shortly after Fireworks'*

*Night, as the sound of rockets and roman candles being loosed off could disturb the cherub. No money was exchanged nor guarantees given.*

*It is therefore very unsettling to discover that the date given is only an estimate, and that the cherub could arrive at any time around that date; this is no way to run a ministry. Both my wife and I pay our taxes on an intermittent basis, and it is this sort of bureaucracy that is crippling the country and dragging the nation back into the dark ages; no doubt it has something to do with the European Common Agriculture Policy.*

*When the cherub finally arrived on the 12th (a day late for Remembrance Sunday), I was at work and had to drive home so as to not miss the delivery, and I may have had to sign for the cherub. My wife has gone to a great deal of effort to plan this cherub, and I feel that your ministry has acted in a high-handed and insolent manner throughout, ignoring my calls and threatening legal action if I do not desist.*

*Thankfully, the cherub is healthy and a delight. We have called him Harris and plan to shorten it to Harry when the mood takes us.*

*Yours with joy,*

Fatherhood the fourth time round was a shock to Damian, and for the first three weeks he hid in the cherub's cot in the hope that the cherub would be quiet for a short while. Nappy changing and feeding were tasks that filled Damian with neither dread nor joy, he was more concerned with his regular tea intake and a decent night's sleep. Sadia and Damian finally came to an agreement, which is still in place today, that states that if the cherub wakes in the night, Sadia shall attend to his needs, and Damian will attend to all Sadia's tea-drinking requirements.

The couple decided to take a very laissez-faire approach to parenting, believing that less is more. For Damian in particular, Harris was an experiment in what a father could do if he ignored things. Damian never trusted people who wore trainer socks, believing that it was a deeply disturbing trend that brought out the worst in ankle exposure. Damian appreciated a well-turned ankle as much as the next person, but this rush to expose ill-formed joints sent a terrible message to impressionable people with ankle dysmorphia. Damian also distrusted enthusiastic people and pushy parents. The very notion of becoming enthusiastic about anything suggested to Damian a neediness bordering on psychosis; excitement and enthusiasm were strange bedfellows, and a phlegmatic approach to life meant fewer disappointments, or so Damian believed. Pushy parents made Damian feel physically sick and quite often lightheaded. Believing your child is bright, or remotely gifted is a recipe for delusion and heartache. Young Jonny being able to kick a ball whilst standing doesn't mean he will be playing for Barcelona in the future. Young Suzie might be able to remember the lyrics to a turgid pop song, but that doesn't mean she should be enrolled in stage school to become an obsessive smiler. Ruinous are the parents who put so much of their own shortcomings into their child's future. Let the fuckers fail. Sadia, who was equally intolerant of parents, believed that the cherub should be allowed to fail in whatever he chose to fail in; it was his failure, so he should take responsibility. It is fair to say that discipline and rules were more important to Sadia than Damian, but they both tried to do as little as possible without actually sub-contracting the parenting role. The cherub, of course, knew none of this, and may well sue his parents when he is older.

Sarah, Damian's oldest parasite, also gave birth in April of the year, supplying Damian with his first child of his child. The infant, a beautiful ball of blond, was Harris's nephew, a Jeremy Kyle dysfunctional family-style arrangement which suited Damian's disordered view of the world perfectly. When the two infants were placed together on a suitably cleansed surface, it was akin to placing a cappuccino next to an espresso: complete opposites. Damian was a father again and also a grandfather. Having never met his own grandfathers due to their premature burials, he had no grandfatherly role model to base his behaviour on, so he quickly bought a walking stick, flat cap and three hundred packets of Werther's Original in readiness for his new position.

The two babies were a constant sore in the peacefulness that adults take so much for granted. Grandchild number one was a flamboyantly curly-haired cherub, whereas Harris had the dark, brooding looks of a well-worn aubergine. Neither child could speak as such in the first three months, which meant their conversation was a little stilted, but what they lacked in fluency they made up for in decibels. Sadia would often take to hiding the pair in a small room and playing hide and seek with herself, just for light relief, and Damian, never a natural father, bought a pair of arm extenders to keep both cherubs at maximum arm's length. This worked for a time, but soon the needs of the babies were such that physical interaction was required. The dispiriting sight of a soiled nappy brought back unhappy memories to Damian's stomach, and he found the whole business rather unnecessary. Surely, in the twenty-first century, there was an app for changing nappies? Short-sighted tech types had missed a trick there, so Damian decided to explore the idea himself. Using his limited brain and a rusty computer, he set about designing an app that would eliminate some of the more tiresome aspects of parenting. After several hours and numerous teas, he had created a prototype — 'The Nappyappy'. Below are the notes Damian made during development of the app.

### _Nappyappy — Wipe away the smears!_

_1/ size selection — based on diet and propensity of baby to crap._
_2/ Masking agent — alleviates the worst odours._
_3/ Vomit suppressant — no one wants to vomit on their own cherub._
_4/ Piss warning alarm — pre-warns unsuspecting parent of imminent fountain of piss._
_5/ screech diverter — towelling nappies still used by small majority — safety pins can kill._
_6/ Find the turd game — smells like shit, but nothing to be seen._
_7/ Handy disposal — best place to discard nappies when on the move, be it on the bus, the outside lane of the M6 or just after boarding a transatlantic flight._
_8/ Nappy crush game — four nappies in a line wins an extra 30 minutes sleep — get a full night's sleep and win cash prizes or alcohol._

*9/ Where's my baby facility — nothing worse than mislaying your cherub in a busy dental practice or florists, so the app will help locate cherub by emitting a high-pitched whine.*

*10/ 'Fuck — the baby has started teething' warning light — complete with virtual ear defenders.*

Damian hawked his app to several of the larger tech companies, but was derided as a fucking idiot. Ironically, several years later, a well-known tech giant produced 'Slappyappy', for those parents who still persisted with slapping their sprogs, and it proved to be a great success with large-handed dullards, but Damian didn't approve.

Deciding that parenthood was something he was vaguely experienced in, Damian started to write a journal to share his insights with other desperate parents.

## Daddy knows Jack!

*Bursting with enthusiasm, like a playful marrow at a horticultural show, many new parents make fundamental mistakes in their journey on the road to being half-competent parents, never pausing to look at the short cuts available to make your cherub feel less wanted and you a little bit smugger. Thomas, my father, who was also a parent, often said that a nurtured child is a needy child, and that the best way to get through parenthood was to think of children as parasites, slowly sucking the life away. Warm words, but it is important to be flippant as well if we are to damage the mental stability of the parasites. Never feel that a compliment given freely to a parasite will be reciprocated; they are unfeeling, blood-sucking vermin whose only purpose is to drain what little life you may have left. But on a more serious note, try not to resent their very being, as that could lead to ulcers and premature balding.*

*Lucky is the parent with short term memory issues; lucky is the parent who is able to forget that they are a parent. Often, with my parasites, I move home frequently to unsettle them; their little faces when they realise Daddy has a new home forty miles away makes my day. Food plays a part in parasite rearing, and the worse the food, the more they want. Taste is anathema to them, satisfied as they are with fast food and any part of a breadcrumb-encrusted chicken, and it is no wonder that the modern-day parasite is prone to panic eating and bouts of gluttony when their guts are fed a diet of congealed hope and bacteria.*

*My own parasites, of which I have four, each bring a little very dull ray of sunshine to an otherwise cloudy existence. None of the parasites smells too bad, they remember birthdays and Christmas, and they know the basics of social interaction. Despite this, I still feel uneasy when I travel to the local tip for fear of one of the parasites desperately clawing through the waste in search of a future. It is a reoccurring nightmare, haunting me even in my waking hours, that one day they will organise a surprise party and invite all the friends I never wanted. A huge cake with ribbons and gallons of sickly ooze, lit up with candles and radiation, the centre piece of a funeral that would kill the sanest of parents. Parasites eagerly sitting around the confectionary abortion with paper plates and a forlorn hat, perched jauntily on their stilted heads. Party my arse — they just came for the free food!*

*However, despite all the kind words I have said, I do love my parasites more than words could ever hope to express, and their love keeps me from drowning in a sea of success. The trick of being a bad parent is to remember that you too were once a parasite, so it's almost inevitable that your own cherubs will be parasitical to a degree.*

It was fair to conclude that Damian was never one of nature's earth fathers, more a desperate man flailing helplessly for any clues on how not to completely fuck the future of his children. Only time would tell. Obviously, Damian wrote a poem as an homage to his four parasites, kindly written in English below.

*Parasites*

*Screaming babies, night-time woes,*
*Sarah, Thomas, Katie's nose.*
*Harris talks, the donkey's legs,*
*Stop your talking, the hind leg begs.*
*Flip and change, bored with lots,*

*Flipping flopping, ticks and tocks.*
*Thomas thought, then thought some more,*
*For the old, the young, the poor.*
*Katie spoke, a single word*
*A silent creature, a mocking-bird.*
*Harris like the babbling brook,*
*Like a record, always stuck.*
*Foibles all, they have so many,*
*Spend too much, don't spend a penny.*
*Can't decide, if up is down,*
*Walks around, a living frown.*
*Despite my words, you are my world,*
*Fuck!*

# Part Six — Some funerals and a wedding
## The Internet

With all things, Damian was open to new ideas and possibilities. Even though he had the appearance of a Luddite, and seldom changed his socks, he was fully aware that standing still would be no good for his Morton's toe. He loved technology and had recently heard of a new phenomenon, YouTubers. This garrulous concept, of talentless people broadcasting their every thought, movement and ineptitude appealed to Damian's flexible mind. He knew Mark was thoroughly versed in the ways of the web and had owned a computer. After many probing questions, Mark revealed a wealth of knowledge on matters, but was fucking useless when it came to cutting-edge things. He did, however, know a man who knew a man who had access to the wonderful World Wide Web. That was Damian's foot in the door, and soon he was up to speed with hard drives, disc drives and long sweeping drives. With a budget of very little, he bought the bare minimum and borrowed the rest from a man who used to clean his windows. After a thorough introduction into the ways of the laptop, the global network and camcorders, Damian felt ready to create his own YouTube channel. Operating from Harris's playhouse, he could broadcast to the masses and influence a new generation, with his off-beat ideas and in-depth knowledge. He had been advised to choose a target demographic, but wanted something that would appeal to kids and pensioners alike. After much deliberation, Damian had a light bulb moment. The name of his channel would be 'Encyclopiedia — An A-to-Z Guide to pie, virtual pies and pie gaming'. Decking out Harris's playhouse to make it look less like a child's playhouse and more like a hi-tech studio was the first challenge. Damian decided to equip the play studio with all the latest technological gizmos, including two

346

high-powered desk lamps, a scatter cushion and a small CD player that he bought from PC World. A quick splash of bleach to eliminate some of the nastier stains, and the play studio was soon ready for its first broadcast to an unsuspecting public.

The next thing Damian needed to do was write the content, which he felt would probably write itself, so he went and did something else. After a few weeks he thought that maybe he could get some ideas down on paper to give the illusion of a polished pie production. Damian had always loved pies, but as he had got older, he was less of a consumer and more of a collector. His knowledge was extensive, and he planned to use the first broadcast to give a brief history of pies, focus on a few world famous and historic pies, and then maybe recite a pie-related poem. Damian prepared his notes carefully, and he has not given permission to reproduce those historic and invaluable notes that he used for the inaugural broadcast.

### The Encyclopiedia Man – Episode One

*Good evening pie lovers of the world, and welcome to my channel – a pork pie of facts for the pie-loving man or woman. I will take you on a magical tour of the pie, stopping at pie accessories and pie games and give a very brief history of the pie.*

*Pie, the opieum of the masses, the giver of cellulite, the bringer of freedom. These days the pie is very much part of our collective eating habits, taken for granted as the go to health snack or welcome stodge. Originally thought to be invented in the early seventeenth century, archaeologists recently discovered something that looked like a pie in a field just outside Droitwich. Dating back to Elizabethan times, this relic pie is thought to have been made for a local glutton. Filled with meat, fruit, and some yet unidentified matter, this pie could be the missing link in the evolution of pie, turning established theories on their head (a sort of meat turnover). If it turns out to be genuine, then pie historians will have to go back to their drawing boards and reline their pastry tins. The pie has a hidden history.*

Across the globe, the pie is seen as a symbol of peace, love and family. In many parts of South America, the pie is a symbol of fertility, used to estimate the number of children a couple could conceivably conceive. In parts of the old Soviet Union, it is thought that pies were used to disrupt American spy planes in the '50s. In the UK, the pie is as British as Prince Albert, with its pomp and circumference, wrapped in a flag of tradition. The names of classic British pies just roll off the tongue: The Gouge, made with eels and strawberries; The Chokie, a gut buster favoured by the bigger-boned; and my personal favourite, The Heart Attack, a heady mix of fat and cholesterol, guaranteed to clog even the widest of arteries.

In recent years, pies have become a symbol of wealth and opulence, with many celebrities squandering their fortunes on outlandish pie parties. Footballers with more pie than sense have been ridiculed in the press for their over reliance on pies, and there are even TV game shows celebrating the humble pie, with pie-themed prizes. Possibly the most popular is 'The Pie is Right', where contestants must guess the ingredients in any given pie, whilst locked in an airtight room, all the while jumping up and down on a giant inflatable pie and wearing a blindfold. Nail-biting drama on prime-time TV.

When the internet was born, the opportunities for pies and pie lovers seemed endless, with an extravaganza of pie sites, offering facts and fun to a new audience. Kids and adults alike could log on to their favourite pie site and spend hours looking at pies, learning fun facts about pies, and downloading useful pie recipes. Fun pictures and clips of pies in hilarious situations offered the pie lover the opportunity to share the lighter side of pie. Pie gaming also became the latest craze among wired-up teens who wanted the buzz of a high-octane pie-related shoot 'em up game. The first, and still the most successful of pie games for consoles and PCs is Pieromatic, a futuristic game set in a dystopian future, where pies are the only way to save civilization. The third person game play allows the gamer to step inside the robotic pie and see the world through the eyes of a pie. Using state of the art graphics, some of the pies featured in the game look good enough to eat. Virtual gamers loved the fact that they could indulge in a pie-based game without the inconvenience of actually having to play and still being able to chomp on their favourite pie. The game has sold nearly twenty thousand copies worldwide, and its influence on popular culture is such that kids now wear t-shirts emblazoned with the legend 'Pie'll be back'.

As for the future, we've hardly broken the crust, and the next big thing for pies will be apps for the busy pie-loving commuter who needs a quick fix of pie before work. 'Pie-to-Go', a new venture, allows eager pie guzzlers to order pies and have them delivered to their door in a matter of hours, making the weekly pie trip redundant. There are suggestions that a pie dating app will be ready in time for the Christmas dating market. Aptly called 'Happie Ever After' the app promises to link up lonely and desperate pie lovers who share a love of crust but an inability to function at a face-to-face human level. Users will be encouraged to get out more and not rely on pies too much. With a swipe to the left, the road to true pie compatibility is assured, a swipe to the right and pie limbo will hammer down, offering very few crumbs of comfort. The possibilities seem limited, but who knows.

When Damian's channel went live, he was unfortunately beset with technical difficulties and lack of interest, meaning he only had three viewers, and one of those was Mark. His intention was to have a live 'Q & A' session at the end of the broadcast, giving viewers an opportunity to pick his extensive crust for juicy morsels of pie-related trivia. However, due to a malfunctioning keyboard, the letters P, O and U did not work, meaning his pies became 'ies' and his you, 'y'. Very disappointing for the three viewers, causing some upset and two viewers left thinking Damian was taking the piss. Mark remained but knew quite a bit about pies anyway.

It was also Damian's intention to launch a line of pie accessories to capture and corner, but not kill, the burgeoning pie accessory market. He had designed and developed a range of pie clothing, footwear and a board game. The clothing had the pie logo, which was a half-eaten pie winking in a cheeky fashion, and included linen trousers for the more mature lady, vests for the more mature gentleman and novelty pie socks for kids. There was also a pie tie, which lit up if you chewed it. The shoes, which were essentially clogs with elaborate pie motifs and scented insoles, offered pie pedestrians the chance to put their best pie forward and dazzle the fashion world. It was also mooted that there would be a range of toiletries. A gentleman's cologne, Pie pour Homme, and a fragrance for ladies Pie for Her, got to the drawing board stage, with a pie-shaped bottle and novelty crust on the base. The scents themselves were reminiscent of a warm day close to an abattoir, with overtones of pork, cherry and ammonia. In the bathroom, there were big plans for novelty pie-on-a-rope soaps, pie-shaped sponges, and a pie shampoo containing real bits of fruit pie. Damian's ambitions were ridiculous, and he even looked into adding an upmarket range of travel toiletries for the busy jet setter: Pie and Go, a subtle blend of lard and warm water to freshen any weary traveller; Pie High and Dry, a lip balm made from organic pork pie and ylang, and a moisturising cream, Pie Fat, rumoured to take thirty years off the face but put twenty on the hips.

The board game, inspired by Damian's love of murder mystery, was called 'Which pie will kill me?', and players had to work their way around a board populated with pie merchants, pie thieves and irate pierates, all trying to lure the unsuspecting player into gobbling too much pie. The last player to have a massive heart attack and die won the game. There were bonus cards included which increased the fat content of pies, a card for genetic heart conditions, and also a vegan get-out-of-coffin card. The game could be played by anyone with a pulse and retailed for an amazing £74.83 including second class postage.

Disaster struck his stillborn venture into cyberspace when he was threatened with court action by not one, but an incredible fifteen different plaintiffs who demanded he shut down his channel immediately. The British Pie and Crust Association actually sent an armed barrister to Damian's place of work and threatened him with an umbrella. The Union of Independent Pie Lovers and Eaters, an organisation whose history is littered with cardiac arrests, stated that Damian was a stain on the pie world. The Ministry of Pies and Pastry demanded that Damian apologise to someone for the shite he was churning out, akin to propaganda which could unduly influence impressionable idiots, leading them into a crusty life of pie drudgery. A major newspaper sent a trainee reporter to get some dirt on Damian, pie related filth if you like, and that was the final crust that cooked his goose. The channel was shut down, the internet remained free of pies, and Damian mourned the nation's unwillingness to embrace his love of pies.

He had written a poem in honour of the pie, and it is published below in its unabridged version:

*Pie R Squared*

*Oh Pie, Oh Pie thy are a must,*
*Oh pie, oh pie, your crusty crust.*
*Large and round, small and squat,*
*Juicy filling, you've got the lot.*
*Oh pie, oh pie, why don't you last,*
*Oh pie, oh pie, you're gone so fast.*
*Meat and potato, chicken and ham*
*Cherry, apple, in they cram.*
*Oh pie, oh pie, puff or short,*
*Oh pie, oh pie, eat not ought.*
*For deep inside, the fillings hide,*
*Eat too much and you will died.*

Following the failure of his YouTube venture, Damian quickly turned his attention elsewhere, focusing on his work as a vaguely useful English lecturer in a further education college. Teaching all and sundry, he was beset with idiots and fools, whose only purpose was to make his life harder. Words were his tools, and only a poor workman blames his tools, but there must be exceptions. His colleagues were a collection of misinformed individuals whose distrust of students, language and efficiency meant that little of value was achieved. Damian's tawdry attempts to impart knowledge to his students were doomed to fail. He decided to teach his students in a more unconventional manner, believing that the considered norms should be discarded for more wayward forms of pedagogy. Adopting a Bohemian hat and fragrant smock, he transformed himself into Monsieur Damian, the French English teacher. Bypassing convention had its risks but living on a tightrope of disaster made each day challenging and alive.

He had five simple steps to follow that meant his lessons would always be, if nothing else, interesting.

*Step Un: Try to start each session with a lunge and a shrug; it keeps the bastards on their toes.*

*Step Deux: Whistling repeatedly like a shepherd in search of sheepdog affection can play havoc with the equilibrium of students. A high-pitched whistle can leave students unsettled and in fear of failure.*

*Step Trois: Anything soiled, be it a shoe, a shirt or a smock, gives the illusion of wisdom, knowledge and reading. Erudite and soiled goes the old saying.*

*Step Quatre: always carry a prop of some sort, be it a soft-boiled egg waiting to be eaten, or an unwritten book, which is essentially just a collection of blank pages. Students will be curious as to why you are using the prop, deflecting them away from your own ineptitude and the focus of the lesson.*

*Step Cinq: Avoid eye contact. Studies have found that one of the major reasons why people are inept and socially awkward is due to eye contact − either too much or not enough. Gazing into the eyes of a slack-jaw who is incapable of understanding the concept of the passive voice will not remarkably imbue them with any more wit than the obligatory half they were born with but have failed to nurture.*

Damian believed that if these steps are adhered to, he would not only become more of a hate figure in the staff room but would also face disciplinary action from those further up the managerial monkey chain. Never one to shy away from bending rules, he had lobbied and campaigned the government to try and get his five steps made obligatory for all those who would like to pass themselves off as a teacher, alive or dead. He felt so strongly that he wrote one very poorly punctuated letter, highly charged with threats and loathing, to The Ministry of Spelling, Grammar and Punctuation. It is reproduced below with the punctuation cleaned up by professional punctuators.

*Dear Mr Colon,*

*I am loathed and full to the brim with bile. You, sir, waste our time sending small individuals to places of education without fully equipping the educators with the necessary tools to frighten the shit out of them. In your ivory tower, you are manifestly unsuitable to serve in any capacity other than as a dull full stop at the end of a meandering sentence. You, sir, are not a simple sentence, nor are you in anyway complex enough to approach being a complex compound sentence. You are an overblown question mark in a world looking for answers.*

*I have taught many things, some of which have responded to my radical five step plan, for enhancing shame in the classroom. I come from a long line of halfwits and fools, so feel fully qualified to spot one when I smell one; you, sir, have been spotted. Colleagues of mine, who may or may not have relevant qualifications, working mouths and slightly overbearing body odour, are far better equipped than you to dictate the correct way to train and arm teachers for the challenges they face on a bi-weekly basis. The radical proposals I have sent to your offices repeatedly, for the last thirty-nine weeks, cannot and should not be discarded in the waste bin of oversight.*

*Men and women like myself have waded through all manner of shite to achieve very little on a daily basis, in part due to our incompetence, but also due to your wanton disregard for my common sense five step proposals. I realise politicians have a role to play in deciding how and when to shaft a cross section of the public, but children are our future. By adopting my wonderful five step proposals you will not only lift a generation of sprogs out of under-achievement and into mediocrity but guarantee a slightly less dim electorate in the future. It's a win-win, Mr Colon.*

*I realise my proposals are expensive, but what price can be put on my happiness? I will obviously charge a small fee that would allow me to retire from this shoddy career and do something far more indulgent with my time.*

*So, Mr Colon, do the right thing and adopt my breathtaking five step proposals and sign that bloody cheque.*

*I am, and always will be, your loyal servant.*

*Yours sincerely,*

Damian's letter sent reverberations around Whitehall, and heads could have rolled, or eyes. When news of his explosive proposals got out, he was hauled down a thin corridor by a large lady and given a severe dressing gown. He was warned not to rock any boats and required to write fifty lines for the principal of the college, who liked lines. His faltering career continued to falter, and he continued to send in ludicrous proposals.

# Breathe, for god's sake!

Lungs: the Amazon rainforest of the body, supplying tropical birds and oxygen, without which we could well die. Damian had two active lungs and was keen to fill them with smoke from assorted smoking paraphernalia. Over time he had smoked all manner of fags, cigars and pipes from around the world. He had also benefited from secondary smoking as a child; both Anne and Thomas kindly shared their smoke with all the children. Not many parents were so giving in the 60s. As was his wont from time to time, Damian would smoke a cigarette with his morning brew, reflecting on the vagaries of life, and then proceed to do sod all if it was a holiday. On the Monday morning before his birthday, he was busily stubbing his cigarette out when he felt a dull pain developing across his back and also on the right side of his chest. His first thoughts were that it was his athlete's foot flaring up again, but after performing several lunges, dropping to his knees and chanting, and finally lighting up again, with no obvious change, he realised it could well be something serious. Immediately he sprang into action, sitting down and reflecting on some more vagaries of life. The pain persisted, and he knew he would have to make the call: 999. On his hands and knees, in some pain, he looked for the phone, which Harris had been playing with the previous evening. Spotting the handset under a cushion, he tapped in the magic number and was immediately connected to a hub located somewhere in a call centre. Explaining his situation, he was assured that an ambulance would be with him as soon as the breakfast dishes had been cleared away. Replacing the handset, Damian took off his shirt and placed his house keys on his lap; he was ready for the blue-lighted mercy dash to the hospital a quarter of a mile down the road. Before the brothers and sisters of mercy arrived, he quickly rang Sadia and gave her the news; his athlete's foot hadn't flared up, but he could well be having a heart attack. Sadia took the news as well as could be expected. He then called Sarah, who always liked to experience new things and visit exciting places. They would all meet in the accident and emergency department. Shortly afterwards, the ambulance crew arrived, and as Damian had kindly left the door ajar, were able to enter without recourse to tools, banging or smashing windows. They quickly scanned the room for no apparent reason, and spotted Damian sitting on the large sofa, topless with his keys at the ready. Attaching several wires and probes, they stabilised something and escorted him to the rear of the charged-up ambulance. Damian wanted the full blue light experience and suggested a detour along the A38 for a few miles so they could really put the hammer down. The driver, a very sensible looking woman called Daphne, had half a mind, and drove straight to casualty. They tied him securely in the back of the ambulance, stuck an oxygen mask on his face and sedately pulled away, Daphne having great clutch control, so much so that the ride was like cruising on a bed of plasma. As he slipped in and out of his shoes, Damian began to hallucinate (powerful oxygen). He could see a small boy standing in front of a large bell, toffee hammer in hand. The boy looked like a younger version of a young Damian. He had curly hair and the bell towered over him. An old man, wearing what appeared to be an Elizabethan outfit and spectacles, approached the boy and stated, "Never send to know for whom the bell tolls; it tolls for thee." Damian, even as a child, had never enjoyed the works of John Donne; he found it too heavy and preferred the subtler poems of Pam Ayres. Nor had he meditated, not even on the toilet, so the meaning of this hallucination was lost on his bleary mind.

The nurse, Trevor, who greeted Damian, quickly connected him to the Wi-Fi and then began the long-winded process of attaching further monitors, wires and probes to machines that bleeped, tweeted and hummed. Shortly after Damian was fully hooked up to the national grid, a doctor approached to give Damian an early indication of the following day's weather. Sunny with a chance of showers, but for Damian, a collapsed lung with severe breathing irregularities. Bugger — smoking could well have caused this massive inconvenience. He would need to be restrained if he wanted to avoid smoking, and Doctor Butt explained that there was a simple procedure that would reinflate his lung and allow him to continue smoking, but with the healthy option, low fat cigarettes. Damian heaved a partial sigh of relief. The procedure involved Damian being injected with air, directly into the target lung and then hoping for the best. This would be done in three different locations. At this point Damian was confused as to why he needed to be moved from location to location; surely it didn't matter in which part of the hospital it was performed as long as it was done. Doctor Butt tried to make it simple and pointed out that it would be three different locations on his body: the first injection would be in his back, the second under his armpit and the final inflation would be via the soft tissue between his thumb and index finger, just in case.

That afternoon a curtain was drawn around his bed, and Doctor Butt, along with two nurses, began by clearing the area around the bed. They then took out an instrument that resembled a football pump with a knitting needle attached at the end, and very deliberately stuck it slowly into the now faint Damian. Damian had been prone to passing out since a childhood incident had damaged his equilibrium. It meant that he couldn't look at butchered meat or enjoy documentaries featuring any type of big cat in its natural environment. As the needle delicately slipped into Damian's unhappy lung, Damian thought of his happy place, just outside Buxton, whilst the nurses watched on with disinterest. Once Doctor Butt removed the needle, he flipped Damian over and repeated the exercise; once again Damian visited Buxton. Finally, Doctor Butt took Damian's hand, poked around with the needle near his left hand and then gave him a sedative. He would return in the afternoon, but Damian was advised to rest and dwell on his past mistakes.

When Sadia and Sarah were finally allowed to see him, they had brought a half-eaten orange and a bottle of a well-known brand of fizzy drink. Seeing Damian in such a state brought the nurse out in Sadia, and she began to plump his pillows and vacuum around the bed. Sadia managed to unplug one of the many probes attached to Damian's body and in doing so caused a full-on crash alert. Doctors and nurses crashed down the ward, sending asunder patients, needles and tablets, reaching Damian's bed just as Sadia completed the vacuuming. Sarah had finished the orange and threw the pith into a bed pan which was by her dad's bed. Once the probes were re-connected, his bedpan rinsed clean, his pillows re-puffed and all things stabilised, Doctor Butt explained the principles of backgammon to a very confused Sarah, who was usually bored by board games. He advised her to look it up on Google and quickly left the ward.

Damian was to be released the following morning once he had been satisfactorily rinsed by the x-ray machine. Doctor Butt needed to be sure that Damian's lungs looked symmetrical and were of a suitable size. If it were the case, he could walk, take a taxi or get a lift from Sadia home, but he must give up his hospital bed for other lung collapsees. A short hop or a long crawl to the x-ray department followed, where he was wrapped in radiation, had his nails manicured and a general tidy up. He was now good to go. He was told to return in a week for a further fly past on the x-ray machine, and if that proved to be a perfect picture of symmetry then he would be fit to play the tuba.

During that week Damian was confined to grunts and semi-audible whistles in order to preserve air. He did go for the odd walk, one foot wrapped in bananas, which was very odd, but he wasn't sure if his lung was co-operating fully. That Wednesday was one of his birthdays, and he was unable to blow any candles out, and Sadia noticed that Damian no longer hummed along to the theme tune of 'Juliet Bravo', which was on repeat on a cable channel. Damian loved humming; indeed, he had spent a lot of his adolescent years humming as a semi-professional hummer on the underground humming scene. Not many people have heard of it or heard it.

. He felt deflated, both literally and metaphorically; he was a walnut in a world full of cashews, unable to complete even simple algebra, or conjugate regular verbs, let alone the bloody irregular verbs. His lung was heading south again and there was nothing he or his left lung could do to prevent it.

When he went back to the lung ward the following Monday, Doctor Butt knew immediately that Damian needed surgery of sorts. Washing him in a wave of radiation to make sure he was fully asymmetric, Doctor Butt explained that Damian would need a tube pushing into his lung to help it along; he had a retarded lung. He was readmitted to the ward and veiled in screens. Initially Damian intended not to be queasy, light-headed or in any way fainty, but once the knife cut into his screaming flesh and he felt the tube explore his lung, his blood pressure dropped to dangerous levels and he was in danger of having no blood pressure at all. Nurses scurried quickly, and flipped the bed ninety degrees, his feet aiming for the ceiling, allowing waves of blood to race to his ashen-faced head. He would be okay. The tube was attached to a large demijohn half full of disinfectant and lemon juice, where it would remain until his lung had pulled itself together and stopped fucking around.

Over the course of the week, as he lay in his grubby corner of the ward, surrounded by energetic asthmatics and grouchy old fuckers with too much phlegm, he contemplated the fragility of life.

The tabard, nature's way of regulating arm temperature and preventing excessive personality, has been a focal point for fools and officious officials the world over. Seen by many as a primitive garment, Damian vaguely remembered sitting at his grandmother's arthritic elbow as she regaled her grandchildren with tales of heroic tabard wearing figures from history. Originally designed as trousers, the tabard was adapted by removing the leg holes and replacing them with arm holes some distance from the entrance of the main body of the garment. Simple yet stylish, the tabard is now the must-be-seen-in garment for the rich and aromatic. Recalling Carter's Cardigans of

Distinction, Damian lay in his hospital bed and decided to set up a small tabard hire business, catering for the man or woman with overly warm arms in need of respect and a place in the world. He asked Sadia, on one of her visits to the 'Lung & Phlegm' ward, to bring along some paper and a pen so he could get to work designing and writing some leaflets for his new venture, 'Totally Tabards'. Below is a selection of literature produced during his heady days coughing and wheezing away the long hours between cold tea breaks and warm jelly surprises.

*Totally Tabards — A cool arm in a world of warm hands!*

*The Cleanser: Made from robust sheep and lashings of wax, this tabard is perfect when cleaning is at the forefront of your agenda. Imagine the admiring looks when you scrub down your enamel bed, or degrease a partner. With pockets front and back, the Cleanser is the utility tabard for the busy scrubber with nowhere to put things. Each pocket comes with a complimentary tissue, along with a small selection of partially sucked boiled sweets.*

*The Good Time Charlie: Scanning your wardrobe for a garment to impress your pals at the social club will be a thing of the past when you choose the Good Time Charlie. Manufactured using the finest velvet, who would not be impressed with its sleek and elegant lines? Entirely non-toxic, so safe around asthmatics, the Good Time Charlie is for the lady or gentleman and is completed by an exclusive book of poor-taste anecdotes to bore companions.*

*The Handy: Ideal to just grab and wear for those busy days looking glum. Inspired by renowned prison guard Enzo Marretti, the Handy is the perfect tabard for exercise yards and chain gangs. Available in sunset orange or an interesting striped motif, the Handy will transform drab gang fights into a glamorous catwalk extravaganza.*

*The Deep-Fried: Batter, fat and fish — the holy trinity of frying. How often have you witnessed a haphazard spillage and wondered why the hapless fryer wasn't wearing the Deep-Fried tabard? Weaved using the finest high tensile cotton, the Deep-Fried is designed not to burn too much, giving the lucky wearer the chance to enjoy their skin. The long sleeves, which strictly speaking shouldn't be on there, make The Deep-Fried a dual-purpose jacket-cum-tabard, ideal for the indecisive tabard wearer.*

*The Wastrel: A wrap-around, beast of a tabard, the Wastrel was designed for the gravity-encumbered gentleman who may well have quaffed a touch too many pies. Strengthened using real timber, the Wastrel can withstand weights of way over the maximum. With its elasticated arm holes and flexible waistline, the Wastrel will fit any body shape and size. So throw away those ugly jogging pants and top and take control of the Wastrel. Your waist will thank you!*

Anne had grown up in and around tabards, and she believed that a good tabard always complemented a good pipe. She had a very minimal wardrobe but was never short of an elegant after-dinner tabard or sporty off-the-shoulder tabard if the circumstances demanded something to surprise and horrify. Thomas, as a child of the 1920s, felt more at home in the all-weather jerkin, despite its obvious chafing potential, and with his elbows being ill-fitting, a tabard would have been the perfect all-purpose solution. Thomas though, believed that a man and his jerkin were like a pie and its crust, separate yet inseparable, and he was in fact cremated with his jerkin, insisting that the jerkin's ashes be sprinkled somewhere on the A38 outside Matlock.

Damian quickly set to work producing very rough sketches of his designs, but due to a significant lack of any design skills his drawings were disposed of by a nurse on the wonky lung unit. Deciding to use a more direct approach, he took to cutting the sleeves off his hospital gowns to see if he could create a buzz around his newly-fashioned Ailment Tabard. Several patients commented on his weak and pallid arms, but unfortunately, not one of the bastards wanted to make the transition from being a side line Jonny to a fully-fledged tabard wearing hipster. Fashion's loss was Damian's loss, and he soon consigned tabards to a small place in his brain.

# On the Fringe

Damian and Mark had spent years laughing, and this year made the decision to travel to the Edinburgh Fringe to laugh in a new location. Careful planning followed, with a swanky guest house booked, tickets bought, and route planned. On the allotted morning, the two laughter junkies hit the road and headed for the devolved capital of culture, with laughter in the heart and a beautiful blue trilby to protect Mark's sensitive follicles. Arriving at the guest house, they were pleasantly surprised by its location, set in the rolling flats of Leith. Climbing to their fourteenth-floor room, they were struck by the rawness of the landscape, with redundant health, smokers strewn randomly and disused people littering the striking backdrop to the culture that lay within the heart of Edinburgh. The room was partially furnished, and Mr Loowit, the owner, pointed out the facilities (two single beds and an ironing board) before informing them that breakfast was served in the morning, on a first come, first served basis. The higher the room, the smaller the breakfast. Unpacking his fourteen pairs of shorts, Mark surveyed the room whilst Damian attempted to get BBC One on the ironing board. The following day would be very busy, so the pair retired in readiness for a day of culture and laughter.

Damian was responsible for the show selection and had decided on an eclectic mix of contemporary theatre and old-school musical hall. Knowing Mark loved musical hall, the first show was a jamboree of musical greats all under one very small roof. The show, 'A Morning of Musical Hall Melodies and Wit', was presented by that legend of theatre, Sir Byron Bussle. Sir Byron had performed in numerous shows, and his reputation followed him around. With his booming voice, churlish demeanour and exuberant waistcoats, he was instantly recognisable as someone who yearned for attention. Also on the bill were Valerie Vague and her performing memory, a tribute to 'The Thirty-Nine Steps', but Valerie just had to remember to not drink too much sambuca and fall off the stage. Her act had featured on a regional TV station's search for a star programme, where she had come a respectable seventh. On stage with Valerie was her sidekick, Hippocampus, a giant of a man with flared nostrils and a propensity to chew his words, making his contribution very difficult to fully appreciate. There were two performing horses, Glue and Dogfood, who were able to discern the star sign of any given audience member using stomps and whinnies. The final act in this menagerie of mayhem, Doctor Grapple and his All-Seeing Eye, was purportedly able to read minds and move objects. Doctor Grapple had recently been released from Ford Open Prison after serving three years for internet fraud and interfering with goats. As they took their seats, the pair scanned the empty seats, realising that they and the elderly gentleman at the rear were the audience. After fifteen minutes of horse play and astrology, the elderly gentleman took his rucksack and walked out, leaving Damian and Mark to enjoy a very intimate forty-five minutes of mind reading and vague memories, interspersed with horse shit and guffaws.

The next show was a one man play set in the bread mills of 1920s Burnley. Its twin themes were despair and bread, a heady sandwich too hard to digest at eleven forty-five in the morning. The writer and performer, Declan Wholemeal, had previously spent twenty years kneading bread, and now his audience needed a break. Dull and lifeless, he really hadn't risen to the occasion, so Damian and Mark rose and left after thirty minutes.

The early evening show was that classic of British comedy, the farce. There was nothing like carnage and ineptitude to tickle the funny bones, and Damian had managed to get tickets for the hottest show in the street, 'Ooops, That's my Collarbone, Vicar', a riotous forty-five minutes of innuendo, fluffed lines and mirth set in and around a seminary somewhere in the south west. Stalwart of farce, Nigel De La Rooftile, played an outrageously short-sighted vicar who had too many hands on his time. Co-starring Thelma Buckethandle as a novice actress in need of spiritual touching, it was a tour de farce. Mark and Damian's obstructed view meant they heard a lot of the action and used their imagination to fill in what couldn't be seen. Suffice to say, the whole seating arrangements were farcical, and they left after fifteen minutes following a dispute with a German woman over what is considered to be touching and what is inappropriate feeling.

The final show of day one was top comedian and star of TV's 'Can't get a Proper Job', Nick Defortunate, a politically incorrect in a world full of correction fluid. His Twitter feed was always buzzing with followers hanging off his every third word, and he had recently featured in an exposé in one of the more sensationalist weekend rags. It was claimed that his material was outdated and only of use if your arse really needed a good wipe. Damian and Mark thought they loved his tightrope walk of controversy, courting infamy like a bigamist courts a pretty woman. Gasps and outrage were in short supply though, as his act was shite, and Mark and Damian unfollowed him.

By happy coincidence, it was also the year when the London Olympics took place. The world's greatest circus of athletic misfortune beamed to every orifice across the globe. As both Mark and Damian had a passing interest, they would occasionally watch some of the events between shows. Two fine athletes would have appreciated the expertise and dedication needed to watch so much drivel on TV, as the pair trawled through some of the most pointless events known to humankind. In breaks between shows, they watched 'Synchronised Running (95 kg)', 'Large Ball Throwing (59 kg)', 'Shooting Things Whilst Wearing an Eye Patch', and possibly the worst, 'Indoor Mopping'. The anthems rang out — tuneless tributes to pointless people. It did kill some time though.

Whilst walking around Edinburgh, it is possible to see real talent on show. In the many bars and cafés, thousands of aspiring actors, singers and devilishly enthusiastic performers vie to be noticed be someone — anyone. Donning bright hair, brighter shoes and hideous clothes, these flocks of forever so-close-but-not-quite-good-enough-ers yearn to be applauded, kissed and hugged with meaningless sincerity. With accents to match their inflated selves, the braying and chortling is enough to put anyone off breathing for days. It was hard for Mark and Damian, two northern fellas from a dirty patch of Yorkshire to fully fit in. They knew not of sonnets and Shakespeare, of Marlow and Proust. The closest they had ever been to culture was seeing Boy George on 'Top of The Pops' in 1983.

Ever dull to the obvious, the pair continued with their long dark journey into the old town. The second day could only get better as Damian had lined up some fabulous entertainment to get the hips cracking and the knees aching. First up was a three-woman show celebrating the life and works of Blues legend, Harriet La'more, known throughout the world as Miss Love. Her wispy vocals set the world alight in the late '20s, and even today, any child will instantly recognise her standout anthem 'Hey Mister, Pass Me My Hat'. Born to a mother, Harriet grew up believing her voice was weak and ineffectual, preferring to whistle instead. It was only when her then boyfriend and occasional driver, Bruiser Bump, heard her singing in a butcher's shop in Harlem that he recognised her insipid voice could be changed. The acoustics in butchers' shops, indeed in most retail establishments, are notoriously out of kilter with reality. The rest, they say, is history. The group performing the show, The Trouts, had performed the show at the Hebden Bridge Blues festival the previous September, where it was hailed as being a show. Following that minor acknowledgement, they then took the show to the three counties show ground in Worcester to entertain blues-loving agricultural types. Once again, they were noticed and not completely dismissed out of hand. The leader of the troupe, Hetty Gusset, was the driving force behind the show, and it was obvious that she had very little else in her life. Her myopic enthusiasm was not to Damian and Mark's liking, and after the opening bars of the first song, they retired to watch men in boats going quite quickly.

Working without a script is considered to be the hardest of all the comedic trades, yet most people manage to do it every day. Improvisation is the pinnacle of reckless entertainment and should come with a health warning. The midday show promised to be the highlight of the day, and both Mark and Damian were eager to be entertained by quick-witted wordsmiths whose imaginations knew no bounds. 'The Improvised Improv Troupe' was a collection of nearly actors incapable of storing anything to memory; they worked on adrenalin and words. Sharp tongues, sharpened on the mean stages of countless shitty theatres around the country, had made them the musketeers of wordsmithery. As Mark and Damian took their seats in the dimly lit dungeon, it became apparent that this really was improv. The stage was missing, there were no lights and a man at the bar said the show had been cancelled due to poor ticket sales and unpaid taxes. Waiting with a mixture of hope and thirst, believing that another hour of women rowing quickly in boats was on the cards, from nowhere, four well-dressed gentlemen marched into the venue demanding to see travel documents. The show had begun!

What followed was a serious misjudgement and very embarrassing for all concerned. The first man, dressed in a crisp pinstriped suit, marched up to Mark and ordered him to leave the theatre at once as he was here illegally. Thinking that this was all part of the performance, Mark began to laugh. In his defence, so did a few of the other audience members who were still awake. This only increased the gentleman's ire, and resorting to name calling and vague threats about deportation and never seeing the bright lights of Bradford again, Mark was manhandled out of the building by the scruff of his very fine hair. Damian quickly picked up Mark's beautiful blue trilby and followed, believing that this was all part of the show. When the bright sunlight lit up their dimmed reality, it was obvious that these four gentlemen were in fact from the Border Security Force in search of undocumented eastern European improvisation artists, a very niche unit. In the clear light of day, they quickly realised that Mark couldn't be a performer as he didn't carry the perpetual scars of nightly performances, nor did he have an eastern European accent. Three months later he received a written apology and a very nice bottle of gentleman's cologne.

Once the rowing had finished, the pair of vultures in search of culture went to the final show of the day, 'Butter No Bread For Me My Love' a blockbuster of a show featuring TV's Mike Journey, a favourite of daytime TV across part of northern Scotland. Journey's Journeys was northern Scotland's seventeenth longest-running show, and everywhere that Mike visited, the TV sheep were sure to go.

The play, set in Inverness, prior to the outbreak of World War One, was a harrowing tale of bread, dry bread and shortages of dairy products. The main character, wee Micky McJourney, is heading off to war to fight someone, and his fiancée prepares his final meal. All the action takes place around a kitchen table at a disused butter factory. Fanny, Micky's bride-to-be, can ill-afford to butter any bread, so instead uses a cheap substitute. Thinking her love for him has waned, he collects his things and is about to leave when a wealthy Englishman, with butter aplenty, offers to butter the bread and send Micky off loaded up with platefuls of cholesterol and a heart full of trepidation. The action then moves forward four years, and Micky is alone in the trenches, surrounded by thousands of evil Huns intent on stealing the rich, creamy butter that Micky has been guarding. In his hand he has a pistol and a slice of well-buttered bread that Fanny had posted to him, but due to delays, had been received only that very morning. The bread is dry, the butter is rancid, but it represents all that is wrong about the war. As the curtain is lowered, and the lights slowly go down, Micky is heard to lament, 'Butter no bread for me, my love.' The audience roared with joy at this magnificent piece of theatre. Both Damian and Mark fancied a sandwich, so headed off to find a suitable place to chomp as the theatre echoed with catcalls and violence.

The final day represented a fortune cookie of entertainment; it could be a brilliant day or absolutely shite. The opening show was a period drama, set in the early nineteenth century, entitled

'The Negligence of Arthur Singleton'. This comedy of manners featured Selma Arthritic and Gavin Strap. The nub of the story was misunderstanding, ill-judged comments and buckets of clichés. Will they, won't they, who gives a fuck — it was not really Mark and Damian's cup of tea, so why Damian had booked tickets was anyone's guess. They sat through several minutes of flustered bonnets and coat tails before leaving discreetly via the stage door.

After an hour of jumping and running with medals to boot, they headed for the next venue, where they were due to see a show entitled 'Blisters and Biscuits'. The show was a timely tribute to athletic legend and pioneer of running, Sir Bertie Treadmill, winner of a bronze medal for running a bit at the 1957 Olympic Games. Sir Bertie was credited with inventing running as we now know it. Prior to his innovative stride, many fast walkers were prone to falling over or slowing down. For years, his work was ignored, and it would have remained that way but for the hard work and idiocy of the writer of the play, Darren Didd. Didd didn't run but did appreciate Treadmill's singular dedication to moving faster without recourse to a horse, a car or a cow. Didd spent thirty years researching his subject, and perhaps on reflection that was thirty years wasted. The play ran for too long, the pacing was stilted, and his performance was wooden. Both Mark and Damian left via a stage door.

After two hours watching Olympic grade kite flying, they walked the five minutes to the next show, a musical extravaganza called 'The Smocks' Story'. This was yet another tribute to some long- forgotten and possibly dead musicians, but Mark and Damian found the tickets to be very cheap. The Smocks were a progressive rock band which shone and faded in early 1970. Lead singer Jessy Smock, and her siblings Francis, Jonny and Sally, topped the charts with the foot tapping anthem, 'Bury Me in my Smock', a tribute to the band's mother, Agnes Smock. They followed this up with the slower, introspective foot stomper, 'Don't Exhume my Smock Darling', which topped the charts in Fiji for an incredible two weeks. Behind the scenes, the band was rife with drugs and disagreements. Jessy did none of the song writing, relying on her siblings to do most of the donkey work. Jessy was using mind-bending aspirin and a heady cocktail of lactose and cookie dough, which inevitably affected her ability to fit into smocks. The three other siblings resented the smocks Jessy wore, and as sure as day will follow night, The Smocks split in March 1970. Their short flirtation with music left a permanent stain on musical history, and even now, the smock is considered a daring item of clothing. Mark and Damian loved it and spent half an hour by the stage door waiting for a smock.

After a spot of food, and it was a spot, they then proceeded to the final show of the day, and it was a humdinger of a show. Like him or loathe him, Rupert P. Blow was Britain's most sought-after chat show host, and his one-man show was a hit with deaf and blind alike. His witty repartee, on-stage gaffes and general inability to make the sane chortle had seen his star rise, splutter, bang and disappear, but Mark and Damian were drawn by the two for one ticket offer. The show was a flamboyant mix of chat, dance and music with the odd special guest brought along to liven up the audience. Taking their seats behind the third pillar from the left directly next to the women's toilet, the pair settled in for fifty-five minutes of fun. Blow is hard to like, with his off-hand humour, derogatory remarks about pies and extreme views on wind farms. As the show rolled along at a very gentle stroll, Mark had to prod Damian several times as he was in danger of snoozing. The special guests, Nina Broom and her sidekick Nana, were more interested in peddling their semi-autobiographical thriller, 'Swept Along', and when they left Blow treated the audience to a five-minute diatribe on the ills of renewable energy sources. The last ten minutes of the show descended into tedium, with Blow and Broom performing a duet — that classic anthem 'I Got the Wind in my Hair and I Need a Broom'. Mark woke Damian and they made their way to a bar to watch some intermediate bucket-filling.

The time in Edinburgh had been fabulous, and the two middle-aged fools made a promise to come again the following year to soak up the warm rain of culture.

The Olympics came to an end shortly after they got back to their respective families, and Great Britain had won an assortment of medals for an assortment of disciplines. Roll on Brazil.

# Fresh start and new curtains

Moving house was something Damian had done many times over the years, and it represented a huge upheaval for Damian, Sadia and young Harris. Moving from their quaint one-storey bungalow would be a wrench, with its withered rooms and fragile décor, but they needed space for Harris to talk more. A suitable property was soon found, and within weeks they were in their new home. Obviously, it needed work, and Sadia and Damian were soon surfing the channels in search of inspiration.

They latched onto a new shopping show, 'Shopping for Loners', hosted by Audrey Bathchair, a cushion of a woman with tassels for hair. Audrey had run a mildly successful cushion wholesalers in the late 80s, supplying cushions to the housebound and uncomfortable, but like her cushions, her business acumen was a little on the soft side. She was soon heading for bankruptcy so sold her business to a large cushion multi-national which was hoping to fill the cushion market with cheap, washable cushions that could be sold in bulk to unsuspecting insomniacs. Audrey had picked her cushion-shaped body up, dusted herself down, and decided TV was where her real talent lay. She had toured the studios, touting her extensive knowledge of cushions and fabric in general, and soon she was spotted by Russian oligarch, Oleg Nokrawski, famed for his flamboyant cushions and love of TV. He was looking for a cushion-shaped presenter for his home furnishings slot, and Audrey was looking for slots. It was a match made in a dusty studio three miles from Luton Airport. Soon they were ready for the pilot episode of 'Cushions and Creases', three hours of TV velour for homeowners who liked shit. She needed a co-host, and following a chance encounter with a tile salesman touting tiles from the back of his Ford Grout, they soon recruited Graham Sponge, a thrice divorced tile-lover in need of regrouting. His natural effervescence was difficult to find. What he lacked in charisma he made up for with buckets of unchecked enthusiasm. Broadcasting is a transient mistress, and initially the viewing figures were shit, but gradually they attracted a dedicated following who would drop most things to watch 'Cushions and Creases', even though it went out at ten p.m. on Sunday evening.

Their stock in trade was tat for the house-proud loner. Thomas would have been delighted that tat was finally getting the recognition it deserved. For too long tat had been the poor relation to the discarded hopes of an avaricious public. Now it was sitting just next to centre stage. Their bestselling product was the waterproof cushion which could be used whilst washing up or cleaning a small family car. It could also be used as a buoyancy aid for inadequate swimmers in shallow water up to a depth of three feet. Most Sundays would witness a surge of calls when the show had specials between the hours of eleven p.m. and one a.m. Audrey would sit atop a huge pile of cushions, and rather like a haemorrhoid infested auctioneer, sell off the unwanted and unsellable tat that most discerning viewers would cross the street to avoid. Items such as the retractable toilet brush and spoon, suitable for most chemical toilets and for removing stubborn stains from hub caps. The portable hat stand was for hat wearers on the move, say on a train or a bike. There was a real demand for a lightweight hat stand that could be folded away in a handbag or lunchbox. A surprise hit that took both Audrey and Graham by surprise was the Pig's Ear DIY kit, designed for the inadequate yet strangely enthusiastic home improver. Thomas would have bought the lot and given them as wedding presents to his three sons.

Damian and Sadia spent hours perched on the family chair, young Harris talking to the light switch in search of a companion to pester, dialling the dedicated number to order all manner of goodies for their new home. Damian was eager to cultivate the garden, and as he surveyed his vast plot of arable bountifulness, he remembered the hours spent with Anne and Thomas, nurturing life-enhancing root vegetables. Turnips were life's forgotten root, so often eclipsed by the more attractive swede. Damian planned to create a huge turnip patch where Harris could play and pick the bountiful harvest. Sadia could then make delightful turnip preserves and chutneys. The neighbours to the left, Joyce and Jeremy, were in their early 60s and steeped in corduroy. On some days Jeremy could be seen at the bottom of his garden by the corduroy bush, carefully harvesting nature's foremost fabric for the over fifty-fives. Joyce loved chickens and would spend hours painting watercolour frescos of chickens throughout history. Their garden was an homage to all things chicken, with just a hint of brown corduroy to satisfy Jeremy. Next door but one was occupied by a retired musician and full-time gravedigger, Dave Crisp, formerly of *Dave Crisp and the Onions*, a 70s glam rock ensemble that had been hugely unpopular in the UK. Dave, or Crispy as he was known in the grave-digging business due to the lingering smell of cheese and onion, had a small shed at the bottom of his garden where he would mix music and rehearse grave digging. He dug graves for most household pets, marriages and failed courtships. Dressed in high-waisted trousers, stacked heels and purple cloak, he was a regular sight around the back gardens and allotments in the neighbourhood. He would compose and then decompose songs that all had a grave-digging theme. He was much in demand, and some of his lyrics are reproduced by kind permission of the Performing Grave Diggers' Society.

*It Ain't Just a Hole — it's a grave*

*Dig it deep and dig it hard,*
*In your garden, in your yard.*
*A home for Tiddles, in the ground,*
*He went and died, no more around.*
*Bury them deep, make it wide,*
*For your husband or your bride.*
*Love has gone, it passed away,*

*When you discovered he was gay.*
*Bring the flowers, dress in black,*
*Around the hole, for the crack.*
*Sentimental words were spoken,*
*All the hopes, in pieces, broken.*
*So bring your dead, your sick, your weedy,*
*Bring your love, don't be so needy.*
*Fill the hole with hopes that faded,*
*Your life is turning oh so jaded.*

# She's how old?

Anne always remembered Thomas's seventieth birthday with a hint of disgust, so she wanted her special birthday (75th) to go without too many hiccups. She had played the role of the merry widow with a dour countenance and misapprehension. She seldom drank, smoked her pipe with renewed vigour, and would spend days only giving one-word answers. She had withdrawn into a world of stiff biscuits and rock-hard fairy cakes: a world where knitted garments represented the height of sartorial elegance; a world before the passing of Thomas. To cheer her up, her remaining breathing children felt she needed perking up, and what better way to perk up a woman who had spent a lifetime smoking pipes than a large whoopee cushion and a day out at the Pipe Factory. Janine vetoed the idea, observing that it would be more appropriate to organise an intimate family gathering where her close family could celebrate seventy-five years of pipe devotion. Janine set about searching for a venue that would most appeal to Anne's frugal nature, and Paul and Damian were given the onerous task of suggesting possible gifts and a guest list that would represent Anne's idiosyncratic idea of a convivial gathering.

After several hours thumbing through an old Argos catalogue, Damian and Paul decided that the best way to select a gift would be to put it out to tender as they did for Thomas on his seventieth birthday. Sealed bids, outlining a gift that Anne would appreciate and be unlikely to return, would be reviewed and the most appropriate and cheapest could be selected. They also thought they could open up the bidding process to any interested parties who may be inclined to make a suggestion. The idea was to keep all the suggestions secret, so all bids were to be sent to Janine, and a review of the ideas could be whittled down by the three children. A two-week deadline was given to ensure that a relatively quick decision could be made.

After just over two weeks, the final bid was received and what greeted Damian, Paul and Janine was an array of weird and wonderful suggestions that were sure to raise a frown on Anne's pipe-holding mouth. The bids are reproduced below and give a flavour of the level of insanity Anne's birthday had encouraged. The first suggestion was from Anne's elder sister, Ruth:

*Anne had a difficult time at school in the late 40s and early 50s, due to rationing, a misplaced pencil case and the lack of a family pet. Whilst her peers would enjoy long walks in the park with their favourite rabbit or cat, Anne could only watch on, pipe in hand, wistfully wondering what life with a dachshund, poodle or terrier might be like for a young girl with hopes of buying a dog lead. During the early part of the 50s, prior to rock and roll, tartan poodles were all the rage in the snack bars and dance halls of Bradford. Anne so wanted to have a tartan poodle of her own, and even tried to knit one using a pattern from a well-known women's magazine of the day. Unfortunately, when rationing ended in 1955, tartan poodles were seen as an unwanted reminder of the struggles and sacrifices that the whole nation had undergone during the war. Without any possible remedy, Anne decided instead to get married and have children, but the longing for a tartan poodle never went away. I know a man who somehow managed to hang on to his tartan poodle after they were outlawed in 1959. The poodle died in 1961 but was stuffed by a semi-retired vicar who also dabbled in taxidermy, and although it has a slightly musty smell, could be given a thorough scrub and brush up. It would be the ideal present.*

The next suggestion was from her brother, John, who stated that he wanted to see Anne fly.

*Anne likes the clouds and the weather. She has spent much of her life looking skywards in search of rain, sun and hope. What better way to remedy that stiff neck than some sort of flight for the old girl? I have an acquaintance who recently bought a trebuchet, fully restored and working, that for a certain fee, could be hired to launch that ambitious sister, husband or enemy into the stratosphere. The trebuchet has yet to receive full safety certification, but I am sure that is just a formality. Imagine if you will, Anne flying through the sky at a phenomenal speed, pipe in hand, not knowing where she would land. Of course, she could damage some of her calcium-deficient bones, but the experience would be memorable.*

The next suggestion was from a neighbour of Anne who often passed her in the street.

*Anne is known for her baking and her beautiful preserves. Her marmalade is almost palatable, and her fairy cakes quite moist. She will often foist them on unsuspecting friends and neighbours, and I for one am sick of it. I would like to apply to the court for a restraining order, stopping Anne from baking and preserving. If she wants some marmalade, I suggest she goes to the fucking supermarket.*

The above suggestion was echoed by several other neighbours in the area along with a vet from Skipton who once had the misfortune to ask Anne for directions. It was a serious contender. The grandchildren then came forward with an idea that some felt was beyond a joke.

*Gran loves ironing and all things laundry, so we thought what better way to celebrate that love of laundry than sending our dirty washing to her, in bulk, to give her something to get her teeth into. Her current washing machine and ironing facilities would need upgrading, but we are sure her pension would cover this. Think of her face when she sees pile after pile of her grandchildren's laundry. Thomas the younger's one good pair of jeans, the Enigma's woollen socks, Sarah's hideous knitwear collection; the list is endless, and what a way to spend her twilight years. We would be prepared to limit the number of garments per week, but we do believe that Gran would be shocked by some of the shit we wear.*

The next suggestion came from her pipe supplier, who had been there for Anne during the lean years when pipe tobacco was rationed.

*Anne was one of my customers, and as such I suppose I could run to giving her some celebration tobacco. Designed to be used at weddings, celebration tobacco gives off a happy smell, often compared to matrimonial bliss. Although it is incredibly inexpensive, I don't think I can spare too much, but I am sure Anne would take anything if it was free. I also have some old pipes that I was going to chuck, so perhaps I could include these just to boost the parcel as it were.*

Janine was hoping to give Anne a magical birthday gift, and her suggestion was a genuine contender.

*Mother has always been a keen pie eater, and she indulged herself in all manner of crust-encased treats as a child. Wartime had seen an increase in prefabricated pies that could be eaten almost anywhere, and the spontaneous nature of pie eating appealed to the wilder side of Anne's retiring nature. I recently saw a report in the local newspaper for 'The Pie Experience Centre', a fun-filled experience centre where visitors could experience the full pie experience. From learning about the birth of the tinned pie, to a fun-filled, mouth-dropping, jaw-spinning ride in the King Pie Waltzer — the largest ever pie tin, which can easily fit a family of six. There is a virtual pie, located near the small gift shop, that eager visitors can explore, and down in the bowels of the centre a state-of-the-art tasting tunnel allows visitors to experience the full range of pie magic. If we can get all the family members and any interested parties to chip in £1.00 each, we should be able to pay for two people to go to the centre and afford a half decent birthday cake.*

Paul wanted the present to reflect Anne's sporting prowess so came up with a very novel suggestion.

*As a girl, Mum would play that sport of kings, indoor hockey. Although Anne had insufficient lungs, she was a keen participant in all sports and could often be seen wandering the streets of post-war Bradford, hockey stick in hand, looking for an impromptu game or fight. Her ankles were the talk of the hockey fraternity, and when she was selected for the Undercliffe under-9 girls' hockey team, her parents realised that they would finally get some peace in their two-bedroom end terrace. Anne would bang around upstairs with her sisters, hitting whatever she could to hone her accuracy with the stick.*

*I ran into some of the members of that team a few weeks ago, and they suggested a framed hockey stick would not piss Anne off too much. I could give it a lick of varnish, knock up some commemorative plaque, job done. I can also get my hands on a 1952 copy of 'Hockey Lady', the essential read for any aspiring stick swinger. Stuffed full of interesting facts and articles, it was the go-to journal for any young stick swinger in the early '50s. Anne almost featured in one edition after her infamous stick rampage in Bingley in 1954, for which she was given a three-month restraining order and has never visited Bingley since.*

Damian had spent little time thinking about a gift for Anne, so his suggestion was very much a last minute, what-the-fuck-were-you-thinking type of idea, but it was made with sincerity and love.

*Mum likes nothing better than a good rummage in a charity shop in search of low-cost jewellery, chipped china and musty clothing. She has kept the diminished high streets alive with her devotion to browsing in the charity shops intent on purchasing somebody else's cast-offs. On one occasion in Ashby-De-La-Zouch, she spent £37.00 on two part-worn shoes (not a pair), a cracked mirror, two wine glasses, a Teasmade with no plug, two Yul Brynner CDs, three videos featuring the best of Countryfile with John Craven and several novels by Desmond Bagley. This dedication to tat is heartening and reminds me of Thomas. Therefore, I would like to get mum a pick-and-mix surprise gift, made up of random tat from a range of her favourite charity shops. Each person who feels the need to get mum a present could visit the charity shop of their choice, choose some tat, wrap it and then present to Mum on her big day. We could set the budget low, so as to not frighten off the more parsimonious relatives and friends — perhaps £1.00 each. This would mean Mum would have lots of tat to wade through on her special day, and no one feels they have spent too much on a person who in all probability, will be dead in a few years. Win, win!*

The final suggestion was submitted by the receptionist at Anne's doctor's surgery, who had been greeting Anne for the last thirty years.

*Anne, and her late husband Thomas, were and Anne still is, well known in and around the surgery and its car park. Whenever they attended the surgery, be it to report a bruise that had mysteriously appeared overnight, or to request a repeat prescription for medication that had little effect on their emotional or physical well-being, they always greeted the other sicknotes and death dodgers with a knowing scowl and a smirk. Anne will often sit for hours in the waiting area, large print Western novel in hand, commenting on the mental health of the staff, the patients, and anyone else who comes to mind. She has an incredible understanding of people's need to be ignored and is always willing to move seats to make her wind less offensive. I would like to offer Anne free car parking for life, or two years, whichever is the shorter, in recognition of her inability to drive.*

Janine, Paul and Damian spent several minutes reviewing the suggestions, and decided that a night mulling over the ideas would allow them to make the right decision. When they met the following day, all three felt that two of the suggestions were head and shoulders above the rest, and indeed genuine. They decided to choose both, as they felt it was difficult to decide which would be cheaper, the charity shop binge or The Pie Experience. The good thing about both suggestions was that it meant the initial outlay for each giver was small. Cheapskates surrounded Anne, and one pound was seen by many as excessive ostentation, so Janine, Paul and Damian hoped that this would encourage at least some people to give what they could find down the sofa, under the microwave or what they genuinely wanted to give.

The birthday meal was to take place at a very run-down restaurant/petrol station three miles outside Halifax. It was chosen for its proximity to food and fuel, two of Anne's favourite things. The restaurant offered a small selection of pies, pasties and sausage rolls, which were also available to be taken away if purchased from the petrol station. Hot drinks were offered but needed to be pre-ordered two days in advance to give the chef time to find a working kettle, and all diners were offered a complimentary car wash if the bill came to more than £12.73. There was no specific dress code, but guests were encouraged to scrub up and make an effort. A family table was booked and, on the evening Anne was to be picked up by Paul and Janine, and delivered to the venue. The rest of the guests were to arrive no later than eight p.m. as the garage kitchen closed at nine p.m.

Once seated, Anne quickly perused the menu and plumped for the Gas Guzzler, a plump pie filled with meat from many animals and served with a mix of trepidation and chips. She had brought a flask of tea, so her drinks were taken care of. Janine, who was experimenting with a new diet, was trying to avoid vegetables, specifically carrots, and any form of freshwater fish. She chose the meat platter, without fish and carrots, and a glass of tap water. Paul spent some time in the petrol station beforehand, and had seen two very plump pasties, so he asked if he could have them reheated and served with some form of gravy. Damian and Sadia both had the curry surprise, which was in fact no surprise. Suffused with hundreds of herbs and spices, the curries were hot and tasteless. Sadia went for the vegetable curry, and Damian chose the lucky dip, a mixture of meat, heat and hope. The grandchildren had all stopped at a well-known fast-food takeaway earlier, so they all settled for a dessert of blancmange with biscuits. Sarah, who had her taste buds removed when she was seventeen, maintained that it was yummy and had two portions. The doctor's receptionist, who was seated on another table with her estranged husband, plumped for the pineapple fritters with tinned ham, whilst her husband sat in silence staring at the fire door. Anne's siblings were unable to attend due to the late hour; they never went out after 6.34 p.m. Two neighbours had promised to come, but an unforeseen mishap with a shower cap, a plunger and a set of bathroom taps had meant that both neighbours had to wait in for an emergency plumber. Once the food had been devoured, the party decided to retire to the small bar at the back of the petrol station for a few after-dinner drinks. Tastefully decorated in 1930s motoring memorabilia, 'The Sump' as it was known, was an ill-lit room with several chairs, an old sofa and a washing machine in the far corner. As the Cinzano flowed, thoughts turned to all those family members who were not there that night. Thomas, who had long since driven off into the pie sunset; Stephen, whose knowledge of pies had been well beyond his years, and several of Anne's siblings, whose names were very old-fashioned.

Party games were always popular in the Carter household, so it was decided that they should play a selection of old-fashioned, nostalgic party games. Anne was given the honour of choosing the first, and with a mischievous smirk as she puffed on her pipe, she suggested that they should try playing 'Where's My Pipe?', a parlour game that was popular in the parlours of '30s Bradford. The aim of the game was to deduce where the pipe was hidden. This seemed simple enough, but quite often the pipe could be hidden where it was least expected. On one occasion as a child, Anne had found a pipe hidden inside a small loaf of bread. How this was achieved remained a mystery to Anne, but she had fallen in love with the game, and her love of pipes had only cemented that love. After explaining the rules to some of the slower grandchildren, Anne took out the Pipe of Mystery, and gave instructions to Janine to hide it in plain sight, with the caveat that it must be located on or near an animal, alive or dead. It goes without saying that few of the guests that evening understood the point of finding a hidden pipe, but they certainly caused a stir in the Sump, as they tossed cushions, flicked ice cubes and ripped up oil-stained carpet in search of Anne's Pipe of Mystery. The next game, which Thomas had played as a child, was called 'Which Pub Is Dad In?', and the object of the game was to guess the name of the pub that any given family member had last been in and if they had made an arse of themselves. Damian always remembered Thomas regaling him with tales of his father being found slumped in a barrel with a haddock for a hat after drinking one too many rum and cokes. Thomas himself had liked a drink-related parlour game, and Damian vividly recalled Thomas hiding in the family fridge during a rather complicated game of 'Who's In My Fridge?'.

As the evening went on, Anne took out her favourite pipe and reflected on the present she really wanted: her husband.

# Gossip, hearsay and rumour

Education: the spittle that lubricates the mind and ensures phlegm-free thinking. Education had played a small role in Damian's underachievement, and he was determined to see his parasites be as equally unsuccessful. Thomas the younger was the first to take the plunge, and he decided to choose a very remote university in central England. His choices were limited as he had spent most of his school days coasting and playing on the PS2. Having reviewed his options, he chose a very esoteric undergraduate course: 'Third World Ribbon Usage and its Impact on the Haberdashery Industry, BSc'. It was a three-year course with a gap year, giving the students the opportunity to get their hands dirty in a real-world ribbon environment. Thomas the younger yearned to see ribbon in its natural environment and be at the cutting edge of ribbon research. Little is known about the origins of ribbon, and certainly in previous centuries, ribbon was viewed with hostility and suspicion. In Victorian times, thanks to the introduction of the controversial but highly significant Ribbon Laws, tariffs were removed from ribbon imports and soon every Tom, Dick and Harry was adorned with colourful ribbons and intricate bows. A huge export market developed, and ribbon was exported throughout the known world. Soon every dandy worth their salt was donning a ribbon and strutting along like a well-dressed Christmas package. Thomas the younger had shown no interest in ribbon as a child and was unable to tie his own shoes until he reached his late teens, so the choice of course was surprising to Damian. Damian was pleased that Thomas had finally decided on a career, and if that meant working for a non-profit organisation in some far-flung place, helping kids and families to access clean ribbon and associated haberdashery, then who was he to object? It might even improve his shoe-tying skills.

Sarah had chosen to follow her father's footsteps and study English alongside film studies, with the view to becoming a fairly competent teacher. Sarah loved books, indeed as a child she had read two, and she was determined to not exceed her self-imposed word limit and read too many books. As a consequence, she relied heavily on her imagination and the power of her bullshit. There was no way in the world she would ever attempt to read 'Paradise Lost', as it would be lost on her, and Shakespeare presented a challenge that even Damian admitted was one sonnet too far. Film studies was an entirely different proposition. Sarah had seen all the Disney films as a child and knew the lyrics for all the songs from 'The Lion King'. She had never seen a black and white film, believing that they were the work of criminals and historians, and although she could sit through short TV advertisements, the idea of watching a film from start to finish seemed like A Bridge Too Far (bloody good film). Her favourite film was Robin Hood, and she believed it to be a true representation of Victorian England.

The Enigma, who was unsure whether to work or study, finally plumped for a carefree life of study, undertaking a degree in psychology, mind-reading and alternative remedies. She had no specific interest in any of the topics, but it meant she could postpone work for at least another three years. The modules on the course were of interest to Damian as he enjoyed learning shit for shit's sake. Mind reading as a science had been debunked many times, yet still society went along with charlatans and quacks who maintained that they could delve inside the mind and read all your intimate thoughts: bullshit.

Harris, still only a young boy, could talk so much that sometimes his ears stopped listening. By the age of two he had registered as a child gossip, and by four was renting out his words to other junior gasbags. Damian and Sadia had considered enrolling him in the prestigious Academy of Gossip, Hearsay and Rumour, said to be located in the area. The academy was the premier hotspot for tittle-tattle, conspiracy and unwelcome speculation. The principal, Hilary Earsay, had spent years working at a downtrodden tabloid newspaper, running its gossip column and spreading rumours about the misdemeanours of management. When Damian and Sadia first heard a whisper that places were available for gifted gossips and chatterboxes, they had sent away for a prospectus, believing that most of its contents would be half-truths. They were not disappointed and below is a flavour of the courses that Harris would have enrolled upon if his parents hadn't been so half-arsed.

## The Academy of Gossip, Hearsay and Rumours
### Bringing lies to life!

*It is the wish of every parent to raise their child with an understanding of right and wrong, up from down and left from right. However, the truth of the matter is, parents often forget the fourth cardinal skill: gossiping. Here at the academy, we pride ourselves on the fact that most of what we say or write could well be a falsification – a half-truth in a world of boundary-less meaning. Children are born with an innate ability to lie, be it to cover up a broken vase that was worth several pounds, or to hide a turd that was left on a priceless rug. This natural aversion to fact should be harnessed and used for nefarious or charitable means, and the Academy is at the prow of a very untruthful ship, surging across the waves of words to produce mystifying spray and froth. We offer a number of courses that focus on a range of skills needed to be a really effective gossip, rumourmonger, or if we aim high, scaremonger. Below are most of the details you think you need, and it has been said that these courses are perfect for the complete novice right through to the lying little bastard.*

### Beginner – Gossip and Tittle-tattle

*This intense course might last many years and could be ideal for the little angel in your life who is forever bullshitting. Each morning the students will be required to create a harmless rumour. Previous students have all stated that the course was of some use and gone on to more advanced tittle-tattle. Testimonials from parents speak louder than lies:*

Jan, 36, parent of some: "I trusted my youngest for a while, but now I don't believe a word he says."

Norman, retired: "My grandson is a little lying bastard now!"

Jean, 87, plumber: "Some fucker stole my hearing aid, so I can't hear the gossip as I used to."

## Rumours – Intermediate

*Having achieved a degree of veracity, a good rumour can cause untold damage and heartache. We at the Academy focus on the vulnerabilities of others to craft rumours that are intended to hurt and upset. With a focus on malice and size, the aim is to make anything sound plausible. Below are some well-written testimonials from people who have been hurt by rumours.*

Glen, 29, chef: "I lost my job and my hat thanks to a rumour about premature baldness – it still hurts now!"

Norman, retired: "My first wife was convinced that I was starting rumours about that lying little bastard of a grandson – I was!"

Jean, 78, builder: "I used to be a plumber until some bastard stole my plunger!"

## Hearsay – Advanced

*Subtle hearsay can undermine the confidence of the strongest in society and be the heavy straw that breaks the fragile back of truth. The Academy aims to equip advanced students with the tools which will enable them to ruin careers, marriages and ambitions. On successful completion of the course, many of our students have gone on to be successful journalists and politicians. Here are a few testimonials, handwritten by puppies:*

Gerald, 52, pianist: "I had the world at my gifted hands, but that was ruined by a wicked lie that suggested my fingers were prosthetic and my ears were merely adornments on an otherwise dull face."

Norman, retired: "My lying bastard of a grandson went to prison thanks to a nasty little bit of hearsay that was swallowed by the authorities."

*Jean, 65, retired: "I was responsible for all the toilet blockages on the London Underground from 1956 to 1971."*

*As principal I know how important education is to some of the pushier parents, but we at the Academy pride ourselves on our focus on half-truths and rumour, eschewing any attempt to be frank. We have no truck with numbers, places or facts, and everything is fabricated on site. Our dedicated team have possibly spent years honing their skills, and they truly are near the top of their game.*

## Earnest Bedevilled: Assistant Principal

*Earnest has spent the vast majority of his career swimming in the puddles of mediocrity, but thanks to a very large donation from his sister's mother, we created an opening for this talentless liar.*

## Francine Frailheart: School Nurse

*On release from prison, Francine spent several days training as a nurse and can supply any certificate that may be appropriate. She speaks 691 languages and understands some of the basics of hygiene.*

## Douglas Quarryhole: Head of Gossip

*After a long career as a string salesman, Douglas retired to the seaside several days ago, but following the urgings of his ex-customers, he decided to use his unique lips and voice box to gossip away from doorsteps. He is currently under investigation by the Serious Twine Division for a string of crimes.*

## Anita Fearful: Acting Scaremonger

*Appointed with a little too much trust, Anita is keen to take and make stamps. Her previous experience is a long list of lies and failure, but she demonstrated enough life to be able to fill the position until such time as we can dismiss her.*

## George Sweeping: Teacher of Exaggeration

*Following 25 years as the best thing since sliced bread, George did some really great stuff somewhere else. He is as tall as a house, as wide as a cow, and as clever as a duck. His feet are rear facing, and his fingers make an unusual noise when he claps. He has so many qualifications that it would take three buses to transport them from his opulent mansion to his magnificent garage.*

## Henry Glove: Head of Research

*Henry has a white coat and many opinions. His love of words has enabled him to collect the largest number of wild words in western England. His knowledge is limited to four and five letter words, but he is currently researching words with hyphens.*

## Oliver Brain: Sanitation and Sweeping

*Not to be mistaken for the cleaner, Doris, Oliver is our go-to guy if a rumour gets out of hand. His glossing-over abilities are legendary, and he was once awarded a Queen's Medal. He did of course return it, thanks to his obvious distaste for flattery. If a rumour becomes dangerous or toxic, he will step in with a large broom and sweep it under the carpet for later.*

## Doris Overwhelmed: Cleaner & Cook

*Doris is a stalwart of the half-truth, and if she maintains that a dish is edible, clean or cooked, it's best avoided. Her efficiency is amazing, and she has often cleaned the whole school from top to bottom within minutes, sometimes before even starting. She is partially sighted so will often work from home.*

*I suspect that not all of the staff attend every day, but they do of course collect a bi-weekly slap on the wrist if they are caught fibbing*

*inappropriately on school time when they should be fibbing appropriately*
*all the time.*

*We look forward to greeting you at the start of the new term for an*
*exciting journey into gossip, hearsay and rumour.*

*Thank you.*

*Hilary Earsay*


Damian and Sadia were torn between discarding the prospectus
and using it as back-up toilet paper in case of emergencies. It
currently sits in a small frame atop the mantel piece as a reminder
to Harris to try harder.

# The door of death

Anne and Janine had been visiting Damian for several years, and at first, they had stayed at Damian's for affordability, convenience and free snacks. However, when Damian's personal hygiene became an issue, and he was reported to the local health and safety department, Anne and Janine thought it best if they found a hotel nearby, allowing them the freedom to come and go as they pleased without the need for smelling salts. Quite often Damian would find a hotel suitably far enough away to avoid indiscriminate meetings, and as the two planned to come down for the Christmas holiday, he had managed to find a small, themed hotel a few miles from his home; it was perfect. The Happy Fall was a twenty-first century coaching inn with eighteenth century plumbing, electrics and service. Both Anne and Janine had mentioned that they loved history, so the Happy Fall seemed like the perfect retreat. Damian made the long journey up to Yorkshire to collect Anne and Janine, and after a very uneventful car journey, dropped the two off at the hotel to settle in and unpack their abundant costumes and trinkets.

Tragedy struck the following morning following an innocuous fall involving a valance sheet, and a radiator. Anne had finished rinsing her pipe, and as she made her way to the bathroom to brush her face, she caught her foot on a floral valance sheet, propelling her forward at speeds that can only be imagined, finally coming to rest on the bathroom floor but not before hitting her hip on a radiator. She was slumped on the floor, unable to move. Janine did the only thing any sensible daughter would do and panicked. She then called Damian, who immediately jumped in his car and sped off. On arrival he quickly assessed the situation, and scanning the room, realised Anne was actually in the bathroom. Insisting to Anne that she stop arsing around,

Janine and Damian attempted to shift their mother to the bed where she could take a nap and be right as rain in a couple of hours. As they went to lift her, Anne let out a visceral scream and told Damian to stop standing on her fucking hand. They tried again; Anne's face was contorted in pain; maybe she had hurt herself and maybe she wasn't taking the piss. Janine decided to call for an ambulance, and Damian sat by his mother and gently sang some tunes from 'South Pacific' (Anne's favourite musical).

When the ambulance crew arrived, Damian left the scene, leaving Janine to ride in the ambulance to the local hospital, St Jude's Hospital and Wellness Centre, a short thirty-minute journey. Anne was quickly seen, or was it seen quickly, and a very broken hip was diagnosed. It would need to be replaced, but with what wasn't clear. Doctors and likeminded individuals had developed a new material, made entirely from sheep's fleece and unguents, which had the potential to save thousands of hips a year. It was still in its experimental stage, but the doctors treating Anne felt she would be the perfect candidate for this revolutionary substance, and if all else failed, they could always pour in some concrete as well.

Anne was under the knife for many hours. Janine, unable to focus, ate pork pie after pork pie, whilst Damian went for a long walk in a local park, or was it a local walk in a long park? His recollections of the day's events are sketchy. Jubilation followed after what seemed like six hours and thirty-nine minutes, when the doctors and their surgeon friend ran from the theatre with failure rubbed out and success inked on their grinning faces. The operation had been a complete partial success, and Anne might still get to drive a helicopter over the Norfolk Broads. She would never be able to skip again, but that was a small price to pay for a woman who wasn't that fond of skipping. Damian and Janine quickly rode to the four corners of the kingdom to share the good news, arriving back in time for evening visiting hours.

Over the following days Anne appeared to be making progress, but on the Friday a seepage occurred. Anne had woken early in the morning to discover the right side of her bed covered in wool and unguent. The hip had failed! The doctors immediately made plans to rush her down to surgery the following Wednesday, when they intended to give the hip a full inspection, change the filters and top up her water. Hopefully, that would do the trick and she would soon get her hands on that elusive joystick. She ended up being in hospital for three weeks, thoroughly annoying the nurses, the doctors and her fellow inmates. The food was the high point of her stay, with a genuine effort to feed the patients adequately with dishes that had not been rejected by the makers of Pedigree Chum.

When her release date was decided on by a junior doctor called Ned, she was poured into an ambulance and forwarded on to Yorkshire, where a detailed care plan was not in place. She was given a walking frame and advised not to fall over. Damian heaved a huge sigh of relief and collected a tenner from the local bookies, who had given him odds of ten to one on his mother flying a helicopter anywhere near the east coast. He intended to splurge his winnings on a 'get well soon' card for his mother.

Anne's recovery was a slow and painful process, and over the following weeks and months she gradually achieved very little, meaning that long walks were something she only saw on 'Countryfile'. Janine bravely attempted a long walk, but all it succeeded doing was creating bitterness and envy. Anne was on the slippery slope to the other side, and as her family watched on, powerless, their thoughts turned to life without their mother. Who would burn the beef? Who would bake incredibly inedible cakes? Who would sit in the armchair, pipe in hand, reading 'Pipe Widow'? Those questions were left hanging in the air unanswered. For now, they had to focus on food and where would be the best place to have the wake.

Damian was at work when he got the call from Janine, busily working his way through a cigarette. When his manager ran to the smoking area, breathless, Damian knew something was wrong with his manager (diet maybe?). He had to call Janine immediately. This he did, and Janine told him that Anne had been rushed into St Elmo's Wayside Hospital following a near-death experience; time was not on Anne's side. He needed to drive up to Yorkshire that very evening before his mother slipped for the final time. Calling Sadia, he then hit the highway and drove within the permitted limits, arriving at the hospital sometime after feeding time. He was starving! As he entered the near-death ward, with its decaying life forms carelessly panting, all he could hear were the grumbles in his stomach. Approaching Anne's bed, he saw his brother Paul, along with his two nephews, Sam and Josh, and Janine, holding Anne's scaly hand, hoping for hope to run into the ward and give her some hope; but it was hopeless. A bedside vigil then commenced.

As the minutes grew into hours, the inevitable happened; Damian needed food. Paul suggested a McDonald's, so Damian quickly performed a small dance and entered a search on Google for the nearest drive-through. There was a twenty-four-hour restaurant only two miles away. Surely Anne would wait whilst her youngest son filled his face?

As with all plans, they never seem to go exactly as wished, and just as Damian had taken all the orders and was about to nip out, Anne stirred, giving the 'V for victory' sign and demanding her pipe. She was obviously delirious, high on cocktails, or just a little bit crazy. Damian decided to wait a little longer, recognising the significance of food, but also the moment; he decided on balance that the moment was a little more important. He waited. Janine waited. Paul waited. Anne refused to die. She clung on dearly, biting the air for life. Damian's stomach needed a bite too, so he decided to nip down to the canteen and grab whatever shit was available. As he made his way down the grim corridor and searched for the canteen, his phone's sat-nav kicked in, advising him that the nearest restaurant was just under two miles away — not too far. Whilst Damian contemplated his next move, he heard Sam call his name. Anne was finally letting go and Damian needed to get back to the vigil. He sprinted along the corridor like an extra from casualty, desperate to get some food later.

Arriving at the bedside it was clear that Anne only had moments, or minutes, whichever was the shorter. Holding

Janine's hand, Damian watched on as his mother finally slipped away. At that very moment, his sat-nav informed him that a U-turn was required. Could they bring Anne back from the dead?

Janine was inconsolable, Paul and Damian very hungry. Their thoughts soon turned to the funeral arrangements, and fortunately Janine knew of a fairly reputable firm, 'Pushit & Hope', who offered a knock-down, budget burial and burn service, with inclusive hearse usage and a top-hatted man with a flag. Anne loved a funeral, and a cheap one at that, so the children went for the low-cost express option as it's what she would have wanted.

As the day of the funeral approached, arrangements were made for flowers (Anne wanted an arrangement in the shape of a pipe), funeral music and of course a venue for the after-show celebrations. Damian wanted to choose music that reflected Anne's indomitable spirit and zest for citrus. He also wanted to prepare a eulogy and so quickly set to work writing down a funeral poem, after he had eaten. The poem he finally vomited onto paper was a moving fusion of words and sentiment, designed to bring the assembled mourners to a cacophony of tears. It was called, 'Anne's Pipe', and is reproduced below:

## Anne's Pipe

*Symbol of wisdom, symbol of peace,*
*A pipe is for all, not just a niece.*
*Anne had a pipe; she used it most days,*
*It was never a fad, a blip or a phase.*
*All of Anne's pipes, they each had a name,*
*They all looked so different, not one was the same.*
*In velvet and leather, in cardboard and steel,*
*The one made of satin, a beautiful feel.*
*Her life had its problems, issues and troubles,*
*She'd sit in an armchair and blow lots of bubbles.*
*Through childbirth and marriage, her sickness and health,*
*In good times and bad, with love and some wealth.*

*She's left us, she gone to the pipe in the sky,*
*Her hip was too heavy, she chose not to die.*
*But age and its burden, along with her pipe,*
*The years took a toll, like an ageing banana, a little too ripe.*
*Pipee, oh pipee, oh take her away,*
*Pipee, oh pipee, it's too late to stay.*
*Pipee, oh pipee, oh heavens above,*
*Oh pipee, oh pipee, you gave so much love.*

The day of the funeral was sunny with just a hint of tears, and as the family drove to the local burning centre there was a sense of trepidation. Would the pipe shape arrangement go up in smoke? Would Damian's moving lament fall flat? Would they have enough tissues? The children needn't have worried as the funeral went down a storm. Some of the mourners liked it so much they suggested they do it every month to give them something to look forward to in their otherwise dull and pointless existence. Damian did like the idea, but work commitments would make it very difficult to juggle laments with full time arsing around in Birmingham.

The next stage of the grieving process is to scratch around in the deceased's home to see if there is anything worth keeping or flogging, and Damian, Janine and Paul realised quickly that Anne had very little of real value. Obviously, her collection of nineteenth century tweed pipes looked like it might perform well at auction, but when they were checked out they were discovered to be cheap Korean imports made in the late 90s. The delicate business of sifting through a lifetime of possessions, some of which were grubby and slightly disgusting was very distressing, particular for Damian as he had very sensitive nasal receptors. Paul was a brick and managed to flog the furniture to a small man he had met on a boating holiday the previous year, and Janine recycled Anne's clothes into some lovely blankets and throws. At the end of the process, Sadia found some semi-useful pots and pans, a couple of cups that didn't have chips in and a half-empty jar of marmalade which could be useful at breakfast time.

As the weeks passed, it was apparent that Anne was still dead, and the children tried to grieve in their own ways. Damian would often jump in his car and sit on the drive, contemplating the dashboard. He found no comfort in this so threw himself into Sadia's car, which didn't help.

Grieving takes many forms, and Damian's approach to loss was to suppress all memories of his mother and make like an orphan. He had used this very same strategy when Thomas had died, disowning his mother for seven years, and he actually approached several children's charities for help, but they all told him to grow the fuck up. His children took the loss of their grandmother with a blasé-ness bordering on apathy. Sarah, keen to stake her credentials as a compassionate grandchild, locked herself away in a luxury five-star hotel in Split, whilst Thomas the younger carried a picture of his gran in a locket, which he hid somewhere in his bathroom. Katie was an enigma. Harris, who only had the one grandparent, lost himself in Cartoon Network, watching 'The Amazing World of Gumball' on a loop. It gave him some comfort.

As spring turned to summer, Damian and Sadia invited Janine down for the week. It was a chance to recharge her depleted batteries in the Staffordshire countryside. Damian had inflated a thirty-year-old camp bed, and Harris had been moved into his treehouse to make room for Janine's extensive luggage. It was the week of Janine's fifty-fourth birthday, and Harris had very thoughtfully made a birthday card from scraps of leaves he found in the garden. Sadia made a wonderful 'Chastised Orange' cake with button mushrooms and just a hint of garlic. Her cakes were becoming very experimental, bordering on the insane. With fifty-six candles atop the cake, Damian, Sadia and Harris gathered to wish Janine a better year and give her the cheapest present available from the pound shop. The day went swimmingly, with fizzy drinks and cheesy puffs for Harris and methylated spirit for the adults. The following morning, Damian drove Janine to the train station, making sure that she caught the right train up to Yorkshire. Previously Janine had boarded the night train to

Istanbul, believing she was living in an Eric Ambler novel, spending four days trying to explain away her passport irregularities. Fortunately, Damian had written the destination on a label which Janine attached to her lapel, to avoid any mishaps.

On the Tuesday of the first week back after half-term, Damian was busily working through a cigarette, contemplating life without eczema and the number of pigeons he had seen recently when once again his frantic manager ran into the smoking area with sweat on her brow (she really was out of condition), demanding that he come and take a call from Sadia. He raced his manager up the two flights of stairs and easily won; she really needed to diet. As he took hold of the receiver, he had a bad feeling in the pit of his stomach; he had eaten three plates of cauliflower cheese and it didn't agree with his sensitive workings. He knew at once that something had happened; it was his third sense, an uneasy feeling, a restless inner turmoil that told him to avoid cauliflower for a while. Sadia told him, when he could focus on the call, that Janine was dead. She had been found seated in her favourite armchair, her favourite copy of Reader's Digest on her lap, a tepid cup of strong coffee on her occasional table. She had died of a massive, and it was massive, heart attack, ending her life instantly. Death had once again clutched a loved one and dragged them off.

Once again Damian had to jump in his car and shoot off up to Yorkshire, but not before going home and informing his children that their auntie had kicked the bucket. Such trials are sent to test us, and Damian, with a resilience bordering on ignorance, went to Harris's school to break the devastating news. As Harris was still quite young, Damian thought it best to break it in the form of a rhyme, dedicated to his defunct sister:

*An Ode to an Aunt*

*Lots of tickles, not a chance,*
*Lots of giggles, not a hope.*
*Book in hand, don't put it down,*

*Never smile, always frown.*
*Hard to know, hard to see,*
*Always coffee, never tea.*
*Little notes, of things to do,*
*Dead relatives, you now have two.*

Fortunately, Harris appreciated the sentiment and was soon busy watching Cartoon Network. Damian knew he would have to go through the rigmarole of clearing the flat, and along with Paul would need to make the funeral arrangements (if only they'd had the foresight to buy the two for one spring offer from Pushit & Hope). This time though, there would be no fucking wake. There are only so many sausage rolls, one mourner can eat. On the drive up to Yorkshire, as Harris diligently sucked his thumb, Sadia and Damian reflected on the fragility of life, plans and butterflies' wings.

Arriving at Janine's one-bedroom flat, they were greeted by Paul, who was sure that the fellow who had bought Anne's surplus stuff would be willing to take Janine's old stuff for a reasonable price. Every cloud! With heavy hearts, they began to sift through the many pictures, books and half-eaten jars of preserve; it was going to be a long and painful task. Brandishing his manly demeanour, Damian dutifully threw out anything that looked vaguely old or unwanted, and he soon had a huge pile of binbags with no obvious means of disposal. Paul had managed to offload some furniture and a framed picture of David Essex but was unable to find a home for Janine's collection of needles and associated sewing equipment. They would have to pass it off as an heirloom.

The funeral arrangements went ahead at a pace, with a celebrant hired to gloss over any unsavoury aspects of Janine's character. Damian was once again delivering a eulogy, as he had some unused words that could well alleviate some of the pain. There were long words, such as predestination and ultimately, which Damian thought would give the eulogy an intensity it would otherwise lack. He also threw in some shorter, pithy words for effect, such as fuck, bollocks and dead, to add some brevity to the proceedings.

On the day of the funeral at the appointed hour, the mourners dribbled up to the chapel, huddled together to protect them from death and sadness. The chapel itself was a breezy little building with no obvious use, with a huge furnace located at the front, masked by cheap velvet curtains. The pews, arranged in the shape of a coffin, offered the viewers a very restricted view of the burning as most of them were set at ninety degrees to the front so as to get more in.

As the service began, it became obvious that not all the mourners were at the right service, with confused expressions conveying sadness and anger at the fact that their late grandfather had been renamed Janine. Damian, ever the idiot, ploughed on with his multi-word eulogy, ending with a few show tunes and five minutes of tap dance. It was incredible, and by the look on the mourners' faces, they were overwhelmed by the breadth of his stupidity. When the service came to an end, the mourners trooped through to shake hands with Paul and Damian. The line went on and on, with some mourners in tears, expressing their deep-felt fears for the future, whilst others kept enquiring as to when granddad had changed his name to Janine. Once the mourners had cleared off, Sadia grabbed some of the least wilted flowers, threw a quid in the collection, and the family jumped in their respective cars and headed home. They had seen enough death.

There had been two funerals, so what Damian needed was a wedding, and as luck would have it, his eldest daughter, Sarah, was due to marry her long-term beard-wearer, Richard, at a glitzy location in the Midlands. The wedding had been many years in the planning. Richard had proposed to Sarah on numerous occasions in various locations, and when Sarah finally said the magic word, the planning went into overdrive: venues, caterers and flowers, along with rings, a dress and the all-important guest list. Deciding who to invite to your special day can be a minefield, wrapped inside a nightmare and then covered in pitfalls. There are those relatives who you wish had been adopted; relatives whose idea of a good time is Marmite on their feet and Coronation Street on the telly; and there are relatives who are just a fucking pain but might owe you money. Then you have to consider friends and partners, which should involve a vetting process that would weed out the obnoxious, the drunks and the maudlin. Sarah and Richard had a long list which needed to become a shorter list.

To help with the cost of the wedding, Damian and Sadia had offered to pay for twenty-five embossed invitations, several flowers and a taxi for two to anywhere within a fifty-mile radius. Family!

Damian spent his time well, preparing a poem for his 'father of the bride' speech, which is not reproduced below as he threw it away after the wedding. However, as luck would have it, he was able to remember the general gist of the poem, and that is bodged together below:

*The Butterfly*

*Flapping, clapping, the butterfly,*
*Up it goes, way up high.*
*Bubbles, troubles, it has none,*
*The prettiness goes on and on.*
*Flying, buying, lots of things,*
*The butterfly has lovely wings.*
*Gentle wings, colours bright,*
*Out all day but not at night.*
*Stopping, chatting, got to fly,*
*Cannot stop, but don't ask why.*
*The butterfly within each one,*
*Every daughter, every son.*
*The butterfly is oh so busy,*
*Enough to make me fucking dizzy.*

The poem was intended to evoke an idea, a notion of the type of butterfly Sarah might have been if her parents had been butterflies too. When Sadia heard the poem, she vomited a little but encouraged Damian to try again. The thought occurred to Damian that perhaps he was not meant to be a poet, but it was such a fleeting thought that he did try again and below is the dog's turd that he came up with, which made Sadia slightly dizzy.

*Daughter, son, son-in-law,*
*I have a family; do I want more?*
*Buy a ring, get a dress,*
*Hope your marriage is not a mess.*
*Twenty, thirty, forty years,*
*All the heartache, all the tears.*
*Is it worth it, a life of gloom,*
*A lonely bride, a lovesick groom.*
*Vicar's here, all the guests,*
*Dressed up nice, Sunday bests.*
*Music starts, tissues in hand*
*She looks fine and he looks grand.*
*Dancing, prancing, drinking too,*
*Seen before, nothing new.*
*Hope your life is full of things,*
*Cars and TV, and wedding rings.*
*This poem for you, I wrote last night,*
*But feel, I know, it ain't quite right.*
*Dad*

Sadia thought that Damian was having pre-wedding nerves, whereas in fact he was pissing around and intended to perform his thoughts through the medium of dance. She knew this to be a stupid idea and advised against the dancing and poem. As it happens, the wedding went off without hitches, and Damian would say it was one of the best days of his life, dance or no dance.

# Europe

As European matters bubbled along via broadcasters across the nation, with piss-poor politicians pontificating endlessly, Damian was ideally placed to have his tooth removed. His teeth were his Achilles heel, and as the sedative slowly took hold of his meagre senses, he reflected on the wonders of Europe. As a young man, Damian had only ever imagined Europe, believing it to be a magical place that only middle-class accents could discuss. When he first saw images of these faraway places, he was awestruck but also afraid. When he was told that they have different languages, cultures and even food, his initial reaction had been to run whilst screaming profanities. On reflection this was a little bit of an overreaction. He pictured medieval rivers with fast-running schlosses dotted along the peaks; lands with truffle trees and pasta farms; exotic hairstyles and well-honed opinions on the avant-garde. Anne, before her timely death, had insisted that first and foremost, no European Jonny would take away her extra-large pork pie; there was no way that she would even consider indulging in a thin sliver of quiche. Thomas, who had seen a little of the world, was equally reticent about the value of moving ever closer to Europe as it would only damage the cross-channel ferry industry. When a cross-channel bridge was mooted in the late 70s, Thomas was one of the three hundred signatories of a letter sent to the Peruvian Embassy demanding action (his geography was shit).

The talk of leaving Europe and of clean breaks made Damian feel a touch of nostalgia for the better times, when all food was considered necessary, and language was merely a collection of sounds and letters. The advent of modern technology had shortened borders, increased time zones had befuddled many. Sitting in that dentist chair, dribble slowly meandering down his freshly laundered smock, Damian tried to recall all his European holidays. His first expedition had taken place in 1982 and coincided with the Falklands War, although they were not connected. He and two friends had travelled to the south of France to experience some of the jet set life. Travelling on a one-year passport, they had boarded the coach at Victoria coach station. The journey took twenty-seven hours and by the end Damian had lost all feeling in his arse and eaten only half a cucumber and a pork pie that Thomas had given him before he left. Speaking of numb arses, he had been in the dentist's chair for some time, and to take his mind off the tugging and grunting that was currently occupying the dentist, he continued to reminisce despite his arse shutting down.

That first continental holiday had proven to be an education for Damian's stunted mind, creating pockets of experience that ran contrary to his upbringing. He had learnt about wine, a vile mix of grapes and soil which had left him stumbling for the nearest toilets. He had ventured into culinary space and discovered quiche Lorraine, baguettes and that crescent-shaped parcel of love, the croissant. The most memorable moment was his trip to Thuir to visit the Dubonnet factory. Before his visit, Damian assumed that an aperitif was the French translation of dentures, but on arriving at the factory he was amazed at the huge barrels containing this magical liquid. Treated to a line of trestle tables with endless samples of the drink, Damian was soon pissed as a fart. What followed was a mystical journey into the depths of his adolescent mind, travelling on a huge wine bottle to scrape the barrel of all its contents. He could hear 'La Marseillaise' as he drank, legionnaires to the left, legionnaires to the right, and Camembert at the ready. He was tripping on Dubonnet.

The dentist swung the chair around and placed a huge ball of cotton wool up Damian's nose to prevent the dribbles, telling him that his tooth was now homeless and to use a saline mouthwash for the next twenty-four hours. As he was unable to drive, Sadia had arranged a bus ticket for the eight-mile journey home. She was all for self-reliance. As he settled down on the ill-advised seat, he began to think back to other faraway places he had visited. In 1984 he had visited the Normandy beaches, along with his part-time girl fiend Claudia. Damian loved history, and aware that it might be a little nerdy to visit so many historical sites in one week, he had attempted to sell the trip to Claudia as more of an opportunity to immerse themselves in French culture. The holiday had been a lacklustre week of showers and shouting; their relationship was doomed. The only take-away from that Norman holiday was a life-long love of France.

With exiled tooth in pocket, reeling from the effects of too much mouthwash, Damian continued his recollections of countries visited and drachmas wasted. He had travelled to several parts of Greece, but he had a very soft spot for Crete, birthplace of Zeus. With its towering mountains, hapless goats and powerful wine, it was an island that held many warm memories. He had first visited the island with Anne and the three older parasites shortly after the death of Thomas. Two weeks of sun, sadness and mourning. Anne had travelled to the Isle of Wight as a young woman, so this flight to a far-off land filled her with bile and wind. Gripping her eldest granddaughter's hand until the parasite cried, the plane slowly descended into Heraklion airport, the mountains to the right presenting a foreboding backdrop. Anne had never been through a custom's check before, so when a rather friendly customs officer asked to see inside Anne's bag, it led to a very long chat between the recently widowed pensioner and a customs official who was keen to explore the contents of this fascinating woman's handbag. Pills, pens, umbrella, tablets, two dictionaries, a road map of Leeds, scissors, nail files, three bottles of hand cream, several combs of differing sizes, a travel iron and two carefully wrapped pork pies; Anne had packed for every eventuality. Following the check and exchange of addresses, Damian escorted the parasites and his over-enthusiastic mother to the car hire desk. There was no fucking way he was travelling by public transport with the herd. A Vauxhall Stupefy was available, so Damian quickly paid, signed and bundled his party into a rusty Vauxhall with beautiful grease-laden seats.

The winding roads of Crete were toe-droppingly beautiful, with vistas throwing caution to the wind and revealing sights that brought a blood-infused tear to Damian's right eye. Arriving at the accommodation, the parasites were unloaded and placed beside a swimming pool. Anne set to work checking her handbag for hand cream — a dry hand is a sad hand.

During the two-week break, they travelled the length of the island, visiting beauty spots that would stay imprinted on the vulnerable memories of the parasites. Possibly the high point was the drive to the Lasithi plateau and visit to the cave where Zeus was born. Driving at speeds that meant the Vauxhall Stupefy spluttered and barked as only an asthmatic dog could, they eventually reached the top, revealing a lace-ridden horizon. To get to the cave where Zeus had first crawled, they were required to ascend the mountain on an antiquated donkey, which after much heaving and groaning, was achieved. The cave was a pit of damp and gloom, but the parasites loved the squalid smell as it reminded them of Granny's house. After a quick whizz around a Zeus gift shop, the group made their way down the mountain, donkey desperately hoping for death, and headed to the beach. Such moments remain long in the memory.

# Recycled

News was often recycled, and this tired Damian. Damian was an avid follower of the news, often forcing himself to listen to recycled news on a loop to keep abreast of developments in the UK and across the globe. He enjoyed the cut and thrust of the live interview, with politicians flailing for credibility at the hands of an aggressive interviewer. He also appreciated the more considered pieces, analysing topics and issues and going underneath the eczema-riddled skin to find the dangerously infected truth behind the headlines. Skirting the airwaves and the news channels, he grew tired of the bland assertions of the weatherman, the mindless rebuttals of the traffic announcer, and the concerted jibber-jab and jingles foretelling future garbage to avoid. The newspapers were no better, packed as they were with lurid tales and blurred truth, so he set about starting his own weekly newsfeed via the internet to bring news straight from the horse's arse to the people. He quickly decided that his coverage would be quite hard-hitting but include quirky takes and sideways glances at stories that were ignored by the mainstream media. He needed a punchy and provocative title for his site, and having dismissed 'Turd Times', 'Say What', and 'Bile', he plumped for the catchy yet thought-provoking 'It's in the Wind'. He set about finding stories that both piqued his curiosity and also had a huge appeal somewhere. Produced below are several of the stories and features that were used in the first six days.

*It's in the Wind —*
*Gossip and Hearsay for the more discerning fool!*

*Local man discovered in bush — police not interested!*

How many times do you hear the refrain that the coppers are never there when you need them, or that they are too busy celebrating at a local takeaway, quaffing copious amounts of booze and savouring the sweet success of capturing a speeding cyclist, rather than sleuthing and rooting out evil from the orifices of our depraved community?

Dan Thorn, 36, has broken the law on several occasions, and on each occasion, he has apologised with a degree of sincerity. For his contrition, the least he could expect is respect and admiration from a police force too intent on judging a man for lurking in a bush in the wee small hours with several of his outer garments missing. Dan, unmarried, was shocked and dismayed to be suspected of nefarious deeds when he was accosted by PC Wold late last Friday night in the vicinity of Screeches Lane, a well-known haunt of trouserless ne'er-do-wells. Dan, Sagittarius, explained his lack of garments to PC Wold, using bird calls and primitive mime, but the said officer was apathetic, stating that he had made a casserole earlier and was eager to get home and share it with his partner, Janice. Dan, semi-homeless, was hoping for a night in the cells and a hot cup of char, but all he got for his sacrifice was a slight chill and a sideways glance from a passing taxi driver. He was led to a bus shelter and PC Wold told him to sod off in no uncertain terms.

Dan, 5ft 7", has since shaken off the chill and is currently looking for warming bushes to undress in. PC Wold remains a serving officer, and when I approached for comment was informed that the casserole was a little on the dry side and needed seasoning.

## The Truth Behind the Headlines –
## The Pie's the Limit!

Pies and pasty, two of life's treasures. So often we skip along the high street into our local crumb haven to pick up our favourite lard-infused delicacy without looking under the crust to see if the filling is all that it appears to be. With time at a premium, who really has the time to send their yummy pie off to a laboratory for detailed analysis? Who carefully dissects and dismembers a pie or pasty when there are buses to be caught, files to be lost and paper clips to be counted? I decided to do the donkey work and lift the lid on the murky world of pies and their fillings.

I approached a local charity to go undercover as a charity pie distributor, working for a large international charity, which sends pies to third world countries. This gave me access to 'Lids and Ladles', the number one pie supplier in the UK. On the drive up to their huge depot in a remote area of Birmingham, I checked my hidden camera and recording equipment, and ate a pie to focus on the task to come.

I was met at the imposing pie-shaped entrance by Tina Bone, lifelong lover of all things meaty and marketing director of Lids and Ladles. A small woman with an unusual spinal arrangement, she dragged herself along the corridors and explained the set up. Lids and Ladles first came to prominence in the late '30s with their ironic take on Hitler, producing a moustache-shaped pie that was very popular on the home front. After the war, their 'egg in a pie' range proved popular with a population desperate for egg and pie after the lean years without eggs due to the German U-boat menace. In the '50s the business thrived, serving up memorable pies, such as the 'Fall Out', the 'Mushroom Cloud', and the unforgettable 'There's a Red in my Bed'. They were a favourite with pie-lovers on the move and those less well equipped to get out and about. The 'Fall Out' was eventually pulled due to a mix up with radiation levels, but not before it had imparted life-threatening glows to some of its more enthusiastic lovers.

The 80s saw the pie industry revolutionised, with new fillings created on an hourly basis, and the crust-breaking privatisation of National Pies and Pastry PLC. This national treasure had pumped out pies for over one hundred and twenty-six years, and the closure of some of its storage tanks, which were sold off to whale harvesters from Japan, led to questions in the House and small riots in and around Batley. The sell-off was a huge success, with everyone able to enjoy a little bit of a very bountiful pie. 'Having your pie and eating it' was the catchy slogan that meant something that already belonged to the nation was sold to the nation — capitalism! The financial markets had pie charts that vindicated the risky sell off, which had been opposed by a stodgy group of MPs determined to keep pie fillings public.

When the UK had joined the EU sometime in the past, new pie regulations meant that stringent controls were introduced on the amount of radiation used in meat pies. Many smaller pie companies shifted their production to offshore rafts, employing French fishermen, who could withstand higher dosages of radioactive meat and potato. The larger concerns invested in new pie technology, so when the new millennium dawned, British pies were the envy of the world. The pie was the limit and had come of age in a virtual world of online eating and consumption. Lids and Ladles was at the forefront, pastry shield at the ready to defend the fillings that were both nutritious and stodgy.

Tina led me to the production and testing facility located in a large potato-shaped building, with images of pies adorning the toilets and walls. This was the nerve centre, with small pie-shaped scientists scurrying hither and thither in search of new flavours and ways to disguise radiation. Deep in the pie hole, specialists worked long hours, exploring their own inner demons and gluttony, all in search of a pie filling that would dominate pies for years to come.

Tina was very keen for me to try some of the newer fillings, still not fully tested, and this was my first chance to understand the processes involved. Starting with kipper and kale, an outrageous concoction for the frugal gamekeeper or spinster, we were soon flitting and flicking between exotic flavours and smells. My personal favourite was the lemon and sage vegan surprise, which left a bitter aftertaste for almost three weeks. Adjacent to the lab was a storage area, and I was keen to take a look inside, but Tina stated that it was off limits for charity volunteers. She had piqued my interest, and I was determined to find a way to access this Aladdin's cave of fillings. I took a few snaps of the lab, and a couple more of Tina dragging herself along the corridor and headed for the canteen to devise a plan to get into the storage area and enjoy a pie.

Tina assured me that there was nothing untoward in Lids and Ladles employing physicists, explaining that pie fillings, although an art form, required the scientist's eye for detail − ('pie r squared' took on a whole new meaning). Sceptical as I was, what struck me was the uniformity of the pies, with each one a perfect circle, and not a square, oblong or triangular pie to be seen. Where did they get all their round ingredients from? There were only so many perfectly plump, round ingredients that were suitable for a family pie. It was my suspicion that Lids and Ladle were importing illegal and illicit round ingredients via an underground network of suppliers, bypassing regulations on the curvature of pie fillings. This would blow the lid off any pie!

Working through the night, I plotted to spy on the pies in order to fill in the gaps and uncover unsavoury secrets that bubbled close to the surface. Deciding that attack was the best form of defence, the following morning I confronted Tina with my hunch. As someone who had unusual spinal arrangements, she knew all about hunches. What followed was both emotional and shocking. Tina broke down and explained that her spinal issues were due to increased radiation in the rear facing part of her body. She was a captive of the pie scientists and seldom saw her family due to their untimely death. For the last three months she had eaten only spherical objects and pies, and her spine was feeling the pressure. Her skin had become flaky and she had developed an unnatural love of peas. What alarmed her the most was a bull horn in the ear. Recording her revelations, I decided to leave Lids and Ladles once I had proof that my camera worked. I made my way to the storage facility, and with Tina's assistance, managed to avoid the pie boffins. Heavily fortified with a large intake of lard, I began to take pictures of sights that no vegetarian should ever have to see. Fruit and vegetables were strewn everywhere, trodden underfoot and spoiled. Large moon-shaped slabs of beef and kidney were liberally sprinkled on disused chopping boards. It was carnage. The boffins had scarpered early to fill up on breakfast pie, and so I snapped away, trying to capture Tina in her best light, gracefully leaning atop a giant onion, or bedecked with plums in what could only be described as unprovocative. Even with the sepia filter, she still glowed a little, thanks to heavy doses of radioactive cherries. Storing the camera in my hand for safe keeping, we made our way to the pie shaped chute that would allow us to escape with a minimum of fuss.

# And finally

Recalling the time Thomas varnished his feet in Fleetwood nearly thirty years ago, Damian reflected on his father's many foibles and ailments. In the 70s, Thomas was convinced that he had contracted Dutch elm disease after visiting an Edam production facility outside Bolton. For over two weeks he had refused to leave the house until a doctor could reassure him that his bark would not discolour and turn to mush. Eventually, after many applications of yacht varnish on his brittle toes, he left the house but avoided long walks near open spaces. Thomas was very aware of his own mortality, and Damian shared this rigid fear of leaving his loved ones prematurely. Thomas worried about the sky, the leaves and the price of peas. The environment was an issue that like many people of his age seemed ever present yet distant. He wanted to do something for the environment, but where to start? It was bloody everywhere! Anne had been very green in her heyday, recycling clothes, food and on one occasion, tobacco smoke. Her recipe book consisted of one recipe typed in twenty-three different fonts. Her buns were still buns, even when burnt, and quite often a rehashed meal would be better the third or fourth time of eating; it couldn't have been any worse.

Reflecting on his life, Damian had so many reasons to thank his parents: their love of pies and nicotine, their awareness of wool and its uses — but what resonated the most was their health-ridden tom-tittery. He recently found a copy of 'Hypochondria Monthly' that Thomas won on an ill-fated game show many years ago. Flicking through the well-thumbed pages, he was drawn to several articles that had been read and reread by his medically challenged parents.

*'Hypochondria Monthly' — Bringing sickness to life! — Issue No. 3*

## Can paper cuts kill?

*Open any sharp magazine or badly trimmed newspaper and the reader is often left bleeding and close to death. Who hasn't run to the newsagents, desperately in search of the latest news or topical pipe magazine, only to be found nearly bleeding to death twenty minutes later thanks to hundreds of tiny papercuts on forefinger and thumb?*

*In a world where many people use their hands for other things, paper shouldn't be so dangerous, and fingers will continue to be cut if the government does not act quickly. Researchers at the Geneva Papercut and Death Institute recently produced a paper, killing five, which stated paper should be reclassified as a deadly material, findings that were immediately rolled into a ball and tossed into the nearest waste paper cut bin. Head of the institute, Morris Mauve, was at pains to show all the papercuts on his delicate digits, testament if testament were needed to illustrate how dangerous paper can be in the wrong hands.*

*Governmental heads, along with letterheads, need to focus on finding a solution to dangerous paper cuts that every year cause some bleeding and hundreds of days off work. Perhaps in the future we will no longer use paper, and all reading matter will be produced using fabrics, but until there is a great leap forward in fabric technology, millions will continue to moan about harrowing paper cuts.*

## "Be safe and self-diagnose," says top neurotic.

*With the advent of larger medical journals, it is now possible to be completely weighed down with endless imaginary ailments. Competitive hypochondriac, Ivor Twinge, has spent many years building up his collection of real and imaginary ailments, winning championships throughout the known world. His most recent success, a virulent case of overactive bowels coupled with incessant scratching, was the pinnacle of a very small mountain of achievements. Speaking via a long piece of twine and two empty paint tins, Ivor explained his thoughts on sickness, sicknotes and neurotic behaviour.*

*"I first realised I was special when my father, Sir Hada Twinge, wrapped me up in cotton wool as a child. Unable to move and sweating*

profusely, I quickly developed imaginary symptoms. At school I was always the boy with draughty pants and involuntary bowel movements, marking me out as an unwitting attraction for flies and vermin. Whilst at university, I was subjected to ailments that in most people would be shrugged off, but I was able to draw out the suffering, moan and whine repeatedly, and was eventually told to fuck off. When father died in tragic circumstances following a protracted argument with a pair of rayon long johns and some wire wool, I knew that if I wasn't more neurotic about my health, I could well die in the future."

Ivor went onto to lament his lack of a life partner or friend, but felt that loneliness had its compensations. "Being alone means I never have to share a thermometer or sticking plaster, reducing costs. If I were to meet someone, they would have to be at death's door and willing to accommodate my niche ailments. I recently spent thirteen days in bed following a bout of scratching on my right knee. I couldn't jump for days!"

We will all die one day, weather permitting, but paradoxically, when life ends, it goes on. Just like illness, you cure one bastard thing and another ailment creeps into your life. Try and embrace the sickness you want to suffer in silence with. Advertise your sickness, shouting from the rooftops that you feel a little under the weather. You might even feel better!

Using a good medical journal or encyclopaedia will enable you to contract a range of sub-tropical diseases, sniffles and limps from the four corners of the globe, impressing doctors and neighbours alike. Imagine the pride you will feel knowing that that patch of dry skin behind your ear could well leave you paralysed from the hairline up and unable to wear any form of headband. Truly life-changing.

## Trivia for the Trivial

1/ Scaly fingers were originally seen as a sign of too much toad stroking, and sufferers would often have to wear elaborate mittens. Nowadays, powerful creams can make any toad feel smooth and soft to touch.

2/ Heart attacks are quite often a cry for help from those whose heart is floppy. In Victorian times, victims of 'floppy heart syndrome' were often sent to work up the chimneys of the well-to-do.

3/ Stroking a cat can induce birthing pains, even if you are not with child. The chemicals given off by some highly strung cats are very similar to those given off by highly strung, first-time parents who want the best start in life for their little cherub.

4/ Wax in ears can be a sign of too much listening and not enough doing. Research conducted during the night found that wax is more prevalent in those who burn the midnight oil eavesdropping on neighbours.

5/ Back pain is often associated with heaving, lifting and weak, inefficient arms, but this area of hypochondria is far more complex. Many back wearers only ever see the opposite side to their front whilst gazing into a mirror, hair resplendent in the morning light, so never truly understand the workings of their back. Grafting a back on to a front was viewed as a viable way of treating back pain, but is now viewed as fucking idiotic.

## Competition Time

*Your chance to win a seven month stay in a top-of-the range iron lung, with en suite toilet facilities and nineteen-hour, almost round-the-clock care. To win this fantastic prize, all you need to do is send in any part of your anatomy that you deem to have suffered the most imaginary ailments. Judging will be completed once we have subjected the body parts to a thorough wash and scrub, and the lucky winner will have the iron lung delivered to a garden of their choice. Two runner-up prizes of a week's stay in a dog kennel will also be awarded to entrants who can produce the most repeat prescriptions for a calendar year.*

*Closing date: 31/4*

As Damian rattles on into middle age and beyond, he knows he has been a lucky man, and can only reflect that if his parasites have half as much love as he had for his parents, then they are truly fucked. No life can be fully remembered, and it is a brave person who would dare to lay bare all their petty inadequacies, foibles and misdemeanours. Damian has attempted to be as frank as possible when writing this memoir. He interviewed himself over a period of several years, often at inconvenient times when the truth was the last thing he wanted to face up to. At times, those one-to-one interviews with himself were painful, uncomfortable and downright strange. Wrestling with a large kebab whilst trying to question yourself on events that might have happened many years ago was and is ridiculous, but Damian persevered and the result, this attempt to wrong the rights and embellish what was and is, in essence, a very dull and meaningless existence, will upset and disturb his remaining family and friends. Many of the characters we meet are now thankfully dead, otherwise the legal implications could be catastrophic. No one wants to be sued by their mother, father, brother and sister for alleged inaccuracies and downright lies. Damian, if nothing else, has tried to be flexible with the truth, and as it is his story, then falsehoods and exaggerations seemed appropriate. His long-standing wife, who finds it difficult to sit down for long periods, along with his children and their children, have questioned his sanity and the wisdom of producing this memoir, but his determination to lay bare the wonderful childhood he experienced, along with his burning desire to put his one-sided side of a many-sided story, has left him emotionally weakened, considerably smaller, and fifty-five pounds down. Readers, make your own judgements, as history will surely do.

Printed in Great Britain
by Amazon